THE HISTORY & DESIGN OF THE
AUSTRALIAN HOUSE

THE HISTORY & DESIGN OF THE
AUSTRALIAN HOUSE

COMPILED BY ROBERT IRVING

RICHARD APPERLY • SYDNEY BAGGS • SUZANNE FORGE • MILES LEWIS • PHYLLIS MURPHY
DAVID SAUNDERS • MAISY STAPLETON • RAY SUMNER • JENNIFER TAYLOR • PETER WATTS

MELBOURNE
OXFORD UNIVERSITY PRESS
AUCKLAND OXFORD NEW YORK

Created and produced by
Mead & Beckett Publishing
139 Macquarie Street Sydney Australia

OXFORD UNIVERSITY PRESS

Oxford London Glasgow New York Toronto
Delhi Bombay Calcutta Madras Karachi
Kuala Lumpur Singapore Hong Kong Tokyo
Nairobi Dar es Salaam Cape Town
Melbourne Auckland
and associate companies in
Beirut Berlin Ibadan Mexico City Nicosia

OXFORD is a trade mark of Oxford University Press

National Library of Australia
cataloguing-in-publication data
The history and design of the Australian house.

Bibliography
Includes index.
ISBN 0 19 554435 8

I. Architecture – Domestic – Australia – History.
II. Dwellings – Australia – History.
I. Irving, Robert 1926 –.
728: 0994

Edited by Elizabeth Dan
Designed by Susie Agoston O'Connor
Jacket designed by Barbara Beckett
Typeset by Asco Trade Typesetting Limited, Hong Kong
Colour reproduction by Bright Arts, Hong Kong
Printed by South China Printing Co., Hong Kong
Published by Oxford University Press, 7 Bowen Crescent,
Melbourne

Although many of the houses in this book are open to the
public, it must not be assumed that the mention of any of
them implies any right of entry, either to the site or the
interior. The National Trust, the state departments of tourism
and the historical societies can usually advise about houses
generally accessible, and local municipal authorities can usually
provide the names of property owners where this is
specifically required.

*Page one: Landscape enframed by architecture – the traditional
homestead prospect, from the verandah of Kangaroobie,
Orange.*

*Page three: Architecture enframed by landscape – Elmswood
House, near Gundy, New South Wales.*

CONTENTS

THIS BOOK IS ABOUT houses – the commonest of all historic artifacts and the most numerous item in the built environment. The starting point is the belief, expressed a century ago by John Ruskin, that buildings are 'documents embedded in time'. Houses especially, being intimately and intensely used by people, are among the most authentic and interesting of heritage documents.

While people are often not aware of the historical significance of houses, they are for most of us inescapable parts of our physical surroundings. We work, play, eat, sleep and die in them, and so they touch us profoundly. They shape our cities and towns, our suburbs and our streets, affecting the whole of our environment. In the words of Winston Churchill: 'We mould our buildings, and then our buildings mould us.'

The historical forces that have shaped the Australian house originated long before 1788. The earliest builders of Australia were already heirs to the Georgian tradition, and had seen the stirrings of the industrial revolution. Thus Classical themes, of necessity simplified and occasionally coarsened, pervaded the early domestic architecture of New South Wales and Van Diemen's Land. The simple and symmetrical Georgian visage for houses lingered longer in

INTRODUCTION

Tasmania, nurtured by a climate more like England's than that of the mainland. The military link with India brought the verandahed bungalow, the earliest of the non-British house forms, to New South Wales. The expansion of the sheep industry promoted both commerce and inland settlement, and stimulated the growth of the homestead. For several generations Sydney and Hobart and their satellites continued essentially as prisons, and a great gulf separated the character of the simple and collective convict domiciles from that of the relatively few houses of the free. Brisbane was likewise a penal town, and it was many decades before climatic forces freed colonial architecture there from its formal austerity. Perth, Adelaide and Melbourne, established as free communities, came more quickly under the new influence of Victorian culture, industry and wealth.

The early years of Queen Victoria's reign were momentous in Australia. First there were the gold-rushes in New South Wales and Victoria, which brought great wealth, rapid migration, and much civic development. The incorporation of local government, begun in the 1840s, was followed by self-government for Victoria and Queensland. Henceforth the gold-rush prosperity of Sydney and Melbourne ensured their steady expansion, which continued virtually unbroken for another forty years. Houses, in great numbers and diversity, filled new suburbs whose growth was stimulated by railways, tramways and better roads. The railways also helped the burgeoning inland towns, and country homesteads multiplied as a result

The affinity of house and setting is well exampled by Walter Burley Griffin's work. This is Coppins, one of his large houses, at Pymble.

of land exploitation. A prosperity boom in Western Australia followed gold discoveries there. Standards of comfort, hygiene, building materials, transport, techniques, services and decoration everywhere improved.

The British influence on house design, which had been dominant in Australia's first fifty years, was shared with many others as the nineteenth century developed. The German settlers in South Australia, the Canadian exiles in New South Wales, the American gold-seekers, the foreign makers of prefabricated houses, and strong personal stylists like J.A.B. Koch and John Horbury Hunt, are representative. Then, towards the end of the century and roughly coinciding with the rise of federation sentiment, the first Australian-born architects began to make their mark, many of them after having travelled in the United States of America. Design which employed Australian rather than foreign motifs appeared in painting and the decorative arts as well as in building. When house-building started again after the great slump of the 1890s depression, Australian-oriented ideas such as open planning were only just discernible among the combined influences of Britain and America, which became known as the Queen Anne style.

The twentieth century heralded not only federation but also the motor car, which aided industry and employment, furthered even more villa suburbs, and fostered the service station, the domestic driveway and the home garage. The new century also brought Art Nouveau, reinforced concrete, new building regulations, Canberra and Walter Burley Griffin. After World War I came an incredibly mixed cultural bag – electricity, hot water, kitchen gadgetry, public housing, and yet another depression. There was more American inspiration such as jazz and the gramophone, and styles such as Spanish and the California bungalow. European influence came by way of the Arts and Crafts movement, Art Deco, the Georgian Revival, and high-rise flats. Rising out of the 1930s depression, the International style typified a new optimism in architecture, which was cut off all too soon by World War II.

The history of the house since the war has been coloured by new waves of immigration, by vast numbers of needed dwellings, by the revitalization of old city housing, by the emergence of the owner-builder and the project house, and by new attempts to imbue houses with a uniquely Australian character. Perhaps the most interesting change is the way the best houses 'fit' their settings, whether urban or rural. It seems certain that one direction for the future is building in harmony with the environment.

Houses have been affected by the Australian environment ever since 1793, when the first verandah was added to Governor Phillip's elemental Georgian residence, so changing its Classical lines. From that time there have been two broad responses to nature: the negative one, requiring insulation from the excesses of the elements, and the positive one, seeking harmony with natural forms and forces. It is almost needless to say that the most satisfactory house benefits from both.

Australia's manifest environmental forces were reflected in the patterns of development of the land, as well as the behaviour of its inhabitants. Among these forces were distance, which brought isolation; topography, where, for instance, mountains became barriers; natural resources, bringing material abundance; and climate, which was the least understood of all.

The great distance from Australia to other centres of civilization has been characterized by concepts like the 'time-lag' theory, which supposes that ideas from Britain took anything from five to twenty years to be absorbed. Remoteness also appears to have been the reason why restrictive building regulations, common in England, were not effective here until a generation later. More significantly the vast internal distances, and differences, between the regions of Australia – long understood by geographers – have only recently been rationalized by architects and designers, so that, for example, it is no longer expected that the houses of Perth should be the same as those of Melbourne, or that those of Darwin should resemble those of Sydney.

Mountains no longer impede the spread of settlement as they did before highways and airlines; on the contrary, their terrain, once almost impossible to build on, now frequently becomes homesites. Steep land, making houses on stilts necessary, was an ingredient in the making of the Queensland style. Later houses, with floors at many levels to fit the slopes, adopted the organic character of the so-called Sydney School. Now, architects are returning to the horizontal-spreading early country homesteads for their inspiration, or discovering the environmental logic of underground houses.

Australia has always been rich in natural resources for building. Their husbanding, however, has varied from careless to criminal. Sandstone and cedar are but two of the many traditional materials which were so seriously squandered that they are now regarded as rare in house-building. Now, as well as seeking to use both natural and synthetic materials wisely, good home design looks for the efficient use of energy resources, including the sun, wind and water.

Climate is probably Australia's most misjudged phenomenon. In earlier times, once the slavish adoption of northern hemisphere habits was overcome, people learned by trial and error to face the problems created by sun, cold, wind and rain. The results were seen in such devices as verandahs, ventilated roofs, wide roof eaves and raised ground floors, and less obviously in innovations like damp-proof courses and cavity walls. Queen Anne houses and California bungalows were intended to express their qualities of protection from climatic vagaries, and bungalows in addition incorporated such summer conveniences as 'sleep-outs'. More recently, the principles of collecting, storing and using solar energy have become important climatic factors in house design. Aspect, shape, volume and materials are all important considerations in solar design, often making for house forms dramatically different from those of the past. Now, the realization that Australia is not one climatic zone, but many, is encouraging even more variety in house design.

There are many ways of looking at houses. One way sees the house as a response to physical needs such as comfort.

In this approach considerations like the arrangement of the rooms, sunlight, air circulation, good views, and adequate equipment, are important: the house should be an ensemble of well-planned and efficient spaces for people to use.

Another is to look at the house as a solid and well-made building, permanent, resistant to attack by weather, decay and insects, and economical: in this view the house should be a sound structure.

A third makes the house a composition of planes, volumes and elements, comparable to a large-scale, live-in sculpture, perfectly related to its setting. Interiors, exteriors and details must provide aesthetic satisfaction: in a word, the house must be beautiful.

These three notions have in fact always applied. Vitruvius Pollio, the ancient Roman architect and theorist, employed them when he described architecture in terms of *utilitas, firmitas,* and *venustas.* In 1624 Sir Henry Wotton seized upon the same elements of good building, which he translated as commodity, firmness and delight. Corresponding fundamentals apply today, though they are likely to be labelled function, structure and aesthetics by architects. If a house works well, is properly built, and is pleasing to the senses, it is apt to be a good house.

Because houses are the most personal and the most immediate of all architecture, they are also the most revealing. Our responses to their function, structure and aesthetics typify the two intentions which throughout history have characterized architecture: to solve the physical problems of providing shelter, and to endow such built spaces with emotional or spiritual qualities. Every house is therefore much more than its physical components. It can divulge its owner's or its builder's character, it can disclose its background of technology and history, and it can display the values of the community of which it is part.

In the course of reading this book it will become evident that its eleven authors, though in hearty general agreement, do not see eye to eye in every respect of interpretation or detail. In the belief that such differences are reasonable, it is left to the reader to form an opinion about the evidence which each contributor presents.

The authors are well aware of their debt to researchers and writers who have already published material relating to houses in Australia. The growing list of published works, and their critical readership, is testimony of an increasing concern about domestic architecture and the built environment generally. The bibliography contains texts which were not only referred to in this work but will also be helpful to the reader seeking further information.

Our grateful thanks are due to those who have shared information and insights, and offered constructive criticism: the State Library of New South Wales, especially the Mitchell Library; the State Library of Victoria, especially the Latrobe Collection; the State Library of Tasmania, especially the Allport Collection; the State Libraries of Queensland, South Australia and Western Australia; the National Library of Australia; the Royal Australian Historical Society; the National Trust of Australia in New South Wales, Queensland, South Australia, Victoria and Western Australia; the Universities of Adelaide, Melbourne, New South Wales, Queensland and Sydney. To the many people and institutions who provided material such as illustrations, and whose names appear in the reference notes and picture credits, we offer thanks. The following people gave particular help which is gratefully acknowledged: Peter Bridges, Ian Stapleton, Harry Stephens, Howard Tanner, Frank Tozer.

The authors agree, and invite the reader of this book to concur, with Roger North, who wrote *Of Building* in 1698. He said that an interest in architecture

is a sober enterteinment and doth not impeach but defend health. Other pleasures which are less despised, as wine, weomen, gaming, etc., have a sting which this hath not. And it is also an exercise of the mind as well as of the body ... he that hath no relish for the grandure and joy of building is a stupid ox and wants that vivacity of sense and spirit that seasons humane life and makes it less insipid.

AUSTRALIA HAS DEVELOPED during the most momentous period of the world's history. The first settlement was an insignificant event compared with the Independence of America or the French Revolution. Yet less than 200 years later Australia, though still one of the smallest nations, can boast of leadership in several fields and excellent world standing in many others, including house design and construction, materials technology and environmental concern.

When Australian architecture began the dominance of Britain was taken for granted. The designers, builders and users of houses were all British; they used local materials in British ways and gave them British names like wattle-and-daub, and built British forms such as cottages, skillions and dormer windows. The first foreign influences also came through Britain – French doors, jalousies, bungalows, verandahs. American sway, which became so important in the twentieth century, appeared in early technology such as the circular saw and brick-making machinery, and in effects such as wall-shingling and the 'piazza' – a vogue-name for a wide verandah. John Horbury Hunt, the first important American architect in Australia, became an influential figure, championing Australian materials. The Boom period brought many other

TWO CENTURIES OF CHANGE

PART ONE

direct foreign influences upon house design, particularly German and French, through travel, migration, and fashionable publications. Yet Walter Burley Griffin, who built eminently successful houses in many different parts of Australia, and also proclaimed the virtues of the Australian landscape, was hardly emulated, and had little direct effect.

These factors all demonstrate the importance of heredity, but what of the equally important influence of environment? Though observers were espousing the *genius loci* of Australia last century, it is only in recent times that house design has admitted the impact of distinctly Australian things like landscape and climate, to redress the evident imbalance of the past. A hoped-for balance between heredity and environment must make better homes in the future.

The first part of this book is a kind of history of the house in Australia. It is built on a spine of high-style – that manifestation of architecture contrived by architects – but fleshed out by reference to the vernacular way of building – that vast majority of houses in both country and city representing the aspirations of a people.

A fusion of Australian and European style in the restrained detailing of Armytage House, Geelong, by Edward Prowse, 1859–60.

In the extensive garden of Ralph Allen's Palladian mansion, Prior Park, at Bath, England, the architect John Wood designed several landscape whimsies, including a temple, a Gothick lodge, a statue of Moses, and this Palladian bridge, which was started in 1755. The merging of Classical and romantic styles in a picturesque setting is a key to the understanding of the Georgian spirit out of which Australian architecture grew.

GEORGIAN AUSTRALIA was the creation of Georgian England, when Australia could be referred to as 'the English Colony in New South Wales'. It lasted for more than sixty years and was, at the end, inundated by the momentous events of the 1850s, when gold rushes, railways, colonial expansion and self-government began a cultural flood that lasted until the end of the century.

In 1850, on the eve of these great Victorian changes, the population of the Australian colonies was a little over 400,000. Virtually all of the adults then alive, as well as those who had died in the three generations since 1788, were born in the Georgian period; about three-quarters of them in Britain. Most were anonymous, and almost half were, or had been, convicts. Yet these were the people who had created the Georgian towns that would soon become Australian cities, as well as the host of thriving rural settlements, scattered around some 4,000 kilometres of the continent's edge.

Cultural origins

These colonial Australians came from several different British Georgian backgrounds, all of which contribute to the story of the Australian house. They are the convict poor, the military, civil officialdom, and the free settlers.

was often less evident in domestic architecture, particularly in the villages and small towns. Fashion was not so important, houses tended to last longer, older traditions lingered, and regional differences were much more pronounced. It is possible that the single-storey cottages of Ireland and the crofts of Scotland − small, simple and single-roomed − were precursors of the Australian one-storey house.[2] They were certainly known to many of our first home-builders. In surviving examples of these vernacular cottages attempts at symmetry, proportion and good detailing are just discernible. When the poor could escape from the trap of abject poverty, as so many emancipated convicts in Australia were able to do, they often entered the stream of taste by building for themselves houses modelled on a Georgian image.

The military influence in Georgian architecture is seen in the sobering effect of utilitarian structures such as army barracks and naval dockyards, where down-to-earth regulations governing sizes, and simple rules of proportion, ensured that buildings would be sturdily handsome. British installations such as Portsmouth Dockyard became models for equivalent industries in many countries, including America. A more subtle influence was exerted by the army, whose buildings, erected wherever British colonies

GEORGIAN BRITAIN   I

The largest group, the convicts, have been dismissed as unworthy of the term Georgian, with its overtones of taste. In many ways, however, they were the most interesting of the pre-Victorians. They were the overt reason for Australia's foundation, and they outnumbered all other inhabitants by nearly three to one.

A general impression of the environments from which the convicts came can be obtained from the drawings of Thomas Rowlandson or William Hogarth, or from the court records of the time. The houses that most convicts would have known were the oldest and meanest slums of the biggest cities. The slums compared starkly with the spacious and stylish houses of the wealthy, just as their crowded and depressed occupants contrasted with the liberated upper classes. In Spitalfields, an inner-eastern district of London, for example, the lodging-houses and packed thieves' dens were pitiable alongside Christchurch, the remarkable Baroque church designed for the fashionable by Nicholas Hawksmoor. Hogarth's *Gin Lane* is a caricature of this district, and it depicts the homeless and poverty-stricken background of many of Australia's early settlers.[1] The centre of Hogarth's stage is full of debauchery, but its architectural setting is unmistakably, attractively, Georgian.

Large numbers of the urban poor, therefore, had only distant access to eighteenth-century culture. Many others, however, through domestic service, or even family connection, were directly familiar with large Georgian houses and their environments. In rural areas the Georgian idiom

were established, not only needed to be common sense and simple in design and construction, but also had to suit all kinds of climates. The British army helped to spread the use of the verandah, window jalousies or shutters, breezeways and portable houses, for example, and probably also the Indian bungalow house form.

British civil officials, being appointments of the Crown and representing the ruling class, tended as a matter of course to set the level of community taste. In England they were often powerful enough to commission the erection of government buildings or the design of government equipment. And their private wealth allowed them to engage architects to build them houses displaying the latest in Georgian taste. Many public servants who came to Australia brought high standards of design with them. Alexander McLeay, already a distinguished Scottish entomologist as well as a government official, was persuaded in 1825 to accept the position of Colonial Secretary of New South Wales. The houses he built and the quiet authority he possessed were important in elevating the standards of Australian building. Other officials appointed to Australia who influenced the architecture of the country were Thomas Livingston Mitchell and Henry Dangar, as well as the colonial architects such as John Lee Archer.

About 14,000 free settlers had come to Australia by 1830, most with barely enough capital to begin development of the land grants that were offered in Britain as bait to emigrants. Most were not landholders in Britain, and their Australian prospects were better than they could

The Georgian device of combining separate houses in a single handsome terrace building can be seen in Bath, an eighteenth-century town familiar to many early Australian settlers including Governor Arthur Phillip. These terraces are in Great Pulteney Street.

The interior of a humble Georgian tenement occupied by an impecunious poet, as depicted by the artist William Hogarth.

Right above: A rural farmhouse in County Clare, Ireland, with colour-washed walls and thatched roof. Even simple vernacular houses displayed the Georgian virtues of balance and good proportions.

Right below: Rows of huts in the Rocks, Sydney, drawn by convict artist Thomas Watling in about 1792. They resemble the houses which many convicts knew in Britain.

have been at home. They became the clients in Georgian building projects and, in rural areas, often the builders as well. Unlike the more mobile military and civilian officials, the settlers generally stayed in the colony, improving their buildings and land as prosperity grew.

The settlers' backgrounds, and the houses they built, were diverse. Robert Campbell, an urbane Scot, joined his family business in India and then moved to Australia to found a mercantile fortune. He built one of the first of Sydney's waterfront mansions in the bungalow tradition. The Macarthur family's many homesteads, by contrast, showed an intensive interest in pattern-book architecture – a typical Georgian preoccupation. Some groups of settlers with shared interests, such as the Australian Agricultural Company in the Hunter Valley, and the Prussian Lutherans in the Barossa Valley, created architecture of special significance.

Even these few examples illustrate the importance of the cultural origin – the British background – of Australia's Georgian home-builders. In Britain, as in Australia, the correct and fashionable houses established the standard, and while only a small proportion of Georgian houses were designed by architects, their influence was profound. Even the most unstylishly vernacular eighteenth-century houses gained from the reservoir of Georgian style.

Georgian Britain: the style reservoir

Georgian is an adjective best applied to a period rather than a style. The period was that of the four King Georges, who reigned from 1714 to 1830. British architecture at this time provided a great stockpile of inspired styles – not one mode of artistic expression but many – which nurtured the opening phases of building in Australia, and positively affected building design all over the world.

Discussing Georgian is like discussing a rainbow; the essence of the rainbow is that all of its brilliant colours are really only components of white light. Or, to change the simile, Georgian architecture is like a large and handsome garden, of great complexity and with many fine specimen plants, which can be seen only through windows, none of them wide enough to encompass the whole panorama. Georgian can be viewed through four windows – Palladian, English Classical, Romantic Revival and Regency. The viewer must merge these four incomplete and sometimes overlapping scenes in order to perceive an entire Georgian panorama. And away in the distance, a colonial version of the garden, full of healthy transplants, grafts and hybrids, extends almost out of sight.

The origins of the Georgian tradition are found more than a century before George I, when knowledge of the Classic world, rediscovered in the Italian Renaissance, reached England. Its appeal was at once compelling. The Classic world was rational, concrete and harmonious. The Renaissance spirit of enquiry illuminated both the broad scale and the fascinatingly minute detail of the ancient world. To the European middle class emerging out of medievalism, Classical culture appeared as the standard and the mould for every expression of life.

Yet England, isolated from Rome by the Reformation, saw the Classic world only fuzzily, through the lens of the

Right top: The first house in England designed wholly in the Italian manner was the Queen's House at Greenwich, built by Inigo Jones. It created a new style which became Georgian.

Audley End, Essex, one of the great Jacobean houses, shows the early influence of the Italian Renaissance in Classical porches.

Renaissance and, even so, largely by its effects in Holland and France. Travellers returned to England bringing glowing reports of new Classical ideas and buildings, new architectural books and drawings. Copied Classical motifs such as the Orders and triumphal arches were fancifully applied to traditional Elizabethan house designs, with results ranging from startling to downright ugly. Then in 1550 the intrepid architect John Shute journeyed to Italy, the Classic fountain-head, where he met Michelangelo, Palladio and Vignola, and on his return

Right centre: The design of the Banqueting House in Whitehall, developed from Palladio's designs for Italian town palaces, was unprecedented in England. The building was started by Inigo Jones in 1619.

Right below: The Earl of Bedford developed his Covent Garden property by building Britain's first terrace houses, above elegant stuccoed arcades, surrounding a fine piazza, with St Paul's church at one end. The Italian-inspired complex was designed by Inigo Jones in 1630. In this engraving of 1720 the first market stalls have appeared.

wrote the earliest instruction book on architecture in English, which was published in 1563.[3] It took only another couple of generations for a knowledge of Roman architecture, art and literature to become essential for every cultured Englishman.

The first-hand impact of the Italian Renaissance upon England was effected quite suddenly in Jacobean London by one man. This was the architect Inigo Jones, Surveyor to the King, who was commissioned in 1616 to build a new house at Greenwich for Queen Anne. Jones had travelled in Europe when the Grand Tour was still unusual and even dangerous, and studied in Italy, the centre of the architectural world. He probably knew more about Italian design than any living Englishman. What interested Jones was not the contemporary architecture of Italy, which was about to enter its Baroque phase, but the principles of design in Classic architecture as enshrined in the work of Andrea Palladio and of Palladio's heir, Vincenzo Scamozzi, whom Jones met in Venice in 1614. Jones idealized Palladio's work as 'sollid, proporsionable according to the rulls, and unaffected'. He had also acquired a copy of Palladio's great treatise, *I Quattro Libri dell'architettura*, published in 1570 and perhaps the most influential architectural book ever written. From this and from Palladio's buildings, Jones derived an intense interest in the harmonic proportions that could be used to establish the length, breadth and height of rooms, as well as the relationships of one room to another.[4]

The house he created for Queen Anne of Denmark was an Italian villa – the first of its kind in Britain – and when it was finished in 1635 it created a sensation. Against its picturesque Jacobean background it was starkly symmetrical, studiously proportioned inside as well as out, chaste in decoration, and surfaced in stucco. Jones gave it a first-floor loggia, a main hall in the proportions of a cube, and an open spiral staircase – all features new to Britain. It was all Palladian, a little like Scamozzi's Villa Molina finished twenty years before, yet not copied from either Palladio's or Scamozzi's work.

The 'Italian taste', so evident in the Queen's House, was even more pronounced in other designs by Inigo Jones, and these profoundly influenced Georgian building. One was the Banqueting House in Whitehall, the first English building in the form of an Italian *palazzo*. Another was Wilton House, Wiltshire, with two features that were to be extremely fashionable in the eighteenth century: a pair of Italianate pedimented corner-towers, and a magnificent main chamber in the proportions of a double-cube. The third, probably the most influential of all, was a speculative development for the Earl of Bedford at Covent Garden. The place was a large rectangular part of Bedford's own garden, which Jones framed on two sides by building joined houses, separated from the Bedford garden on the third side by a low terrace walk, and punctuated on the axis of the fourth side by a church with flanking gateways. The church, built at the insistence of King Charles I, was in the form of a plain but noble Tuscan temple with a portico – the first of its kind – and wide roof eaves. It was called St Paul's, and it must have been familiar to Francis Greenway, for he echoed it later in some of his Australian buildings. The two ranges of row houses were built above spacious ground floor arcades – the forerunners of verandahs in Britain – which were so innovative that they became known colloquially as 'the piazzas'. The Piazza (to give the whole development its proper name) marked Britain's adoption of Italian taste and design, and was the first integrated group of terrace houses, and the first great example of English urbanism.[5] Here, the essence of Classic style, as distilled by Palladio, was revived in a distinctively English way. The Georgian tradition had germinated.

Georgian through the Palladian window

By the time the first King George was on the throne, a century after the Queen's House and two centuries after Palladio, the authority of the great Italian had grown stronger than ever. Inigo Jones was regarded as the first

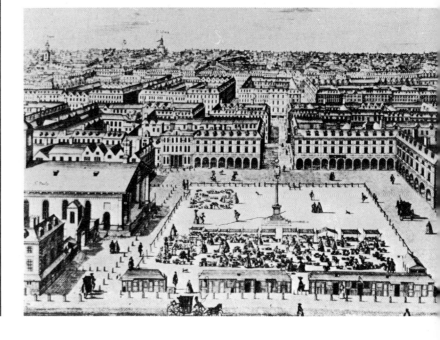

of a long line of designers, dedicated to purity in English architecture and known collectively as the Palladian School. Architects such as William Kent and patrons such as Lord Burlington built houses that were austerely plain by comparison with the current Baroque style, which they considered false and artificial.

The visual essentials of Palladianism were order (as seen in the correct relationships of the parts to one another and to the whole), symmetry (the careful integration of the house and its setting – for example by linking the main block and its dependent wings by low colonnades), and the rightness of proportion. Elements like temple fronts, grand formal staircases and loggias, techniques such as stuccoing and plastering, and innovative detailing including the 'Venetian window', were important. Many designers were dilettantes, happy to be bound by architectural rules and content to imitate the works of the past.

landscape garden, in complete contrast to the formal garden which had long been popular, became fashionable, largely through the work of William Kent. Scenic and irregular, it 'had the appearance of beautiful nature', as Kent wrote. From this time on the country house was designed to harmonize with the landscape, rather than to dominate and control it. Lancelot ('Capability') Brown, Kent's even more famous successor, extended this artful informal manner, devising lush park-like settings for his wealthy clients' formal houses. Even as late as 1835, in Sydney, Francis Greenway reported in the *Australian* newspaper that he wanted a 'tamed nature' landscape for his proposed Government House:

The government domain was to have been planted in the manner of the celebrated Brown, the landscape gardener, it having *great capability* about it, with a bold and grand mass or rich plantation in the back ground as a fine relief to the build-

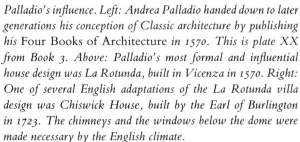

Palladio's influence. Left: Andrea Palladio handed down to later generations his conception of Classic architecture by publishing his Four Books of Architecture *in 1570. This is plate XX from Book 3. Above: Palladio's most formal and influential house design was La Rotunda, built in Vicenza in 1570. Right: One of several English adaptations of the La Rotunda villa design was Chiswick House, built by the Earl of Burlington in 1723. The chimneys and the windows below the dome were made necessary by the English climate.*

Mereworth Castle, for example, designed in 1723, was a copy of Palladio's Villa Almerico (La Rotonda) in Vicenza. Though very handsome, the mansion was quite inappropriate for the cold English climate. Nevertheless the intellectualism and elegance of the Palladian idiom was compelling, and its qualities could be found in many well-designed buildings. Palladianism became the underlying theme of Georgian residential building. Local squires copied what the grander families were doing, and the yeomanry copied the squires,[6] so that Palladian was absorbed into the vernacular, in both Britain and in her colonies.

With these developments a new concept of the English

ings; in the *foreground* a lawn, diversified with elegant shrubs and flowers of different climates, with groups of deciduous and native trees.

The phenomenon that spread the principles of Georgian style even more widely than the architects' buildings was the pattern-book, the equivalent of the twentieth century's 'how-to-do-it' manual. Among the early examples was Sir Henry Wotton's work of 1624, called *Elements of Architecture*, in which he enunciated his famous dictum:

> The *end* is to build well.
> Well building hath three Conditions:
> COMMODITIE, FIRMNESS, and DELIGHT[7]

a philosophy that became a vital part of the Georgian tradition. Colen Campbell, the designer of Mereworth Castle and a protege of Burlington, wrote *Vitruvius Britannicus*, a telling record of English architecture under the influence of Italy, in 1715. Another notable manual was *A Complete Body of Architecture*, by Isaac Ware, which was published in 1756. Ware cautioned the reader against the desire 'to transfer the building of Italy right or wrong, suited or unsuited to the purpose, into England', and his

warning to would-be Palladians is very practical:

In studying a design of Palladio's, which we recommend to the young architect as a frequent practice, let him think, as well as measure. Let him consider the general design and purpose of the building, and then examine freely how far according to his own judgement, the purpose will be answered by the structure. He will thus establish in himself a custom of judging by the whole as well as by parts; and he will find new beauties in the structure considered in this light.[8]

Ware's large folio is full of practical information about construction, design and decoration, and it was one of a number of its kind that were brought early to Australia. A host of books like these, nearly always packed with drawings and descriptions of buildings and advice about designing, promoted the dispersal of Palladianism all over the English-speaking world.

The English Classical window

Parallel to Palladianism a very different architectural tradition occurred. Its progenitor had been Sir Christopher Wren, the scientist who took to architecture at about the time that Inigo Jones died. Wren never visited Italy, but he did meet the great Baroque architect Gianlorenzo Bernini at the new Louvre project in Paris, in 1665. 'Bernini's

The 'Palladian motif'. Left: The use of arch and lintel together as in the ancient Roman arch of Titus is an inspiration for the Palladian motif. Above: The tower of James Henry Fox's Werribee Park mansion shows the Palladian motif remaining fashionable well into the nineteenth century in Australia.

Design for the Louvre,' he wrote, 'I would have given my skin for, but the old reserv'd *Italian* gave me but a few Minutes View'.[9] Wren made a study of the works of Bernini and the Baroque architects of France, and of pattern-books such as that by Sebastiano Serlio, the first of the 'practical' rather than theoretical manuals, and the first to codify the five Roman Orders. Wren mainly designed public buildings, but his influence upon all kinds of architecture was extraordinarily wide and profound.

Wren was no mere servant to the Italian vogue. His use of distinctively English materials, such as Portland stone, red brick, tiles, slates, wrought iron and oak gave the Classical style a national character. He exploited some of the Dutch features then fashionable in England, as well as many of the common vernacular forms, and integrated them into his designs. Thus he used the hipped roof, the roof cupola, and massive chimneys, with great skill. His designing was always sane and practical, always English, and he promoted the ideal of excellent craftsmanship.

Classical design in England was modified by the use of Dutch-inspired motifs. Above: a decorated, pedimented breakfront and roof cupola at the College of Matrons, Salisbury. Right: The central pediment of the Ironmongers' Almshouses, London.

The list of domestic style components that were popular at this time provides a key to the character of incipient Georgian design. It includes the Classical Orders, usually used as applied decoration; a strongly marked cornice line right round the building; sash windows rather than casements; roof dormer windows; hipped roofs rather than gables; refined forms of mouldings, such as on cornices and around door and window openings; and better quality decorative work, especially in plaster.[10] The 'breakfront' house, its slightly projecting central bay crowned by a pediment, was a Dutch-inspired form much exploited in English Classical design. This axial pediment, often with the arms of the owner carved into its tympanum, became a status symbol, as it had been in ancient Rome.[11]

The Wren-initiated English Classical style was extended by many distinguished architects, among whom were Hawksmoor, Vanbrugh, Gibbs, Chambers and the Woods. Nicholas Hawksmoor and Sir John Vanbrugh, stimulated by the Italian Baroque, experimented with massing, scale and space to invent dramatic and often excessive effects, which displeased the Palladians. Their work was known to architects who came early to the Australian colonies, including Francis Greenway, but their influence was slight. James Gibbs trained in Italy in the Baroque main-stream, and this was reflected in his much-copied public buildings such as St Martin-in-the-Fields, London. In his houses he employed Italian-Swiss stuccoists to carry out interiors of great richness. Gibbs became one of the most influential architects through his publications, especially his *Book of Architecture*, published in 1728. Here the intention of the typical pattern-book was stated:

Such a work as this would be of use to such Gentlemen as might be concerned in building, especially in the remote part of the Country, where little or no assistance for Design can be procured. Such may here be furnished with Draughts [drawings] of useful and convenient Buildings and proper Ornaments which may be executed by any Workman who understands Lines, either as here Design'd, or with some Alteration, which may be easily made by a person of Judgement.[12]

Gibbs's widely-used book contained designs that were similar to some of Greenway's Australian work.

The John Woods, father and son, are inseparable from the development of Bath and its fine urban townscapes,

which many early Australians, including Governor Phillip, knew well. The work of Sir William Chambers belongs firmly to the English Classical tradition but it may be viewed through several of the Georgian windows. His style was Palladian, yet his inspiration came from ancient Rome and his work in this mode is said to have inspired John Lee Archer in Van Diemen's Land.[13] Chambers's most notable publication was the *Treatise on Civil Architecture*, 1759, copies of which reached the Australian colonies early in the nineteenth century, including a later edition in the possession of architect Henry Ginn; yet his earlier work, *Designs of Chinese Buildings, Furniture, Dresses, &c*, was a key document in popularizing Chinoiserie. The picturesque layout and the buildings he designed for Kew Gardens, which included the Pagoda and the Alhambra, mark his architecture as part of the Romantic Revival movement. This diversity is a salutary reminder that categorizing architects and their work according to styles and movements is artificial, useful only to promote understanding through comparison and analysis. Chambers, like so many Georgians, was an all-round architect.

The most pervasive aspect of these Anglo-Classical modes was, without doubt, the way they were adopted and 'vernacularized' in the multitude of lesser houses of the eighteenth and early nineteenth centuries. This was the case not only for free-standing cottages, but for town residences of the kind destined to become the most typical Georgian building form: the speculative terrace house.[14]

The terrace house was at first unique to Britain, but there were early counterparts in some of the colonies, and in Australia it had appeared by the 1820s. The social and physical forces that shaped it, wherever it was built, were surprisingly similar. In England, even before the eighteenth century, what we call terraces had become so common that they were known only as 'houses'; it was the separate dwelling that needed another name, such as cottage or villa or mansion.

Most terrace houses were not architect-designed; they were scaled-down versions of the fastidiously elegant town houses that eminent architects built for the rich and powerful. The appearance of their facades was governed by vertical proportions rather than the horizontal ones of wider detached houses. Within this vertical rectangle the details of each house – doorcase, windows and cornice – were arranged just as carefully according to rules as were those of the grander houses. There were plenty of pattern-books to provide guidance, and with the onset of the industrial revolution, manufacturers made available the necessary quantities of repetitive details of all kinds: doors, doorcases, fanlights, windows, keystones, chimney-pieces, columns, balusters, balconies, cornices and paints.

Above left: The Rectory at Windsor is a simplified Australian version of the English Classical idiom.

Above right: Governor William Bligh was born in one of these unassuming brick terrace houses in Lambeth, London.

Left: This 1826 view of George Street, Sydney, looking north from Grosvenor Street, shows Underwood's Tenements, thought to be the earliest terrace houses built in Australia.

The increase in residential density that resulted from erecting joined houses on a single block of land threatened community safety and hygiene. The crowded wooden city of London was levelled in the great fire of 1666. Its rebuilding provided a great impetus for speculative redevelopment, and spawned the first building regulations to affect the way houses looked. The 1667 London Building Act, explaining itself as 'an Act for the better, preventing mischiefs that may happen by fire', limited the construction and height of houses according to the width of the street and demanded that outside walls be of brick or stone, thus incidentally promoting uniformity. The Act of 1707, still concerned with fire prevention, made brick party-walls separating houses extend upwards as parapets, separating the roofs of terraces. It also banished timber cornices and overhanging eaves, along which flames might have spread from house to house, and recommended masonry front parapets instead. Two years later a supplementary Act had further simple but profound results: it required that door and window frames of timber be set one brick-width (100 millimetres) inside the face of the wall, revealing thereby part of the wall thickness. The shadow lines made by these 'reveals' had an important visual effect. By the Act of 1724, downpipes for roof drainage were required, and designers began to use these vertical attachments visually to divide the continuous terrace front into individual bays.

The 1774 Building Act was the last comprehensive building legislation enacted before Australia was colonized. It consolidated all the previous legislation, and in addition divided buildings into seven different Rates according to their volume, cost, use and position. A First Rate house, for example, had to exceed 9 squares (900 square feet or 84 square metres) in area, to cost at least £850, and comprise at least four storeys above the ground. All front, rear and party-walls were to be of brick or stone, and all timber external decoration except frontispieces to doorways was forbidden. Furthermore, window and door-frames now had to be not only recessed, as in the earlier Act, but tucked in behind the outer brickwork of the opening, so that from the outside they appeared much finer than ever before. The distinctive 'terrace' look had now emerged.

Peter Nicholson was one of many architects who compiled pattern-books of terrace house designs after the 1774 Act and some of his titles were brought to Australia early in the nineteenth century. But not all terrace building was bound by regulations. What is interesting is that the improving techniques they symbolize, expressed through an accepted Classical tradition, had so satisfying an effect upon the vernacular architecture of so many towns and cities of the world.

Georgian through the Romantic Revival window

Two of the four windows on Georgian architecture have been opened. The first revealed the Palladian theme which, like a foundation, underlay the movement towards the Anglicizing of Classical architecture seen through the second window. The third view is more complex because it shows a series of trends that washed like waves over the whole scene: the revivals of past styles. By the time George III came to the throne in 1760, this idea was so attractive that almost all designers were dipping into the past for inspiration, and before the end of the Georgian period eclecticism was rampant.

The first wave was hardly a revival at all. It was the resurgence of Gothic, which had never died out, but only subsided. The English had always enjoyed taking a romantic retrospective look at the days of chivalry; now a whimsical form of medievalism (today called Gothick to distinguish it from the real thing) began to infect architecture. A sham ruin in the Gothick taste was designed by Sanderson Miller for Hagley Hall, Worcestershire, as early as 1748. The Gothic novel became something of a cult when Horace Walpole wrote *Castle of Otranto: a Gothic Story* in 1764 and Sir Walter Scott's Waverley novels followed later. The literary and architectural streams converged in examples like Walpole's house, Strawberry Hill, at Twickenham, a medieval fantasy begun in 1753 which earned its own style-name, 'Strawberry Hill Gothic'.

One of the earliest Gothick 'how-to-do-it' books was written by Batty Langley in 1742. This was an attempt to 'improve' Gothic architecture by rules and proportions, and it presented 'many grand designs ... geometrically expressed', invented by its ingenious author. Langley eventually published more than twenty such books, some of which were brought to Australia. A pioneer example of an 'improved' – Gothick – house was begun in 1745; it was Inverary Castle in Argyllshire, erected for Archibald Campbell, Duke of Argyll and kinsman of Mrs Elizabeth Macquarie.[15] Its designer was Roger Morris, who was responsible for many houses in a correct Palladian taste. The square-block symmetry and axially-placed tower of Inverary make the influence of Palladio obvious beneath its mock-medieval decorative overlay. This reveals the essential difference between Gothick – the Picturesque, romantic and delicate revival which belongs to the Georgian period – and the scholarly interpretation of true Gothic principles which came to be so important in Queen Victoria's time. Gothick creations were not required to conform to precise rules of style; their purpose was to evoke images of the past by mood and association. It is easy to understand how early Australian colonists, far away from home, were comforted by such evocations.

The reference to Gothick as Picturesque is significant, for it fits the eighteenth-century fashion of contriving buildings and their settings as though they were elements carefully placed in a landscape painting: Nature imitating Art. The Gothick ruin in the garden of Hagley Hall was built with this intention. So too was a Doric 'temple', added a little later, making it clear that the Picturesque Movement was not limited to the Gothick taste. Among the earliest writers to encourage people to look at a building and its setting together was the Reverend William Gilpin, whose visual 'rules' were published in such works as *Observations, relative chiefly to Picturesque Beauty ...*, from 1782. At least one copy of a Gilpin book found its way to the Australian colonies.

Picturesque Gothick continued as a seductive fashion in Britain until the production of meticulous measured studies of medieval buildings made it easier for architects to design in the correct Gothic manner. The end of the Picturesque vogue and the beginning of the systematic Gothic Revival with all its moral and religious overtones, was signalled by the appearance of A.W.N. Pugin's books *True Principles of Pointed or Christian Architecture*, 1841, and *Contrasts between the Noble Edifices of the Middle Ages and the Corresponding Buildings of the Present Day*, 1836. Such high-minded Gothicism was not readily applicable to house design, and for a while the builders of stylish residences looked elsewhere for enlightenment.

The second wave of revival, as romantic in origin as the Gothick, began in the middle of the eighteenth century with an upsurge of interest in the forgotten antiquities of ancient Greece. Ancient sites such as Paestum were drawn into the circuit of the Grand Tour and their archaeological interest was publicized. Some of the early pioneers in Greece itself were Frenchmen like J.D. Le Roy, whose book *Ruines des Plus Beaux Monuments de la Grèce*, published in 1758, contained the earliest drawings of Greek buildings. But in fact the most avid votaries of Greek were the British. James Stuart, who with Nicholas Revett wrote *Antiquities of Athens*, the first volume of which came out in 1762, was nicknamed 'Athenian Stuart'. He had designed the Doric garden 'temple' at Hagley in 1758 – the earliest Greek building in Britain – and built, in 1763, a house in London with an Ionic front, thought to be the first of its kind. Stuart and Revett were the twin arbiters of the new fashion. Their publication was so comprehensive, and so simplified, that it enabled other architects to embrace the Greek Revival without the necessity of visiting Greece.[16] Architect Henry Kitchen, a contemporary of Francis Greenway's, apparently brought a copy of *Antiquities* with him to Australia in 1814.

Up to about 1800 the Grecian style developed in Britain as one of several waves generated by the romantic impulse, and only after the turn of the century did it achieve any real importance. But by the 1820s – the period of the Greek War of Independence – it was the very criterion of architectural distinction. The style reached a climax with the building of the British Museum, which Sir Robert Smirke designed in 1823 – 'the Erechtheum re-created in London'.[17] Before this there were some remarkable Grecian houses, including 'the most complete Greek-temple house of all time',[18] Grange Park, in Hampshire, which was designed about 1808 by William Wilkins as an adaptation of the Theseion in ancient Athens.

The first essentials of the style, then, were forms derived from the structure of Greek temples. The pedimented temple shape was ideally suited to the gable-roofed house, while Classic colonnades, sometimes with Orders two storeys high, lifted the verandah out of the ordinary. Of the three Greek Orders, Doric, the simplest, was considered to be more 'masculine' than Ionic or Corinthian. The Doric Order was chosen by the great engineer John Rennie, because of its 'structural nobility', to embellish his magnificent design for Waterloo Bridge in London, begun in 1812. At this time John Lee Archer, who later came to Van Diemen's Land, was working in Rennie's office. Greek decorative motifs such as the anthemion (buds of the honeysuckle plant), the rosette, the fret, the spiral and the egg-and-dart embellishment, were interpreted in a wide variety of materials, which included stone, artificial stone, terracotta, stucco, metals and plaster. Even a short list like this makes the style seem rich, yet ornament was applied usually with elegant restraint.

Benjamin Latrobe, who learned both architecture and engineering in England, emigrated to Virginia in 1795, was befriended by Thomas Jefferson, and introduced the Greek Revival style into America. It set a pattern for the official architecture of the United States, and in the golden years before the Civil War it became something of a national style. Thomas U. Walter (who later became architect for the United States' Capitol) designed for the wealthy banker Nicholas Biddle 'a formal academic man-

sion as close to a copy of the Theseion as a house can be'. Biddle wrote, 'the two great truths in the world are the Bible and Grecian architecture'.[19] Australia first witnessed the style in 1828, when Surveyor-General Thomas L. Mitchell built a Grecian mansion at Darlinghurst. Henry Kitchen was advocating the style even earlier.

The Neoclassic movement must now be mentioned, for the Greek Revival was a part of it. An understanding of Neoclassicism can help in appreciating the wider significance of the Romantic Revival in Georgian architecture. The essence of Neoclassic architecture lay in the scholarly and precise revival and abstraction of antique motifs – it was a synthesis of archaeological detail and geometrical forms. It is easy, therefore, to regard the Greek Revival as the culmination of the Neoclassic phase. Wren and the English Classical designers, who extended Renaissance

A Gothick Picturesque fantasy built for the wealthy Ralph Allen as an eye-catcher crowning the hill opposite his town house in Bath. It was designed about 1755 by Sanderson Miller.

Top: Lady Franklin's Museum near Hobart is a tiny, scholarly Australian example of the Greek Revival style started in England by 'Athenian' Stuart in 1758. It was built about 1842 and is attributed to the convict architect James Blackburn.

and Baroque traditions, represented the opposite approach: they refused to be bound by the strictures of archaeology and geometry. For example they used the Orders decoratively rather than functionally, and took their Classical examples at second or third hand, *via* Vitruvius or Palladio, or from Italian Renaissance buildings. The Neoclassicists repudiated this approach and went back to the original evidence, demanding for instance the 'truthful' use of the Orders – their columns *appeared* to support something rather than being merely applied to walls.[20]

Neoclassic architecture was by no means all Grecian. The search for accurate Roman models intensified during the second half of the eighteenth century. Giovanni Battista Piranesi was made an honorary member of the Society of Antiquaries in London in 1757 in acknowledgement of his great output of engravings of Classic Roman buildings and ruins. Piranesi designed almost no buildings, but his drawings were deeply persuasive to generations of architects, especially in France and England, as much for their overpowering scale as for their wealth of accurate detail. When the results of archaeological excavations in Italy – including Pompeii from 1748 – were published, and with the recovery of Etruscan art from northern Italy, the variety and efficacy of antique models increased. Robert Wood's *The Ruins of Palmyra*, the first of many English texts on the subject, appeared in 1753.

The greatest British architect of the later eighteenth century exemplified this broadened Neoclassic palette. He was the Scot, Robert Adam, who with his brothers, James and William, founded the most fashionable residential practice of the day. After a tour of Italy and Dalmatia, Robert Adam published a folio volume called *Ruins of the Palace of the Emperor Diocletian at Spalato ...* in 1764. In this book and in his work a new wealth of ornamental sources appeared, full of subtle colour, light and gaiety. Adam popularized the more feminine Ionic Order and introduced a new elongated-leaf capital and other motifs from Dalmatia. His designs in plaster decoration were both brilliant and elegant and with his brother William he promoted a new proprietary material called Liardet's stucco. The Adam brothers aimed to create spatial drama and complexity in their interiors by juxtaposing rooms of contrasting shapes and sizes, often made mysterious by columned screens, semi-domes and apses, freely adapted from the ruins of the Roman world.[21] In the process they made their mark on every element, from carpets and furniture to candlesticks and lock-plates. Their attention to detail was remarkable. In all these ways – by concentration on domestic architecture, by intense interest in interior design, and by sheer variety and vivacity – the Adams greatly extended the repertoire of Neoclassicism. The brothers explained their ideas in *The Works in Architecture of Robert and James Adam, Esquires*, published in London in 1778. Rebelling against 'frequently minute and frivolous' convention, they wrote:

The great masters of antiquity were not so rigidly scrupulous, they varied the proportions as the general spirit of their composition required, clearly perceiving that however necessary these rules may be to form the tastes and to correct the licentiousness of the scholar, they often cramp the genius and encumber the ideas of the master.

The Adams's optimistic and extrovert philosophy was the antithesis of the strict Classical style expressed in sober and conservative tones in the *Treatise* by Sir William Chambers, their chief rival.

Robert Adam had many imitators, the most successful of whom was James Wyatt. His eclecticism culminated in a rash of official 'restoration' work on historic monuments which earned him the nickname of 'Wyatt the Destroyer'. One of Wyatt's pupils was Henry Kitchen.

It is not surprising that the Adam manner, with its slightly revolutionary overtones, caught on in America and, in the early nineteenth century, made important contributions to the styles of Federation there.

The Romantic Revival movement, its Classical rationale becoming less relevant as its Picturesque tendencies grew, flowed into the nineteenth century. It was accompanied by a rash of architectural literature, further waves of eclecticism, and the pretensions of the *nouveaux riche* who had done well out of the Napoleonic wars. To the Gothick, Etruscan and Chinese styles were added revivals like thatched Elizabethan, and exotics such as Norwegian, Egyptian and Hindoo, as well as new combinations and inventions. All of these became evident before the end of the Georgian period, all were the subject of interesting experimentation by architects, and all were applied enthusiastically to domestic architecture.

Georgian through the Regency window

There are two reasons why the Regency period is worth a window of its own. Georgian architecture in Britain then reached its final expression; and, at about the same time, awakened by the realization that the colony was not merely a penal settlement, and nourished by newly arrived architects, the Georgian style made its first confident appearance in Australia.

The true Regency period – when the Prince of Wales ruled as Regent during his father's insanity – lasted only ten years, from 1811–20. But it is usual to think of it as starting in the architectural sense rather earlier, at about the beginning of the new century, and lasting until the end of George IV's reign in 1830.[22] The two great figures of the architectural scene were Sir John Soane and John Nash, and their subtle influence in Australia may be discerned among the effects of the buoyant Regency culture.

The strands of style outlined earlier in this chapter – Palladian, English Classical and Romantic Revival – mixed and overlapped more than ever in the early nineteenth century. Picturesque Gothick was changing into studied Gothic Revival and would later become a favourite residential style. The Picturesque movement waxed as Palladianism waned: Sir Uvedale Price's *Essay on the Picturesque*, 1794, was an important Regency influence. The Greek Revival attained its peak. The Industrial Revolution accelerated the growth of cities and towns, so that at the same time terrace housing achieved its Regency perfection, the cause of its debasement was imminent. The strongest Georgian style keys in the work of Soane and Nash were Neoclassic and Picturesque.

Sir John Soane was a creative eclectic who selected motifs mostly from Grecian ones and from the Adam brothers, and from them made his own idiosyncratic style, where

Left above: No. 7 Adam Street, built in the late 1760s, is the sole surviving house of the Adelphi residential development in London, built by Robert Adam. Adam cared little for conventional 'correctness' but dressed his buildings in full decorative finery.

A rustic Georgian cottage orné, complete with thatch roof and flint walls, in the Picturesque manner. It is The Lodge, in Codford St Mary, Wiltshire.

Sir John Soane remodelled his house, the middle one in this terrace of three in Lincoln's Inn Fields, at the end of the eighteenth century. His was a very personal, romantic interpretation of Classicism.

Left below: The Otis house, in Vernon Street, Boston, is an example of the restrained late-Georgian manner that was known as the Federal style in the newly-formed United States of America. It was designed by Charles Bulfinch in 1800.

proportion and light and shade were more important than colour and decoration. He reduced Classical architecture to its essentials and replaced the traditional members of the Orders with curious mouldings and grooves. Soane's most renowned designs were those for the Bank of England, but his innovative houses were almost as well known, particularly to other architects, many of whom regarded him as the most original living genius in architecture. Many practitioners in Australia in the Regency years must have admired Soane's work, for there are numerous Australian echoes of his very personal style. At least one of his books, *Sketches in Architecture*, published in 1793, was in Australia before 1822; a copy was then in Henry Kitchen's library.

John Nash became George IV's favourite designer and thereby a leader in architectural taste. He was an impressario, a creator of townscape, and an organizer of genius who knew little, and cared less, about the finer points of architectural scholarship.[23] He and the land-

Robert Adam adapted an ancient Roman triumphal arch design for the garden front of Kedleston Hall, Derbyshire, about 1760.

scapist Humphrey Repton became partners, and together created Picturesque houses and gardens that were startlingly new, making use, for example, of Gothick, Rustic, Classical and Italianate styles. Nash's 'Italianate', which became almost a universal vogue, was based on vernacular buildings in the backgrounds of seventeenth-century paintings by Claude Lorraine – a source recommended by Payne Knight, one of the most effectual advocates of the Picturesque.[24] Even more remarkably, Nash became a brilliant town planner who brought the compositional techniques of the Picturesque to the centre of London by building the Regent's Park scheme, lined with grand terraces and dotted with villas. It was a foretaste of the Garden City, but many of the terrace houses contrived by Nash were poorly constructed and conformed only minimally with the building Acts.

The conversion of a modest villa into the fantastic Hindoo-style Royal Pavilion at Brighton typified one end of Nash's creative range, while his design of 1811 for

Blaise Hamlet, a village of nine wildly differing *cottages orné* scattered around a central green, shows the other extreme of his Picturesque style.[25] The English *cottage orné* fashion was one of the inspirations of the domestic Gothic Revival much later in Australia.

Apart from the general inspiration of Nash's genius, which was very widely felt, one specific link with Australia must be mentioned. Francis Greenway worked for John Nash at the time of his partnership with Repton, an experience which must have made a great impression upon the young Greenway.[26] Greenway's subsequent practice in Bristol provides an instance of the way the Regency manner spread into the English counties. It is also a reminder that the extension of the Georgian idiom to the remote colonies was almost as natural, if not quite so direct, as its dispersal over the countryside of Britain.

Though Nash and Soane have been singled out, there was a large body of good designers practising in Regency Britain. Many a town had its equivalent of Nash, and housing projects like Regent's Park appeared at Cheltenham, Plymouth, Tunbridge Wells and many other places. Outside London the use of Classical motifs was less blatant, and house forms were simpler, relying upon good proportions and sparse detail. External walls were usually articulated by simple pilasters or slight projections and recessions, which made subtle shadow lines. The most obvious characteristic of Regency architecture was the exploitation of Roman-cement stucco – an economical means of protecting brickwork and producing decorative effects, as well as imitating ashlar – that could be freshened up by repainting. There were other distinctive Regency motifs: delicate balconies and verandahs, often cantilevered above the ground floor and with delicate iron treillage, roofed with concave sheets of metal, ribbed or painted in wide stripes like the coloured canvas awnings from which they developed; segmental projecting bays, often with window hoods and fine glazing bars; and simple undecorated parapets concealing hipped roofs.

Most constituents of this diverse architectural stockpile made an appearance in colonial Australia before the dramatic changes of the 1850s which encouraged other kinds of growth. The multitude of transplants, grafts and hybrids, metaphorically plucked or carefully transported from the garden of Georgian styles to the new country, on the whole fared well in their new setting. A typical Georgian aid in this transfer was one of the most-used of all pattern-books – John Claudius Loudon's *An Encyclopaedia of Cottage, Farm and Villa Architecture and Furniture*, first published in 1833 – which spread the philosophy as well as the practicalities of the Age of Enlightenment far and wide beyond Britain. Loudon acquired a great following in the Australian colonies, offering every kind of help and advice to the colonist, wealthy or not. In the transitional years leading to self-government, the gold rush, rural expansion, city growth and the railways, the *Encyclopaedia* provided the most common architectural education one could obtain.[27]

Adam's eclectic admiration for the colour and splendour of ancient Roman decoration is evident in the antechamber of Syon House, London.

John Nash has been called the father of Regency architecture and the greatest British architect of the Picturesque Movement. Above: Carlton House Terrace, 1829, displays his mastery of large-scale townscape effects; its finish is mostly stucco, which covers up cheap brickwork. Right: In Park Village West, Regent's Park, Nash established the tradition of the small suburban villa. These houses, typified by asymmetrical towers, are among the earliest in the Italianate style. Far right: Houses such as those around Chester Terrace completed by Nash's assistant Decimus Burton, were exemplars for colonial designers.

GEORGIAN ARCHITECTURE took more than 200 years to develop in Britain. Its orderly flexibility, firmly based on Palladianism and bound by Classical rationale, was ultimately strained by the forces of romanticism and industrialization. The onset of the age of Queen Victoria made Georgian old-fashioned, and it died away, to be revived again in the twentieth century.

In the Australian colony the much shorter tenure of Georgian began tentatively, with the first settlement at Sydney Cove. But it grew, in the bush as well as in the towns, echoing British changes, adapting to suit the environment, and incorporating ideas brought from the other colonies. Then, starved by the withdrawal of convict labour, strangled by Victorian eclecticism, and abandoned for the prosperity brought by gold, it finally withered. Early in Queen Victoria's reign a publication appeared which showed the tenacity of Georgian architecture. It was Joseph Fowles's *Sydney in 1848*, a lively microcosm of this small colonial city; in its carefully drawn townscapes, all of the hundreds of houses, and nearly all of the other structures as well, clearly displayed their Georgian character. The status of Sydney as a remote but confident centre of late-Georgian culture, is revealed in one of the advertisements for the Fowles publication:

or designed, which are always a minority; and the untutored, or vernacular, which form the majority. The two were probably closer in the Georgian period than at any other time in the history of architecture.

Aboriginal habitations

The European view of architecture as a physical necessity makes a striking contrast with that of Australia's original inhabitants, to whom the building of structures seems to have been singularly unimportant. Being mostly hunters and gatherers, the Aborigines did not want permanent architecture; their shelters were few and elemental, and almost none survive. The most substantial evidence of the way the natives built is found in the descriptions and illustrations made by white observers and explorers.

Early observers, applying Western values based on material culture, often evaluated Aborigines as particularly primitive and 'brutish'.[1] In 1688 William Dampier, the buccaneer-author, offered this opinion:

The inhabitants of this country are the miserablest people ... They have no houses, but lie in the open air without any covering, the earth being their bed and the heaven their canopy.[2]

Cook, who met Aborigines on the east coast a century later, saw them through more charitable eyes:

GEORGIAN AUSTRALIA 2

The principal object of this work is to remove the erroneous and discreditable notions current in England concerning this City, in common with every thing else connected with the Colony. We shall endeavour to represent Sydney as it really is – to exhibit its spacious Gas-lit streets, crowded by an active and thriving population – its Public Edifices, and its sumptuous Shops, which boldly claim a comparison with those of London itself ... It is true, all are not yet in a state of completion; but, be it remembered, that what was done gradually in England, in the course of many centuries, has been here effected in the comparatively short period of sixty years ...

Architecture is shaped not only by conscious design and developing technology, but also by environmental forces such as climate and the available materials. The Australian Georgian period is especially interesting because the impact of all of these factors upon building in this new and unfamiliar environment may be seen for the first time.

Though the essential character of Georgian architecture was established by professional architects or educated owners (often with the aid of pattern-books), its continuity and consistency were provided by builders, entrepreneurs, speculators and craftsmen, as well as impecunious owner-builders, whose contribution to Australian building became evident in the days of the First Fleet. In every age there are two basic kinds of houses: the tutored,

The adaptation of Georgian architecture to conditions in colonial Australia is seen in these two Tasmanian examples. Left above: Somercotes, at Ross. Left below: A two-storeyed house at Oatlands.

These people may appear to some to be the most wretched on earth, but in reality they are far happier than we Europeans. They live in a tranquility which is not disturbed by inequality of condition, the earth and sea furnish them with all things necessary for life, they covet not magnificent houses and they sleep as sound in a small hovel or even in the open as the king in his palace on a bed of down.[3]

Watkin Tench, the urbane First Fleet military officer, was puzzled both by the natives' disdain for shelter and by their refusal to wear clothing.

They are seen shivering, and huddling themselves up in heaps in their huts, or the caverns of the rocks, until a fire can be kindled. Than these huts nothing more rude in construction, or deficient in conveniency, can be imagined. They consist only of pieces of bark laid together in the form of an oven, open at one end, and very low, though long enough for a man to lie at full length in. There is reason, however, to believe, that they depend less on them for shelter, than on the caverns with which the rocks abound.[4]

In numerous accounts these structures are described as deserted, suggesting temporary, perhaps seasonable, occupation, appropriate to nomadic life. Thus First Fleet surgeon George Worgan reported that:

We believe mostly in ye Summer ... they take up their Lodgings for a Day or two in a miserable *Wigwam*, which they make of the Bark of a Tree ... these are dispersed about the Woods near the Water, 2. 3. 4 together ... While they had Lodgers the whole stock of Furniture consisted of a Bundle of Spears, 3 or 4 fishing Lines, Shields & Baskets made of ye Bark of a Tree.[5]

An Aboriginal 'hut' and its occupants, as pictured by a First-Fleeter and published in 1789. Bark is bent into a roof shape.

Augustus Earle's graphic watercolour of a camp in New South Wales shows tent-like gunyahs of bark and leaves, each with a fire in front.

There were also houses displaying more advanced technology where mobility was less essential. In 1799 Matthew Flinders described three huts at Shoal Bay:

They were of circular form, of about eight feet in diameter. The frame was made of the stronger tendrils of vines crossing each other in all directions and bound together with strong wiry grass at the principal intersections. The covering was of bark of a soft texture, resembling the bark of what is called the Tea-tree at Port Jackson; and so compactly laid in, as to keep out both wind and rain: the entrance is by a small avenue projecting from the periphery of the circle and does not go directly into the hut but turns sufficiently to prevent the rain from beating in. The height of the under part of the roof is about four and a half or five feet and those that I entered had collected a coat of soot from the fires which had been made in the middle of the huts. Those who have been in an oven will have a tolerable exact idea of these habitations, but the sides of these are nearer to a perpendicular than those of ovens usually are. One of the three huts was a double one ... containing two recesses with but one entrance ... This hut would contain ten or fifteen people.[6]

Settlements like these were obviously semi-permanent, and their habitations more solid. In 1828 Captain Rouse, during a survey of the Richmond River, reported three huts, 30 feet (9 metres) long and 6 feet (1.8 metres) high. In 1839 Captain Perry told of a 'village' on the Clarence River, and commented that the natives appeared to possess 'habits of industry; their fishing nets, baskets, water vessels, and cooking utensils being constructed with peculiar care and neatness'. In describing another New England tribal group, Sir Thomas Mitchell wrote,

Each hut was semi-circular, or circular, the roof conical, and from one side a flat roof stood forward like a portice, supported by two sticks. Most of them were close to the trunk of a tree, and were covered, not as in other parts, by sheets of bark, but with a variety of materials, such as reeds, grass and boughs. The interior of each looked clean, and to us passing in the rain, gave some idea, not only of shelter, but even of comfort and happiness. They afforded a favourable specimen of the taste of the gins, whose business it usually is to construct the huts.[7]

In South Australia, according to Professor A.P. Elkin, well-made huts of saplings and mud, and of saplings and grass, were used mainly as a means of escape from mosquitoes, by closing up a very small opening which served as a door, or by lighting a smoke fire near the opening.[8] Fire itself was precious, and one function of the hut was undoubtedly to protect it. Other writers have observed wood structures (presumably logs or branches) covered with brush or skins, mud huts,[9] huts plastered with clay over sods, beehive-shaped log huts, log houses 16 feet (4.8 metres) long with recesses in the walls for implements and floors carpeted with seaweed, and several kinds of dwellings having stone walls and sapling roofs covered with bark and grass thatch. There were also reports from Queensland in 1906 of two-storeyed pole-framed huts, and even huts with window openings. It has been claimed that stone-walled houses found in Queensland could have been influenced by Malay or Indonesian examples.[10]

A hint of the complexity of native architecture is given by the Aboriginal words used to describe it. For a start, there are dozens of words that mean both 'hut' and 'camp', such as *arura*, *bulgunna*, *kanowindra*, *wilpena* and *yaralla.* (The New South Wales town of Canowindra was named for an Aboriginal hut or camp.) *Yanga* means to make a hut, while *torokolya* is a shade hut. The habitation itself had several names: it was called a *gunyah* by the Aborigines of New South Wales, a *mia-mia* by those of Victoria and Western Australia; in Queensland it was an *oompi* (the word 'humpy' comes from this), and the South Australian natives called it a *wurley* or a *bungaree*.[11] Even from this evidence, which is far from complete, it can be seen that, while Aboriginal houses were less important than in most other cultures, there was much greater variety, and more substance, than is generally realized.

A 1965 study cited the ideal Aboriginal residential unit as a composite family of a man, several wives, unmarried daughters and uncircumcised sons. The same study claimed that, despite the richness and complexity of Aboriginal symbolism, there is no indication that dwellings filled any symbolic function, other than that each was for one family, and outsiders did not enter a dwelling without invitation.[12]

The black man had lived in co-operation with nature for thousands of years and could have taught the white men a great deal about land and resource utilization if they had wanted to learn. But building was a different matter, and the Aborigines had as little of value to offer the Georgians as the newcomers had to offer them. There were of course the ancient middens, which from 1796 onwards the settlers plundered for burning into shell-lime. The experience of the Coal River settlement was typical. In about 1815 W.C. Wentworth wrote:

The lime procured at this settlement is made from oyster shells, which are found in prodigious abundance. These shells lie close to the banks of the river, in beds of amazing size and depth. How they came here has long been a matter of surprise and speculation to the colonists. Some are of the opinion that they have been gradually deposited by the natives in those periodical feasts of shell fish, for the celebration of which they still assemble at stated seasons in large bodies . . . [13]

The one building technique that the nomadic natives gave to the Europeans was that of stripping sheets of tree bark. Andrew Crombie, a Riverina settler, recalled how he employed Aborigines to supply bark for his station outbuildings, using what was probably an age-old method:

After selecting a box tree, straight, and in sappy condition, he would chop a ring around it thus ///// then again crossing XXXXX making the ring in criss cross fashion. This line, though chopped by eye only, would often be as precisely accurate as though marked with a chalk line. Then, taking two forked sticks, and resting them against the trunk of the tree, he would place a stick in the forks, and using this as a movable platform upon which he would stand, he would repeat this ring, making it six or seven feet higher up. Finally he would chop a straight line from top to bottom ring, and the result was that a clean sheet of bark, say, six feet by seven feet would, after a little levering with a tomahawk handle, slip safely to ground, and the boy be provided with half the material required for a good weatherproof, winter gunyah.[14]

There is one remarkable little structure, indelibly linked with Aboriginal history, which should be examined. It was the house built for Bennelong: symbol of the Georgian relationship between black and white.

Bennelong's hut

The first Aborigine to occupy a European building was a young man named Arabanoo, who, on the orders of Governor Phillip, was seized and kept under a kind of house arrest in a hut especially prepared for him, not far from the governor's new house under construction. The capture, curiously, was part of Phillip's plan for integration, all of his earlier efforts at friendliness having proved fruitless. After his first shock had subsided, Arabanoo's reaction to his captors' buildings was interesting. He was astonished and horrified by the tinkling of the bell over the governor's door, and expressed 'extravagant surprise' at the sight of people leaning out of the first floor windows of Phillip's partly-built house.[15] After a while Arabanoo began to enjoy the colonists' friendship; but his untimely death, of smallpox, in May 1789, brought to a close the governor's first serious desegregation experiment.

Six months later Phillip ordered a second expedition, in which Colbee, who was a chief, and Bennelong, were captured at Manly. They were shackled and kept in the same hut. Colbee escaped, but Bennelong gradually gained a degree of trust in his captors, and began to enjoy the patronage of the governor and the attentions of the others as they studied him. Lieutenant P.G. King, who later became governor, wrote that Bennelong:

is a stout, well made man, about five feet six inches high, and, now that the dirt is washed from his skin, we find his colour is a dark black . . . He sits at table with the governor, whom he calls 'Beanga' or Father; and the governor calls him 'Dooroow', or Son. He is under no restraint . . . [16]

Aborigines helping explorers with the construction of an overnight lean-to shelter by cutting bark sheets from a tree. This is a detail of a lithograph, published in 1826.

By 1790 food supplies became scarce and rations were reduced. Bennelong's 'civilized' life became less attractive, and he made his escape. It was not until the end of 1790 that he and Colbee were seen again – at Manly. In broken English, Bennelong expressed a desire to see the governor again, and upon hearing this Phillip went straight there to meet him. During the encounter one of the many other natives who were present, apparently taking fright at Phillip's gesture of friendship, speared him through the shoulder. Everybody scattered in confusion, and the official party embarked and dashed back to Sydney with the badly injured governor. About a week later Bennelong and others visited the outskirts of Sydney and, after various formalities, friendly relations were resumed. Phillip met Bennelong and his new wife Barangaroo outside the town and invited them to dine at Government House. In due course Bennelong and three companions arrived. Bennelong was uninhibitedly glad

Bennelong's hut, on the east point of Sydney Cove (extreme left) was one of the earliest brick houses in Australia.

to see the place again. He 'seemed to consider himself quite at home, running from room to room with his companions, and introducing them to his old friends, the domestics, in the most familiar manner'.[17]

To Watkin Tench this dinner signalled the success of Phillip's attempts to assimilate the Aborigines. 'From this time our intercourse with the natives, though partially interrupted, was never broken off. We gradually continued, henceforth, to gain knowledge of their customs and policy.' It is in the context of such encounters that the building of Bennelong's hut must be seen.

Bennelong's visits to Government House became quite frequent. At length, he solicited the governor to build him a hut at the extremity of the eastern point of Sydney Cove. This the governor readily promised, and gave the necessary directions for it to be built. Thus Bennelong Point obtained its identity. Watkin Tench confirmed that the hut was built at Bennelong's request:

Farther to please him, a brick house, of 12 feet square, was built for his use, and for that of such of his countrymen as might chuse to reside in it, on a point of land fixed upon by himself.[18]

Sergeant James Scott, of the Marines, wrote in his diary for Tuesday, 19 October 1790:

The natives Come in frequently & the Governor has building a house for them ... the Natives get Quite femillier & Great Numbers of them are daily in town ...

By the middle of November, Bennelong's hut was complete. It had a tiled roof, the first such roof used on a residential building in Australia. It also had a fireplace and a chimney, a doorway and one window. Early views of the town show the little building with a pyramid-shaped roof, the door facing west, the window overlooking the north shore, and the chimney on the south side. At the handing-over ceremony, a leather shield, double-cased with tin 'to ward off the spears of his enemies', was presented by the governor to Bennelong. He was elated by the additional status the house and the shield gave him among his fellows, and attached himself even more warmly to the society of the white man. After moving in, Bennelong and his wife and two children offered almost daily hospitality to their black friends.

As far as is known the hut had no furniture, no door, and no window sash or shutter. The evidence suggests that Bennelong did not need these niceties any more than he needed the fireplace; he preferred to light his fire just outside the doorway – the traditional Aboriginal location for a hut fire.[19] He and his family did not live continuously at the hut, but stayed in the Sydney Cove area for only a few days at a time. Bennelong is on record as liking 'his house at the point', and so did his friends, for on at least one occasion the hut was so crowded that he and his wife asked for, and were given, permission to sleep at Government House. The most spectacular event at the hut was a corroboree staged by Bennelong and Colbee in March 1791. Lieutenant William Bradley wrote that the dancers numbered twenty-four men, women and children, and the main dance lasted for an hour.[20]

By May 1792, for reasons unknown, the hut was being used less often; it seems that the natives 'went walkabout' more frequently. Then, at the end of that year, Bennelong left Sydney with Governor Phillip and another Aborigine, named Yemmerrawanie, bound for London. Phillip did not return to the colony, nor did Yemmerrawanie, who died in Kent in 1794; but Bennelong, after an eventful stay in Britain, returned with the new governor, John Hunter, in 1795. His remaining years were not happy, and the *Sydney Gazette* of 9 January 1813 reported his death at an age estimated to be forty-nine years:

Bennelong died on Sunday morning last at Kissing Point. Of this veteran champion of the native tribe little favourable can be said. His voyage to and benevolent treatment in Great Britain produced no change whatever in his manners and inclinations, which were naturally barbarous and ferocious.

The tragedy of Bennelong is that, while on the one hand he was in the end regarded as an incorrigible savage by the whites, on the other he was no longer wanted by his own people. Governor Phillip's experiment in integration, of which Bennelong's hut stood as a symbol, was a failure.

There is no record of anyone living in the little hut after Bennelong went to England. It was still standing unused when, in 1793, the Spanish expedition of discovery, led by

Malaspina, arrived in Sydney. The Spanish scientists requested permission of Lieutenant-Governor Grose to erect an observatory, and for its location:

They chose the point of the cove on which a small brick hut had been built for Ben-nil-long on Governor Phillip's orders, making use of the hut to secure their instruments. Ben-nil-long was absent from the colony at this time in England.[21]

The story of Bennelong's hut ends with its dismantling and recycling, the first recorded instance of the reuse of building materials in the colony. Lieutenant-Governor Collins reported, in October 1795, that:

The bricklayer and his gang were employed in repairing the column (signal station) at the South-head; to do which, for want of bricks at the kiln, the little hut built formerly for Ben-nil-long, being altogether forsaken by the natives, and tumbling down, the bricks of it were removed to the South-head.[22]

The conciliation of the two cultures, symbolized by this little Georgian building, has been attempted countless times since then with little success. In December 1798, Bennelong Point began its long life as a defence installation with the building of a gun battery. And when Governor Macquarie built his fort there in 1817–19, the name of Fort Macquarie ousted that of Bennelong. Only since 1959, when the fort was demolished, has the name Bennelong Point been restored.

Government houses before Macquarie

The optimism of the first settlement is graphically shown in Governor Phillip's 1788 design for the town of Sydney. It was a grand, orderly arrangement of streets 61 metres wide, focused on a civic centre, and with firm proposals for land development. Phillip wanted to:

preserve a kind of uniformity in the buildings, prevent narrow streets, and to exclude many inconveniencies which a rapid increase of inhabitants might otherwise occasion hereafter ... When houses are to be built here, the grants of land shall be made with such clauses as will prevent the building of more than one house on the allotment, which is to consist of sixty feet in front and one hundred and fifty feet in depth.

So Phillip wrote in the journals which were later published in his name. But his Georgian vision was thwarted by the hardship of the settler's situation and, evidently, by the lack of support he received from the officials of the colony. The prospect of planned growth disappeared, and Sydney was destined never again to have a semblance of order in its growth. But although Phillip's expedition was ill-prepared to build an outpost of empire, before he returned to England at the end of 1792 he saw more than 200 buildings, most of them houses, erected in Sydney and its satellites, establishing the Georgian idiom.

The very first house erected in the colony was a miniature herald of the industrial revolution. This was the governor's 'portable house', a ready-made building ordered and paid for in London by the Navy Office in 1786, its cost being £130.[23] Its design has been attributed to the young Jeffry Wyatt, nephew of 'Wyatt the Destroyer', but there is no documentary evidence of this. It was in fact made by Nathan Smith, the London inventor of 'oil-cloth', a precursor of linoleum. The house consisted of timber-framed panels covered with oilcloth, which was

Lieutenant William Bradley's drawing of Sydney Cove early in 1788 shows the small prefabricated house which Governor Phillip brought to the settlement. It is depicted with four windows on a site above the flagstaff, in what is now Macquarie Place.

The first substantial Government House was completed in 1789. It was built of brick, in a simplified Classical style. The kitchen block is at the right, linked by a covered way to the house. The spike on the roof is a lightning arrestor.

A British Georgian landscape and its Classical house, in a man-made landscape setting, with water and a 'folly' in the foreground: Prior Park, at Bath, about 1756.

essentially canvas impregnated with pigmented linseed oil.[24] Its components were brought ashore on 29 January 1788, and a number of carpenters immediately set to work assembling it on a site that is now Macquarie Place. The work went on slowly, and it was not until 19 February that the governor moved from his ship to his residence on shore.[25] The unpretentious structure was a rectangle of four rooms, of which the Marine, Daniel Southwell wrote, ''Tis very compact'; but it was large enough to allow a sit-down dinner to all the military and civil officers of the settlement, including Southwell, to celebrate the King's Birthday on 4 June 1788.[26] Months later, when the governor's permanent house was finished, the portable house was taken apart and reassembled as one of its outbuildings.[27]

Until the end of the eighteenth century the leaders of taste were the governors and their senior officials, but in the decade preceding Macquarie some houses of surprising quality, surpassing the vice-regal residences, were created by emancipists and free settlers.

The first Australian house that could be thought of as architectural was the one whose foundation plaque was laid by Governor Phillip in May 1788. Though none of the structure above the ground remains, there are significant archaeological remnants at the site, and a wealth of historic documentation survives to tell its story. Its demolition in 1845 prompts the observation that a history of Australian architecture could be written from the evidence of buildings which no longer survive.

As built by Phillip, the first Government House was a symmetrical, two-storeyed, hip-roofed and stuccoed-brick rectangle, situated overlooking Sydney Cove on the rising ground just south-east of the portable house. The front, facing north, was designed in three bays, the centre one projecting slightly as a 'break-front' which was surmounted by the building's most distinctive feature, a gable in the form of a pediment, in the tympanum of which there was a circular recess. The front door had a semicircular fanlight and sidelights, grouped together under a larger recessed arch. The ground floor windows were twelve-paned, and the first floor ones were nine-paned. There were decorative quoins, a string-course dividing the facade half-way up, and the whole house rested upon a stone plinth, in which small openings were placed to provide daylight to the cellar under the western half. At the rear, on each side of a projecting double-storeyed stair hall, there was a skillion-roofed appendage of additional rooms. Linking the central rear door to the separate kitchen block was a covered way, and across the rear courtyard were service buildings, including stables.

In front of the house was a low-walled courtyard containing two cannon, two sentry-boxes and some formal planting. The land between this and Sydney Cove was made into a garden, with paths, fences and shaped beds of vegetable crops. Thomas Watling, the convict artist who portrayed the house many times, summarized its appearance in about 1792:

His Excellency's indeed, is composed of the common and attic

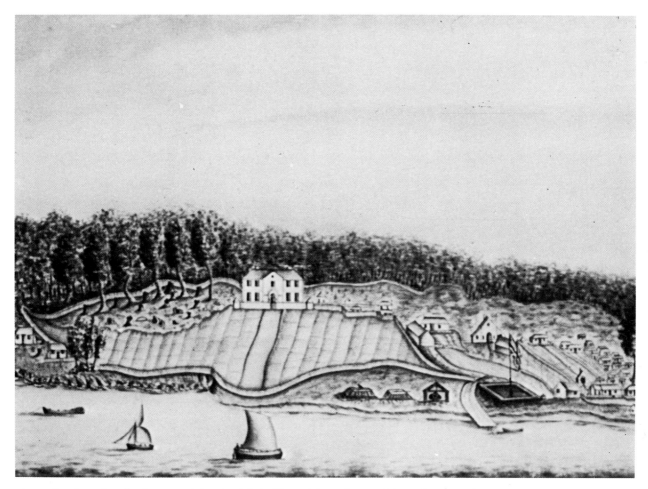

orders, with a pediment in front, and commands the most exalted station, but as neither the wood, brick, nor stone . . . are good for much, it is simple and without any other embellishment whatever.[28]

Phillip brought 5,000 English bricks with him, and it is presumed that he used them at Government House. The rest of the needed bricks were made at the Brickfield Hill brickyard. The mortar and stucco for the brickwork were made partly with English lime and partly with shell-lime burnt in Sydney. The First Fleet also brought a large quantity of crown glass cut into window panes, of which three or four hundred would have been used in the governor's house. Some of the joinery and interior fitting-out was done with Norfolk Island pine timber, and this probably included the staircase, which was the only one in the colony for some time.[29]

When looking at illustrations of Phillip's residence in its park-like setting, the comparison with stately Palladian mansions such as Prior Park, at Bath, is inescapable: the differences, of course, are obvious, but the similarities are even more fascinating. Four elements are common to both the English and the colonial images: the formal house, the 'tamed' landscape contiguous to it, the 'wilderness' beyond, and the foreground of water with a 'feature' at its edge. If the style of the Sydney building had to be named, it would be 'simplified English Classical'. Phillip's house was a peculiar Georgian symbol. It was not only the

focus of the colony; it also represented order, security, permanence, taste and, inevitably, subordination.

The designer of this first house is unknown. Fifteen years after its completion the *Sydney Gazette*, in reporting the death of James Bloodsworth, Superintendent of Buildings, stated that: 'The first house in this part of the Southern Hemisphere was by him erected, as most of the public buildings since have been under his direction.' Bloodsworth was a convict and a master bricklayer, who was emancipated in 1790 and died, a much-respected tradesman, in 1804. But just as likely a candidate for designer of the house is Henry Brewer, a companion of the governor's, who is described as an architect, and was appointed as Superintendent of Works within a few days of the first landing.[30] It is a pity that no documents have yet been found to credit either of these two men with the introduction of Georgian architecture into Australia.

Governor Hunter, the second bachelor incumbent, made the first of a series of alterations to Government House. He added the five-bay northern verandah – a single-storey skillion-roofed climatic necessity – which modified the English character of the building. Philip Gidley King, the next governor, was accompanied by his wife, who found the accommodation inadequate and accordingly added a 'long drawing-room' to the east end of the house, wider than the earlier rooms and needing a higher ceiling to make it conform to Georgian proportions. When the verandah was extended in 1802 to protect this room, the house lost its symmetry. Francois Péron, of the French expedition then visiting Sydney, described it in his journal as: 'the governor's house, which is built in the Italian style, surrounded by a colonnade, as simple as it is elegant, and in front of which is a fine garden'.[31]

The next residents were William Bligh and his widowed daughter Mary Putland. They ordered floor coverings of 'oilcloth' for all the main rooms, large mirrors to 'suit the Paintings of their Majestys', new state dinnerware, and decorative candlesticks. Bligh also greatly altered the garden. Surgeon Harris wrote that it was 'all laid out in Walks with clumps of trees . . . all the Rocks in the Garden is blown up and carried away . . . carriage roads are now all around Bennelong Point'.

During the trial of Major George Johnston, which followed the Rum Rebellion, the participants in the dramatic events at Government House described their movements on 26 January 1808. From the detailed proceedings of the case the functions of all the main rooms can be determined. The central drawing-room was connected with the long drawing-room on the east as well as with a 'dining-parlour' on the west, behind which was another parlour connected with the hall. From the west window of this parlour 'in the back section', the main guard could be seen approaching the house ahead of Johnston, to arrest the governor. East of the hall were Mrs Putland's two rooms, one of which was a bedchamber. Upstairs, the governor's room and two other bedchambers were under the main roof. Also upstairs, 'at the back of the house, formed the same as a skilling', was the governor's steward's tiny suite of two rooms, one of which had a small window. From this window, Bligh testified, 'it was my contemplation how I could possibly get clear of the troops . . . and get to the Hawkesbury'. He was arrested in this plain little attic room. Five more governors occupied the house, each of them changing it, until its metamorphosis, from a simple Classical design to a complex and vaguely Italianate Picturesque composition, was at last complete.[32]

The large house built for the lieutenant-governor, across the Tank Stream on the 'military' side of Sydney, was the opposite in style to the prim Georgian visage of the governor's mansion. Robert Ross, Marine Major and Phillip's second-in-command, started construction of his long, low residence facing 'the principal street of the intended town' in April 1788. Behind it were the barracks buildings and in front was the spacious parade-ground. In twentieth-century Sydney the site is at the corner of George and Grosvenor Streets. The house was the first to be built of hewn sandstone and it was the first of many building jobs to run into difficulties caused by poor mortar and a capricious climate. On 7 August, Lieutenant William Bradley wrote in his journal that: 'The Lieut-gov's house, which was a building of stone and several feet above the ground, gave way with the heavy rain and fell to the ground.'

A drawing of the settlement done in 1792 shows his house completed as a single-storeyed L-shape, with a hipped roof, its floor elevated well above the Parade. Francis Grose became lieutenant-governor in that year, and took over the administration of the colony when Phillip left. He liked the house and the ample subsistence garden that Ross had established. He built stables and other outbuildings and also, by 1793, added a verandah –

the first to be seen in the colony – along the full 22-metre frontage facing the Parade. This transformed the house into something like a big bungalow, with a wide roof, and verandah posts so closely spaced that they were more like vertical louvres. Impressive new steps led up to the entrance, above which, by way of emphasis, the verandah roof was canted up into a little gable pediment. The horizontal lines and elevated 'galerie' now made the lieutenant-governor's house look like one of the French-American plantation houses which he could have seen during his travels while on service in the War of Independence, before coming to Australia.

The exotic garden, for which the lieutenant-governor's house became famous, was begun by Captain William Paterson when he moved in during 1794. Science was Paterson's chief interest. He maintained close contact with Sir Joseph Banks and other scholars in England, collected botanical specimens for them as well as for cultivation in the colony, and even directed a small 'botanic garden' in Parramatta. Planting in his Sydney garden included English and foreign trees, and there were large numbers of fruit trees, grape-vines, shrubs, flowers and vegetables. Paterson was interested in oak trees as a timber resource, and introduced an early-flowering peach variety in a successful bid to overcome destructive blight. He also built in the garden the first example of a dovecote, a strictly functional structure in which birds were reared both for ornament and for table. The French expedition visiting Sydney in 1802 reported that:

The whole of the western side of the square is occupied by the house of the Lieutenant-Governor, behind which is a vast garden, which is worth the attention both of the philosopher and the naturalist, on account of the great number of useful plants and vegetables transported thither from all parts of the globe by its present respectable proprietor . . .

In 1820 the spacious house was opened for 'Public Accommodation as the Sydney Hotel and Coffee House', and Governor Macquarie attended a ball and supper there in 1821. When it was demolished in 1831, to make way for new roads, the passing of Australia's first bungalow house and first verandah went unnoticed.[33]

None of Sydney's other pre-Macquarie residences built for the use of the governors or commandants was as impressive as these two, but all were Georgian in form, and some have survived to display remnants of eighteenth-century colonial taste. Old Government House at Parramatta was first built by Phillip in 1790, as the focus of an axial vista town plan which, though quite different from Sydney's, was just as unusual. Its main street was 'of such breadth as will make Pall Mall and Portland Place hide their diminished heads', and it extended from the landing-place on the river to the foot of Rose Hill, on which the small, symmetrical, hip-roofed villa was erected. The land around the house was used to graze the government cattle and for farming. One writer described it as 'so situated by nature that, in my opinion, it is impossible for art to form so rural a scene'.[34]

After Phillip's departure the lath-and-plaster house fell into disrepair, and on his arrival Hunter decided to build a new residence at the same site. It was 'large and elegant . . . spacious and roomy, with cellars and an attick storey'. Its

Left: The Classical lines of the first Government House were softened by the addition of a single-storey verandah, and the house lost its formal symmetry when it was extended eastwards.

By 1828, when Augustus Earle published this picture, the house and its garden had become quite Picturesque and Italianate. The Classical addition at the east end, left, was probably designed by Francis Greenway in 1816.

Left: Parramatta's Government House as it was in 1809. This simple Classical house, built by Governor Hunter, remains today as the centre of a Palladian composition designed by Lieutenant John Watts.

walls were of brick, coated with lime stucco and marked with grooves to imitate stone, and its roof was shingled. By 1799, still not finished, it was damaged in a severe storm, and the house was not complete until after Governor King arrived. George Caley, the enthusiastic botanist, occupied it and made it the base for his scientific work, at King's invitation.[35]

This 'Hunter' building survives, somewhat altered, but a painting done by G. W. Evans in about 1809 shows it as it was in King's and Bligh's time. The main block of the house was symmetrical, two-storeyed, and designed in the proportions of a triple-cube. The roof was hipped and shingled, with close-cropped eaves. The ground-floor windows were 'double-cube' (twice as deep as wide) and those on the first floor were one-and-a-half times deep as wide. The windows were positioned beautifully in the facade. The central door had sidelights and a semicircular fanlight, all framed by a slender Classical frontispiece. Outside the window above the front entrance there was a slim balconette with a filigree balustrade, probably of iron. Like Sydney's Government House, this building was a simplified version of the English Classical style. These delicate proportions and details suggest the hand of a knowledgeable designer. It is unlikely to have been Henry Brewer, for his health was failing and he was no longer active in building; perhaps it was James Bloodsworth who was then Superintendent of Buildings.

David Collins's Government House in Hobart is shown in an 1806 sketch as a small single-storey three-roomed hip-roofed building. Before 1817 it had been enlarged into a two-storeyed structure with a symmetrical frontage of seven bays, the centre one containing the entrance, and around the house a new square, named after the King, had been created.[36]

At Kingston, Norfolk Island, a fine Georgian house, which must have been the commandant's, dominates the view drawn by William Neate Chapman in 1796. It is a single-storey building of five bays, symmetrical about a doorway with a fanlight, sidelights and a surrounding frontispiece. The roof is a double-pitched or 'mansard' shape with five dormer windows. In front there is a balustraded gallery, without a roof. What happened to this house is unknown, but by 1803, 'on a gentle eminence', there was a new house under construction for Major Joseph Foveaux, the new commandant. It was made of the island's porous limestone, with joinery of Norfolk Island pine. Reinstated and enlarged during the Second Settlement, it now forms the western part of the Administrator's house.

At Coal River, Newcastle, the most dreaded of all the penal settlements, the first commandant, Lieutenant Charles Menzies, built what was called 'Government House' about 1804. In a watercolour by an unknown artist it is portrayed as a single-storeyed stone building, with a hipped, shingled roof, and a central entrance comprising door, fanlight and sidelights. A five-bay verandah has a pavilion room at each end, lit by windows with segmental arches, and in each of the bays there is a curved valance, linking the verandah posts at eaves level. This little residence, with its arches, valances and end rooms is a very early example of Regency in Australia.

Left above: The remarkable, remote little settlement of Norfolk Island, with 'Government House' (the commandant's house) occupying a prominent and symbolic position.

This detail of an 1817 sketch of Hobart shows Government House as a symmetrical two-storeyed building. On the left is Mr Birch's impressive Gothick house with a crenellated parapet.

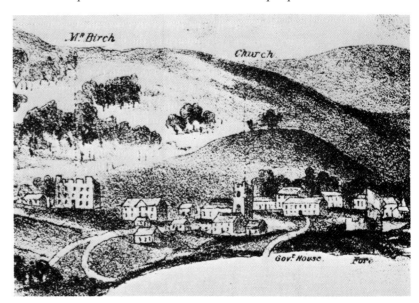

A watercolour of about 1804 shows the Government House at Newcastle as a gently Regency-style building, with a pavilioned verandah.

Left below: Government House at Norfolk Island is today the residence of the island's administrator. It is simplified Classical in style, single-storeyed and verandahed.

Houses of the first settlers

At the end of the eighteenth century Australia's building resources, of materials as well as taste, were being developed as thoroughly as the little populace could manage. Sydney was the largest of the settlements and the pictures of the time reveal its astonishingly confident character. Two large oil paintings, done at the turn of the century and attributed to Thomas Watling,[37] when studied together, give a detailed impression of the buildings of the town. The Rocks area (so called from about this time) while dominated by the skyscraper town clock and the windmills, was crowded with variegated houses which clearly illustrate how Georgian taste was adapted.

Almost every dwelling was one-storey high, with a facial arrangement of central nose-like doorway and two eye-like windows: a naive and childlike offspring of the parent style half a world away. Significantly, there were no joined houses, nothing even remotely like terraces; each was a private house, even though they were built in

In 1800 residents of the Rocks lived in rows of small vernacular town houses, most of them primitive versions of Classical villas.

'rows'. Vernacular town houses, typified by those in the Rocks, were not built of brick or stone, but of less durable materials such as wood and wattle-and-daub, with whitewashed walls and thatched roofs. One reason for this was that these settlers had no security of tenure, as the land was not granted or even leased. Another was that the lesser occupants built their own houses, using whatever materials they could get. The range of occupiers included free settlers, alone or with families; some military personnel; convict families; and convict work gangs. There were houses also of slightly better quality, with shingled roofs, skillion extensions and more than one fireplace. Some had lofts or attics, with 'bed-closets' upstairs. For example Thomas Randall, a tinsmith, had a house 13 metres long and 7 metres wide, but most were smaller than this.[38]

Isaac Nichols, an emancipated convict, built his first house beside Sydney Cove in about 1800. It is shown in one of the Watling paintings: a storey-and-a-half high, with a rear skillion, a gable roof with its top half nipped off by hips, and two dormer windows. The tile-roofed house built by Judge Advocate Collins, also shown by Watling, had a tall gable facing the street, balanced by a skillion on each side. The front doorway and six windows of this house were symmetrical, and it resembled a simplified miniature of a pedimented villa by Palladio. In 1800 it was whitewashed, but in earlier views it was painted blue. A house occupied by Thomas Moore, Governor Hunter's master boat builder, was also exceptional. It was of stone, on a podium, with steps leading up from the waterfront to an arched central doorcase which included sidelights. But its hipped roof of shingles was a mansard – a double-pitched form originating in France – and had many dormer windows lighting its attic rooms.

In 1800, apart from Government House, there were only

A large oil painting of Sydney in 1799, painted by Thomas Watling. The wide street to the right of centre is Bridge Street, at the far end of which is Government House. The single-storey building in the right foreground is the lieutenant-governor's house. The dwellings on the left are in the Rocks.

two double-storeyed houses in Sydney. One of them belonged to John Boston; it was built of stone, with a shingled roof, and was identical in form to the governor's house at Parramatta. Almost nothing is known of this house, but John Boston was one of the most colourful of Australia's early settlers, whose fortune came from making beer, salt and soap, and from Pacific trading. He was murdered by natives at Tongatapu in 1804.[39]

The other two-storeyed house was built in 1799 by William Kent, a naval officer and nephew of Governor Hunter. It is shown in the Watling paintings and in many other early pictures, and is the subject of a very early professionally done but unsigned working drawing. The house was described later by Rowland Hassall as the 'best house in all Sydney, none excepted'. It was the first example of a residence designed in the manner of the English Palladians, with single-storeyed wings extending outwards from its two-storeyed centre block. It was a single-pile building of stone, with close-eaved shingled roofs. The principal floor of the central core comprised two rooms, one each side of a hall which contained a geometrical cantilevered stair. Upstairs there were two large rooms, and a smaller one over part of the hall added spatial interest to the staircase. The two dependencies contained servants' quarters, kitchen and store-rooms. The arrangement of the elevations, including the garden-front doorcase and the pairing of the windows, was the same as that of Governor Hunter's Parramatta house. Kent, however, added a string course above the ground-floor windows (as had been done at Sydney's Government House) which improved the proportions of the double-storeyed block. The garden which Kent developed between the house and the Cove was impressive – a formal, axial arrangement of regular plant beds separated by paths, and divided into two equal parts by a straight walkway leading to the water's edge.

After Kent's departure in 1800, Governor King decided to purchase the house for an orphanage. James Bloodsworth was one of the valuers who assessed its worth as £1,539, and it was opened as the Orphan House in 1801.

The house was enlarged in 1803, without damage to its Palladian character. It was sold in 1827 to James Underwood and, as shown in Joseph Fowles's *Sydney in 1848*, was replaced by late Georgian buildings.[40]

John Macarthur's original Elizabeth Farm cottage, simple but soundly built, survives partly within the more complex structures which enveloped it later at Parramatta. Macarthur described it as:

a most excellent brick house, 68 feet in front, and 18 feet in breadth. It has no upper storey, but consists of four rooms on the ground floor, a large hall, closets, cellar, etc.; adjoining is a kitchen, with servants' apartments and other necessary offices.

As was usual in single-pile houses, the centre hall and the two rooms on each side were connected by doors to facilitate internal circulation. The modifications made during the next thirty years transformed this box-like beginning first into a bungalow form, and subsequently into one of the lesser Regency masterpieces.

Lieutenant William Kent's Palladian house had a formal waterfront garden laid out in geometrical beds of vegetables.

William Neate Chapman's house at Norfolk Island, redrawn from a letter written to his brother on 20 November 1795. Both the house and the separate kitchen are symmetrically shaped.

Plan of my house, no scale is observed, it is only to shew you the different appartments

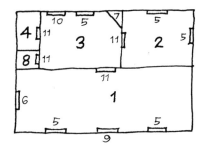

KITCHEN

№ 1	Chimney & oven	№ 1	Parlour
2	Door	2	Bed room
3	Windows	3	Passage room
4	Dresser, Shelves &c.	4	Stair case
5	Cupboard	5	Windows
6	Temple	6	Chimney
		7	Corner Cupboard
		8	Cupboard under the Stairs
		9	Front Door
		10	Back do.
		11	Doors

Detail from a painting of Sydney done about 1825, showing Robert Campbell's bungalow house, built around a courtyard. The roof lights are notable.

Right: An engraving of Sydney in 1813, by Absalom West. At the left is James Underwood's flat-roofed Regency-style house, and to its right is the George Street front of William Kent's Palladian-style house. Beyond this, just across the bridge, is Simeon Lord's four-storey stone mansion.

One of the few surviving eighteenth-century annotated house plans is included in a letter written by William Neate Chapman from Norfolk Island in 1795. It shows that under the main roof of his house there was, untypically, only a single room, which he called the parlour. Its front facade, as might be expected, was symmetrical. Behind, opening off a 'passage room', were a bedroom and a small staircase leading to loft rooms above the main block. The kitchen was a separate rectangle, also symmetrical, but placed at right angles to the house. Some distance away was Chapman's pit closet, the 'temple'.[41]

These few but varied examples of eighteenth-century houses clearly display their sources of style. In the main these were Palladian and English Classical, but Indian bungalow and even French influences can be discerned. In Sydney there is no sign of the Regency influence.

The optimism of Governor King's regime, which opened with the new century, encouraged a great deal of building by free settlers and emancipists, whose numbers increased to about 15 per cent of the population. In the same period less government building was being done, but there was more private building, much of it assisted by the system of convict assignment.

Robert Campbell was the first truly independent merchant in Australia. He established his business in 1800 after some years of experience in India. His Sydney house was part of his trading complex 'at the water's edge ... where a ship of large dimensions can load or unload, with any tide alongside his wharf'. It is depicted in paintings as early as 1802 as a long, low single-storey house, 'finished in an elegant manner with colonnades and two fronts', and the seven-bay front facing Sydney Cove had the now customary centre entrance and balanced window arrangement. Campbell's was the first house to have its verandahs incorporated under the main roof rather than being added later, as in all the earlier examples. Campbell may therefore be credited with introducing a whole-hearted Indian bungalow form into Australia. Nevertheless this idiom, so suitable for the colony, was not popular, and very few examples can be found before Macquarie's time.[42]

The emancipists' stylish designs

Most of the interesting houses in this first decade were built not by free settlers or military officers but by emancipated convicts who had prospered. The following examples were among the best and most fashionable in the colony, yet they were built, it seems, without the benefit of professional designers. No architects had yet come to Australia, and no evidence has been found of pattern-books being available to builders as early as this.

James Underwood was a convict whose early career is obscure, but he became a shipbuilder, distiller and merchant. He probably began his career through a connection with an officer-trader, but established his fortune in partnership with Henry Kable and Simeon Lord. His house, built in about 1804, occupied waterfront land next to the Orphan School and for a time his boat-yard sheds stood on the same block. In this house Underwood introduced Regency design to the colony. It was built upon a stone-faced base storey, which not only formed the plinth of the street elevation but also was extended outwards from the waterfront elevation to form a balustraded podium. Above this the house was a symmetrical block two storeys high, of brickwork limewashed in stone colour, with quoins, string courses and window dressings. It was flat-roofed, and a little turret gave access to a 'captain's walk' which was edged with a filigree balustrade, probably of iron. There were balconette railings on the five upper windows of the street facade and along the street boundary there was a masonry fence of piers, panels and balustrades. No house of such delicacy and stylishness had been seen before in Australia.[43]

Simeon Lord's house was more conservative. Lord had

including a counting house and auction room. There were four bedrooms and three dressing-rooms in the second storey, while the upper floor had fourteen single rooms opening off a 3-metre wide passage. In the basement were the servants' hall, pantry and cooling cellars. The house had external walls of stone, internal ones of brick, 'lined with cedar on the ground and first floor', and an M-shaped hip roof of shingles. Lord later claimed it cost him £15,000 to build. Externally, apart from its unusual size, the house was very simple. Of seven bays width, the front, across the road from Macquarie Place, was protected by a two-storey verandah, which gave the

been transported in the Third Fleet, and was assigned to Thomas Rowley, a prominent officer-trader. By 1795 he had a liquor licence, and in 1798 bought his pub, the Swan, which is possibly one of the buildings standing on what was later Macquarie Place. Lord became a retailer, auctioneer, sealer, pastoralist, timber merchant, manufacturer, wholesale merchant, captain's agent and merchant banker. In 1803 he began building the large house by the Tank Stream bridge which became a Sydney institution as much as a residence. A boon to ships' officers who wished to sleep ashore near their merchandise, it was a rendezvous for captains and supercargoes for the next twenty years. Three storeys to the front, four to the rear, the house had four large rooms on the ground floor,

building a Regency air. Its doorcase included a huge semicircular fanlight embracing the door and side-lights. The house was demolished in 1908.[44]

John Redmond was less prosperous and his house was much humbler, though hardly less interesting. After his emancipation Redmond became chief constable in Sydney, and afterwards a shipowner and merchant. His house, built before 1810, on the waterfront of Sydney Cove not far from Underwood's, had a symmetrical front facing what became George Street, but on the water side there was an L-shaped wing, on two sides of which was a cantilever verandah, in the Regency manner.[45]

The Sydney house of Thomas and Mary Reibey differed from all of these. Thomas Reibey was the first free settler

outside the military ring to engage in trade. He and Mary Haydock, a convict, were married in 1794, and lived for a while in the Hawkesbury area. Reibey acquired property in Sydney, set up as an importer, and named his establishment Entally House, after a suburb in Calcutta, to symbolize his earlier Indian experience. In 1811 Tom Reibey died, as did his partner Edward Wills, and Mary was left with seven children and numerous business concerns to control. She prospered, and her trading operations and property holdings increased. In the forty-four years between her husband's death and her own, Mary Reibey and members of her family built many houses, in New South Wales and Tasmania. An 1806 rendition of Sydney by John Eyre shows Entally House as a two-storey stone building but during its life this house was modified many times. Before 1817, when it was the venue for the opening of the Bank of New South Wales, it had been enlarged into an impressive double-pile house, three storeys high at street level. Five bays wide, the building had a breakfront embracing three bays and surmounted by a gable pediment with a circular motif in its tympanum, and there were double entrance doors under a large fanlight. Though it was undoubtedly better built than Governor Phillip's house twenty-one years before, the Reibey house was almost as conservative in style: a colonial version of English Classical.[46]

Strong elements of Palladian, English Classical and Regency taste, as well as the Indian bungalow tradition, came to Australian house design before 1810. The expansion and mingling of these styles, and the advent of the Romantic Revivals, had to wait for the architects, and for the expansion that Governor Macquarie encouraged.

A page from Joseph Fowles's microcosm, Sydney in 1848, *showing Macquarie Street. The prominent house in the second line is Burdekin House, demolished in about 1933. Two of the Horbury Terrace houses, and one from the terrace in the fourth line, still survive. Fowles claimed that Sydney's houses could 'boldly claim a comparison with those of London itself'.*

Building a society

In the thirty years that started with Macquarie's governorship the vision first seen by Phillip and Tench began to materialize. They were years of expansion, of order, and dignity, and just as architecture at all times reflects the aspirations of society, so now the house became the dominant building type, the symbol of settlement, the family, community, and confidence in the future.

Macquarie was a builder. The exploration he promoted is typified by the crossing of the Blue Mountains and the foundation of Bathurst. He built on his predecessors' start by naming Windsor and the other Macquarie towns, founding Liverpool, and giving Hobart Town a new vision of itself. His public building programme and the building codes he introduced improved the quality of architecture. The town plans he promoted affected the way Sydney, Hobart and towns throughout his realm developed. And as though to make Macquarie's dreams come true, the first professional architects arrived during his time.

Brisbane, the astronomer governor, came armed with instructions to reduce public building and to favour the free settler rather than the emancipist. He also encouraged growth in Van Diemen's Land, which became a separate

Town house and country house compared. Above: Bligh House, Sydney, is an urbane Classical residence of the 1830s. Right: Mountain View, outside Richmond, New South Wales, however, is a simpler rural house in a more spacious setting.

colony in 1825. In his time the town that became Brisbane was settled.

Governor Darling's effect on building was characterized by the regulations he issued in 1829, directed at the setting-out of new towns. East Maitland was one of the first of these, but the influence of the regulations was seen long after and Melbourne's street layout is one instance. Western Australia was settled in Darling's time.

Governor Bourke introduced state aid for all religious denominations, encouraged the foundation of Melbourne, and established a system of licences for land squatters. His brief term of office ushered in the prosperous period for New South Wales and Van Diemen's Land that Morton Herman called the Golden Thirties.

In Governor Gipps's tenure Adelaide was founded, and Sydney and Melbourne were incorporated as cities; convict transportation to New South Wales ended, while in Van Diemen's Land, Port Arthur was established. Victoria was crowned Queen

Australian mainstream Georgian

There are several great themes that pervade the Georgian mainstream of domestic architecture. The first is that through the growth of the colony two kinds of houses emerged – the town house and the country house. Houses now appeared which had a definitely 'metropolitan' character and belonged to a streetscape. A great many of these performed a second function, that of a shop, or a pub; and many – those built before Macquarie's regulations, for instance – were on tiny blocks of town land, tight against the street alignment. Examples of the two extremes of town houses were tiny joined houses like Glover's Terrace in Kent Street, in the Rocks of Sydney, and Tusculum, one of the 'villas of Wolloomooloo', which, despite its spacious setting, was close enough to be regarded as a town house. Country houses, on the other hand, tended to symbolize the agricultural importance of the colony, in particular the wealth that the wool industry was bringing. Nowhere was this better expressed than in the homestead, and its associated structures such as the shearing shed – building types that became distinctly Australian.

Rocky Hall, near Wilberforce, is a house of vernacular character. Its half-hipped roof, characteristic in the Hawkesbury region of New South Wales, meant that the gable-end walls did not need to be built as high as the roof apex.

The second theme centres on the people who built and used the houses. Some, like the Macarthurs, the Coxes and the Archers, established dynasties. Emancipists of the previous generation did this too: the Reibeys, the Lords, the Kables. Accordingly, the currency lads and lasses increased in numbers. But it was also true that the flow of free settlers and, proportionately, the capital they brought with them for building, increased. In 1830 about 22 per cent of the population were free settlers; by 1840 this proportion had gone up to about 60 per cent. While most of them were subsidized immigrants, there were also the well-to-do. The population of the Australian colonies in

Right: Variants on the Georgian theme. Top: Two Sydney houses whose designs came from the same English pattern-book. The nearest is the Colonial Secretary's house of 1814, and to its right is the Judge Advocate's house of 1812. Centre: A two-storey house and shop in Campbelltown, with an ogee-roofed verandah. Below: The Doctor's House at Raymond Terrace, a single-storeyed later house with roof dormers and a concave verandah.

1830 was 70,000 – a substantial resource of knowledge and ability. The considerable range of vernacular architecture in the Georgian years is due to the great variety of backgrounds from which the settlers came and the ranges of skills they possessed. And to the limited funds of the 'bounty immigrants' who did not have the money to spend on large or stylish homes. Whether they lived in town or country, they all had to satisfy their need for shelter, often by building for themselves.

Popular pattern-books

Many new Australians needed to construct buildings, particularly houses, and were helped by the pattern-book – the next theme. Pattern-books were the ancestors of architectural magazines. They comprised design-books for cottages, villas, mansions and farm buildings, as well as handbooks and encyclopaedias. Many a sensible settler brought one with him, and they were a significant factor in colonial domestic architecture. One favoured book was David Laing's *Hints for Dwellings*, first published in 1800, copies of which were owned by several Australian families, for example the Macarthurs, the Oxleys and the Campbells. Mrs Macquarie owned a copy of Edward Gyfford's *Designs for Elegant Cottages and Small Villas*, 1806, and Design No. 1 in this book was the inspiration for Judge Advocate Ellis Bent's new house in 1812. Replacing the Palladio-inspired house built earlier by David Collins, this was a three-storeyed residence with flanking bow-ended wings.

Alexander McLeay possessed a copy of Loudon's popular *Encyclopaedia of Architecture*. Loudon's works were particularly influential among a professional group in Sydney, comprising Surveyor-General Mitchell, his deputy John Thompson, and colonial architect Mortimer Lewis. Thompson adapted one of Loudon's designs for his own house, and encouraged immigrants to adapt pattern-book designs to suit Australian conditions. Pattern-books were also important in the dissemination of aesthetic attitudes, particularly the Picturesque. Governor Gipps owned a copy of Richard Payne Knight's *Analytical Enquiry into the Principles of Taste*, 1805.

Some of the other titles used in Australia in the Georgian years were Peter Nicholson's *The Builder's and Workman's New Director*, 1836, J.B. Papworth's *Designs for Rural Residences*, 1818, and Count Rumford's *Chimney Fireplaces with Proposals for Improving them*, 1795.[47]

A climatic necessity

The fourth theme concerns the Australian climate. The first settlers were affected by the summer heat and the periods of dense rain. Yet it seems, from pictures of the earliest houses, that they included no adequate protection from either, but built their dwellings as much like their British counterparts as they could. Eventually wider roof eaves became usual, to throw roof water clear of the walls and prevent erosion damage, and surface and perimeter drains were used to carry rain-water away to underground wells. The remnants of such a system have been found at the site of the first Government House in Sydney. The collection of drinking water by means of eaves, gutters and downpipes was still a generation away.

Apart from building steeper roofs, which cast off rain more quickly and enclosed a volume of air to insulate against the heat of the sun, the characteristic Australian response to the climate was the verandah. Originating centuries before, possibly in Portugal, the idea of the shaded gallery was taken by Iberian colonists to the New World and to India, where it was absorbed into tropical architecture. The encircling verandah was common by the beginning of the eighteenth century. British colonists extended its use wherever the climate made it desirable, and the Dutch took the idea from the Indies to South Africa. Houses enveloped in verandahs were being built in the southern states of America by 1740. In England in 1795 John Plaw published designs for houses with extensive verandahs which he called 'American Cottages'.

Whether William Fielder's Sydney house was anything like this is not known, but he advertised it in the *Sydney Gazette* of 26 May 1810:

To be sold by Private Contract, the well known and eligible Premises situate at the Back of the Bonded Store, near the Church . . . comprising a neat American built House, Shingled, glazed, the floors neatly laid, the garden extensive . . .

Although it was never really a climatic necessity there, the verandah became fashionable in Regency Britain. In 1801 the Prince Regent had verandahs installed at the Brighton Pavilion, and in 1805 Mrs Fitzherbert built a house in Brighton with a two-storeyed verandah on which the

Two contrasting Tasmanian Regency houses without verandahs. Top: The Poet's Cottage at Stanley is an elemental house of stone with a symmetrical stuccoed front and attic rooms in the roof space. Above: Hythe, near Longford (now sadly demolished), a sensitive and delicately-detailed design was described as 'among the most architectural of villas'.

Prince was often to be seen breakfasting with her. The Brighton Pavilion was significant in the development of the verandah, for it appears to be the first to have had boldly shaped fascias, giving what was described as a 'seaside effect'. This Regency device persisted in the form of scalloped valance boards in England and the colonies after about 1810. The pattern of the valance board is clearly that of the drapes of a canvas awning, the so-called 'rustic verandah'. The use of curved rafters to support such awnings – itself the result of a seaside fashion – is probably the precursor of the Australian concave verandah roof. One of the first of these was the eastern verandah of Elizabeth Farm House at Parramatta, added by John Macarthur after he returned from England in 1805.

In Regency England the verandah also began to be used as a means of access from room to room and from room to garden. This meant converting Georgian sash windows, with sills at or near floor level, to French casements. The earliest known example is at Bromley Hill, Kent, where an 1811 remodelling included the substitution of casements (called French windows in Australia) in order to give access to a trellised conservatory. J.B. Papworth reported this new fashion in *Ornamental Gardening*, 1823:

> The chief apartments are now placed on the level of the ground, and have free access to the lawn or terrace by casements that descend to the very floor. This has been attended by the intro-

duction of colonnades and verandahs that throw agreeable shade on the apartments and which become new ones for reading and study.

Such casements may be seen in many Georgian homes. The earliest known surviving examples are those at Glenfield Farm House at Casula, built about 1817.

In the Sydney area, where temperature variations are steadied by the sea and the harbour, verandahs sometimes followed fashion at the expense of utility. Inland, the tendency was for verandahs to be larger and more functional, and the verandah-dominant bungalow form was common. In Van Diemen's Land the countryside as well as the climate was more English than anywhere else in Australia, and verandahs were less frequent. In the cool

Two contrasting verandahed houses. Top: Laguna House, near Wollombi, New South Wales, was built by Richard Wiseman in 1831. It is a robust vernacular farm house with a broken-back roof and details very loosely derived from the Classical repertoire. Above: Henry Handel Richardson's house, Lake View, at Chiltern, Victoria, is a style survival, built well after the Georgian period had ended.

south where farming was less dominant, town houses, such as those in Hobart, abounded; in the north, where agriculture flourished, country houses became the norm. The climate of Tasmania was described as 'Grecian', as though to explain the settings of beautiful Greek Revival buildings like Lady Franklin's Museum, near Hobart.[48]

The arrival of the architects

Well over thirty architects came to the Australian colonies in this mainstream period, about twenty of them to New South Wales, eight to Van Diemen's Land, and a small handful to each of Victoria, Western Australia and South Australia. There can be no doubt about the beneficial effect of their skills on the culture of the growing colony, yet not all of them prospered.

Daniel Dering Mathew was the first architect to arrive, and he is singled out in this survey simply because, as far as is known, only one of his projects was ever built. His unrealized design for a combined town hall and court-house reveals his interest in Palladian symmetry. It was a simple English Classical scheme, unusual in having round-arched windows at ground-floor level. But the only house Mathew is known to have worked on was the Colonial Secretary's house and office, built in 1814. It too was Palladian in form, with a two-storey centre block and single-storey flanking wings. In the Regency manner it had stuccoed walls, curtailed front corners which required a complicated roof with double hips on each side, a Classical door surround within a framed recess, and two front rooms with unusual curved interiors fitted to the cut-off corners. The surprising thing about the house is that the source of Mathew's idea was Design No. 2 of Edward Gyfford's *Design for Elegant Cottages . . .* , the one following that used for the Judge Advocate's house next door. Mrs Macquarie is believed to have lent both Mathew and the Judge her copy of Gyfford's book. Daniel Mathew did not persist with architecture, and he later took up sawmilling on the north side of Sydney Harbour.[49]

Architectural styles in Georgian Australia

A number of styles that became distinguishable in the Georgian period in Britain – Palladian, English Classical, Gothick, Greek Revival, Neoclassical, Regency and Italianate – retained similar characteristics when introduced into Australia, though in the colonial context they were always simplified in size or detail. All had the

Top: Old Government House at Parramatta, as enlarged for Governor Macquarie, is a strongly Palladian composition.

Centre: Narryna, in Hobart, is a house in the simplified Classical style, built of brick, with a three-bay pilastrated facade of stone.

Left: Rouse Hill House, on the Windsor Road, was built in 1813 as a severely simple Classical house. The encircling verandah was added in about 1858.

common theme of symmetry except Italianate, which relied on balance. The bungalow style, however, had no direct equivalent in Britain, for essentially it was shared by the colonies and the New World. Because of the strong influence of fashion, eclecticism and copyism, the style categories often overlapped, and there were many buildings which displayed the characteristics of more than one style, or were examples of transition from one to another. 'Pure' examples were in a minority.

Palladian

The essence of the Palladian style is order: the business of relating the parts of a building to one another and to the whole. A Palladian house is likely to consist of a dominant block containing the 'public' rooms, and is carefully proportioned, often in accordance with a simple ratio, such as 1:1 or 1:2. The English Palladians enjoyed dealing with more complicated ratios such as the double-cube (1:1:2) or the 3:2 rectangle, but these are harder to detect. The court room of Windsor Court-house, one of the calmest and most satisfying of Greenway's interiors, is virtually a double cube. There are probably many examples of such proportions waiting to be discovered in Australian houses. The Palladian designers also 'ordered' the relationships of solids and voids in their facades, and were very conscious of the effects of deep shadows. The dominant centre block was often supplemented by balanced wings, or by dependencies linked to it by colonnades or corridors. The other principal quality of a Palladio-inspired house was its garden, usually set back in order to display the three-dimensional and sculptural form of the building, as though man had 'tamed' nature.

One of the best Georgian examples of the Palladian style is Old Government House at Parramatta, as enlarged by John Watts in 1814. The good proportions of the main block, erected in Governor Hunter's time, were considered worthy of development by Watts. He extended the eaves by bell-casting the roof, giving the house its distinctive shadow-patterns. Greenway's portico and doorway arrangement echoes, in Palladian form, the earlier frontispiece probably built by Hunter.

Glenlee, at Menangle, is a sophisticated design of 1824 attributed to Henry Kitchen. It has a recessed ground floor portico reminiscent of Palladio's Palazzo Chiericati in Vicenza which, like Glenlee, has the upper part of its facade supported on columns.

The Palladian theme occurs and recurs, and is recognizable even when overlaid with the accoutrements of other styles.

English Classical

Typically rectangular forms built of masonry, plain rather than stuccoed, and decorated with details derived from the Classical repertoire: these are the essentials of the English Classical style. The details often included the Orders or their components or variants, such as pilasters, pediments, mouldings and rustication. The style usually incorporated hipped roofs, dormers, sash windows and, occasionally, cupolas.

An obvious example is St Matthew's rectory at Windsor – attributed to Henry Kitchen, 1822 – which has the typical breakfront and pediment, the embellished doorway and, overall, a compelling sense of scale. The rectory is of plain brickwork, which was favoured in Britain as well as in Australia.

Douglas Park, at Campbell Town, Van Diemen's Land, is a chaste English Classical design of about 1835 by Hugh Kean. Its plain ashlar form is parapeted, marked by a plinth, string course and cornice, emphasized by quoins, and given a beautiful Ionic portico, above which the central window is entablatured. Rouse Hill House, built about 1813 near Windsor, is one of many simplified English Classical houses which illustrate the change in style brought about by additions such as verandahs.

Gothick

This style was essentially Picturesque, eminently suited to harbour headlands and settings with potential or contrived romantic associations. Symmetry was often varied

Douglas Park, in Tasmania, built to the design of Hugh Kean, is a very English-looking simplified Classical house with a parapet and an unusual Greek Ionic portico. It was built in about 1835.

by asymmetrical details. The most obvious characteristic was the application of medieval motifs – pointed arches, crenellations, pinnacles – without the discipline of historical accuracy. Gothick houses often had a thin, unsubstantial, cardboard-like appearance. Stucco was sometimes used to imitate stone, and roofs were often steep. The *cottage orné* belongs to this same associative idiom. The Gothick mode faded after the depression of the 1840s.

An early example, though not a house, sets the tone of this style – the Government House stables in Sydney, designed by Greenway in 1817 in a 'castellated' style at the request of Mrs Macquarie. Its form is really symmetrical, and the courtyard elevations were originally Classical.

An early example of the Greek Revival style is Dalwood, in the Hunter Valley. Part of this vineyard homestead, behind the front entrance seen here, is flat-roofed.

Top: Carthona, at Darling Point, is a Gothick Picturesque villa based on a design in Loudon's Encyclopaedia *of 1833. Sir Thomas Mitchell commissioned it in about 1841.*

Vaucluse House was made Gothick by W.C. Wentworth from 1829, when the architect George Cookney built the Tudor-Gothick stables and coach-house. The house itself is one of the earliest Gothick examples in this country, but it was never finished as Wentworth intended.

Sydney's new Government House, designed in England by Edward Blore and started in 1837, popularized the style. Lindesay, on the headland of Darling Point, was started in 1834 to the design of Edward Hallen. It has a 'perversely asymmetrical' plan and a rather cardboardy look owing to its painted stonework. Carthona, nearby below the same headland, was Sir Thomas Mitchell's second house, a Gothick 'marine villa' derived from Loudon's *Encyclopaedia*.

In Van Diemen's Land, James Blackburn designed The Grange, at Campbell Town, in a similar Tudor style, in 1848. Built of brick, it is like an oversized *cottage orné*, with Picturesque asymmetry and romantic details such as tall decorated chimneys, all inspired by an 1836 pattern-book.

Greek Revival

The main requirement of the Greek Revival style was the use of authentic forms and details from ancient Greece; but the name is loosely applied to houses which incorporate Greek details, whatever their form. Strictly speaking, the only Greek Revival building in Australia is Lady Franklin's Museum, near Hobart: a totally convincing copy of a Classic temple.

Sir Thomas Mitchell's first house, Craigend, built in 1828, no longer survives. It was a large, single-storeyed house on a big triangular grant of land in Darlinghurst. Its main portico was in the form of a Doric temple with four columns, and there were similar expansive wings on each side, with the house itself beyond. The Doric Order was authentic in detail but not in form; for instance the columns were too far apart and too slender, and the pediments were too low pitched. Nevertheless it was a convincing and very fashionable pastiche, a 'splendid specimen of the simple Doric order'. Its architect, if any, is unknown.

The architect of Dalwood, an 1830s vineyard estate house built by the Wyndham family at Branxton in the Hunter Valley, is also unknown. As at Craigend, forms such as pediments diverged from the Doric Order. Dalwood was an early example of flat roof construction using bitumen waterproofing, behind Greek pediments.

Fernhill, the house at Mulgoa attributed to Mortimer Lewis and completed in 1840 for the Cox family, has been called Greek Revival, yet the only Greek details are the widely spaced unfluted Doric verandah columns. Many other so-called Greek houses, though well designed and using elements from the Antique, have little Greek character. Panshanger, near Longford, and Lauderdale, at New Town, both in Tasmania, are examples. Another, now gone, which exemplified the great subtlety of the style, was Burdekin House in Sydney, built in 1841, which was probably designed in England.

The architect Mortimer Lewis built Richmond Villa, Sydney, in the late 1840s. It has an asymmetrical bow front and Tudor detailing, including the 'eyebrow' barge-boards above the top windows. The house was moved to this site in the 1970s.

Top: Fernhill, at Mulgoa, was designed as a commodious two-storeyed bow-fronted mansion, but only the ground floor was completed. Doric columns support the wide verandahs.

Right above: Vaucluse House was greatly enlarged and made Gothick by W.C. Wentworth in the 1820s. Its Picturesque landscaping originally extended over some 200 hectares.

Panshanger, near Longford, Tasmania, was built about 1831 possibly to the design of John Lee Archer. One of the most stylish Georgian houses, it is Palladian in form, pilastrated and entablatured in the Regency manner, and has a Tuscan portico.

The house designed for Robert Campbell Junior by Francis Greenway (now demolished) was a large and symmetrical Regency building with a bow-fronted centre and Greek details.

Right below: Sometimes described as a cottage orné, *James Blackburn's The Grange, at Campbell Town, Tasmania, is really a Tudor variation of the Gothick style.*

Overleaf: Two verandah types. Above: Kilgour, at Longford, Tasmania, with excellent Regency treillage of the kind more common in Tasmania than on the mainland. Below: At Hunters Hill, a verandah with a cut timber valance like the vestige of a Regency canvas awning.

Neoclassical

The Neoclassical style was both an accurate revival of ancient Classic motifs and an abstraction of the shapes of Classic buildings into new geometric forms. Authenticity of detail went hand-in-hand with the purity of form expressed in the Greek or Roman temple. Some architects extended this ideal to include all forms derived from the Antique, provided that they were simple and bold, while others extended the decorative vocabulary well beyond the Classic. Henry Kitchen's unbuilt design for the Pyrmont house of John Macarthur, of about 1820, was probably the best example. It was to have been a half-cube with a Greek Doric portico, the entablature of which extended as a frieze around the eaves. The design was similar to one in a pattern-book by Sir John Soane which Kitchen owned. The simplicity of the half-cube, and columns which actually held up a roof, provided Kitchen's design rationale.

One of the most convincing Neoclassical houses owes its inspiration to the French. It is Clarendon, at Nile, Tasmania, built for James Cox in about 1838. While the house has an underlying Palladian character, its cubiform proportions are changed by the remarkable portico of widely-spaced double-height Ionic columns. Its pure but unclassical shape, adorned with Classically derived details, is reminiscent of France's Petit Trianon at Versailles.

Regency

The complexity of the Regency period became a part of Australian architecture. Regency emerged from a mixture of all the Georgian styles, but the mixing was seldom complete, and the result was often very eclectic. Even so, house forms tended to be simpler and Classical details more sparse. Subtle projections and recessions, exploiting fine shadow lines, were used to divide facades into panels according to desired proportions, and marks were indented to imitate stone. The vehicle most used for this was stucco, in Australia made of lime and not of the hard Roman cement available in Britain. Thus painting for weather protection was common. Balconies and verandahs abounded, embellished with timber treillage (especially in Van Diemen's Land) or iron panels (especially in Victoria and New South Wales), and roofed with sheet metal. Parapets to conceal roofs, and porticoes to decorate doorways, became more common.

Greenway's work is typically Regency, though he rarely used stucco, presumably because of the lack of Roman cement. Cleveland House, built about 1814 for Major Thomas Sadleir Cleveland of Macquarie's 73rd Regiment, is attributed to Greenway. It seems a simple stuccoed vernacular villa, but a closer look reveals its subtlety.

Greenway's largest domestic commission, which no longer survives, illustrates Regency complexity. It was the Sydney residence of Robert Campbell, Junior, built in 1822. The three-storey centre block was bow-fronted in the Regency manner, and colonnaded with a Greek Doric Order. Wings on each side gave it a Palladian flavour. The three-storeyed servants' barracks, a large block with gable-pedimented ends, was given an elaborately parapeted centre frontispiece reminiscent of the Baroque work of Nicholas Hawksmoor in England.

A marvellous Regency 'naval pavilion', called Henrietta Villa, was built in 1820 for the hospitable Captain John Piper, just over the crest of what is now Point Piper. A single-storey sandstone mansion, it was one of the most original buildings of Australia's colonial period. Its design has been attributed to Henry Kitchen. Symmetrical about a diagonal axis, the house was L-shaped. From each end of the building there projected a pedimented pavilion, and between these, running along the two main sides of the house, there were verandahs supported on fluted Doric columns. The identical facades of these pavilions were articulated by pilasters and panels to suggest temple fronts. Where the axes of the end pavilions crossed the arms of the L, there were two spacious domed rooms, one a saloon

Camden Park House, at Menangle, New South Wales, is a Regency masterpiece by John Verge, built for the Macarthur family in 1835. The Doric portico and the large panes of cylinder glass in the casement windows are noteworthy.

Top: A house in Quality Row, Norfolk Island, of the 1830s, when military officers designed the island's buildings.

Previous page: European influence. Above: Burrundulla, Mudgee, designed by William Weaver in 1865, with a central block and flanking wings in the Palladian manner. Below: Clarendon, Nile, Tasmania, about 1838: a unique example of the influence of France, with a giant Ionic portico.

Right: Springfield House, at Oatlands, Tasmania, is a stuccoed house built about 1840 for the police magistrate John Whiteford.

and the other a ballroom with large rectangular apses. Ten sets of French windows opened on to the verandah. Internally the domed rooms were unique evocations of Sir John Soane's exquisitely plastered domes and vaults. Henrietta Villa was unaccountably taken down before it was forty years old.

Henry Kitchen also designed Regentville, at Penrith, for Sir John Jamison. This was a large double-pile house with a pedimented breakfront, surrounding colonnade, and balanced outbuildings in the Palladian manner. Regentville was demolished in the 1860s, but another house by Henry Kitchen still stands. It is Hambledon, at Parramatta, which was designed as a kind of *cottage orné* with timber treillage, but developed into a Regency composition.

Australia's range of Regency houses is extensive: from Camden Park House and Elizabeth Bay House, both by

John Verge, the best-known Regency architect, to Horbury Terrace in Sydney at the other end of the scale. In between there are elegant residences like Lake House at Cressy, Tasmania, and Hawthornden in Hobart.

Italianate

The Italianate style in Australia represents a transition from Georgian to Victorian. It owed its origin to John Nash and the Picturesque tradition. The style was characterized by irregular massing and by elements reminiscent of Renaissance Italy, such as towers, round-arched windows (often grouped in pairs or threes), arcades, and loggias. Italianate became very popular in Australia because it was Picturesque and because it seemed an ap-

designed houses, so as to become an Australian idiom.

Though the varieties are endless, there have been four main types of Australian bungalow. All of them were single-storeyed, and all incorporated verandahs. The first type had the verandah under the house roof, and often on one side only, with the end bays of that side either enclosed or treated as pavilions, giving the verandah a restricted character. The best known example is Horsley, at Horsley Park, New South Wales, built for Lieutenant George Weston of the East India Company in about 1832. An earlier example is at Glenfield Farm, which Dr Charles Throsby built at Casula in 1817.

The second type also had the verandah under the house roof but there were no pavilions, and the verandah some-

propriate style for a warm climate. The best example is Rosedale, near Campbell Town, Tasmania, Italianized by James Blackburn in 1848. The pioneering Victorian example is Bishopscourt, in East Melbourne, designed by Newsom and Blackburn and built from 1849–53.

The bungalow

One of the most persistent influences in Australian domestic architecture, and particularly in homestead design, has been the bungalow form, which originated in India and was dispersed by the army as well as by British migrants. There are two particularly fascinating facts about the bungalow: one is that it is roof-dominant, which makes it eminently attractive for Australian conditions; the other is the way in which it has interacted, like a strong vernacular force, with stylish or

times extended around more than one side. A good example is Epping Forest, at Minto, built before 1832 for another East India officer. Denbigh, at Narellan, was built in 1817 by Charles Hooke, once a Calcutta merchant.

The third type of bungalow had a separately pitched verandah springing from the main roof plate at a lesser slope. An example is Somercotes, at Ross, Tasmania, built about 1840 by Captain Samuel Horton; an earlier one is The Cottage, at Mulgoa, built about 1820. This form became the epitome of the homestead roof.

In the fourth type the verandah roof was pitched from a wall plate below the main roof eaves. Verandahs like this were easily added to the main block of a house. Such an instance is at Ormiston House, Cleveland, Queensland, built about 1850, while an earlier example is Entally House at Hadspen, Van Diemen's Land, built in 1821.[50]

THE ERA OF Queen Victoria in Australia was amazingly eventful. It coincided with the greatest journeys of exploration, the opening-up of the land, and the consequent migrant explosion. It saw the separation and self-government of the colonies culminating in federation, and the rise of local government in autonomous municipalities. It became synonymous with the great gold rushes in Victoria, New South Wales, Queensland and Western Australia, and with a general tendency towards colonial wealth and well-being.

As life became more complex, new building types emerged to cater for new or different activities. Rural expansion brought wool stores, shearing sheds, warehouses and banks. Local government promoted the building of countless town halls. Railway expansion meant not only stations but also hotels for travellers. Compulsory education brought a great increase in school building. City growth caused a boom in retail trading and in buildings such as shops.

Victorian technology was a dominant factor in architecture. An obvious instance was cast iron, one of the earliest materials used in the mass production of building components. It was used for structural items like columns as well as for an amazing variety of repetitive decoration.

constant features – as evident in the late Colonial style as in the architecture of Federation. The Australian colonies became, over this period, marginally less British and more American in technology and in style almost cosmopolitan. The culminating Federation style, however, was to be a British/American hybrid. Aesthetically the Victorian age saw the continuous development of the Picturesque principles that were first clearly expressed in the work of James Blackburn in the 1840s, and dominated the Federation style – probably the first or only distinctive Australian style of architecture. Indeed, if there is a way to make sense of the stylistic diversity of this period, it is by understanding it in terms of the search for the Picturesque.

Before the mid-1850s there had been few houses of any very distinct stylistic character. Occasional excursions had been made into Gothick of an eighteenth-century type, as well as into the Palladian and the Greek, but these were now if anything on the decline. On the rise were more superficial styles with origins in the pattern-books of the preceding decades, but these formed a small minority. The typical house of the period had a symmetrical facade, with some details of a Renaissance, or at least loosely Classical character. Details like the concave sweep of the verandah roof reflected a continuing Regency influence.

THE VICTORIAN HOUSE

3

Another new product was corrugated galvanized iron, the wonder material of the age. It was cheap, plentiful, versatile and, because of its light weight, particularly useful in remote areas. The new composite material, reinforced concrete, appeared at the end of the century.

Machinery, now installed in purpose-built structures, also transformed building processes. Steam-powered saws, moulding machines and lathes made factory-produced joinery components like doors, windows, posts, beams, tongue-and-groove flooring and cupboards more readily available. Brickmaking was mechanized, resulting in harder, stronger, reliable and more plentiful bricks, as well as the variety of brick shapes that made fancier buildings possible. Traditional materials such as plaster, stucco and paint improved, enriching interior design, while the use of Portland cement promoted even more lush exterior treatments. The list of Victorian improvements that affected architecture is long: plate glass, gas and electric light, sewerage, cavity walls and interlocking roof tiles are just a few.

Towards the Picturesque

The Australian house, in the sixty-four years of Victoria's reign, changed its character entirely. The greater proportion of single-storey dwellings and the more extensive use of verandahs than in Britain or the United States were

Left: A splendidly eccentric Victorian house in the Greek manner. Rossiville, at Goulburn.

A colonial continuity

Robert Russell's design for Yarra Cottage in Flinders Street, Melbourne, typifies the middle of the range of stylistic elaboration. The house was single-storeyed and symmetrical to the front, with a drawing-room and dining-room flanking the entrance hall. The formal visitor would not have gone further into the house than these rooms, for the only other reception room was a second, smaller drawing-room, probably intended for less formal family use. The main block contained in addition a large pantry, convenient to the dining-room, and two large bedrooms. Behind the main block the planning was not at all symmetrical. The two back wings were quite disparate, one containing the nursery, two bedrooms and a small closet, the other a bedroom and *en suite* dressing-room and, straggling out from the side of the house, a kitchen, servant's room, scullery and (accessible only from the outside) a laundry. The idea of two back wings with a space between, in the form of a U, is logical enough, admitting light to the back of the main block. It remained common, especially in larger single-storey houses and in farmhouses, where the rear space may be enclosed by a fence and gates to become a service yard. In houses of social pretension this rear space was sometimes temporarily roofed as a ballroom, and in some cases a permanent roof was added later to give a top-lit room.

Yarra Cottage effectively provided for separate circulation through the house for servants, though such separation was less of a problem in a single-storey house where no stairs were required. Here each of the main reception rooms was accessible from the transverse passage, so that the path of the servant need never intersect that of the formal visitor. The privy is a water closet, which is a mark of some sophistication before the advent of reticulated sewerage systems, and is reached only from the exterior, but it is so contrived that access can be had under cover of a verandah from all the living areas of the house. From the bedrooms it cannot, especially from the one in the kitchen wing, but this was of less concern in the days of chamber-pots, though the servants who had to carry these noisome utensils through the elements may have suffered. The kitchen is not detached as it was sometimes in British colonies in hotter climates because of heat and fire, and as it often was in Australian farmhouses. Here, to isolate cooking smells the route from the kitchen to the dining-room passed first into an airlock with direct external access, and then through another elbow in the passage with a back entrance.

The architectural treatment of the house is simple but attractive. The main block has a hipped roof with shallow eaves, and totally plain wall surfaces. Touches of style are added by the design of the verandah and of the doors and windows. The verandah is concavely roofed – possibly in canvas, oilcloth or zinc – and carried on columns with rudimentary suggestions of capitals and bases. These columns are placed in pairs but, remarkably, the corners which in a later house would often have three columns – a pair in either direction – have none at all. This seems to be because the width of the verandah return is much less than the normal column spacing (determined by the distribution of openings in the facade), and so here the design is not typical. What was entirely typical, however, was that the only architectural elaboration was concentrated at the front door. The surviving drawing conveys the suggestion of a Classical surround, possibly with side pilasters and a simple cornice above the transom light. Apart from this only the joinery gives any suggestion of quality; this consists of the panelled entrance door, and four pairs of French doors each with a solid lower panel and three glazed upper panels, and a top-light to match. There is no narrow margin glazing, and there is little more than the concave roofed verandah to indicate that Regency is the most apt description of the style of the building.

Houses of a larger size than Yarra Cottage were relatively scarce and more individual in character, and their plans tended to be close to those of contemporary English mansions. Smaller houses were plentiful, and sometimes similar to Yarra Cottage in form. One of these figures in the competition designs obtained by the Victoria Freehold Land Society and published in the *Australian Builder* in 1855–56 (others of the group are distinctly Picturesque). The house in question, by T.J. Crouch, was essentially a rectangle with the entrance facade on one of the short sides, and a verandah across this. At the opposite end, or back, the plan cut inwards in a U-form with two short wings (a kitchen and a bedroom) and a verandah around the three sides of the space in between. There were three more bedrooms in the main block, making four in all, and a parlour and dining-room flanking the entrance hall. There is no indication of any privy, laundry, bath-house,

servant's room, pantry, store or closet, whereas other designs entered in the same competition show all or some of these. There is no separate circulation for servants, though the public areas of the house are again confined to the entrance hall and two flanking rooms. The privy is presumably detached and reached only through the open air, and the kitchen, though under the same roof, is reached only by way of the open rear verandah.

If the plan form of Crouch's house is a simplified version of Yarra Cottage, so, to a great degree, is the elevation. The roof is hipped and the facade is symmetrical, with four double-hung windows symmetrically placed around a central four-panelled door, but with no Classical door-case or architraves. The verandah has a concave hipped

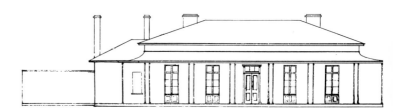

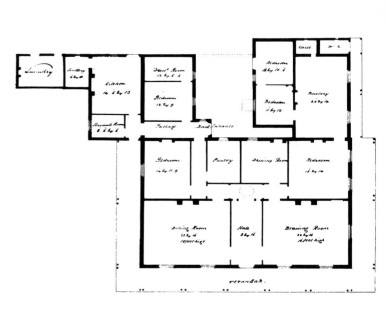

Robert Russell's drawing of Yarra Cottage, Melbourne, 1839.

roof and it is carried on five evenly-spaced pilaster-like supports of an openwork design containing circles and crosses. These are presumably of timber, though they may be of wrought iron, and the corner ones are L-shaped with a similar face to the side. The elevation seems to show the traces of four other pilasters differently spaced, the result of a change of intention. The concave roof and the pilaster supports indicate continuing Regency influence.

The same theme can be followed even further down the scale. A two-bedroom house by Charles Laing in 1856 is similar, with a hipped roof, symmetrical facade, and concave verandah roof, but the door is flanked by only one window on either side, and the verandah is carried on four sets of paired timber posts and decorated by pieces of fretwork suspended from the eave at intervals. While Laing's house is smaller than Crouch's, it does have a servant's room, opening off the kitchen. The main block has the familiar central passage, with a dining-room on one side and parlour on the other, and the two bedrooms behind, also placed symmetrically. The service wing is attached to the back of the house at one side but the kitchen can only be reached by a short dash through the open air. The privy is at the very back of this wing and accessible only by a long route through the open.

Even two-roomed cottages might have their verandahs, though those in Melbourne described by F. Lancelott[1] in about 1851 were shingled, and presumably not concave in profile. The front door, and possibly others, would be panelled, and the exterior joinery painted green, black or stone colour. There were two rooms, one behind the other, each measuring perhaps 4.2 metres by 3.3 metres by 2.7 metres high, with a single window, plastered walls, and lath and plastered ceiling, none of which were papered or coloured. The rooms were close to ground level, the doors opened directly into them, and there was no passage. The front room would have a wooden floor; the back one, containing the only fireplace, served partly as a kitchen and was paved in brick. There were no dressers, sinks or drains, but there might be a cedar topped bench and a wooden safe with a perforated zinc door.

This series of houses of different sizes shows a remarkable continuity, and one would expect that they would derive from equally standard English types. Single-storey houses, however, were exceptional in England, especially in urban areas. Most of the architects were English, though often from provincial centres with their own marked architectural character, which is sometimes reflected in their Australian work. Some of the smaller cottages, however, are of two rooms aligned parallel with the street rather than one behind the other, with a hipped roof and a low parapet, and with stone quoins and dressings. These seem to derive from Scotland, for they are not typically English, and Loudon's *Encyclopaedia* describes a similar form as being 'in the common Scotch manner'.[2]

The Victorian verandah

The verandah, ubiquitous in houses of various types and sizes, calls for more detailed consideration. It was, of course, established in the early colonial period, analagous to, if not derived from, similar forms in other British colonies, and from the more frivolous awnings of Regency England. It was by no means universal, but it was very common, especially in country farmhouses, where it often surrounded the house completely. What was new was the development of the verandah into a 'piazza' or open air living-room. The derivation of this meaning from the Italian word for an urban square stems from the Covent Garden development in London, where the term 'piazza' was properly used, but where the public in Britain came to understand it as referring to the novel covered loggias around the perimeter, not to the square itself.

The piazza had come to mean the recessed loggia at ground-floor level on the street frontage of a multi-storey Glasgow tenement house, and the word was applied to some sort of verandah on the Government Offices in

Victoria Square, Adelaide, in the 1840s.[3] In the context of domestic housing it is used in 1846 by Louisa Meredith, who describes 'a verandah or piazza' as a universal adjunct in front of Sydney houses.[4] It is interesting that Mrs Meredith should regard the two words as interchangeable, for in the United States later in the century there was a definite distinction and a single portion of a verandah might be designated a piazza. This was usually a wider area, often more fully protected by trellis-work, and regarded as an outdoor living area, in contrast with the rest of the verandah which was used for shade space and corridor. To some extent it was apparent in Queensland houses, and in American-influenced houses in other colonies at the end of the century. By 1887 John Sulman was advocating the introduction of American-type piaz-

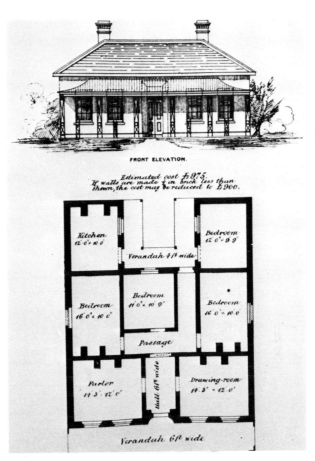

FRONT ELEVATION.

Estimated cost £975.
If walls are made 9 in. brick less than shown, the cost may be reduced to £900.

A house design by T.J. Crouch, 1856.

zas, and there was no longer any question that the term was interchangeable with 'verandah'.[5]

Australia did have some buildings with a loggia of the Glasgow or Covent Garden type. Those in G.S. Kingston's houses in Adelaide, however, were distinctive – they were placed within the main perimeter of the house and under the main roof, rather than being verandah-like attachments. The most probable source for the idea is Loudon's *Encyclopaedia of Cottage, Farm and Villa Architecture*,[6] which illustrates small cottages of this character, but in the other colonies, and in Adelaide at later dates, this form was very much the exception in other than terrace houses. There are examples, especially in the 1860s, of terraced houses with the ground floor loggia fully recessed below the one or two storeys above it. In general, however, the loggia is associated with detached asymmetrical houses in the Italianate style, and, whether it is of one or two storeys, it is provided with its own roof distinct from that of the body of the house. The rise of cast-iron decoration was to allow lacy screens to supersede the arcaded masonry loggia, although there were those who saw the iron lace as meretricious and shoddy. Thus the architects Terry & Oakden wrote in 1885 disparaging ornamental cast ironwork in favour of 'the Italian system of stone balconies and balconettes'.[7] When the arcaded masonry loggia was carried through two storeys, and even through three on a few Melbourne terrace houses, it created an effect unknown in contemporary English work but sanctioned, by historic models such as Bramante's Cortile of S. Damaso in the Vatican.

Despite the rise of decorative ironwork, elaborate cement castings and polychrome brick, and notwithstanding the increased popularity of the Italianate and other more sophis-

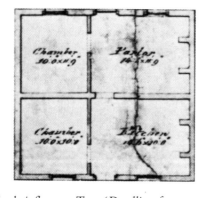

Pattern-book influence. Top: 'Dwelling for man and wife', from Loudon's Encyclopaedia, 1833. Above: Plan by Charles Leroux of a house like Loudon's, in Melbourne, 1839.

ticated styles, the single-storeyed four-square Georgian/ Regency houses persisted throughout the century. In Tasmania earlier examples such as Kilgour, Longford, built in about 1850, stressed their Regency character with elaborate verandah fretwork imitating, in timber, designs executed in wrought, or occasionally cast iron, in their English prototypes. The decoration reduced or disappeared but the concave and often striped verandah roof remained in examples like Yarra Yarra homestead near Holbrook, built in about 1870, and, with the verandah along the front facade only, at Richmond Villa (later The Elms), Yass, built in 1866. Even when the verandah roofs become convex or bull-nosed, as they do around the turn of the century, they often incongruously retain their Regency striping.

In more vernacular examples the verandah roof is not concave, nor does it butt the wall below eave height, but rather it is a continuation of the main roof surface, either at the same slope or more commonly at a shallower one which gave the rural and charming broken-backed profile. The latter gains its authority from Elizabeth Farm, Parramatta, which in its evolved form is attributed to John Verge, Henry Kitchen's Hambledon of 1824 and Experiment Farm Cottage. But the cruder straight profile was also used at Parramatta, in Roseneath Cottage built in about 1827. Both forms long retained their popularity in rural areas and there are many examples in New South Wales such as Kirmington, Milton, built in about 1840, and Dyraaba station to the west of Casino, built in about 1853. Across in Western Australia, and presumably quite independent of any Parramatta origins, are examples like St Leonards, West Swan, from 1842 onwards, and Southampton, near Balingup, built in about 1861.

The persistence of Georgian form

The two-storeyed Georgian form is seen at its most rudimentary in houses like Woodbine near Port Fairy, Victoria, built in about 1846, with a strange boxy effect due to the lack of any eave overhang, and a verandah (now gone) across the front ground floor only. Almost identical, except that Woodbine originally had dormer windows, is Gundayne at Booral, New South Wales, of about 1860. These houses have three windows across the facade. The same basic type achieves a more generous effect at Minninup near Capel, Western Australia, built in 1848, for the proportions are broader, the roof has eaves, and the verandah returns at the side. A grander specimen, with five windows across but with close-cropped eaves, is Campania House, Campania, Tasmania, built in 1840. Here there are dormers in the short ends of the roof, and the corners of the building are emphasized with quoining.

Campania House is a mean Classic Georgian house form of great durability. The same theme was carried out with much greater refinement at Glenrock, Marulan, New South Wales, in the 1840s: here again there was quoining, but there was also a slight eave overhang, a variation – albeit symmetrically – in the window spacing, and an imposing Doric colonnaded verandah with shuttered French windows opening onto it. Very much the same design (with small variations such as a higher roof) appears as late as 1870 in Golden Vale (later Golden Valley), Sutton Forest, New South Wales. This standard Georgian form is still current, but is often camouflaged with an enveloping balcony as well as a verandah, as at Baerami, Denman, New South Wales, built in 1875. But in spite of any Victorian or other stylistic elaboration of the doors and windows, the overall effect is still dependent on the balustrades, friezes and columns of the verandah and balcony. These superficial elements sometimes show a surprising degree of Georgian continuity. The eighteenth-century Palladian rail motif, which occurred in an etiolated, almost Chippendale form in Melbourne's Lucerne Farm (built in the 1840s but long demolished), is still found at Roseneath, Armidale, New South Wales, built in 1854 – here with a concentric square within each criss-cross panel. While it soon passed out of fashion in the southern colonies, it achieved a new lease of life in the timber houses and commercial buildings of far north Queensland in the later years of the nineteenth and the early years of the twentieth century.

Other elements of Georgian stylistic detail appear before the middle of the century. The use of pilasters, which had characterized much of Greenway's work in New South Wales, was particularly prevalent where brick was the building material, such as in northern Tasmania, where there is little freestone. This quite practical constraint, combined with the positive factor of the availability of lime, had tended to cast northern Tasmanian architecture into a more Regency pilastrated and stuccoed mode, as at Hagley House, Hagley, built about 1848, and occasionally with overtones of the Greek Revival in details like incised lines in pilasters, with elaborations suggestive of a Greek fret. Some few houses were still being built in a more explicitly Greek mode at the beginning of Victoria's reign, notably Aberglasslyn at Maitland, New South Wales, built

decorative devices in this work show that he was more interested in the Hellenistic period than the Golden Age.

In a more general way, much that was Greek Revival in origin found its way into the evolving local version of the Italianate. Most interesting in this context is the house Sunnyside in Newtown, outside Hobart, built in 1847 and attributed to W.P. Kay, the Tasmanian Director of Public Works. It is a single-storey house of sandstone with a projecting pedimented portico flanked on either side by a timber-posted verandah which appears to have been built, or at least substantially modified, at a later date. The sandstone is among the first from the Kangaroo Point quarries, which were to export extensively to Victoria in the 1850s and 1860s.

The style of Sunnyside is Classical, but an ambiguous Classical form. The main wall surfaces are sheer ashlar stonework with projecting panels rather too wide to be read as pilasters, and with cap and base mouldings con-

Sunnyside, Hobart, 1847, attributed to W.P. Kay.

about 1840–42. The Greek was to reappear only sporadically later in the century, though often in a more formal fashion, as at St Aubin's House, Scone, New South Wales, completed in 1880, where the Doric columns more realistically approach the proper Greek proportions, even if they are crude and perhaps more Roman in detail. The most splendidly eccentric example was Rossiville at Goulburn, owned by the even more eccentric F.R.L. Rossi (later the Comte de Rossi). Its gutsy Doric portico set against a sheer stone facade, with a gentle curve in plan and near-slit windows, had overtones of the French Neoclassicism of Ledoux, which were carried through internally in the stone vaulted entrance hall. Greek details like the Ionic portico columns at Langford near Walcha, New South Wales, of 1900, appear almost randomly as part of an eclectic repertoire. And in Victoria, J.A.B. Koch at the end of the century often used Greek details such as the key pattern, though the masks and other lush

tinuous with those of the adjoining walls. The corner of the house is turned by a quadrant of curved wall appearing as it were from behind the end panels of the two elevations – very much in the manner of J.L. Archer's Customs House (now Parliament House), Hobart. On the basis of these features the house can be defined as Greek Revival and to some extent explicitly Neoclassical. The portico is consistent with this because it is carried on two pairs of columns with Ionic capitals of the Greek type, although the shafts are unfluted and Tuscan in character, and are raised on simple pedestals. Crowning the whole, however, is a balustrade – a device unknown to Greece and Rome, explicitly invented in the Renaissance, and rare in Australia for about another three decades. Its next appearance seems to be in Charles Webb's Park House, Brighton, Victoria, built in 1856 – a two-storey four-square symmetrical building that is not Picturesquely massed, but is much less formal in character than Sunnyside, and has Italianizing details including balustrades to the balconettes of the *piano nobile*, and over the portico.

The essence of Italianate

The Italianate style did not arrive in Australia fully formed, and there are some transitional specimens that illustrate the stylistic evolution which was taking place in England. There John Nash was not the originator, but certainly the leading proponent of the Picturesque house, and his Cronkhill in Shropshire, of 1803, introduced the elements which were to become so familiar in Australia – the asymmetrical composition, tower, loggia, stuccoed finish, and detailing in a Renaissance or vernacular Italian manner. Nash happily translated most of these into a loose medieval version of the same house, and the only essential aspect was the Picturesque massing of the whole. Others were to stress this in pattern-book designs, like the 'Irregular House' by J. Thomson, who states that 'each elevation differs from the rest'.[8] This example has nothing very specifically Italian about it unless it be Classical Roman. The porticos are trabeated, not arcuated, the windows have aedicular surrounds, and the squat tower has broad pilaster-like elements at the corners. Other examples are more explicitly Greek in character, but changes in taste in about the 1830s meant a swing from

rectangular and Greek in spirit, with formal architraves and corniced heads to the main ones. The colonnaded verandah appears on closer inspection to be strangely cardboardy, for the columns are in fact free-standing timber pilasters with very little thickness back to front.

If Rosedale is still not very explicitly Italian in character, it closely relates to a house that is. Bishopscourt in Melbourne is officially credited to Newsom & Blackburn, the partnership of James Blackburn, Junior, but it probably has a substantial input from his father, who had migrated from Van Diemen's Land and who became town surveyor of Melbourne, and hence could not acknowledge his private practice. Another Tasmanian, H.D.G. Russell, was also involved in at least the supervision of this house. Bishopscourt is a much simpler design, but again asymmetrical with a square tower carrying a low pyramidal roof, and a cardboard verandah treatment. This verandah, however consists of superimposed trabeated and arcuated systems, and hence has become a proper Italianate loggia. The eaves of the house are bracketed, the corners are quoined, and the top storey of the tower has a bank of three arched windows in each face, in an appropriate

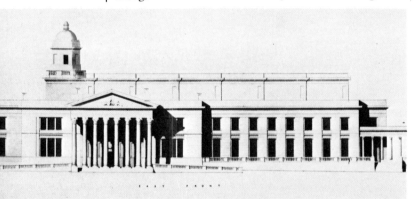

Designs by James Blackburn. Left: The 'Grecian' design for Government House, Hobart, about 1840. Above: Rosedale, Campbell Town, remodelled by Blackburn in 1846.

Greek to Italian. It is, this context that the work of James Blackburn in Tasmania must be understood.

Blackburn prepared schemes for Government House, Hobart, exploring a range of styles. One scheme, broadly Palladian, had a central Corinthian portico and a slightly Baroque touch because of its end pavilions with giant corner pilasters. In two other designs his search for the Picturesque is evident. One of them was a powerful Greek-inspired arrangement including an off-centre portico and an octagonal cupola. The other was a striking Italianate version with a Picturesque massing of symmetrical parts incorporating a terrace, a campanile, and two pyramidally roofed pavilions.

Blackburn's Greek and Italian Government House designs are based on essentially the same Picturesque composition, and neither is at all stylistically pure – one being Graeco-Roman, the other being Graeco-Italianate. The latter has only one arched opening and is otherwise trabeated. These aspects help to explain one of the first Picturesque designs actually carried out by Blackburn, the redesign and extension of Rosedale, near Campbell Town, from about 1848. Here again there is the Picturesque composition and the tower, and colonnades flanking an arched entry through the verandah, this time carried up into a mini-tower with an arched attic opening above. Here too most of the remaining openings are

campanile fashion. If the sombre colour and texture of the bluestone walls are ignored – they were possibly meant to be stuccoed – this is a conventional mid-century Italianate house. It approximates to a design by the Americans A.J. Downing and Calvert Vaux, which was published soon afterwards,[9] and which seems to have been the prototype for the anonymous Tasmanian house, Northbury, Longford, built in 1862.

The now-evolved Italianate style contained conventional elements crystallized from various English influences, but in particular from the publication of Parker's *Villa Rustica* in 1832. More pretentious designs drew upon the more formal Renaissance Revival spearheaded by Sir Charles Barry. The Italianate style is not defined by any one universal characteristic, but is a syndrome of characteristics that tend to be found together: Picturesque massing; tower; loggia; quoining; bracketed eaves; Renaissance window surrounds (from simple architraves to complete aedicules; balconettes; balustrades; stucco finish; and a use of astylar planar surfaces within which Renaissance elements float and can be distributed according to convenience. An example of the looseness of the Italianate syndrome is J.H. Pettitt's drawing for Clydebank House near Sale, Victoria, built about 1856, where a symmetrical and perhaps vaguely Georgian-derived elevation with two pedimental gables had added to it a proposal for an asymmetrically positioned tower which, had it been executed, would have made this building one of the earlier instances of Italianate design.

One of the most charming of these mid-century Italianate designs is the Observatory building at Sydney, by the Colonial Architect William Weaver, but executed under Alexander Dawson, in 1858. Here the material is sandstone but the massing, quoining, bracketing and other details are true to type. Athelney in St Peter's College, Hackney, South Australia, is another good example, designed by Edmund Wright or by Wright and Woods in 1858 or 1864,[10] with outer walls mainly of squared rubble, but with freestone dressings including corners treated not as quoins but as rusticated piers. Edmund Blacket's Retford Hall, Darling Point, Sydney, of 1865, is another example of this phase. This was far from being the end of the Italianate evolution. We may pass by the few committed Renaissance and Mannerist designs of the 1850s, which led nowhere, and consider instead those that grafted formal Renaissance elements onto the standard vernacularizing Italian such as Queen Victoria's Osborne on the Isle of Wight, for which Thomas Cubitt was responsible with Prince Albert. It showed how the style could be used for larger houses, introduced formal elements, and made the style highly fashionable. Then came buildings like Barry's Walton House in Surrey, a Picturesque composition with an especially strong tower. These towers were not mere ornaments and lookouts, but often housed water tanks, if anything more necessary in Australia than in England, and smoking-rooms, which were then sensibly banished from the house proper.

In Melbourne the chance acquisition for the use of the Governor, Sir Charles Hotham, of Samuel Jackson's Italianate Toorak House, built in 1848–50, set the seal of approval upon the style. The house was renovated in 1854, and later, after its official use was over, it was further modified in a way which nicely illustrates the evolution of the style. This change consisted of adding to the tower another storey, containing archways, which has since been removed again. The replacement of the overhanging eave of the tower, minor as it might seem, was enough to alter the tone of the whole design from the vernacular Italianate to a formal Renaissance version. At the same time a balcony of High Victorian iron lacework was added on top of the verandah colonnade. Toorak House was not unusual in preferring a Classical verandah colonnade to the more appropriate arcaded loggia. J.F. Hilly's Carrara (later Strickland House) at Vaucluse, Sydney, built in 1854–56, was a two-storeyed house with a single-storey Tuscan colonnade wrapped around its bow-windowed front; a few years later the single-storeyed Drummoyne

Three Italianate houses. Top: Bishopscourt, Melbourne, by Newsom & Blackburn, 1850–53. Centre: Northbury, Longford, Tasmania, 1862. Below: An 1861 view of Toorak House, Melbourne, attributed to Samuel Jackson, about 1848.

Charnwood, St Kilda, Victoria, by Samuel Jackson, 1855.

was given another; and still later in Melbourne Lloyd Tayler used a colonnade for both ground floor and balcony levels of Kamesburgh, Brighton, built in 1872.

Toorak House is almost contemporary with Rosedale, but whereas Rosedale's idiosyncratic tower can be barely identified as a part of the Italianate idiom, that of Toorak House, squat though it was, was quoined and recognizably Italian in character, though not so much so as that of Bishopscourt soon afterwards. The appearance of the tower in Australian Italianate houses is a matter of more moment than the number of examples would suggest, for in this style more than any other there is a continuum of scale and pretension in which the lesser examples aspire at least in principle to the characteristics of the greater ones. In Victoria this was all the more true because the greater ones included the two successive Government Houses.

Another in this seminal group was Charnwood, St Kilda, designed by Samuel Jackson in 1855 in a very formal and essentially Renaissance-derived style, with a sort of mini-balustrade over the portico containing a criss-cross pattern in place of balusters. It seems, however, from the one surviving illustration to have been more or less completely symmetrical and with only a taller pavilion to suggest a tower.[11] Frogmore in Caulfield, an 'Italian villa' designed by Joseph Reed in 1856, would probably have been just as important, but no illustration seems to survive. Charnwood, however, was a very prominent and elaborate house, and so it happened that when the Reverend Joseph Docker began to build his Bontharambo, near Wangaratta, in 1858, it was reported that it

would be identical to Charnwood. This it certainly was not, but it was Italianate and it proved to be remarkably advanced in concept. A clue appears in the loggia with its use of the stilted segmental arch – a form effectively introduced in England by C.R. Cockerell and to some degree popularized in fashionable London suburbs in the previous decade. Bontharambo is two-storeyed, Picturesque in composition, and with other stylish details like the chimney backs with the flues flanked by scrolls, probably inspired by illustrations in Parker's *Villa Rustica*[12]: but the important aspect is the tower.

All the earlier Italianate towers in Australia, and indeed the great majority of Italianate towers up to the 1880s, had overhanging and often bracketed eaves in the vernacular Italianizing tradition. At Bontharambo the tower had a balustraded parapet – a factitious nineteenth-century combination that immediately gives the whole building a much more formal air. An important antecedent of this form is Sir Charles Barry's remodelling of Highclere Castle, Hampshire, designed in 1837 and executed in 1842–44, with five towers, a large one at the centre and smaller ones at the corner. Far from being Italian, it was Elizabethan, and the towers were finished with a decorative balustrade carrying a strap-work motif, between corner pedestals carrying spiky finials. It is largely through this unlikely prototype that the parapeted, and more specifically the balustraded parapet, reached Australia. But there is another source more relevant to Bontharambo.

Mona Vales, Ross, Tasmania, by William Archer, 1867.

Parker, in *Villa Rustica*, illustrated a design which would perhaps at first be taken to be Italian, but it is actually explained as being modelled on the new Poor School at Bruges, and it has a square tower surmounted by a balustrade.[13] This second source is also non-Italian.

In Britain, Highclere Castle was followed by John Thomas's refacing of Somerleyton Hall, near Lowestoft, built in 1844–51, where there is a tower with a perforated but not balustraded parapet, and an overall Renaissance style. Owen Jones's design for 8 Kensington Palace Gardens, of about 1850, had something of the Italian character about it, though the parapet was corbelled out on imitation machicolations, and surmounted by spikes rather than urns. Whether it was perforated is not clear, but perforated balustrades were used on balconettes lower in the building. But we must return again to Barry for the critical example – his remodelling of Trentham Park, completed in about 1850, where at last the tower has a proper balustrade and is surmounted by urns. The lower detailing is Renaissance-derived, and the top storey has a trabeated structure overlying an arcaded form with a loggia behind, and so relates directly to Bontharambo.

The older Italianate tower with a low-pitched pyramidal roof remained the norm in Australia, as at Eskleigh, Perth, Tasmania, built about 1870; Kenmore, Rockhampton, Queensland, designed by James Flint in the 1870s; Struan House, Struan, South Australia, by Coke and Pannell,

1873–75; and Retford Park, Bowral, New South Wales, 1887. One parapeted tower, by contrast, occurs at Woodfield, Fullarton, South Australia, with a parapet of linked circles rather than a balustrade proper – it has been attributed to James McGeorge's renovations of about 1857,[14] but this is neither substantiated nor probable. In Tasmania, William Archer's Mona Vale, a contemporary of Retford Hall and probably of Athelney, still has the eave, but achieves a degree of formality by reducing it to no more than a coping. This is not very difficult in a house so large – fifty-two rooms and three storeys high – and of such superior freestone finish and detail. With this partial exception, the evolution from Bontharambo is next taken up in Victoria in the early 1870s, in the new Government House designed by Peter Kerr and J.J. Clark of the Public Works Department, under William Wardell.

Government House, Melbourne, clearly descends from Osborne in its overall spreading Picturesque composition and in some of its detail – indeed, so the story goes, the architects were instructed to reduce the size of the ballroom to avoid exceeding that at Osborne. The tower rises to a bracketed projecting balcony extending around all four sides, above which rises an open loggia level, steep and with a single arch to each face, flanked formally by Corinthian columns set more or less *in antis* between Corinthian corner piers, and with a balustrade above. This precise form of tower was not often used, but it does reappear rather mysteriously in the renovation (previously mentioned) of Toorak House, which was living

on its reputation as the former governor's residence – to the extent that the owner, at the point of selling it, sought to enhance the connection by giving it the same tower as its successor. The tower is shown in a painting by William Tibbits of 1878,[15] which was thought until recently to reflect only a proposal, but contemporary pictures[16] confirm that the extended tower was actually built.

Two mansions designed just after Government House revive the parapeted tower of the Bontharambo type, which was to become widespread in another four or five years. One of these was probably an English design, by J. Macvicar Anderson of London, for it now seems[17] that he supplied a scheme for the mansion Werribee Park, 1873–78, and that J.H. Fox, who is normally credited with the work, may have been merely the local supervising architect. The design is certainly unexpected in local terms. Firstly, the house is symmetrical and the tower forms the apex of a striking pyramidal composition in the front view, but diminishes in its successive upper stages. Secondly, the tower and the house are worked out in fine architectural detail, which is enhanced by the use of Barrabool sandstone. The upper floor is pilastrated Ionic, and the loggia around the ground floor is trabeated Roman Doric superimposed over piers and arches. This is the only mansion in Victoria executed in freestone, and is to this extent the equivalent of Tasmania's Mona Vale.

A less refined design, but one more relevant to the general development of the domestic Italianate in Australia, is Lloyd Tayler's Kamesburgh, Brighton, built in 1872–73. The tower is again parapeted, but it is asymmetrically placed in a Picturesque manner. The house is stuccoed, and the lower part of the tower quite fanciful, but the overall effect is made more serious by the two-storey Doric and Ionic colonnades forming a verandah and balcony across the garden front and returning partway along the sides. This contrasts with the more conventionally Renaissance arcaded loggia of Werribee Park.

The spread of this mode in Victoria occurs in the period 1876 to 1890. Lloyd Tayler, now in partnership with Frederick Wyatt, followed Kamesburgh with the more humble Dhurringile in northern Victoria in 1876–77 – smaller in scale, with only a simple single-storey arcaded loggia, but a roofed balcony above it with columns and frieze of decorative cast iron. Not far from Dhurringile a member of the same family, the Winters, had a grander mansion, Noorilim, designed by James Gall and built in 1878–79. Once more a two-storey verandah/balcony treatment in the form of masonry loggias can be seen, formally treated with trabeation superimposed upon arcuation like the single-storey loggia of Werribee Park, and, in addition, a pedimented pavilion set into the garden front. While Noorilim is not finished in freestone like Werribee Park, the effect of the finely finished cement in contrasting tones (doubtless using Keene's as well as Portland cement) must have been almost as impressive.

Italian and beyond: Top: The towered asymmetry of Bontharambo, Wangaratta. Far left: The Renaissance loggia of Werribee Park, faced in Barrabool sandstone. Left: A villa in Balmain with a bayed verandah of the kind later called a 'piazza'.

James Gall's less imposing houses in the mode were to include Mintaro, Monegeetta, built in 1882, and Frognall, Camberwell, in 1889. In 1881 Frederick Williams built a matching pair in Brighton: Bona Park and Ratho (now respectively Chevy Chase and the St John of God Hospital). Another important Melbourne example was Raheen in Kew by William Salway in 1884, exceptional in its use of face red brick, with cement for the dressings only. Prominent, but not yet attributed examples were Linden and Tyalla in Toorak, and a late one is Ulimaroa in St Kilda Road. Ulimaroa is a surprise because it is the work of J.A.B. Koch, a German architect inclined to use more exotic Second Empire and Hellenistic motifs. The tower is conventional, and the personal motifs – swags of fruit, key pattern verandah frieze, and a particular form of iron balconette – are not obtrusive. What might seem remarkable is the use of the polygonal or canted bay window.

Towards Boom architecture

Because the Italianate depends so much for its evolution upon elements from varied and often non-Italian sources, it is worthwhile pinpointing one more of these in detail – the canted bay window, typically with two sides angled back at forty-five degrees or less from the central light. It is found in the later nineteenth century as a standard feature of the asymmetrical Italianate facade in Australia. Its sources are Picturesque Gothic designs, themselves not so much Gothic as we would now understand the term, but of Tudor and later periods. An example is Turretfield, Rosedale, South Australia, designed by James McGeorge and built in 1854. In style it is castellated Tudor, with four-centred arches, label moulds, machicolations and a square tower with a higher octagonal corner turret, a descendant of the Beauclerc Tower of Strawberry Hill. The canted bay window appears here with its own castellated parapet consistent with the style of the house. At T.R. Yabsley's Barwon Bank, Geelong, Victoria, built in 1853, a pair of such castellated bay windows appears on a house that is essentially symmetrical and more or less Georgian, with a Tuscan portico. At about this time the canted bay window, without castellations, appeared in other Victorian contexts such as a hotel in Flemington Road, long demolished.

The canted bay had become accepted as a Picturesque but stylistically neutral element, and therefore acceptable in an Italianate context – it was only after the mid-1870s that it became a fairly universal feature of the style. A two-storey window bay appears on the front wing of Henry Hunter's Glenelg, near Hamilton, Tasmania, of 1878, but does not look totally at home against the austerely treated carcase of the building, and contrasted with an inadequate iron-fringed verandah. The same motif appears more convincingly in Yallum Park, Penola, South Australia, built in 1879–80, where it is accompanied by a two-storeyed iron verandah and balcony – yet it looks as though it belongs not in rural South Australia but in suburban Melbourne. This is not surprising as it was designed by the Melbourne builder-turned-architect Edward Twentyman, who was probably responsible for a number of the houses in this mode that proliferate in Melbourne's eastern suburbs. A late and more distinctive and idiosyncratic example is Andrea

Stombucco's Palma Rosa, Hamilton, Queensland, of the 1890s. This has one two-storeyed and one single-storeyed polygonal bay, both rather flat in plan and treated with austere Tuscan pilasters – in contrast with the slightly eccentric pyramidally roofed tower.

The bay window was more capable than the tower of being applied to smaller houses, and so, while the tower remained the aspiration of all, the bay window was used in a huge number of medium and small villas, and even occasionally in terrace houses. The balustraded parapet – dissociated from its tower – was even more versatile, as was the stilted segmental arch. This motif, which we saw in the loggia of Bontharambo in 1858, was used overpoweringly in the loggias of some Melbourne examples of the 1880s, and likewise in both levels of the loggia of Edina, Waverley, Sydney, of the 1880s. The smaller elements of the formal Renaissance repertoire, the door and window pediments, urns, spiked balls, consoles, masks, and panels of vermiculation, were even more ubiquitous. What has sometimes been called the Boom style is, at the lower end of the spectrum, little more than this: the more formal Renaissance, Mannerist, and Baroque elements which were used more or less appropriately in the more formal designs of major mansions, were now used in lesser buildings which lacked the formal structure to carry them. But this lack of formal structure was no less a part of the original Italianate concept. The idea of an informal and vaguely vernacular astylar wall surface, showing off a few more formal Renaissance elements placed in it according to convenience, had evolved into the idea that the wall surface was a *tabula rasa* waiting to be filled from a cornucopia of Renaissance and Post-Renaissance devices.

It is often claimed that this so-called Boom style architecture is the work of the speculative builder rather than the professional designer, and that it is the result of decorative elements being available for purchase off the hook. But these are half truths. Architects of this period were associated with projects of even a very minor nature, and it would seem that proportionately far more houses were designed by architects than is the case today. The term architect', however, was much more freely used – members of the institutes of architects had qualified by serving articles and only very few had taken some proportion of a university engineering course. Non-members of the institute might call themselves architects even without this training, and were often self-promoted builders or tradesmen. Moreover it does seem to have been the latter category who were most easily seduced by the more meretricious and opulent products of the cement caster.

When we come to look at the elements purchased in this way we find that the palette used by any one designer tends to be relatively limited. A given form of casting in cement or iron tends to be used continually by the same architect. In some cases we know that he supplied the original designs; in others, undoubtedly, he commissioned them from a modeller, and in others again he drew upon stock. In a minority of cases designs were given some protection by registration. Among these there are architects' names as well as those of modellers and manufacturers. An example is the work of Norman Hitchcock, who practised in Melbourne and then in Fremantle. Hitchcock was a builder turned architect, and his Melbourne work in the 1880s is easily distinguished by its lushness and by its solecisms, such as the evil taper which serves as entasis in his Corinthian pilasters, but most of all by certain characteristic motifs. Prominent among these is a form of scroll used on the parapet, typically flanking a name or date-plate. The scroll is large and it finishes on a central ribbed boss with a projecting spike (which rarely survives today) and, most unusually of all, this central boss is surrounded by radially placed openings which penetrate right through the scroll. In no case has such a scroll been found in a building attributable to another architect, but it is found again and again in Hitchcock's work, not only in Victoria, but in Western Australia, where his vocabulary remains essentially unchanged until well into the twentieth century.[18]

The term Boom style is appropriate enough for this hectic loading-on of decorative elements but it is sometimes used indiscriminately of any type of late nineteenth-century eclecticism. Most relevant in this context is the French Renaissance or Second Empire style, which we need not discuss in detail here because it was introduced in public buildings, and never became very widespread in houses. It is distinguished by little more than high mansard roofs and pavilion planning, but these aspects are generally combined with a fairly lush development of the wall surfaces, often with baroque motifs, belted columns, swags and so on – hence its early association with the Boom style as a whole. In one of the earliest manifestations of these tendencies, John Grainger's house for Robert Barr-Smith at Mount Barker, South Australia, (now known as Auchendarroch) of about 1878–79, there is little more than the prominent mansard roof on the extraordinary belvedere-cochere on the front of the house. The overall rambling Picturesque composition is English rather than French, and the details are more or less Greek. In Melbourne, meanwhile, many architects during the 1880s, such as David Askew and William Salway, adopted aspects of French Renaissance detailing without the mansards. None approached the correct pavilion planning. It is appropriate to mention one prominent example, J.A.B. Koch's 1890 remodelling of Ontario (later Labassa) in Caulfield, Victoria, because of its great flamboyance, because of its explicit connections with German designs in this mode, as illustrated in Hugo Licht's *Architektur Deutschlands*, and because of Koch's use here, as elsewhere, of Classical Greek and Hellenistic motifs such as key patterns and giant masks. There are other less remarkable examples, such as William Ellis's Lathamstowe, Queenscliff, built in 1882–83, adjoining which Ellis had already designed the Ozone Hotel in 1881–82 in the same style – and it was for hotels rather than houses that the Second Empire style had been most adopted in England. Thus the tower mansard again appeared, rather crudely, in the Osborne Hotel, Perth, built in 1895, although the overall design is more or less domestic in character.

Decorative iron and brickwork

Ornamental cast iron in its characteristic Australian forms, unlike cast cement, is not a logical development of Italianate tendencies, but its evolution can be traced

Left above: A detail from a block of shops in Carlton, by Norman Hitchcock, about 1886.
Left below: Houses in Fremantle. Notice the parapet scrolls on the nearest house, by Norman Hitchcock.

The Second Empire style. Top: J. A. B. Koch's extravagant design for Ontario (now called Labassa) in Caulfield, 1890. Above: The Villa Knoop, at Bremen, Germany, by J. G. Poppe, illustrated in Hugo Licht's Architektur Deutchlands, *1882. The Second Empire style influence is seen particularly in the mansard roofs.*

from the ironwork, both cast and wrought, of Regency England. In Regency work the mass of the building is simple and abstract, and much the same as in the earlier Georgian except that the segmental bow had become common, and the use of stucco based on Roman cement enhanced the simplicity of the building. Verandahs were light, frivolous appendages, more or less like awnings, and were often roofed in canvas or oilcloth – from which the tradition of painted stripes on iron verandah roofs was to persist in Australia throughout the century. The supporting ironwork was also light, an easy accompaniment rather than a challenge to the mass of the building proper. While it was sometimes of a Gothick character, far more commonly it was influenced by the contemporary Greek Revival. The supports might be open-work pilasters with Doric or Tuscan capitals, rather than being single posts, and the decorative patterns might incorporate such Greek motifs as the anthemion and the palmette.

become dense by New South Wales standards, but the repeating motif is a sort of lyre containing an anthemion in each interstice – still overwhelmingly Greek. As a later example, compare a Sydney house at the corner of Liverpool and Forbes Street, Darlinghurst, where the pilaster persists but the Greek detailing does not, and friezes and brackets give an effect of overall decoration at each level. The effect, however, is much lighter than late nineteenth century work in Melbourne, particularly the balustrade panels with their circle-based design.

There is a definite contrast between Sydney and Melbourne styles. Melbourne, for example, never used the pilaster support, though it was produced by one provincial foundry at Ballarat. Ironwork, however, was at times imported to Victoria in the mid-1850s from Dawson's foundry in Sydney. The columns of John Mills's house at 54 Gipps Street, Port Fairy, have the Dawson brand. They are of the open-work pilaster type,

Ironwork of this English Regency type was the first to reach Australia. Sometimes it was imported, like the porch of Brickendon, Longford, Tasmania, made by Cottam and Hallen of London, allegedly to William Archer's design. The supports here are vertical rectangular panels rather than pilasters, and the decorative work includes the most delicate scrolls and tendrils, as well as abstracted lyres. J.L. Archer's extension in the of 1840s of Highfield at Stanley, was designed with a delicate iron verandah of Greek Revival character, with panels more like pilasters. Sometimes these characteristics would have been the result of castings taken direct from sets of imported English iron, which was apparently the practice of the early Sydney foundries, Dawson's and Russell's. Certainly the pilaster-like support was to remain very common in Sydney ironwork, as was the Regency characteristic of lightness and openness. In detail, however, the continuous curvilinear forms, adapted from wrought iron technique and imitated in cast iron, were replaced by the more elaborately modelled shapes easily achieved by the casting process. The cast iron of Josieville, Richmond, New South Wales, is a good example: it has the pilaster-type supports, with Doric bases and capitals. The balustrade has

Highfield, Circular Head, Tasmania, as shown in Henry Hellyer's elevation drawing of 1832.

and the upper part is filled with a simple Regency-type geometric arrangement of uniform section bars. By contrast the lower part contains a panel of dense vegetable decoration cast in relief – a truly transitional example. Architectural castings were rare in Victoria until in 1859 a temporary slump in quartz mining caused founders who supplied the mining machinery market to look elsewhere. From then on iron was produced not only in Melbourne but in the mining centres of Ballarat, Bendigo and Castlemaine, and it was exported widely, mainly from Melbourne because of its access to the sea. What looks like Melbourne iron is found at Tahara in Deloraine, Tasmania, built in 1883. Shop verandahs not only of the prescribed Melbourne form, but bearing the City of Melbourne crest, are found right across country Victoria and at Corowa and Broken Hill in New South Wales. In the same way, the ironwork of Hillside in Albany, Western Australia, built in 1886, bears the brand of Revell Adams & Co's Vulcan Ironworks, Adelaide. Most widespread of all, and exported even to South Africa, was a form of column invented in 1873 by the Melbourne modeller and caster Angus McLean, and introduced to Sydney about 1880. This column was a cylinder of galvanized sheet iron containing a core of iron pipe, angle or T, with the space between packed with cement and sand. The base and the capital were commonly of cast zinc.

It is possible, in at least broad terms, to summarize the stylistic development of Victorian cast iron. At first it was the iron palisade fence with the bars and caps cast in one, or a cast-iron cap shrunk onto a rolled wrought-iron bar. Como, South Yarra, has such a palisade fence/balustrade, dating from the 1850s, but with the central bar in each bay expanded into a narrow decorative open-work panel. At this stage the frieze or arcading, if any, and often the columns themselves, were of timber rather than iron. Next in logical, though not always chronological order, come decorative balustrade panels, at first either very broad ones with a basically criss-cross pattern derived from the old Palladian rail, or much narrower ones, less than 250 millimetres broad, and sometimes cast in a sway-bellied profile. Often these panels, of whichever sort, were alternated with plain or ornamental iron bars. These panels were common in the 1860s, and by 1862 Mayes's *Australian Builder's Price-Book* could list four types made locally: large honeysuckle, plain Gothic, richly ornamented Gothic, and plain diamond pattern. The cast-iron frieze, often designed to complement the balustrade pattern, was introduced later in the 1860s, and until about 1880 usually was placed above a timber cross-rail. Modest brackets, central pendant drops, and in due course even a fringe or valance might be attached below the rail.

During the 1870s balustrade panel design developed more and more into a continuous pattern rather than a series of discrete decorative rectangles, and this continuity of pattern was to produce the well-known lace-like effect. This effect, which was fully evolved in the 1880s, also depended upon the elimination of the cross-rail below the frieze, so that the frieze, fringe and brackets also appeared perfectly continuous. Other developments included hollow backed casting to reduce the weight of iron in a given pattern – this became common in the 1880s. The trend to greater modelling was only reversed in the early twentieth century with the introduction of castings that were totally flat on each face, like timber fretwork, and usually influenced by Art Nouveau in their designs. These, however, were only a small minority among the patterns which by and large continued almost unchanged from the 1880s until World War I. The range of design motifs during this evolution is too great to summarize, but it can be said that the range of Regency-inspired patterns with Greek Revival motifs and criss-cross or other simple devices tended to be replaced by modelled vegetable motifs such as leaves and grapes, and especially in the frieze with the continuous rinceaux patterns of scrolls of foliage – all more or less Roman or Renaissance in conception. The 1880s and 1890s saw the rise of specifically Australian themes, and particularly of a great range of balustrade panels based upon ferns. Such a summary necessarily ignores a large range of different patterns based on geometric forms, Gothic designs and so on: still more it ignores the persistence over many decades of some of the early designs and the introduction of others like the Greek fret frieze in the 1880s, which seems to look back to the Greek motifs of the earlier designs, though it had not in fact been among them.

Apart from ornamental cast iron, the other decorative technique that was grafted onto the Italianate from totally foreign sources was polychrome brickwork. Polychrome work in churches was promoted in England at the middle of the century by the writings of Ruskin and Street, influenced by Italian examples, and by the buildings of Street and Butterfield. The bichrome or polychrome work of the 1850s in Australia, however, mostly reflected an Elizabethan tradition which had been revived by English architects like S.S. Teulon in the 1840s.

The watershed came in Australia when Joseph Reed in 1863 paid a visit to northern Italy and returned to promote a new style – not the polychrome Gothic of the Ruskinians, but a polychrome Romanesque which he claimed was Lombardic. This represented a dramatic change when Reed introduced it into ecclesiastical architecture with the Independent Church in Melbourne, but the three major houses that Reed did in this style in Melbourne suburbs, Euro-Reko, Canally and Rippon Lea, do not show a great difference from the Italianate in overall form (Euro-Reko has been demolished; Canally, now Koorine, is much altered; and Rippon Lea is also altered, rather more deceptively, for an Italianate tower was added in about 1881, probably by Lloyd Tayler). These houses stress round-arched openings, simplified Romanesque capitals, and most striking of all, multi-coloured brickwork in black, brown, red, yellow and near-white. Only the brickwork was to descend into the suburban lingua franca, and this it did with a vengeance in the Melbourne suburbs, though it was less significant elsewhere. Its spread was partly dependent upon and largely supportive of two technical developments, the production of coloured bricks, especially the browns of Hawthorn and the whites developed by John Glew of Phillipstown (now West Brunswick), and also the cavity brick wall, which appears, with varying systems of bonding, in about 1870. The cavity wall was more necessary as a way of stopping water penetration once the skin of cement was omitted from the exterior.

Planning and massing

Developments in planning are harder to analyse than development in decorative detail. To discuss at length the plans of the largest mansions would be unrewarding, because they are so much the exception rather than the rule, and because they are so complex, and remain so much in the English mould. William Archer's Mona Vale, Tasmania, was probably planned in accordance with the principles laid down in Robert Kerr's *The Gentleman's House* of 1865. The same can be said with even more confidence of Davidson & Henderson's Barwon Park, Winchelsea, Victoria, built in 1869–71, for though the drawings do not survive, an account of the rooms does, and their names and functions can in most cases be assigned with a fair degree of certainty.[19]

At the smaller scale the effects on plan of Picturesque massing were not always as great as might be expected –

The mansion Euro-Reko, St Kilda, had Italianate form, Romanesque detailing, and polychrome brickwork. It was designed by Reed & Barnes in 1865.

The street front of Friesia (now called Oxford) in Hawthorn, a deceptively simple design by J. A. B. Koch, 1888.

Right: A pattern-book application. Above: a cottage design from J.L. Tarbuck's The Builder's Practical Director, published in the 1850s. Below: The Lodge, Glebe, New South Wales, built about 1855 and based on Tarbuck's design.

the plan might remain organized about an axial hall or passage but that one room was enlarged in relation to its counterpart and thrust forward at the front, or one or more rooms similarly expanded to the sides. The more fundamental changes tended to be only towards the end of the century with firstly, in only a few cases, the development of a central geometric top-lit hall. This was important as a key to understanding the succeeding tendencies to regroup the rooms onto a diagonal axis, and to reduce the degree of compartmentalization and allow spaces to flow into each other *en suite*, circumferentially about this central focus. At the same time advances in plumbing, and especially in water-born sewerage in urban areas, were encouraging kitchens and bathrooms to become more integrated into the main body of the house.

These tendencies towards a geometric central hall, a circumferential organization of rooms and a diagonal axis had all been to a greater or lesser degree foreshadowed in England in the proto-Italianate houses of John Nash, like Cronkhill (and castellated ones, like Killymoon Castle). The central hall containing a geometric stair was a leitmotif of the Regency in England, and of the houses of John Verge in Australia. In Australia, these stairs quickly disappeared in favour of a conventional dog-leg plan along the back of the hall, or breaking off from it sideways, though the stairs were often grandly treated, especially when lit by great stained-glass windows – common in the 1870s. In the largest houses the stair might rise axially to the landing and then divide and return up each side. Here the space might be a hall, with curved corners and statuary niches, though still essentially rectangular.

In single-storey houses, which were of course far more common in Australia than England, there was still less incentive to maintain such a central space. It was done quite grandly in W.P. Kay's Sunnyside, Hobart, built in 1847, with a segmentally barrel-vaulted hall, rectangular in shape but with curved corners containing niches, but this was exceptional. A revival of interest in the central space did not occur until the 1880s. J.A.B. Koch's Oxford, in Hawthorn, Victoria, built in 1888, has a fine octagonal lantern-lit hall with statuary niches and a fine encaustic tile floor. This hall has been used as a pivot around which the house plan has been partially rotated. The arcaded loggia which extended across the front of what looks like a perfectly symmetrical rectangular block actually returns part-way along one side to the position of the front door. Thus the entry hall runs laterally from here to the octagon, and the complete front is occupied by the library and dining-room with no hall or passage between.

An even more significant development occurs in Lloyd Tayler's Mynda in Kew, designed for his daughter and son-in-law in 1886. Mynda also has an octagonal top-lit hall, but rather than being domed like that at Oxford, it has ceiling panels of diagonal boarding sloping towards the lantern. It is in all respects a humbler house, but more forward-looking in taste, and while its entrance is conventionally located at the front it incorporates one striking innovation – a square window bay projecting from the drawing-room at forty-five degrees at one of the front corners of the house. By 1890 a design by Butler & Ussher for a house at Brighton Beach, near Melbourne,

has an octagonal hall, and like that of Oxford it is entered laterally from the back end of an L-shaped verandah, so that the principal rooms occupy the full width of the front elevation with no interrupting hall or passage. In this case the octagon is not top-lit, for there is an upper floor in which the same shape is repeated, and on top of this again it appears as a roof-top belvedere of the type that was to become a standard Edwardian feature. By comparison with Oxford, also, the grouping of the circumferential rooms has a new informality and, even more critically, the massing of the hipped roofs develops an overwhelming diagonality totally absent in its predecessor.

The Brighton house became the progenitor of the numerous ingeniously planned diagonal houses of Ussher & Kemp in the later 1890s and the early part of this century, notwithstanding that the central octagon, having served its catalytic function, is abandoned almost entirely. The same diagonality is soon reflected in the work of lesser practitioners, and becomes almost universal in the Edwardian period. To pursue this topic we must take up the thread of medievalizing architecture which ran parallel with the Italianate and the Boom style – not nearly so widespread, but more pregnant with the ideas which would rise to prominence at the end of the century.

Medieval and Picturesque

Picturesque medievalizing houses spring from the same English roots as Picturesque Italianizing houses, and John Nash's castellated houses were composed and planned on just the same principles as his Cronkhill. The term *cottage orné* was applied indiscriminately to any smaller house conceived as an object of Picturesque interest, regardless of whether its style was vernacular, Gothick, indeterminate, Italianate, or even Greek. This term, however, was increasingly used for vernacular houses with elements like thatched roofs, undressed timber columns and half-timbering; for Gothic or Tudor houses with pointed windows or small sections of castellation, or elaborately patterned chimney-pots; and most of all for those which combined a little of each tradition.

It is probably in this more limited sense that the word should be understood in Australia, and it seems likely that the *cottage orné* known to have been designed by Francis Greenway was of this general type. It is in this sense too that the word was still being used in Australia as late as the 1850s.[20] It is not so easy to find surviving examples which retain any explicit link with the designs of Nash, George Repton, P.F. Robinson and their contemporaries. One, however, is Charles and Louisa Meredith's house, Malunnah, at Orford, Tasmania, which has verandah posts and brackets of undressed and knotty Oyster Bay pine trunks and branches – undoubtedly from familiarity with English prototypes, and it would seem, giving rise to a minor local school of Picturesque knotty pine architecture.

Far more common are conventional Picturesque, ostensibly Gothic cottages, without explicitly rustic overtones, and comparable with published English designs of the 1840s and 1850s. Some can be shown to be actually copied from these sources, as is the case with The Lodge, 9 Toxteth Road, Glebe, Sydney, based on an illustration in J.L. Tarbuck's *Builder's Practical Director*. It is important to

appreciate that there are no true Gothic cottages of this sort, for the nearest prototypes are Elizabethan, and this is more especially true of the lush loopy bargeboards and finials which become such a leitmotiv of this mode. Apart from the bargeboards and the steep roofs these houses are characterized by Picturesque massing, just as with their Italianate contemporaries. The loggia of course was unsuitable and verandahs tend to be limited in extent or even reduced to a small porch. The bay window, being more authentic to the style, was more common than in Italianate houses of the 1850s, and commonly projected from the parlour which came out at one side of the facade.

More elaborate or larger houses in this mode in Sydney include the Dower House of Ascham School, Woollahra, and Greycliffe House, Vaucluse, both built in the 1840s. Later, at some time before 1871, is the remodelling of Thomas Woore's Pomeroy in a more Tudor Gothic mode – with parapeted rather than bargeboarded gables. In Victoria there are a number by Charles Laing, notably Coryule, near Drysdale, built in 1849–50. In Tasmania there is the anonymous Inglewood at Needles, built about 1850, and, of a rather more exceptional character, James Blackburn's The Grange at Campbell Town, built about 1847. Later examples include Brougham Lodge (now Callooa), Darling Point, designed by Francis Clarke in the 1850s, and the former Bishopscourt, Bathurst, built about 1862, to choose from many in New South Wales, and as late as 1883, G.A. Morell's Rona, Woollahra.

This style persisted with little evolutionary change for nearly half a century. In Tasmania it was seen in T.P.A. Monds's house at Carrick, built in 1875, as well as a number of Gothic wooden houses which tend to be elaborate but not sufficiently distinct in style to merit the specific term 'Carpenter's Gothic' (which is sometimes applied to them on the basis of American analogy). In Battery Point, Hobart, there are Vernon at 11 Mona Street, and Hillcrest at 19 Runnymede Street, the latter with a strange little American-looking concave-roofed central pavilion. Still more is American influence apparent in Garthowen, Launceston, a beautiful wooden gingerbread house of 1882 with every window different, and one wooden hood taken directly from Calvert Vaux's *Villas and Cottages*. In Westella at Ulverstone, built about 1885, the roof pitch is reduced, bringing the form more into line with contemporary English practice. The same is true of the more sophisticated stuccoed Shaftston House, Kangaroo Point, Brisbane, of 1883.

Victoria does not persist so long with this conservative Gothic style, but follows more closely on the latest English trends. Houses like Benjamin Ferrey's Wynnstay in Denbighshire of 1858–61 had introduced French pavilion planning with steep pyramidal roofs of bellcast profile. Something of the same spirit appeared in J.L. Pearson's Quar Wood, Gloucestershire of 1857, together with the depressed Gothic arch with the two segments almost straight and at a low angle. This form of arch, often stilted above the capital or impost line, appeared on London suburban villas at this time, as in the work of T.K. Green. In Victoria the same features appear in certain school buildings and in some houses by Reed & Barnes – Barragunda at Cape Schank of 1868, Kolor, Penshurst, of

A Queen Anne design by Arthur H. Fisher, published in the Building, Engineering and Mining Journal *in December 1892.*

Top: An influence of the American Romanesque, in Cestria, Hawthorn, by E.G. Kilburn, 1891.

1869, and Heronswood, Dromana of 1872. Reed's employee, the decorator and landscaper Edward La Trobe Bateman, possibly contributed to these.

This was symptomatic of a new attitude to the Gothic in England, and to some extent in Australia – that it was a style to be developed rather than imitated, that the more gutsy, chunky qualities were those to be used, and that new materials and techniques should be assimilated into it without inhibitions. This new style was described by terms like 'Modern Gothic' or 'Modernized Domestic Gothic'. The latter description was applied to a house near Manchester by H.W. Paull and Oliver Ayliffe in 1864–65, which was published in a book *Villas and Cottages*, in 1868, and copied by two of Australia's most eminent architects – Henry Hunter of Hobart, of 1869–70 and Lloyd Tayler of Melbourne. Hunter's copy, Bellona in Davey Street, Hobart, is reversed but otherwise fairly exact. Tayler's copy, Blair Athole in Brighton, is less slavish. The details of this design, particularly the portico with its depressed Gothic arch supported at one side on a sturdy Corinthianesque colonette, show the style to be similar to that of Frank Furness in America with its compressed, strengthened and exaggerated Gothic forms. In a more general way the work in Australia of the American John Horbury Hunt took the same approach, but with much more concern for abstract masses of brickwork, in the manner of William Butterfield, than for specific Gothic details.

The incipient Federation styles

There were various exaggerated offshoots of the Gothic later in the century and varied medievalizing combinations with eclectic Renaissance sources. They are not numerous or influential though they did tend to develop the diagonal axis, especially with corner towers or conical roofed turrets. The more significant trends were the English Queen Anne Revival, Old English and Arts and Crafts, and the American Stick style, Romanesque and Shingle style. The Art Nouveau and cognate European modes had virtually no influence in the nineteenth and very little in the early twentieth century. The American Romanesque is of great interest because, though it produced few significant houses – perhaps the most notable is E.G. Kilburn's Cestria, Hawthorn, Victoria, built in 1891, following Kilburn's visit to America – it was seen as a basis for the development of a national Australian style. Nothing much was to come of this apart from some later examples of round arches fringed with moulded gumnuts and other Australian motifs, though in domestic work even this was largely confined to interiors.

The American wooden architecture of the Stick and later the Shingle style was of local relevance because, to some extent, it incorporated the balconies and verandahs popular in Australia – we have already seen Sulman advocating the American piazza. It gave the lead, moreover, for the elimination of the old cast iron in favour of turned and modelled wood, a process which began in the 1890s but was barely complete by 1914. In other respects the Americans had themselves been much influenced, since it was first promoted to them by Hudson Holly, by the English Queen Anne. Not only were Australians naturally predisposed to look to the English sources, but there

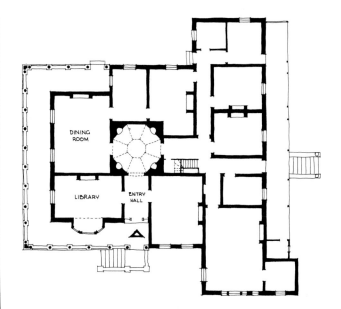

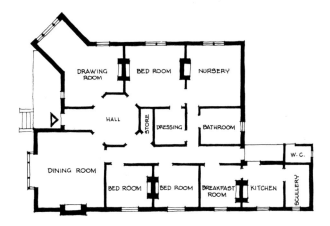

Central, circumferential and diagonal planning. Top: Friesia (Oxford), Hawthorn. The octagonal hall is a pivot around which the house plan rotates. Centre: Mynda, at Kew, a humbler house, also has a polygonal hall, and a striking bay window gives some diagonal emphasis to the front of the house. Below: A design by Butler & Ussher has a differently shaped hall, around which the rooms are informally grouped. The resulting roof arrangement, prominently hipped, gives the house a strongly diagonal character.

Ashfield Castle (now a convent), with typical Victorian confidence, combines the elements of Classical and Gothic.

were in Australia two or three gifted English-born practitioners who had supped at the fount itself. The earliest of Norman Shaw's classicizing Queen Anne Revival, with its rectangularity and broad paned windows, had no impact in Australia, but as he turned to a more medievalizing steep-roofed and Picturesquely massed mode, his influence on Australia became greater. Only a handful of houses of a distinctly Queen Anne character were built before the end of the century, but all the elements were there for the creation, under that unlikely English name, of the Australian Edwardian style that was to follow.

Two English emigrants who were to make major creative contributions to that style had shown their hands a decade earlier. North Park, later Woodland, Essendon, Victoria was built in 1888 to the design of Oakden Addison & Kemp. It was a two-storeyed house with a balanced but not symmetrical facade with gabled pavilions at either end, half timbering in the gables, and banked Tudor windows. Separated from these by recessed verandah sections was a square entrance tower surmounted by a timber arcaded belvedere with a steep French roof and cresting. Henry Kemp had migrated from England in 1886, and this design was derived explicitly from one by his former master R.W. Edis.[21] His partner G.H.M. Addison also played a part in the design and perhaps in the decision, for almost the first time in Australia, to roof a building in the newly available

Marseilles terracotta tiles. The combination of an English Queen Anne design with a Marseilles tile roof was a harbinger of the future.

Even more up-to-date in an English sense, and roofed not in Marseilles tiles but in terracotta Roman tiles from Bridgewater, England, was Blackwood near Penshurst, by Butler & Ussher, built in 1891–92. This was a different concept, a long one- to one-and-a-half-storey house stretching along the crest of a hill, with half-timbered side gables branching out from the enormously long ridge. This spreading form paralleled – without any specific connection – Edward Ould's Wightwick Manor, Staffordshire, built in 1887 and 1897 and C.F.A. Voysey's Walnut Tree Farm built in 1890. Walter Butler had moved in the Arts and Crafts circle of Morris, Shaw and Lethaby, and had worked for J.D. Sedding until his emigration to Australia in 1888. The significant aspect of his design for Blackwood is the way in which his surviving design development drawings for the house take each separate section of it and present on one sheet a discrete plan, elevation, section, and any relevant detail, thus making clear the designer's intention of allowing the whole to develop out of the detailed requirements of each part – an organic approach to planning.

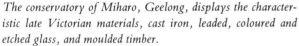

The conservatory of Miharo, Geelong, displays the characteristic late Victorian materials, cast iron, leaded, coloured and etched glass, and moulded timber.

Right: Fernleigh Castle, Rose Bay, is a house of Classical form with a crenellated Medieval skyline and iron lace decoration.

The last decade of the century, when these new impulses were fermenting, is particularly difficult to assess. Melbourne, which had set the pace in High Victorian architecture, tottered under financial scandals involving some of the major building and property speculations of the time and directly implicating one or two prominent architects. It then entered a deep depression in which, characteristically, the building industry was the most seriously affected. While other eastern capitals had their own difficulties, the Western Australian gold discoveries suddenly moved that colony from a long period of stagnation into a boom. As a result, a remarkable number of Melbourne architects left for Perth in the middle 1890s, though only a smaller number returned gradually as normality returned in the early years of the twentieth century.

There were already some gifted architects in the west, notably George Temple Poole, who, after ten years as Director of Public Works, during which he showed a distinct flair for the Picturesque, left for private practice in 1896. There are few major innovative houses in this period. Poole's 1896 portion of the Albany post office, however, is quasi-domestic, and illustrates some of the new trends, with its Picturesque massing; its tendency towards diagonality, with a small corner turret and a larger adjoining tower; its conical tower roofs, one of which is bellcast in profile; and its red brick walls with cement dressings. As in other work of the Department of Public Works there is an American Romanesque component. Also quasi-domestic is the Weld Club in Perth, built in 1892 to the design of the Englishman J. Talbot Hobbs but nonetheless with American Stick style and Shingle style influence and with an angled corner bay once again developing a diagonal axis.

These six decades of development were characterized by the search for the Picturesque, and Picturesque principles, which were exceptional at the outset, were almost universal at the close of the period. The precise manner of building was no longer a matter of choice between conservative colonialism and the imitation of British pattern-books. The imitation of Britain, through the building journals, could be much more related to current practice, and through trained emigrants could be much more autonomous. Add to this the imitation of America, the occasional imitation of France and Germany, and the increasing theoretical search for a national architecture, and the scene is set for the birth of a new style, but inevitably a Picturesque one.

Kirkham, designed by John Horbury Hunt in 1888, was renamed Camelot in 1900. It is a Picturesque agglomeration of shapes, including two candle-snuffer roofs and a profusion of hips and gables. Hunt's personal style influenced the course of Federation architecture in Australia.

The swinging of the great globe is bringing us nearer to tomorrow's dawn. When its sunlight silvers the vast panorama of this continent and the richly jewelled islands that lie within its seas, it shall shine upon a territory which by the act you will then perform, and the solemn compact into which you will then enter, will be bound once and forever in a united Commonwealth, an indissoluble union, everlasting and strong – into an Australia, one and indivisible.[1]

Alfred Deakin's words drew cheers from his enthusiastic supporters on the night before the 1899 referendum which, it was hoped, would ratify the proposed federal constitution. On the following day, however, 40 per cent of the electorate lacked sufficient motivation to cast a vote either for or against the proposal.

Nationhood came to Australia easily, undramatically and at a leisurely pace. The main task faced by the fathers of federation was to convince six self-governing colonies scattered around the perimeter of an island continent that it was in their best interests to join forces, at least in matters which concerned them all. Defence, 'White Australia' and economic self-interest were the main arguments for, if not the causes of, the moves towards federation which began in the early 1890s. A disastrous depression and years of severe drought caused the movement to

which shone on their continent, to the subtle monotony, the ochres and grey-greens of the landscape. 'The Bush' had acquired its mystique and legends. The archetypal Australian could now be recognized: he (a man, of course) was lean, wiry, self-reliant, pragmatic, laconic, fiercely loyal to his mates and unenthusiastic about non-white races. His mould had been shaped on the goldfields, in the shearing sheds and around swagmen's campfires. The Eureka flag symbolized his abhorrence of authority and the *Bulletin* was his bible.

The growing awareness of the nature of the country and its people was being expressed. Tom Roberts, Arthur Streeton and Frederick McCubbin sensed the special qualities of Australian space, light and colour: they went out into the bush, painted it and got it right. Locally written verse was eagerly consumed by a large reading public. It ranged from the bush ballads of 'Banjo' Paterson to the wartime rhymes of C.J. Dennis and it told ordinary Australians about themselves in a language everybody could understand. In prose, rural yarns such as Steele Rudd's *On Our Selection* won enormous popularity, and Henry Lawson's best short stories told with poignant economy of the struggles of the battler against daunting odds in the outback. But Lawson did not write only about

THE FEDERATION PERIOD

4

lose momentum, but a more stable economic and political climate in the last few years of the decade enabled 'Australia' to become a political reality on the first day of the twentieth century. All that remained was, in the fullness of time, to invent a national flag, a national anthem and a national capital.

While they inched their way towards federation, the politicians of the 1890s were also erecting the framework for an egalitarian democracy. By 1900 manhood suffrage had been written into the statute books of each of the colonies. Moves were also afoot to abolish plural voting, this goal being achieved in all states by 1907. Women could vote in South Australia in 1893, in Western Australia in 1899, and in every state of the Commonwealth by 1909. The voice of the working man was heard in parliament for the first time in 1891 when thirty-five newly elected Labor members held the balance of power in the Legislative Assembly of New South Wales.[2]

The politics of the 1890s were clearly of great importance in shaping the future nation's destiny. Nevertheless, political federation did not arouse much passionate interest because most Australians realized that 'social federation' had already been achieved. By 1891 three-quarters of the population were Australian born. One could move throughout the continent noting fewer differences in speech and behaviour than could be found between English counties. Australia's cricket victories over England were celebrated from Albany to Cooktown.

Australians' eyes were now attuned to the harsh light

the hard life of the country areas. His own experiences of city life produced tales of squalor, inequality and human exploitation in the metropolis. Lawson's inability to avoid contact with the city was symptomatic of the larger situation: the bush had provided the setting for much of Australia's growing self-awareness but it was 'the big smoke' that would matter in the future.

The city and suburbs

At the turn of the century all of the state capitals were flourishing seaports. From them and from other strategically located coastal cities railway tracks radiated like iron tentacles to the pastoral and agricultural hinterlands. The seaports were linked to each other by relatively cheap and efficient coastal shipping services, consequently each railway system tended to remain independent of its neighbours. As the produce of the rural areas grew in volume and the railways correspondingly increased their mileage, the capital cities handled and processed an ever-increasing influx of goods and grew fat. New stores, wharves, factories, warehouses and offices were needed, and with them a swelling army of storemen, labourers, factory hands, clerks and managers. These people and their families needed somewhere to live, and already the city cores were surrounded by tightly packed residential districts at more or less walking (or bicycling) distance from their inhabitants' workplaces. The solution to the problem was found in improved and extended public and private transport systems to serve new suburbs that sprang up beyond the dense belt of nineteenth-century housing. Before 1914 the iron rail was still in its heyday and it was the suburban railway and the tramway (powered by horse, then steam, then electricity) which made possible this move outwards to the new suburbs. And, even as the twentieth century began, the motor car was becoming more than a new-fangled oddity. In 1909 the first Model T Fords were imported from the United States and Australia was on the threshold of the motor age.[3]

Once he had been liberated by the mechanically-driven wheel, the Australian in search of a suburb soon realized that outside the city limits vast tracts of empty or thinly

The semi-detached house combined elements of both the terrace and the bungalow. Houses were built in pairs: two houses shared a party-wall which ran from front to rear on the dividing boundary line but each house was kept about 900 millimetres clear of its other side boundary, creating an open passageway from the small front garden to the rear yard. In unsewered localities this side passage allowed night-soil to be removed from the earth-closet at the back of the house where there was no rear service lane. In plan, semi-detached houses usually had no option but to follow a standard arrangement. From the front door a corridor ran towards the rear, alongside the party-wall. The front

populated land stretched beyond the horizon. The need for compactness had gone and there was more than enough land for everyone. It was little wonder that the new suburbs straggled outwards at far lower densities than had previously been necessary. Houses could now sit freely on their own blocks of land as they had always done in country towns. The two- and three-storeyed terrace houses that had proliferated in the inner suburbs of Sydney and Melbourne were abandoned in favour of single-storeyed villas or bungalows, except by those who felt that their social status was better reflected by the impressive bulk of a two-storeyed house.

The transitional semi

While the terrace house was being phased out in favour of the bungalow, a transitional type of dwelling appeared.

Semi-detached house pairs such as this typified the transition from terrace to bungalow.

room – usually a 'parlour' or 'drawing-room' – had a window facing the street. The bedrooms beyond it opened off the corridor and had to rely on windows opening on to the side passage. Having passed the bedrooms, the corridor opened into a living-room or dining-room which occupied the full width of the house and also had its windows on to the side passage. The bathroom, kitchen and laundry lay beyond, close to the rear yard and the clothes-line.

Compared with the terrace house, the 'semi' was a doubtful quantity. Benefits included having all its rooms on a single level close to the ground, eliminating the need for a staircase to be negotiated many times each day. And, as with the terrace house, the party-wall gave privacy from one's immediate neighbours. On the minus side, privacy, outlook and the access of sunlight were all severely diminished for those rooms with windows on to the side passage: there was every likelihood that these windows would be directly opposite the corresponding windows of an identically-planned 'semi' next door. However, in its exterior expression the semi-detached house offered its inhabitants a rather unquantifiable bonus – each pair of 'semis' could at first glance be mistaken for one relatively commodious dwelling. A single roof system covered both occupancies and often the party-wall did not penetrate the roof as it had done in the terrace house. In fact, a gable or ornamental parapet feature was sometimes provided in the centre of the elevation, its only justification being to further the impression of 'oneness'. In other cases minor gables and other excrescences broke the line of the main roof in a deliberately asymmetrical arrangement to suggest that the Siamese-twin houses had been conceived as a composed totality rather than as a pairing of mirror-imaged units.

In the two-and-a-half decades between 1890 and World War I, speculative builders put up large numbers of single-storeyed semi-detached houses, mostly in working-class suburbs. Much more rarely, a two-storeyed version appeared among the conventional detached houses in the streets of more affluent suburbs. But at best the 'semi' did no more than mark the halfway point in the inevitable transition from the terrace to the bungalow.

Suburban space

The growing demand for bungalows clearly separated from their neighbours brought about substantial change in the suburban environment. The street composition shifted from the 'corridor' effect that was formed by two-storeyed terraces, to the twentieth-century suburban street with detached houses swimming in a sea of open space. The roadway became wider than it had been in the pre-automobile era; the footpath acquired a grassed 'nature strip'; the front gardens of the bungalows extended as much as 8 metres back from the front fence. This new suburban environment may be deplored for having abandoned the traditional model of the compact, enclosed, socially interactive street. On the other hand, it is a manifestation of a way of seeing buildings as 'objects in space', a concept which is more relevant to Australian conditions than the European tendency to see buildings as 'objects which define and enclose space'.

The Australian suburban householder was not worried about spatial concepts. Nor was it his concern that the 700 or 800 square metres of land on which he built his house would become the endlessly repeated module for a vast sprawling suburbia in the distant future. He did know, however, that the free-standing house, with its own front garden and backyard, offered better opportunities for family life than anything he had seen. Whether he realized it or not, he was being caught up in the broad stream of the Garden City movement which had for some time been gathering strength, especially in Britain. Bedford Park, a speculative development begun in 1875 by Jonathan Carr at Turnham Green just outside

London, was a widely admired estate of red-brick Queen Anne houses in a leafy environment, with its own shops, church, club and inn.[4] In 1898 Ebeneezer Howard provided the theory and the model for the Garden City in his *Tomorrow: A Peaceful Path to Real Reform*. Letchworth in Hertfordshire, started in 1903, became the first planned Garden City to demonstrate Howard's ideas.[5] Expressing a disenchantment with nineteenth-century industrialization, the Garden City owed much to William Morris's dream of a semi-rural Arts and Crafts utopia.

The concept of the Garden City, or at least the Garden Suburb, was the result rather than the cause of a growing

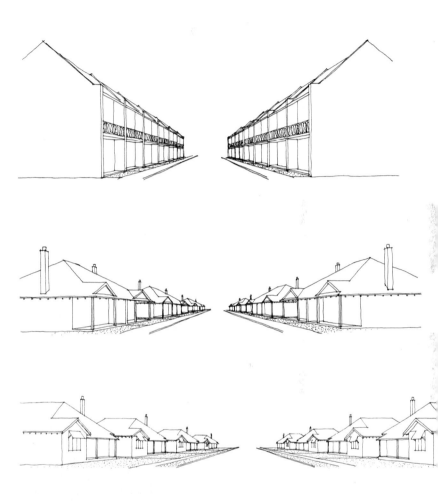

As the demand for separate bungalows grew, the residential environment changed, for good or ill, from corridor street to spacious suburbia.

middle-class urge to escape from the congestion and cacophony of the urban workplace and live peacefully in a mini-Arcadia where each family could proclaim its own identity through the medium of the detached house. In Sydney, conscious attempts to implement Garden City ideas were made by both private enterprise and the State. The first subdivisions of 'Haberfield: The Garden Suburb' were offered to the public in 1901 by the real-estate entrepreneur Richard Stanton,[6] and Dacey Garden Suburb (now Daceyville) was conceived and commenced in 1912 by The Housing Board of New South Wales.[7] The Adelaide Workmen's Homes of 1899–1900 (Charles

W. Rutt, architect) show the same forces at work, surprisingly, in the heart of the South Australian capital.[8]

In the ideal Garden City each house was an entity, recognizably different from every other. This criterion was enthusiastically adopted in Australia, not only in residential developments where there was some measure of design control but also in the *laissez-faire* world of the 'spec' builder. In practice, however, a house was given its sought-for identity by the variation and manipulation of details rather than essentials, making it feasible to examine a hypothetical 'typical' suburban house at the turn of the century, bearing in mind that a host of local variants occurred across the length and breadth of the continent.

House plan and form

The house was single-storeyed. It was complex in its shape, silhouette and details, but relatively simple in its plan. It was placed towards the front of its site, allowing about a quarter to a third of the available open space to be devoted to the front garden and the remainder to the backyard. While the side and rear boundaries of the site were defined by a head-high paling fence, the front boundary was demarcated only by a low wall or fence of brick, stone or timber – or combinations of these – so that passers-by might view the house across the carefully contrived foreground provided by the front garden. The backyard, by contrast, was treated as a strictly functional area. A considerable amount of it was occupied by the clothes-line, which consisted of a pair of parallel wires attached at each end to a horizontal timber crossbar pivoted on a bolt through the top of a hardwood post about two metres high. When the wires sagged under a heavy load of damp washing they were given extra support by fork-ended poles, sold by the itinerant 'clothes prop man'. Also in the backyard there might be a vegetable patch, a citrus tree or banana plant, a small shed and a narrow garden bed alongside the fence containing a few hardy plants. The rest of the yard was planted with buffalo grass, providing a rugged, flexible and safe place where children could play under supervision from the kitchen and laundry.

The house itself consisted of a number of rectangular-shaped rooms, access to which was gained by a central corridor running from front to rear. Where the planning was tight, the main entrance was directly into the front end of this corridor, but usually the corridor was widened to provide a more commodious entrance vestibule. 'Front entry' was by no means obligatory, and where the entrance was at the side of the house the central corridor took a ninety-degree turn to address the front door. A verandah extended across at least part of the front wall of the house, often returning for some distance along a side wall. The front door usually opened off the verandah, part of which then assumed the role of entrance porch.

The kitchen, laundry and bathroom were located towards the rear of the house, for practical as well as aesthetic reasons. The laundry needed direct access to the clothes-line; the copper in which the clothes and household linen were boiled needed to be close to the fuel store at the back of the house or in the yard. Some houses had a back verandah – a useful place to hang wet washing in bad weather – and an 'open' laundry might be placed here. In

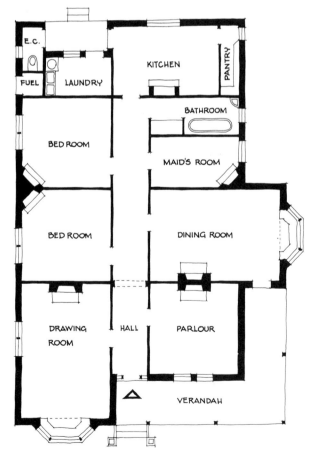

any case, the laundry was a hot, steam-filled room on washing-days and it was naturally banished to the rear of the house. Similarly, the kitchen was often unpleasantly hot in summer and the fuel stove needed access to the fuel store. Lastly, the bathroom relied on a supply of hot water from a large kitchen kettle or from the laundry copper, so it also gravitated to the back half of the house, especially in unsewered areas where an outside earth-closet was necessary. With this concentration of service rooms at the rear of the house, it was not unreasonable for tradespeople of all kinds to be directed firmly along a side path to the back door. Nevertheless, the social gulf between 'front door' and 'back door' indicated that egalitarianism in Australia had not yet progressed to a stage where middle-class householders could happily receive their peers and their tradesmen through the same entrance. As the twentieth century advanced, young women who might otherwise have sought employment in domestic service turned in growing numbers to more lucrative and less restrictive jobs in factories, department stores and offices. Some middle-class families, however, still found it possible to employ a live-in maid. She could easily be accommodated if a small additional bedroom were provided at the rear of the house near the kitchen and laundry – the kind of room for which there were many other uses if a suitable occupant could not be found or afforded.

Looking at a plan of one of today's houses it is possible to identify living-rooms, dining areas and bedrooms by their relative sizes, their location, their relationship to other rooms and by the cupboards or fitments which are built into them: each room is designed specifically for its purpose. This was not so at the turn of the century. Four or five rooms of roughly equal size were provided at the front of the house, served by the central corridor or the entrance hall. The rooms facing the street might have been fitted out with slightly more elaborate ceilings and overmantels. South of the Queensland border it was not uncommon for each of these rooms to have its own fireplace. In rooms of modest dimensions the fireplace was frequently set diagonally across a corner of the room, its flue sharing a chimney stack with that from a similar fireplace in the adjoining room. Usually at least one of these front rooms featured a polygonal-sided bay window with a low ceiling and a built-in window-seat. On the architect's plan these front rooms were labelled 'drawing-room', 'parlour', 'dining-room' or 'bedroom', but functions were generally allotted to rooms to meet the occupants' personal preferences. The flexibility afforded by this system had definite advantages. Usually a front room looking on to the verandah (but not necessarily having direct access to it) was chosen as what today would be called the 'living-room' but was then the 'parlour'. The

Above: An artist's view of the Garden Suburb: the opposite of the nineteenth-century industrial city.

Far left: The floor plan of a hypothetical 'typical' suburban house at the turn of the nineteenth century.

Left: The three planning axes of an L-shaped house on a corner allotment. The diagonal emphasis was often the strongest.

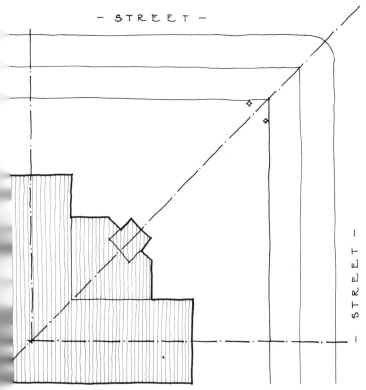

- STREET -

STREET -

room contained a studied arrangement of the family's best furniture, carpets and ornaments and was kept in a constant state of tidiness for the reception of visitors.

If most features of the plan arrangement just described were present in medium-sized houses at the turn of the century, the designer's constant pursuit of variety was always likely to modify the typical plan. A tower or turret introduced for its Picturesque three-dimensional effect could give rise to, for example, a large octagonal bay on the external corner of a front room or to an unusual treatment of the entrance hall or porch. The provision of an upstairs room – in a tower or within the main roof space – would also affect the planning to a minor degree. On corner sites, which allowed the house to have two frontages, an L-shaped plan was often favoured, with an element placed on the diagonal axis between the two arms of the L. The play of angles generated by this plan led to its frequent use on non-corner sites of sufficient width.

Foreign influences

It would be simple and gratifying to say that Australian domestic architecture at the turn of the century reflected the upsurge of nationalism found in the work of some radical writers of the 1890s, and to claim that a new style was born to express Australia's national identity. There would be, however, little truth in such a claim.

The rich vein of nationalism that emerged in literature and painting was also reflected in the applied arts. The use of Australian themes was vigorously championed by R.T. Baker, botanist and museum curator, leading to the application of waratah, flannel flower and gum-nut motifs to artifacts of many kinds.[9] It seems hardly surprising that, after a century of European civilization in Australia, artists should show an interest in local flora and fauna. But architecture, the social art dependent on the expenditure of large sums of clients' money, produced no passionate, tragic Henry Lawsons, no carefree, lyrical Streetons.

Houses could and did respond to more mundane influences. They expressed the climatic differences between, say, north Queensland and Tasmania; they inevitably reflected the materials and constructional techniques available in different regions and localities; they equally inevitably responded to the increased breathing space allowed to them by larger building blocks in new suburban subdivisions. All of these factors played a large part in shaping the house but they did not finally determine its appearance. Here 'style' stepped in to add the finishing touches, and style was very largely a matter of powerful overseas influences rather than local traditions or aspirations.

By the 1860s in Britain, Europe and the United States of America architects were suffering from (or enjoying) a surfeit of self-imposed academic eclecticism: they went to considerable trouble to design their buildings in 'correct' versions of Classical (Greek, Roman or Renaissance) or Gothic styles. At the same time, the factories of the great industrial cities were spewing out huge quantities of products manufactured by repetitive mechanical means. Foremost among a number of younger artists, designers and architects in Britain who reacted against this was

William Morris, around whom the whole Arts and Crafts movement grew and flourished. Looking back to some of the more attractive facets of the Middle Ages, Morris sought to re-establish what he saw to be the specifically medieval virtues of fitness for purpose and the honest use of materials.

Red House, designed in 1858 for Morris by his close friend Philip Webb, has been enshrined by twentieth-century historians as a lonely progenitor of Modern architecture – a distinction which the uninitiated might well fail to recognize when confronted with its warm red brickwork, tiled roof, white-painted sash windows and occasional pointed arches. The sensitive, publicity-shy Webb became the behind-the-scenes leader of the architectural arm of the Arts and Crafts movement. He drew his inspiration from traditional English buildings of the kind which for two or three hundred years had been largely unaffected by the shifts of fashionable style but which was several notches above the level of earthy artlessness generally implied by the word 'vernacular'.[10]

Far more in the public eye was the brilliant, versatile and successful Richard Norman Shaw, probably the most influential architect of the last three decades of the nineteenth century. Unconcerned with theories but blessed with talent, charm and a keen eye for the picturesque, he cheerfully selected motifs from whatever sources suited him and wove them together with unerring skill. During the early years of his popularity he employed two basic styles – 'Old English' and 'Queen Anne'. The former style was reserved for houses in the country and made use of a wide range of traditional elements and materials – complex pitched roof systems, bay windows, ingle nooks, tile-hung walls and gables, tall brick chimneys, leadlights and half-timbering. While they in no way sought to be historically accurate, Shaw's Old English houses usually had a vaguely Tudor look.

Queen Anne was the style used for London town houses. It had its sources in English urban houses of the seventeenth and eighteenth centuries, with more than passing reference to the Dutch and German models from which these had originated. Its main elements were plain red brickwork, white-painted timber sashes, discreet touches of not-too-correct Classical ornament and stepped or scalloped brick gables on the skyline. Shaw mixed and varied these elements with considerable elan and the style soon became the fashionable choice of fresh, wholesome, 'aesthetic' families of the kind so delightfully depicted in the books of Kate Greenaway (herself a client of Shaw's).[11] The only trouble with the vastly popular Queen Anne style was its name, which had been fairly irrelevant from the start and which soon came to be used indiscriminately to describe any buildings (including those of Old English derivation) which owed even the slightest stylistic debt to Norman Shaw or other leading architects working along similar lines.

By the turn of the century what became known as the 'Domestic Revival' in Britain was held in high regard internationally, and not solely because of the great popularity of Queen Anne. C.F.A. Voysey's houses, with their white roughcast walls sheltered by spreading hipped or gabled roofs, had something of the styleless quality of traditional farmhouses; Charles Rennie Mackintosh took as his model the old sturdy Scottish house and added to it his own idiosyncratic brand of ornament; Edwin Lutyens, then at the start of his long and varied career, was using a rich palette of time-honoured materials to create some of the loveliest English country houses ever built.

At the height of the Domestic Revival in the 1870s, English ideas started to flow freely across the Atlantic to the United States, where they were enthusiastically received. Leading American architects – among them Henry Hobson Richardson, Charles Follen McKim and Stanford White – spent considerable time in Europe and were well aware of developments in British domestic architecture. But a more widespread and constant influence came from the weekly flow of information, ideas and images in British architectural and trade periodicals such as the *Builder* and *Building News*. In the early 1870s *Building News* introduced a new technique – photolithography – which made possible the accurate reproduction of the highly detailed and richly textured pen-and-ink perspective renderings favoured by Norman Shaw and his followers.[12] Interpretation of these influences and discussion about their relevance to America became possible when the *American Architect and Building News* began publication in 1876. So it is not surprising that, by and large, the United States adopted Queen Anne and proceeded to Americanize her.

The American response to Queen Anne in some ways foreshadowed Australian developments a decade and a half later. It was marked by a number of differences from the British models on which it was based. Chief among these was a blithe disregard for restraint – an eagerness to 'lay it on thick'. Steeply pitched roofs were brought together in complicated relationships and towers and turrets were added to produce a busy, piled-up effect. The verandah, conspicuously absent in Britain except at waterside pleasure resorts, was an almost universal feature of American houses. At ground floor level, it wrapped itself around several sides of the house and widened out at an appropriate vantage point to form what was usually called a 'piazza'. Smaller verandahs and balconies were also common on upper floors. The architectural treatment of the verandah reflected the American penchant for the lavish use of timber and it also demonstrated the growing use of power-driven saws, lathes, drills and planes by which the wood could be cheaply and easily formed into elaborate shapes. Stout wooden verandah posts were square in cross-section at top and bottom, changing to circular in the mid-section where they bulged, curved and tapered as the lathe-operator decreed. Between each pair of posts were timber balustrades, braces and valences which displayed equally exuberant machine-

Three important foreign houses which contributed to the development of Federation architecture in Australia. Above: Leys Wood, Sussex, an 'Old English style' house by Richard Norman Shaw, 1868. Centre: The Shaw idiom imported into America – the Joseph H. Berry house, Detroit, by Manson and Rice. Below: The development of the American model into the Shingle style of the 1880s – the S.P. Hinckley house, Lawrence, Long Island, by Lamb and Rich, 1883.

A striking chair designed by A. H. Mackmurdo in the 1880s, with the curvilinear motifs that epitomize Art Nouveau.

Right: A Queen Anne development of the traditional 'oeil-de-boeuf' or round window, edged in fine brickwork.

Far right: Tinted glass leadlighting was an effective medium for curvilinear Art Nouveau decorative motifs. This iris window is in Cottesloe, Western Australia.

formed shapes. The elements which remained closest to their English origins were the soaring chimneys enriched by brick pilaster strips and corbelling. The rich complexity displayed by these Queen Anne houses was reinforced by the wide range of materials used – brick, stone, terracotta, slate, timber, ornamental plasterwork, weather-boarding, plain and fancy shingles.[13].

The 1880s in America saw the now-absorbed eclecticism of Queen Anne become a distinctly American idiom which was destined to have some effects on Australian architecture. The Shingle style was evolved in the north-eastern seaboard states, and flowered especially in large seaside houses for wealthy clients of a partnership that would leave its imprint on American architecture for several decades to come – McKim, Mead & White.[14] The Shingle style adopted the loose-knit picturesqueness of Queen Anne but dispensed with its pretty fussiness and substituted broader, more sweeping effects through timber balloon framing. The wood shingles which gave the style its name were used not only for roofing but also for wall cladding, where they replaced the traditional English technique of clay tile-hanging.

While the Shingle style was being evolved in America during the 1880s, there were signs of radical change in some fields of the decorative arts in Europe. Designers of the younger generation were coming to regard historicism, even eclecticism, as a millstone around their necks and they searched for new forms of expression which would signify a clean break with the past and in some way reflect a positive attitude to modern times. Around 1883 Arthur Heygate Mackmurdo, a disciple of Ruskin and a leading figure in the Arts and Crafts movement in Britain, produced some startling designs featuring asymmetrical compositions of curvilinear shapes.[15] In 1884 the Frenchman Emile Gallé exhibited art glass of striking originality, drawing on themes from the dark recesses of the animal and vegetable kingdoms.[16] These early leads were taken up and developed on the Continent – especially in Belgium, France, Germany and Austria – as well as in Britain, and a new, extremely successful decorative style came into being. Art Nouveau was 'new' and stimulating, often bordering on the erotic. For decorative motifs it drew heavily on the 'natural' and the 'organic', making use of vegetation of all kinds and, all too frequently, women's hair of inordinate length. The style's trademark was the sinuous asymmetrical curve. Art Nouveau flourished in decorative arts such as jewellery and fabric design where functional considerations imposed little restraint on the designer's freedom of expression. Buildings were less able to swoop and sway in response to an architect's emotional input, but Victor Horta in Belgium and Hector Guimard in France were able to create masterpieces of Art Nouveau architecture. The British Arts and Crafts movement, having played a significant part in planting the seeds of Art Nouveau, was inclined to disown responsibility for the blossoming tree when it whiffed its aroma of slightly salacious amorality. Nevertheless, much Arts and Crafts decorative work by men such as Walter Crane represented a wholesomely Anglo-Saxon aspect of Art Nouveau suitable for consumption by respectable middle-class families.

Favoured Federation materials and motifs. Left: Red brick and orange terracotta at Verona (now called Sorata) in Burwood, New South Wales. Above: The roofs of single storey houses, being closer to eye level, lent themselves to showier ornamentation, sometimes with native motifs.

All of these developments had relevance for Australian architecture at the turn of the century. While most Australians saw federation as a desirable and necessary step towards independence, they nevertheless felt vaguely threatened from the Asian north and were acutely conscious of their link with English-speaking and European cultures. They looked for protection and guidance to the other side of the world from which they were physically so remote. Architectural channels of communication with Britain, the United States and Europe were kept open in several ways. Books and periodicals flowed steadily into Australia, together with the occasional pattern-book[17] and trade catalogue.[18] Substantial quantities of building materials and accessories still were brought in from overseas although local manufacturers were starting to supply some of the demand. Roofing tiles, ceramic tiles, sanitary ware, many items of hardware, light fittings, furniture, fabrics, wallpaper and floor coverings were among the most frequently imported products. Most importantly, many architects from abroad who had trained and worked in their home countries had comparatively little trouble assuming leading places in the profession when they emigrated to Australia where effective architectural education was still in its infancy. (The first academic qualification in architecture to be granted in Australia was a Diploma awarded by the Sydney Technical College in 1896.)

An Australian style emerges

Australians thus became aware, in a rather piecemeal way, of the developments that had occurred overseas from about 1870 onwards – but Australian architecture took about fifteen years to respond to these influences. During the prosperous 1880s, elaborate stucco work and frilly cast iron admirably expressed the current mood of ebullient optimism; there was no need to go looking for other modes of architectural expression. The financial crashes of the early 1890s, however, brought people back to earth with a resounding bump. As so often happens, after the disaster there was an instinctive urge to wipe out bitter memories of what had suddenly become 'the bad old days' and the down-to-earth homeliness of the Domestic Revival and its American offshoot seemed to offer a reassuring path on which to make a new start.

During the 1890s Australian architecture started to exhibit symptoms of 'multiple eclecticism' as it absorbed features from both British and American eclectic architecture (the latter, of course, already having borrowed elements from the former). The stylistic mix was completed by a dash of second-hand Art Nouveau. But it also acquired a distinctive and easily recognized Australian flavour through the combination and interaction of several factors. The borrowed elements were applied to the Australian suburban house which, as we have seen, was single-storeyed rather than two-storeyed. This alone had important visual results because the roof became more dominant and was closer to the viewer's eye level. Some of the materials used in Australia were different from those used overseas; the Australian designer often imparted his individual twist to imported themes; and functional and climatic demands in some parts of Australia – notably Queensland – produced solutions that were far removed from the overseas models.

The structure of the suburban house

The ordinary house in the suburbs was indisputably an Australian product made for Australian suburbia, even if it used ideas, devices and materials from abroad wherever they seemed to be appropriate, desirable or convenient. A turn-of-the-century 'typical suburban house' might be found in Hawthorn (Melbourne), Burwood (Sydney), New Town (Hobart) or Mount Lawley (Perth).

Brick was the preferred material for exterior walls. This, of course, was not new, but, in response to the popularity of the urban Queen Anne style in Britain and America, it was decreed that brickwork should be seen to be such. The layer of painted stucco which masked exterior brickwork in the 1880s had given some protection against moisture penetration: the new fashion for face brickwork made cavity wall construction highly desirable if not mandatory. By the turn of the century an external wall sheltered by a wide verandah might still be built in solid brickwork, but it had become normal practice to separate the inner and outer skins of a wall by an air gap of about 50 millimetres. In localities where building stone was available at reasonable cost, the brick cavity wall was built on a 450 millimetre-thick rock-faced foundation wall that reached just below ground floor level. Such foundation walls, in sandstone, are especially noticeable on sloping sites in Sydney's harbourside suburbs, their rough texture and sandy hue contrasting with the darker tone of the brick walls they support. For brickwork exposed to view, red was the favoured colour; medium to dark brown was acceptable. Bricks of a contrasting colour or tone were often used for string courses, window surrounds and imitation quoins. Brickwork was required to be smooth in texture, uniform in colour and tone. Flush mortar joints were therefore used and, especially with red bricks, the mortar was tinted to match the brick colour. Tuck pointing was not universal, but its use was very widespread. Combined with even-coloured brickwork and hardly-visible flush joints, tuck pointing gave an impression of immaculate precision which echoed the quality of seventeenth-century Anglo-Dutch work. Where economy was important, face bricks were often confined to the front elevation of the house, the side and rear walls being executed in common brickwork.

Roofs of suburbia

The roofs of Australian houses displayed a complexity which belied the basically simple shapes of the buildings they covered. They echoed, on a smaller scale, the roofs of Norman Shaw's large Old English houses of the 1870s and

Left above: Terracotta tiles and decorative timber work were common in all Federation architecture, but sandstone basework and wood shingle roofing were used more in Sydney. This house is in Mosman.

Left: Federation brickwork was often tuck-pointed. Tile-hung gables and crested roof ridges were commoner in Victoria. This house is Molmo, in Bendigo.

their American derivatives. Shaw's Picturesque roofscapes were a natural outcome of his predilection for 'agglomerative planning' where the separate parts of a building were deliberately expressed rather than merged into a unifying envelope. Denied the opportunity to ramble, the Australian suburban house sought to establish its identity by means of complicated Shavian roof geometry. In the typical instance illustrated, a simple hipped roof was placed over the main body of the house and a gablet was inserted at each end of the ridge. A short length of gabled roof was then run out over the room which projected forward at the front of the house. The main roof was continued down over the verandah at a slightly flatter pitch, the free end of the verandah roof being finished with a hip and tucked back in under the main eaves. As something of an anticlimax, the service rooms at the rear were roofed with a low-pitched skillion, giving the back of the house the appearance of a sagging bustle. For additional complexity if required, another gable could be thrust out from the main roof or a pyramid-roofed tower could be introduced for vertical emphasis. While such roof configurations were common, the urge to make every house different led to an almost infinite number of variations.

replaced if broken. Hot air was not trapped in the space between ceiling and roof as the tiles 'breathed' through their interlocking joints. As a bonus, the skyline of a tiled roof could be enlivened by decorative terracotta accessories of varied design. Many patterns of crenellated or filigreed ridge tiles were available, together with scrolled or pillar-and-ball finials. Most splendid were the winged dragons: some of which still survive slightly the worse for wear in suburbs of Melbourne, Hobart and Perth. Terracotta hip and ridge tiles were used on both tile and slate roofs. These crudely functional accessories at least had an affinity with Marseilles tiles, but their clumsiness was accentuated when they were used in combination with slates.

Between the mid-1890s and World War I slates and tiles competed on fairly equal terms. Tenderers were frequently asked to provide alternative quotations before it was decided which roofing material would be used. Sometimes the contrasting visual qualities of the two materials were exploited by speculative builders and estate developers. For example, during the first decade of this century when Mr George Hoskins created the charming Appian Way in the Sydney suburb of Burwood, orange

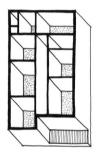 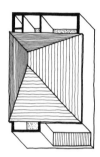 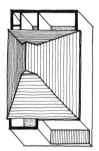 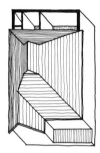 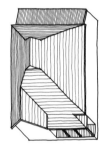

In the boom years of the 1880s slate was the only 'prestige' material to be widely used for domestic roofs: where it was not available or could not be afforded, corrugated iron was used. *En masse*, grey slate roofs imparted a sober, somewhat dreary air to a locality. This situation changed dramatically with the importation from France of terracotta Marseilles tiles. Regular shipments started to arrive in Melbourne in the late 1880s, in Sydney in the early 1890s and in Perth about 1900. Imports of tiles increased steadily in volume until they were stopped by World War I, and thenceforth supplies were maintained by large-scale local production by firms such as Wunderlich Ltd.[19] For two decades slates and tiles fought for dominance of the market, with tiles eventually winning. Visually the two materials were poles apart. Slates were smooth and grey, the unglazed tiles were knobbly and orange. Slate roofs could cope more crisply and cleanly with complicated roof geometry, especially if hips were mitred. Marseilles tiles looked coarse and clumsy where roof planes came together, as on a pyramid-roofed tower.

Aesthetically, the sallow orange of the Marseilles tile may not have been the ideal complement to red Queen Anne brickwork, but to the speculative builder and his customers the tile had much to recommend it. A tiled roof could be laid quickly and easily. Tiles interlocked only along their edges whereas slates, to be waterproof, had to be extensively overlapped, resulting in a heavier roof. Tiles kept out the rain effectively and could be easily

A simple house shape was often given a complex agglomerative roof treatment which included hips, gables, gablets and skillions.

roofs alternated with grey along both sides of the street.

An array of chimneys penetrated through the tile, slate and corrugated iron roofs of suburbia. They were welcomed for the contribution they made to the picturesqueness of the roofscape. As in America, the basic inspiration came from Old English models which were remarkable for their height, slenderness and sculptural qualities. In even the cheapest 'spec built' cottage, plain brick chimneys were avoided and some gesture was made towards elaboration of shape and variety of texture. Face brick and roughcast, alone or in combination, were the most favoured materials. The shaft of the stack was enlivened by bricks projecting to make geometric patterns, horizontal bands or narrow vertical pilasters. The top of the stack was enlarged by means of several courses of corbelled brickwork and capped with one or more terracotta chimney pots, depending on the number of flues.

So many houses featured at least one gable facing the street that it is not surprising to find that this element was singled out for special attention. Indeed, the treatment of the gable could give a house something akin to a facial

Right above: Fashion outdoes function at the Moorings, Bellerive, Tasmania. Verandahs are appropriate in warmer areas.

Right: Local materials are used in this Adelaide bungalow.

expression which clearly differentiated it from its neighbours. It was almost universal practice to project the end of a gabled roof beyond the face of the wall below, and to finish the edge of the roof with a timber bargeboard about 200 millimetres wide. The finish of the bargeboard at the eaves was resolved in many different ways, the most common being the straight vertical cut and the rarest being the straight horizontal cut favoured in Britain and America. Widely overhanging 'flying gables' were supported on cyma-shaped timber brackets and had an open framework of ornamental woodwork set flush with the bargeboards in the apex of the gable-end, hinting at structural complexities lurking in the roof construction behind. There were many ways of treating the triangular piece of wall at the top of the gable under the overhanging roof. Stained or painted shingles were a popular choice, contrasting in texture with the brickwork of the wall beneath. Another common practice was to fix flat boards to the face of the wall, set in rectangular, diagonal or curved patterns for a half-timbered effect or arranged radially in a 'sunburst' configuration. The wall surface itself could be finished in face brickwork, roughcast, or pargetting with ornamental scrolls and strapwork.

The simplified verandah

The verandah was introduced to Australia in the early days of European settlement. It continued to be an important element in both rural dwellings and large suburban houses during the second half of the nineteenth century and its value in the humid heat of Queensland was never in question. But it had become emasculated in the more compact forms of housing which clustered around the cores of the capital cities. By the end of the century, however, the relatively larger allotments available in the new suburbs allowed the verandah to be firmly re-established as an essential part of the ordinary suburban house. Architects sang its praises, noting both its widespread popularity in America and its long-standing contribution to Australian architecture. The suburbanite responded with cautious approval. Care had to be taken to shield delicate complexions from the sun's rays. Flies and mosquitoes were often a great nuisance. Still, it was nice to sit out on the verandah to catch the breeze after a long summer day had made the house hot and stuffy.

In its architectural treatment the turn-of-the-century verandah differed from its late Victorian predecessor principally in the materials from which it was constructed. For the floor, tongued and grooved hardwood boards were preferred to encaustic tiles set in geometric patterns. The slender cast iron columns and lacy balustrades and valences so widely used in the 1880s were banished from the scene and the verandah was constructed entirely of wood. Especially during the 1890s, the influence of American timber verandahs was strongly evident: a visiting Yankee would have instantly recognized the sturdy lathe-turned posts, the valences and balustrades filled with closely spaced square sticks or round spindles. After 1900, verandah details were gradually simplified and strengthened. Posts became square in cross-section and were sometimes mounted in pairs on waist-high masonry piers or balustrades. The intricate valences disappeared, replaced by

brackets or braces set in the angle between post and verandah plate. They were cut from flat pieces of timber, 40 to 50 millimetres thick, and their tautly curved profiles suggested Art Nouveau. The simplification of the verandah continued until, by World War I, most of the non-essential elements had been discarded.

Windows of all shapes and sizes

With eclecticism and the Picturesque permeating domestic architecture, windows were arranged with considerable freedom. Quaintness was the admired quality, taking precedence over uniformity and regularity. Window frames and sashes were of wood and, in deference to hazy ideas about 'Queen Anne', were painted white, ivory or cream to contrast with the dark colour of the brick walls. Both casement and double-hung windows were popular and it was common to find them used together in the one building. Casement sashes were usually combined in banks of three or four with a row of small toplights above a transom. Double-hung windows were generally used singly: if they were combined in a bank the intermediate timber mullions became inordinately wide, having to accommodate the pulleys and lead sash-weights for a pair of windows. The double-hung window was relatively tall in relation to its width and frequently had a very flat segmental brick arch over the head of the window opening. Horizontally sliding windows were favoured on side and rear verandahs, especially in locations exposed to the weather. The sashes slid in recesses formed in the head and sill of the window frame, sometimes straddling a small metal guide rail on the sill. Consequently they were stiff to operate, the compensation being that there was no complicated hardware to go wrong. In many houses a small window of unusual shape was located near the front door, as a visual accent. The circle was the most widely used shape, but many variations can be found – the ellipse, the diamond, the equilateral triangle with convex-curved sides and even the asymmetrically shaped quarter-ellipse. Their shape was emphasized by a surround of voussoir-like bricks.

The admission of direct sunlight into rooms was not regarded as a blessing. Furnishings, carpets and wallpaper had to be safeguarded from fading and people regarded the interior of the house as a shady retreat from the heat and glare of the outdoors. By the standards of the late twentieth century, rooms were dimly lit, the windows shrouded by a double layer of heavy and light curtains. Windows exposed to excessive sunlight were individually shaded by fixed external hoods sloping down and out from the wall above the window and supported by shaped timber brackets. The upper surface of the hood was covered either by the roofing material (slates, tiles or corrugated iron) or by timber shingles or flat sheet metal.

Style and technology came into conflict in the detailed design of windows. On the one hand 'Queen Anne' demanded that windows be divided into small panes by a grid of slender glazing bars: on the other hand it was perfectly feasible to glaze a sash with a single sheet of good quality glass. In a compromise calculated to make the purist shudder, large panes of glass were used in the lower sections of windows and small panes with glazing bars were introduced above eye level. Coloured glass was often featured in these small panes, in alternating tints of rose, amber, green, blue and violet. Those who have been conditioned by a modern architecture notable for its excruciating blandness may sneer at such practices, but the impure and fuzzy philosophy of turn-of-the-century architecture was at least sure that it wanted intricacy, interest and variety to extend through all parts of a building, right down to the details.

Nowhere is this desire more evident than in the use of coloured glass and leadlights to adorn windows and glazed doors. There was no overseas high-style precedent for this. In Britain, the Old English branch of Queen

Anne made use of lead cames to divide sashes into small rectangular or lozenge-shaped panes of clear glass: urban Queen Anne also occasionally used cames in decorative mesh patterns. However, in the High Victorian era the coloured glass leadlight was a 'popular' favourite in Britain, Europe and the United States as well as in Australia, where it retained its popularity until the 1930s. During the Federation period, the leadlight window took as its point of departure a rectangular grid of lead cames, overlaying it and modifying it with flowing lines depicting stylized leaves, flowers, fauna and landscape scenes, picked out in glass of bright, cheerful colours. The curving lines suggested Art Nouveau, but the main influence was from the British Arts and Crafts designers who had turned their hands to stained glass. Walter Crane, Selwyn Image, Brangwyn and others produced many designs for domestic windows.[20] The stained glass of the American, Louis

Country houses were often conservative in style. Belltrees, at Scone, is a fine homestead surrounded by an ample two-storeyed verandah that is decorated with cast iron, which by then was becoming old-fashioned.

Top: Eubindal homestead, near Binalong, was built of camerated concrete, an invention of the Federation period by H. A. Goddard. His system utilized timber shuttering for building cavity walls, the shuttering being raised after each concrete pour. Owners of Goddard houses complained that their walls were 'so hard that it is impossible to hang a picture'.

Comfort Tiffany, was also widely admired. The objects depicted in the great majority of Australian leadlight windows were not specifically related to native flora or fauna, but there were some splendid examples which used waratah, flannel flower and eucalyptus leaf motifs. Coloured glass leadlights were frequently used in casement sashes (especially in 'front windows'), rarely in double-hung windows. They also appeared in the small 'accent' windows placed near entrances, in the sidelights to front doors and in the doors' glazed upper panels.

The general characteristics of suburban houses of the Federation period were modified by local conditions. A good example is Adelaide, a city not usually regarded

long since passed out of favour in suburbia. Queensland, however, departed most from the norm. It is difficult to imagine anything more different from the red-brick, tile-roofed bungalow than a house raised on stilts, framed in light timber studs, roofed with corrugated iron and surrounded by a latticed verandah. The common element was the decorative woodwork associated with the verandah. In Queensland it became more prominent visually (often there was almost nothing else to be seen), more fancifully elaborate and more functional.

Allowing for all of the regional and local variations which occurred, it is still possible to generalize by saying that the great majority of houses for families living on

as rich in houses of this period. Many, however, can be found in suburbs of such diverse character as North Adelaide, Unley and Fitzroy. Local limestone was a popular material for walls, with quoins and dressings in face brick or stucco. Marseilles tiles had to be brought by rail from Melbourne, consequently corrugated iron was frequently used for roofing. These two factors alone were enough to make many Adelaide houses look very different from those in Melbourne, Sydney or Perth. In country areas corrugated-iron roofing was the rule rather than the exception. There was also an inherent conservatism shown by the established pastoral families which may account for the use of decorative cast iron on large homesteads built in the decade after 1900 when the material had

Carclew, North Adelaide, is an exuberantly complex house of 1897 which shows not only some French provincial details such as the round tower, but also the strong influence of the American Stick style of the 1870s.

modest incomes shared some common characteristics.

Number of storeys: one.
Massing: asymmetrical.
Scale: small, with many elements relating comfortably to the size of the human being.
Planning: compartmentalized. Central corridor access. Living-rooms and bedrooms at front, service rooms at rear.
Roof configuration: Picturesque, with visually prominent gables, bargeboards and chimneys.

Materials: ideally, walls of red-brown tuck-pointed brickwork, roofs of tile or slate. Alternative materials used as appropriate for local conditions.
Verandah: timber post-and-beam construction, with machine-formed elaborations incorporated and/or added.
Windows: vertical proportions. Timber casement and/or double-hung sashes. Selected windows embellished with coloured leadlights or panes of coloured glass.

The Queen Anne mainstream

What name-tag should be applied to houses of this genre? 'Federation' aptly identifies the two decades from the early 1890s to World War I and has appropriately Australian connotations for Australians (if not for Americans). However, an examination of the domestic, commercial, institutional and public architecture of these decades reveals that several distinct styles were operating concurrently. It is therefore best to use the catch-all 'Federation period' to define the era as a whole and to find other labels for the various styles in vogue during the era. 'Queen Anne' was used in Australia for houses of the kind described, and the name was given a new lease of life by Robin Boyd in 1952.[21] The virtue of using 'Queen Anne' in the Australian context is that it acknowledges the links which existed with domestic architecture of the late nineteenth century in England and America. From the 1870s on, 'Queen Anne' was used on both sides of the Atlantic with blithe imprecision. Strictly interpreted, the term implied a revival of the English domestic architecture of the period from 1702 to 1714, an impossibly narrow definition for an idiom which drew its motifs from any century from the fifteenth to the eighteenth. This has long since become irrelevant. Through common usage over a long period, 'Queen Anne' (or 'Australian Queen Anne' when necessary) readily identifies the predominant domestic style of the Federation period, now free, one hopes, of the disparagement heaped upon it by the anonymous writer in *Building* who in 1908 attacked what he (or she) called The Queen Anne Atrocity:

This type of cottage came into fashion quite ten years ago in all the growing suburbs of the Greater Sydney area. They are the special goods of the usual villainous building company, which attracts by its alluring announcements of Queen Anne style. It is a pity the poor Queen should have her memory thus assailed.

While most Australian houses were immediately identifiable despite the overseas influences which helped to shape them, there were some interesting and important exceptions. Caerleon, a two-storeyed house on Bellevue Hill, Sydney was (and still is) one of the most authentic Queen Anne houses in Australia. It was built for Charles B. Fairfax, a grandson of the first Fairfax to own the *Sydney Morning Herald*, and completed in 1887. Fairfax commissioned a preliminary design for his residence from the Sydney architect Harry C. Kent. However, while visiting England he consulted Maurice B. Adams, the editor of *Building News*, and apparently with Kent's concurrence, engaged Adams to develop the design in detail – in other words, to clothe it in fashionable Queen Anne dress. Kent assiduously supervised construction in Sydney.[22] Maurice B. Adams was a well-known figure on the English scene. He had worked with Norman Shaw and he was responsible for several houses (including his own) in the predominantly Shaw-designed Bedford Park Garden Suburb estate. Caerleon, the outcome of the slightly odd Kent-Adams association, turned out to be a charming essay in Shaw's Bedford Park manner. The walls of the lower storey are of red brickwork with flush joints of red mortar; the upper storey displays the traditional English technique of plain and scalloped tile-hanging. A continuous dentilled cornice forms the small eaves overhang, above which rise simple white-painted pediments at each gable. The roofs are covered with terracotta plain tiles which became known in Australia as 'shingle tiles'. Symmetrical when viewed from the street,

A tower in Toorak. The house's candle-snuffer roof and the imported terracotta of the main roof are French influences.

the house becomes comfortably asymmetrical on its other elevations. Superb craftsmanship is evident where local sandstone is used to accent particular features. For example, in the bay window on the garden front the remarkably slender mullions and transoms are of this material. The central semicircular transom, used here, is one of Norman Shaw's favourite motifs. Apart from the single-storeyed verandahs on the garden front, the house is English in style and detail. It is interesting to note that Kent's work in the years following Caerleon's completion owed much to his exposure to Adams.

Caerleon was an early example of true Queen Anne in Australia. Dalsraith (now Campion College), in the Melbourne suburb of Kew, appeared relatively late. It was built in 1906 for Samuel Gibson of Foy and Gibson's emporium to the design of the Melbourne architects Ussher and Kemp. Dalsraith is a direct descendant from the Old English side of the Queen Anne family and it bears a slight resemblance to Loughton Hall, Essex, designed in 1878 by W. Eden Nesfield, Norman Shaw's friend and office-sharing 'partner' during the 1860s. While the house is redolent with Old English picturesqueness, the entrance front exhibits an unusual degree of formality, approaching complete symmetry but deliberately withdrawing from it at the last moment. A two-storeyed sandstone loggia securely straddles the centre-line of the facade flanked on either side by a steeply-pitched gable projecting forward from the main roof. Under the right-hand gable a bay window rises unbroken through two

Chirritta, at Peppermint Grove, Western Australia, by J. J. Talbot Hobbs, 1896.

storeys; under the left-hand gable there is an oriel window in the overhanging tile-hung upper storey, with a bay window below. This 'nearly-but-not-quite' play with symmetry is probably to reassure the viewer that he is not being confronted with a piece of strait-jacketed 'high style' architecture but rather with a building which appears to have been built over an extended time and to have acquired slight irregularities in the process. Dalsraith has some fine details. The carving of the sandstone loggias is crisp and the decorative motifs on the string course are varied in a way which would have pleased Ruskin. A lively buff-coloured terracotta frieze with writhing chimerical beasts adorns the bottom edge of the tile-hung upper storey. There are some excellent leadlight windows in the principal rooms and the hall.[23]

Nine hundred kilometres and nearly twenty years apart, both Caerleon and Dalsraith were high-class manifestations of overseas influences. Each house clearly proclaimed its English parentage. This was obvious in the case of Caerleon, designed by a well-known London

architect, but Henry Kemp, the designer of Dalsraith, was also born in England. The majority of Australian architects of this period whose houses were of significance or interest were born in Britain, and in most cases they had practised there before coming to Australia.[24] It is difficult to maintain that stylistically the architect-designed houses of the Federation period reflected an outpouring of Australian national sentiment – unless it is argued that the 'convert' is often more passionately zealous than one born into the faith. It was only to be expected that these men would bring to Australia the first-hand experience and knowledge they had gained and that they would continue to keep closely in touch with overseas developments.

While the eastern states were suffering from drought and depression in the early 1890s, the sparsely populated western half of the continent was on the ascendant. Discoveries of gold in the late 1880s culminated in fabulous finds at Kalgoorlie in 1893. Australia's second major gold rush led to a building boom in many parts of Western Australia, not least in suburban Perth. Naturally enough, many architects migrated to the west, both from the eastern states and from abroad.[25] George Temple Poole, an able and versatile Englishman, was the architect responsible for the design of public buildings in Western Australia from 1885 to 1896. Competent and at ease in many styles, he designed several buildings at near-domestic scale which demonstrated his familiarity with the Domestic Revival in Britain. Buildings such as Albany Cottage Hospital, 1887–96, York Hospital, 1894–97, and Pinjarra Post and Telegraph Office, 1896, provided a strong lead for those of his colleagues in private practice who specialized in domestic work.[26]

J.J. Talbot Hobbs, whose houses in suburban Perth showed how the Australian Queen Anne idiom could be applied to the commodious residences his clients could afford, was influenced by Poole's work. An interesting variation from Hobbs's usual style, however, was seen in Chirritta, 1896, a single-storeyed stone house in Perth's pleasant riverside suburb, Peppermint Grove. The Queen Anne component was played down and emphasis placed on a hipped-tile roof which dominated its subsidiary gables and swept down over an extensive and simply treated verandah. This sophisticated, suburbanized version of the traditional Australian homestead might well have been a model for architects searching for a distinctively Australian idiom, but contemporary taste demanded greater complexity of massing and detail.

The finest architect-designed Queen Anne houses are to be found in the suburbs of Melbourne, due largely to the work and influence of the firm of Ussher and Kemp, which flourished from 1899 to 1908. Dalsraith was the most formal house designed by the partnership, almost certainly as a result of Henry Kemp's firm hand. Some of

Right above: Caerleon, Bellevue Hill, is a highly disciplined design by Maurice B. Adams, who had worked with Richard Norman Shaw in England. The house was commenced in 1885.

Right: Dalsraith, Kew, 1906, probably designed by Henry Kemp. A sensitive house with studied asymmetry and a fondness for finely wrought materials. It is now Campion College.

Left above: Haberfield was established as a Garden Suburb of
Sydney in the Federation period. This house, dominated by
stepped and bracketed gables, is set in a leafy garden.

A house in Moruya of timber and corrugated iron. The conservative L-shaped plan has been dressed in Queen Anne
details — the gabled hip roof, the bay window, and particularly
the elaborate barge and balustrade timberwork.

Left: Tay Creggan is a large Queen Anne house in Hawthorn
whose bay windows and decorative barges look back to Tudor
architecture. It was designed by Guyon Purchas in 1897.

Ussher and Kemp's other houses may appear to be almost excessively romantic and Picturesque, but there is usually more discipline and order than immediately is seen. The Cupples house built in 1899 in Camberwell is at first sight a rather confused jumble of disparate elements. On closer examination it is revealed to be an orderly enlargement and elaboration of the basic 'corner site L-shaped plan'. From the large central hipped roof, gabled wings project to address each of the street frontages. A candle-snuffer roof emphasizes the diagonal axis between the arms of the 'L' and the verandah roof is punctuated by appropriately scaled gablets. The reasonableness of this arrangement is disrupted, however, by two large and aggressively dissimilar dormers (one of them flanked by a pair of chimneys) that project from the main roof. This interplay of the predictable and the unpredictable exemplifies the theme of 'basic order modified by occasional quirks'

The Queen Anne Cupples house in Camberwell is a subtle design suiting a corner site.

which is often noticeable in Queen Anne architecture, both in Australia and abroad.[27]

The houses of Beverley Ussher and Henry Kemp marked the apogee of Australian Queen Anne, but there were many other architects throughout Australia who worked in the style. As a rule, their houses were distinguishable from those of the suburban 'spec' builder by their size and cost or by the greater degree of expertise evident in their details. John Sulman, who arrived in Sydney from England in 1885, was one of many such architects whose work in the idiom tended towards the pedestrian rather than the spectacular. At Ingleholme, a two-storeyed house for his family in Turramurra, built about 1896, Sulman went through the motions of being Old English without displaying the enthusiasm and flair needed to lift the anachronisms and artificialities of eclecticism into the realm of credibility. The work of J. Spencer-Stansfield, another English architect who came to Sydney, was more closely geared to the demands of expanding suburbia. He was employed by Richard Stanton to design most of the houses in the Haberfield Garden Suburb development. Prospective home-buyers had three choices: they could purchase a completed house on its own block; they could buy a vacant block and have one of Spencer-Stansfield's stock designs built on it; or they could arrange for the architect to design a house incorporating some of their ideas on the block of their choice. Most of the Haberfield houses were of modest size and were designed to suit middle-class budgets. Spencer-Stansfield's task – and it was a rare opportunity – was to produce a large number of designs to provide the visual variety sought by the promoters within the conventions of Australian Queen Anne. Spencer-Stansfield was equal to the task.[28]

Out of the mainstream

The architects who ventured away from the mainstream generally looked outside the Queen Anne style. A few, however, like Haddon and Annear, took it as their point of departure. The Englishman Robert Haddon came to Australia in 1891 and worked in Perth and Hobart before settling in Melbourne in 1900. He was an educator as well as a practitioner. While he talked about simplicity and the truthful use of materials, he was clearly not immune to the sensuous delights of Art Nouveau. The puritan within him battled with the hedonist. In his own house, Anselm, built in 1906 in Caulfield, Haddon tried to reconcile these influences. The simplified, no-nonsense brand of Queen Anne which emerged was perhaps a worthy achievement in itself but it provided an unduly sober setting for the scattered touches of Art Nouveau which Haddon introduced. Anselm was more successful and innovative in its planning. A large living-room occupied half of the ground floor, extending from the front of the house to the rear. As a foil to this big space, a semi-octagonal bay with vertical slit windows was set diagonally on the front corner of the room. A small entrance lobby was virtually part of this living-room, through which one 'circulated' to the rooms at the rear. In one simple stroke the ubiquitous central corridor had been eliminated.

Haddon's bold step in disposing of the corridor had, however, been pre-empted four years earlier by Harold Desbrowe Annear in his own house on a hillside in Eaglemont, Melbourne. Annear was the first Australian-born architect to make a creative contribution to this country's domestic architecture. 'Importation cannot help us; the ideas must be our own, born of our own necessities, our own climates, and our own methods of pursuing happiness.' He was certainly not the only architect to make such assertions in the early decades of the twentieth century, but in 1902 he alone had the unfettered talent to translate words into buildings. To the few passers-by who frequented outer suburban Eaglemont at the turn of the century, Annear's house would have appeared to be mildly eccentric but not especially radical. The 'half timbered' stud frame walls, the timber balus-

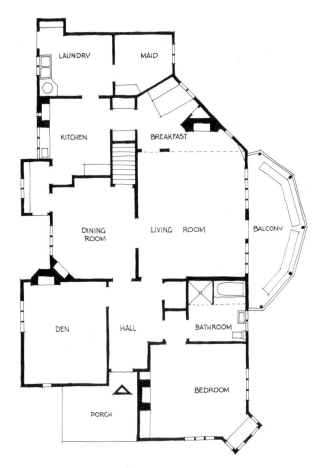

The exceptionally open and flexible floor-plan of Harold Desbrowe Annear's house in Eaglemont, 1902.

trades and valences and the roughcast chimneys were a token acknowledgement of the current Queen Anne style. Although Annear roofed his house with corrugated iron, he reverted to terracotta tiles when he built two very similar houses lower down the hill a few years later. As Robin Boyd clearly recognized more than thirty years ago, it was the plan which gave the house its exceptional quality. Apart from the entrance lobby which led directly to the living-room, dining-room, den, bedroom and bathroom, there was no space given to circulation. Allowance was made in the planning for a built-in buffet, benches, cupboards and wardrobes. In the bedroom a bay containing the dressing-table was pushed out diagonally from a corner of the room, almost thrusting its user out into the tree-tops. The dining-room was linked to the living-room by a wide sliding door which slid away into a cavity in the wall. But the *pièce de résistance* was the living-room. A skewed wall at the far end of the room created a wedge-shaped space which formed a small breakfast alcove, partially screened by a triangular-plan fireplace. Picking up the line of the skewed wall, a balcony bulged out towards the view outside the glazed eastern wall of the living-room. As Boyd observed, the plan contained 'most of the devices of the daringly progressive architect 45 years later'.[29]

Robin Dods was the cultured, discerning, eclectic architect *par excellence*. Working in Britain between 1886 and 1894 he numbered among his friends such luminaries as Robert Lorimer, Giles Gilbert Scott and Norman Shaw. Returning to his native Brisbane in 1894 to enter partner-

Rangemoor, a house at Clayfield built by Robin Dods in 1903. It is an accomplished Federation-period example of the Queensland style, with emphatic verandahs and ordered timberwork.

A house by Howard Joseland, built in Wahroonga in the first decade of the twentieth century. The paired gables are typical of the idiom developed by Joseland which became popular on the North Shore of Sydney. The style is an amalgam of the Horbury Hunt legacy and the Arts and Crafts movement.

ship with Francis Hall, Dods designed many non-domestic buildings which reflected the catholic attitude to style evident in the work of most architects at that time. Greatly to his credit, he recognized the well-established Queensland vernacular domestic style and proceeded to design houses which refined and extended this local idiom. He did this so successfully that only the *cognoscente* could differentiate between a Dods house and an 'ordinary' one. His chameleon-like personality was clearly revealed when he moved to Sydney to join the firm of Spain and Cosh. Fenton, his own house in Edgecliff built in 1919, was an essay in symmetry, cream stucco, twelve-pane double-hung windows and green louvred shutters – homage to his friend Hardy Wilson.

Canadian-born John Horbury Hunt stepped ashore in Sydney in January 1863. From the early 1870s onwards he bullied, cajoled and inspired his fellow architects until they formed themselves into the Institute of Architects of New South Wales. His acrimony and his incredible tactlessness almost destroyed the infant institute on several occasions, but his drive, coupled with financial support from his own pocket, also kept it alive at times when all seemed lost.[30] Hunt lived architecture with great intensity. He had none of the innate ability to plan interior spaces which Desbrowe Annear was to demonstrate at the turn of the century, but his grasp of materials, construction and detailing was unsurpassed. Hunt was a self-confessed American Anglophile and influences from both sides of the Atlantic can be detected in his work. His important houses were built a few years too early to be strictly classified within the Federation period, but they exerted a powerful influence on many Sydney architects throughout the 1890s and early 1900s. Booloominbah, 1887, a large country house at Armidale in the New England region – now the administration building of the University of New England – was a linear arrangement of many elements of diverse shape and height. Its long, broken silhouette was reminiscent of some Shingle style houses of the 1880s in the United States of America. It was most definitely a brick house, however, with a few medieval touches, and its deliberate eschewal of conventional 'beauty' recalled the work of the English architects Philip Webb and William Butterfield.[31] Kirkham, 1888, renamed Camelot in 1900, at Narellan outside Sydney, was an even more Picturesque agglomeration of shapes, with two candle-snuffer roofs jostling for a place among a complex array of hips and gables.[32] In its piled-up profusion of elements, Kirkham had an affinity with American Queen Anne houses of the 1880s and it was a far more valid model for Australian Queen Anne than Caerleon, its 'pretty' contemporary in Bellevue Hill.

The full flowering of Horbury Hunt's domestic work was seen in five shingled houses built in the late 1880s and early 1890s – Pibrac, the Phillis Spurling house, Trevenna, Hamilton House and Highlands. Highlands, in Wahroonga, Sydney, was perhaps the finest of them. No architect but Hunt could have convinced a wealthy client that his substantial home should be built of hardwood stud framing with timber shingles covering both the roof and the walls. The connection with the American east-coast Shingle style was strong. Hunt understood that, with the

Hamilton House, Moss Vale, is one of a series of generous and ample shingled houses which John Horbury Hunt created in the 1890s. They clearly demonstrate a derivation from the American Shingle style.

materials he was using, big, sweeping surfaces and a broad simplicity of treatment were called for.[33]

Hunt's career petered out pathetically after the depression years of the early 1890s, but the next generation of Sydney architects absorbed something of the robust masculinity of his architecture. When these younger men used good 'honest' plain brown brickwork, shingled surfaces and sturdy timber detailing, they were acknowledging, perhaps unconsciously, their debt to Horbury Hunt. Many large houses built in the wealthier suburbs of Sydney in the early 1900s do not lend themselves easily to clear-cut stylistic classification: they reflected the search for a 'free style' which preoccupied many architects during the Edwardian decade. These houses mixed so many themes so freely and so loosely, that they acquired

Crafts influences were also evident in the small, shingled police station and residence built in 1896 at Claremont by George Temple Poole and in two interesting houses with shingled upper storeys by William Williams.

Finally, it is not difficult to cite a number of unusual houses that defy classification. What, for instance, does one make of Nee Morna built about 1910 on Port Phillip near Sorrento? It was an impressively bold and forceful design for its time, suggesting that there could have been an Australian equivalent of the Shingle style in stone, asbestos cement and corrugated iron. And what of George Sydney Jones's premonition of a flat-roofed, cubic, modern architecture which he published, rather endearingly, as 'My Home' in 1906?[34] Houses such as these make it clear that the domestic architecture of the Federation

a strangely original quality in the process. They incorporated something of Queen Anne, something of the Shingle style and H.H. Richardson, something of Art Nouveau and something of British Arts and Crafts architecture (including Lutyens' pre-1900 houses). In addition, there was possibly a hint of the American Colonial Revival of the 1890s to be seen in the occasional use of Tuscan columns, usually no more than 2 metres high, to support verandah and balcony roofs. Among the many architects whose work fell into this category were Edward Jeaffreson Jackson, James Peddle, John Barlow and Rutledge Louat. Howard Joseland's houses left a strong imprint on Wahroonga and, during the World War I period, E.H. Orchard's houses dominated Clifton Gardens. B.J. Waterhouse favoured roughcast walls and big, simple roofs, giving his houses some visual affinities with the work of the English Arts and Crafts architects C.F.A. Voysey and M.H. Baillie Scott. In Perth, Arts and

A house in Mosman by Rutledge Louat, now demolished, which was a free interpretation of the English Arts and Crafts style.

period cannot all be thrust into a single pigeon-hole labelled 'Queen Anne'. At the dawn of the new century there was at least the illusion of a 'free' Australia in which a 'free style' of architecture might be evolved to express the optimistic pragmatism of its citizens. Further research into the architecture of the era will undoubtedly reveal even more of its rich and complex variety.

Right above: Nee Morna, near Sorrento, built about 1910, is a bold and simple version of the Shingle style but instead built of stone, asbestos cement and corrugated iron.

Right: William Williams, an Englishman, built this house in Claremont, Western Australia, in about 1905. It is a direct and unusual example of the English Arts and Crafts influence.

Belvedere, Cremorne, built by Alexander Stewart Jolly in 1919 with the long, low California look. Its protective roofs were originally covered with bituminous felt.

Top: Troon, in Toorak (demolished in 1960) was hailed as Australia's first 'Modern' house. It was designed by H. Desbrowe Annear in 1916. In a period of imitation and eclecticism Troon was uniquely functional.

IN THE TWO DECADES between the wars, the Australian house developed from a cosy traditonal bungalow, with a pitched roof, cottage casement windows and a beamed and panelled interior, full of chintz-covered chairs and carved wooden furniture, to the embodiment of a ship on land: a streamlined form, with flat roof deck, curved walls and port-hole windows, its interiors sparsely arrayed with chrome furniture, circular mirrors and all the conveniences of the electrical age.

This transformation was by no means straightforward. In the inter-war period Australian housing styles exhibited schizophrenic changes. There was the all-pervading bungalow, the influence of the Mediterranean styles, the romance of the Tudor and English cottage and reminiscently Georgian and Colonial buildings, the glamorous fantasy of the Spanish Mission style and later, the introduction of modern machine-like buildings, stripped of all traditional stylistic associations, but reflecting instead, the influence of modern ideas of beauty. All these styles developed against a background debate about which was the most suitable for our climate, appropriate to our way of life or satisfied the needs of modern living. While architects extracted from a lucky dip of styles of the past, they also faced more practical considerations and the need

As the size of houses shrank, their comfort became increasingly important. Appliances, well-regulated services such as gas, electricity, hot running water and central heating, efficiently planned kitchens and well-appointed bathrooms became the ideals of domestic design. In post-World War I years the 'servant problem', or growing lack of domestic help, had an immense impact. There was an emphasis on planning to minimize labour and effort in housework and on mechanical, press-button substitutes for the disappearing race of servants. In the cant of the day, appliances 'replaced drudgery by convenience' and labour-saving design transformed the home into a 'labour eliminating paradise'.

Built-in fittings were one solution – both labour and space saving, unlike bulky dust-catching furniture. Built-in book shelves and glass-fronted cabinets were common in the living-room around a fireplace. Window-seats with box storage, linen presses along a back hallway and fitted wardrobes in the bedroom appeared.

As passageways were reduced or eliminated, holes were opened between rooms and floors. There were serveries from the kitchen, service hatches for deliveries, and clothes chutes to the laundry. Ingenious devices were to be found. There were china cupboards and drawers

BETWEEN THE WARS

5

to develop an architecture of suitably Australian character in a rapidly changing world.

Shrinking in comfort

One aspect of change to be faced soon after World War I was the general levelling of society, an increasingly important factor after the effects of the Depression. Though the well-to-do still had large houses and household help, this was rarely more than a maid who frequently had her own lodgings and did not need to 'live-in'. Houses had to be more compact when the burden of their upkeep fell on the shoulders of one or two females in the house.

Nor was the house used in the Victorian sense, as the hub of activity for a large family. Families were smaller, and work and pastimes kept members more frequently away from its rooms. House sizes diminished rapidly and though there were still homes which reflected the upper and lower ends of the economic scale, the days were past when grand mansions were the prerogative of the wealthy and large villas that of the upper middle classes.

Instead of creating endless suites of rooms, architectural thinking concentrated on planning to minimize wasted space. Long passages and halls were eliminated, picturesque nooks and corners were chopped away and the functions of many rooms were combined. At first, living- and dining-rooms were made into one. Then the two were joined with an L-shaped plan or with a dining alcove. Later, the eat-in kitchen—once the fate of servants or the wretchedly poor—became acceptable.

between kitchen and dining-room that allowed items to be washed and stored on one side and taken out for use at the other. Ventilated cupboards were installed in the kitchen and heated serveries were designed for the living-room, where you could boil a kettle for tea. Alexander Jolly designed a remarkable sliding table between kitchen and dining-room for a house in Lavoni Street, Mosman. It ran on wooden tracks between the two rooms and slid in, set and laden with food, and later could be pushed out to the kitchen with the debris of the meal.

The kitchen of this period showed the most remarkable changes in planning. Once it had comprised single units, scattered seemingly at random in a vast space. Ideas of labour saving, however, soon created logical 'work stations' for each stage in food preparation and introduced fitted cupboards and sufficient storage, so that cooking equipment lay close at hand. The size of the room was also reduced to limit movement. The scrubbed wooden benches and deep sinks were replaced by stainless metal sinks and stainless bench tops with tiled splashbacks. Rubbish chutes lay outside the back door, insect-proof blinds guarded the windows, and kitchen built-ins often included a folding down ironing-board, a broom cupboard and later perhaps a breakfast table and seats.

The all-electric dream house

By the 1920s, a sizeable number of houses were connected to gas and used gas stoves and a gas hot water heater over the bath, though chip heaters were still used. The household was fortunate if it was also connected to electricity and had an electric iron, radiator and fan – the most common appliances. Other appliances were rare, mostly imported from America and relatively expensive to operate.

The next two decades introduced some remarkable changes. While gas remained the main source of power for heating and cooking, the all-electric dream home seemed to symbolize the development of the future as one by one miraculous appliances were introduced. In the kitchen the electric toaster, cooker, and kettle, and a small electric range, which could be set to start automatically, appeared. There was even a crude electric dishwasher available for purchase, while the laundry was equipped with an electric wringer and washing-machine. Among the persuasive advertisements for electrical goods in the

A magazine advertisement of the early 1930s.

1920s was one for a quaint and no doubt highly dangerous radiator-cum-boiling-device, with a revolving face that could be turned upwards to boil kettles and keep water hot and turned back again to heat the room. It was ideal for do-it-yourself tea in the parlour when there were no servants to appear from the kitchen.

Integrated electric hot water services were also developed to allow hot water to gush from every tap, and by the mid-1930s a more economical off-peak hot water service was offered. Vacuum cleaners had been available from pre-World War I. And between the wars, refrigerators began to replace the dripping ice-chests for cold food storage, although their use did not become widespread until after World War II. Early refrigerators were built in wooden cabinets with metal linings. Later they were

manufactured from enamelled, stamped steel, with an 'air cooled electric motor'. With some misgivings for this age of convenience, a writer in the *Australian Home Journal* of 1936 wondered 'What effect a steady diet of refrigerated foods will have on the organism of man?'

Central heating could be powered electrically and fan-forced ventilation cooled the house in summer. As well as a telephone, the house could be fitted with an internal intercom system. With their electrically operated piano player, a phonograph bleating out the latest dance steps and the radio, introduced in the 1920s broadcasting the latest serials, Australian householders began to feel a part of the Modern Age. It took some years, however, before the external appearance of housing reached the same identifiably modern character.

The bungalow was the ubiquitous housing form of this period, a small detached, single-storeyed, rectangular building with a jutting front porch, built of brick with a red tiled roof that had evolved from the Federation villa. Its scale and compact size were ideally suited to middle-class housing – fulfilling the Australian ideal of a home of one's own. Its character could be altered to adopt the prevailing fashionable style. Geometric Art Deco paned windows and a stepped motif over the porch created a Jazz Age building, a twisted stucco column linked it with Spain and square paned windows lent a Georgian stamp; while the roofline, the composition of the facade and the interior planning remained virtually the same. Its chameleon-like qualities provided the ideal basis for mass housing. Though when bungalow design was allied to 'back-to-nature' movements or the aesthetics of the Arts and Crafts movement, bungalows appealed to the wealthy – at least as an appropriate holiday residence – and were viewed as healthy housing for the poor.

The California bungalow

The California bungalow originated in the traditional American timber house. When the Arts and Crafts philosophy at the end of the nineteenth century was combined with interest in Oriental design, stylishly crafted wooden residences were produced, dominated by wide porches and bracketed gables.

The leading American proponets of the style were Charles and Henry Greene, based in Pasadena, California. The individual character of their work evolved from a study of timber craftsmanship, an appreciation of Japanese design and a love of nature and natural materials. This was expressed in the dramatic use of heavy timbers, projecting rafters, broad sloping roof lines and overhanging eaves, rough masonry, stained board and batten siding, and the inclusion of the garden into the design.

An article in *Building* magazine in 1908, 'The Building of a Bungalow: a Style that Should be Popular in Australia', introduced the style to Australia. Further reports followed, while regular advertisements for the roofing products of the Malthoid Company of the United states, illustrated a California bungalow with a low pitched spreading roof. A full-size bungalow cottage was featured in Sydney's Ideal Home Exhibition held in the Town Hall in 1916 and wide publicity was also given to a pre-fabricated 'Pasadena' bungalow imported in 1916, and erected in developer Richard Stanton's model suburb, Rosebery in Sydney. It was named 'Redwood' by its promoters who wished to test the response to the style and demonstrate the versatility of American timbers.

Australians were quick to adopt the style. However, except in Queensland or centres where timber construction predominated, the Australian version of the California bungalow was translated in brick, which tended to create solid and weighty buildings, lacking the elegance of the originals. The rustic homespun quality was maintained in the use of pebbly roughcast walls and gables, shingles and hefty sloping pylons supporting the inevitable front porch. Clinker-brick walls were often combined with river cobble stone chimneys and the shuttered, small-paned casement windows might be glazed

1908 in Melbourne, to the Queensland bungalow variation, its association with the ground denied as it perched high above the ground on stilts; its timber decoration incorporated in traditional lattice-work and carving.

Direct links with the California style were found in Sydney in the work of the firm Peddle and Thorp. James Peddle was English trained and came to Sydney in 1889 to furnish the interiors of the new Australia Hotel. He designed in a Queen Anne and Arts and Crafts manner until a business recession in 1909–10 when he left Australia and set up practice in California, leaving his Sydney office in the hands of his assistant, S.G. Thorp. Peddle opened an office in Pasadena in 1911, within a ten block radius of most of the Greene and Greene houses. When Thorp won the competition for the design of 'single cottages' at the

Glyn, Toorak, is a house of the English Arts and Crafts tradition, which was to be swept away by the advance of the Modern movement.

with squares of thick homely glass, often featuring a decorative rondel. Timber was limited to the 'trim' of projecting timber beams and purlins and slatted balustrade or frieze decoration in porches or verandahs, painted dark brown or green. The low spreading roof, with shallow gables and overhanging eaves, seemed to tie the building firmly to the ground. Inside, timber panelling was used and the rustic feeling maintained with glazed tiles in the hearth, plain brick or simply painted wall finishes and Picturesque features such as window-seats.

The California bungalow form spread across Australia, from the work of Kenneth Milne in South Australia from about 1906 and of Oakden and Ballantyne from about

proposed Daceyville Garden Suburb in 1913, he cabled his partner to return. Peddle was back by 1914, his design approach strongly influenced by West Coast housing which he felt could be aptly transferred to Sydney. The subsequent work of Peddle and Thorp reflected qualities of the Californian style.

One of the most interesting aspects of the Californian style was the development of a set of standard details for bungalow houses giving remarkable consistency despite different plans and sites. The walls were generally of brick, sometimes with clinker bricks introduced for greater rustication, and the roofs of small terracotta shingle. Timber was emphasized in the boarded gables and projecting rafters, and internally, in extensive use of panelling and ceiling beams. The living-room was given a high ceiling, lowered over ingle-nook recesses. Glazed bookshelves and cupboards lined the walls and a plate

The California bungalow influence spread throughout Australia. This is a Tasmanian example, clad in weatherboards and shingles, with a corrugated-iron roof.

Right: The Cobbles, Neutral Bay, 1918. This is the architect S. G. Thorp's own house, a rustic bungalow of great charm.

A house designed by Alexander Stewart Jolly in Balmoral, in the manner of an American hunting lodge.

shelf circled the major rooms. Chintz curtains, patterned rugs and beaten copper jugs, accompanying slatted wooden 'Craftsman' type furniture, was thought appropriate in such a setting.

S.G. Thorp's own residence, The Cobbles built in 1918–19 in Neutral Bay, Sydney, is an excellent example. A winding path leads through a modified lich-gate, past lush vegetation, down brick-edged steps to the house. The dark hued brick walls are ivy clad, their texture enriched by the insertion of large chunks of specially glazed terracotta. Windows frame large circles of handmade glass, set in leaded patterns; heavy hinged shutters hang from the openings. A large cobble-clad chimney tapers skywards, above a roof of unglazed terracotta shingles. The front of the house opens out to the terraced gardens and paved paths. The effect is rustic and in tune with nature.

An unusual interpreter of the bungalow style was Alexander Stewart Jolly. The son of a Lismore timber merchant and furniture maker, he was apprenticed in the furniture trade before first coming to Sydney in 1908 to train as an architect in the office of Wardell & Denning

and returning later in 1919 to set up his own practice. His knowledge of timber and romantic approach to design created a small number of fine houses.

One of the most successful is Belvedere in Cranbrook Avenue, Cremorne, built in 1919 when the California bungalow style was at its height. Jolly's version, with a wide, low-pitched gable, deep eaves, massive dark timbers outlining openings and the sheer bulk of the white roughcast pillars and walls, is a striking variation. Its spreading plan, centred around the dining-room and fireplace, with open verandahs flung out at extremities is more reminiscent of Chicago-based 'Prairie School' work, than that of the brothers Greene. The massive verandah pylons have large timber beams branching out from their crowns and an excessive amount of timber was used in the roof framing.

Interest within the house lies in the ceiling forms. The living- and dining-rooms have coved plaster ceilings with dark-stained beams at the centre. The master bedroom has a pyramidal plaster ceiling. There are many built-in fixtures and labour-saving devices in the house, including a 2-metre rotating servery cupboard between kitchen and dining-room, an elaborate built-in dressing area off the master bedroom, and a tea-leaves waste disposal unit in the kitchen.

Other Jolly buildings of this era are more romantic and individual exercises. At Lavoni Street, Balmoral, he created a shingle-roofed house of rubble stone for an American couple who wanted their home to look like an American hunting-lodge. Later, in the 1930s, retiring from architecture to speculate in land subdivision on the Palm Beach peninsula, he designed a series of stone and timber houses, incorporating natural rocks, tree trunks, logs with bark still clinging, and forked branches. These were built into strangely organic and often whimsical forms, resembling boulders or animals (one is called the Elephant House), rather than the angles and planes of conventional architecture.

In about 1926, some years before Jolly's bush forms, Cedric Ballantyne in Melbourne had created a bungalow, Skelbo, at Mornington. Its form was more traditional, though the materials were similarly rustic, featuring a cobble-stone chimney, split timber balustrades, architraves of bark and logs, and tree trunk verandah posts.

Right above: Alleuria, Wahroonga, by Bruce Dellit, 1928, is a symmetrical house with a subtle echo of the Mediterranean. It has a beguiling largeness of scale, and an unusual plan arrangement in which the arcaded central section is one large room – a 'living hall'.

Too easily dismissed as a mere decorative appliqué, the Spanish idiom brought a new interest in sunlight and shade, climate and colour. This is a ventilating wall panel in a house at Rose Bay.

Right below: Forms and details from the Spanish Mission style enliven an otherwise mundane block of flats in Sydney.

The enclosing timber walls of this cottage were stained green, the furniture was contrived from rustic logs, and boomerangs were hung over the doorway. In buildings of such rustic charm, the bungalow showed itself as architecture allied to nature.

Spanish and beyond

Another American-inspired housing style gained popularity in the 1920s, introducing a note of romanticism to suburbia. The Spanish Mission style developed from the churches and mission stations erected by Spanish religious orders in Mexico in their attempts to convert the local population. They bore the hallmarks of the Spanish Baroque: fullblown writhing decorations, such as twisted columns, coloured tiles and elaborately ornamented bell towers, albeit often translated in rough stucco naivety.

These formed the inspiration for the houses of neighbouring California in Los Angeles, San Francisco and more importantly Hollywood, where sprawling richly furnished, mission-inspired villas with their palm trees and courtyards housed stars such as Maurice Chevalier in much publicized luxury. These buildings were also ideally suited to the warm Australian climate. Their courtyards and shady, tiled verandahs protected the house from the heat and encouraged cooling cross draughts through its rooms – a concept later espoused by Professor Leslie Wilkinson, first Professor of Architecture at Sydney University. The decorative aspects of the style, its richly modelled ornament and glowingly tinted colours, if a somewhat exotic and foreign transplant to the gum-treed shores of Australian cities, fared well in the harsh light. The hot sun faded bright colours to soft tones and sharply delineated the ornament with crisp shadows, enlivening the mass of housing with a touch of romance.

Spanish Mission nicknamed 'Auspano' and described as 'the Mediterranean via the Golden Gate', took little advantage of traditional mission layout, except in a few well-planned instances, and relied on a translation of its outer forms, portrayed with a wide range of skill and artistry. The roof was of curved interlocking pan or 'Cordova' tiles, multi-coloured in shades of brown, purple, cream and red. The chimney often featured as a bell tower, with gabled top and arched opening. Walls were roughly textured in imitation of smeared stucco and painted in bright pastel shades of lavender, lemon, hot pink or warm cream, with turquoise or jade shutters. Arched openings featured as small paned windows, as porch openings designed to resemble loggias or as ornamental recesses in a wall. Ornament was contrived, often grotesque, featuring twisted and heavily stunted columns with ornate capitals, pierced screens, overhanging balconies balanced on ornate corbels and wrought iron trappings, such as twisted balusters, fake hinges and decorative grilles set in arched openings.

The Mission style was found in the suburbs of Melbourne, Sydney and Brisbane, where Queensland versions were strangely elevated above the ground. An early example of the style, Windermere, in Hobart, designed in 1926 by Lauriston Crisp, was a restrained interpretation. A traditionally spreading house given arched windows,

A house built by the Federal government's War Service Homes Commission in about 1926.

gabled chimneys and pierced screens could provide a Spanish flavour. This was typical of many Mission buildings to follow. The best versions of the style were like A.E. Stafford's Stuart Doyle house, Biscaya, built about 1926 above Rose Bay, Sydney. It was depicted in an intriguing and lavish style, with ornate stone decoration, iron-railed balconies and hooded sun-blinds, striped yellow and blue.

Neville Hampson's Boomerang, Elizabeth Bay, Sydney, built in 1926, was the most complete and elaborate example of Hollywood Spanish Mission. Built for mouth-organ and sheet-music magnate, Frank Albert, it was certainly the most luxurious version of the style and included its own underground cinema and stretch of Sydney waterfront. Hidden behind a high wall, the house could be glimpsed through its wrought-iron gates and iron grilles in small arched peep-holes. The house, now half hidden by giant palms, was an elaborate balanced composition of arched openings, iron railed balconies, columns and decorative screens, topped by two layers of coloured tiled roof. Its entrance skirted still pools and tiled dishes set with water jets. Fountains played to either side of the front door. Inside, the large double-storeyed lobby, with its oval gallery lined in travertine, was lit by a huge metal lantern at night and by arched leaded windows by day. A flight of marble stairs led up to elaborate bathrooms and rooms lined with polished timber closets. The exterior pushed out into sun porches, paved gardens, and arcaded walks, and curved stairs led out to the swimming-pool, tennis-court and lawn from which could be seen the Albert yacht moored in front of the house.

Everyone a home owner

The reality of building during the period was unfortunately much more mundane, as the acute housing shortage at the end of World War I spurred the rapid development of suburbia. Construction had lapsed over the war years, and returning soldiers and growing families increased the pressure for more housing. There was little opposition as land developers sliced out new subdivisions, radiating out from the city centres, while speculators and builders, much to the horror of architects, followed with houses of assorted styles that spread like a motley blanket around each city. The dream of 'a home of your own' filled with modern conveniences, fuelled the imagination more than visions of fine architecture. And commercial and government organizations were ready to assist in turning the dream into dull reality.

The typical house was usually of solid, almost fortress-like construction, in brown or dark liver brick. Despite a display of leaded glass in the drawing-room, or perhaps a bay- and window-seat, it could rarely be called homely and was often duplicated as a row of detached houses, separated by paling fences and a narrow strip of no man's land between the side walls. Each house overlooked its neighbour and each individual neat patch of buffalo grass at front and rear was relieved by a display of annuals, a clothes-line and a lemon tree.

The federal government committed itself to funding housing for ex-Servicemen through the Commonwealth

A tiny house in Castlecrag designed by Walter Burley Griffin and built in 1934 with 'Knitlock' components.

War Service Homes Commission, founded in 1918. Many state governments followed suit, often linking financing schemes to standard and inevitably dreary sets of house designs. There were also schemes to assist low income earners to purchase their own low-cost house. In South Australia, the State Housing Scheme, monitored by the State Savings Bank, lent up to 70 per cent of finance required, developed its own plans for houses and called mass tenders for construction, considerably lowering the cost of individual buildings, if not increasing their architectural merit.

A proliferation of unimpressive and uniformly dull buildings was thus assured. *Building* magazine of October 1925 remarked of a featured War Service home in Darwin that 'the actual appearance of the building is not beautiful and the rooms look small'. The *State Advances Corporation of Queensland Manual* of housing designs, published in 1934, showed typical mass housing designs for variations of bungalows, perched on stilts. The standard formula for all was a front living area, a front and back bedroom, a rear kitchen and bathroom, a central hall and a front porch or verandah fitted into a compact rectangular area beneath the roof. As the cost of the house increased, the verandah area was enlarged, the room sizes were marginally bigger and the facade became more decorative.

But public housing also offered attempts at total and often enlightened planning solutions, such as Colonel Light Gardens in Adelaide and Daceyville in Sydney.

'Dacey Garden Suburb' for instance, initiated by the State Labor government in 1912, was planned along broad avenues with crescents, circles, parks, recreation and service facilities and a variety of bungalow dwellings. The Matraville Soldiers Garden Village, in New South Wales, begun in 1917, was similarly based on the English Garden City concept, while Way's Terrace, Pyrmont, where workers' housing was designed by Professor Leslie Wilkinson and opened in 1925, gave its inhabitants romantic, Mediterranean-style housing on a spectacular promontory site overlooking the city.

The architect Walter Burley Griffin, winning designer of the Canberra competition, was also responsible for a community housing scheme at Castlecrag in Sydney based on unique principles. In 1919, distressed at the quality of Australian housing, Griffin and other members of the Greater Sydney Development Association purchased land on this rocky promontary overlooking Sydney's Middle Harbour. Buildings were to be designed in harmony with nature, with 'no fences, no boundaries, no red roofs to spoil the Australian landscape'. A fifth of the landscape was dedicated to reserve and parkland, including an open-air theatre, where drama and dance were performed. There was to be a community social centre, hospital and school, for the Griffins and Griffin's associate Eric Nicholls and his wife were followers of Rudolf Steiner's anthroposophical movement. To Griffin this philosophy was rooted in two principles: that average people need a full, clean, beautiful environment, and that nature is the uniting factor between man's material efforts and his social behaviour.

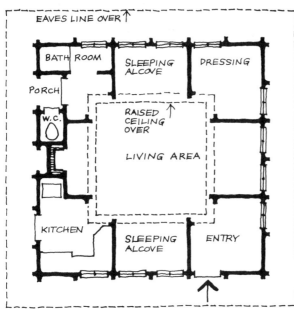

The 'Knitlock' house. Above: Some 'Knitlock' concrete wall components. As the wall was built up, the cavities between these interlocking tiles were filled with a concrete grout. Below: Floor plan of what became known as the basic 'Knitlock' house. It was a diminutive bungalow in form, 6.4 metres square, with small recesses surrounding a central living space.

The site was laid out with encircling roads; pathways were kept away from vehicular traffic and housing plots were grouped to follow the natural contours, or enhance special natural features and allow spectacular views from each house. Griffin also ensured he had the final approval of any building planned for the area.

Indeed, most of the initial buildings were his own design. Built primarily of stone, or later of his modular concrete construction units, 'knitlock', the flat-roofed houses appeared as squat, squared boulders, difficult to distinguish from the rocky outcrops, through the screen of native vegetation that was rigorously preserved even during construction. They were unlike any other building in Australia. Blocky and planar in form, with massive architraves defining the openings, they were built flat on the ground, with flat roof terraces often hidden behind high, tooth-like parapets. Decorative crystalline forms were worked over the windows, and window frames were divided with sloping rails.

Inside, the houses were planned with simple ingenuity in a range of sizes. Some were laid out around open courtyards. Compact houses were enlarged by rooms that opened into each other with walls of folding doors. Varying ceiling heights were used to define different living spaces and Griffin often introduced special quirks, such as sky-lit stairs, panes of glass set into a chimney so the room beyond was visible and even an illuminated fish-pond above a dining-room table, which with crystalline lights and other specially designed internal fittings, gave the buildings a delightful and individual character.

Unfortunately, though Griffin had direct links with the Chicago Prairie School and the work of Frank Lloyd Wright, his buildings, unlike more popular styles, had little contemporary influence on Australian architecture. He was dismissed from work on Canberra, reviled by publications such as *Building* magazine and eventually, left Australia for work in India. His buildings in Castlecrag received little support, and even his large-scale domestic work, such as the Pratten Houses in Pymble built in 1934–36 and the Mary Williams House, Toorak, built in 1923, which bore direct allusions to the work of Lloyd Wright (and to his own early work) in America, had little immediate impact beyond influencing his associates such as Frederick Ballantyne, Leslie Grant, Eric Nicholls, Edward Billson and Roy A. Lippincott.

The period revivals

Despite attempts at rationalization, a more popular vision of suburbia prevailed. The upper end of the housing market offered a wide choice of period styles. Thus in the leafier suburban areas, set on oversize blocks, amid shrubbery and wide stretches of lawn, a conglomeration of styles ranging from Colonial hipped-roofed mansions to Dutch gabled villas, were placed out of sequence like a jumbled history of architecture.

The Tudor manors were particularly impressive with their nailed-on half-timbering, studded doors and fake armorial crests, worked into the diamond-paned casement windows. The English country cottage also won favour for its steeply pitched roof with a featured gable over the front porch, flaring out on stepped eaves. The

quaint bay windows and boarded door were, however, often confusingly topped with castellations, and despite their size, these dwellings displayed mean proportions, with pretentious suites of small rooms crammed into the picturesque shell.

The most important period influence was the Georgian, which had enjoyed a revival in the United States from the late nineteenth-century work of McKim, Mead and White, and in the English work of Sir Edwin Lutyens and his contemporaries. In Australia, this revival of the Classical domestic style of the late eighteenth and early nineteenth centuries was portrayed in hipped-roofed buildings of formal compositon, their shuttered small paned windows balanced around a central opening, with a panelled door and fanlight, set off by a pillared porch. The building, generally stuccoed, was painted white or ivory and enhanced by green shutters. Though there were some modified Georgian bungalows, the style tended towards the grandiose: double storeyed, with elaborate detailing and high stuccoed front walls, topped by stone urns or cement balls.

The final work of Melbourne architect Desbrowe Annear, was indicative of this trend. His Ince House, Glenferrie Road, Malvern built in 1935, was an austerely dignified representative of the Georgian revival. Its double-storeyed facade had a central *porte-cochère*, set before a pedimented breakfront; an interpretation of a Georgian device. On either side an assortment of windows were displayed: large, six-paned sashes, arched windows and circular *oeils-de-boeuf*, the latter strung with moulded stucco garlands. The interiors carried on the same theme. They were panelled in an 'Adamesque' manner, hung with tapestries and brocade, with pelmeted curtains at the windows and a suite of Hepplewhite revival furniture in the dining-room. The result was a romantic interpretation that only faintly echoed a true Georgian character. However, the equally romanticized associations of Georgian refinement, dignity and charm, rather than historical accuracy, were all that the owners of such edifices sought.

In Sydney, the architect F. Glynn Gilling, designed even more opulent Georgian fantasies, to the delight of his

A fine Tudorbethan house in Armadale, Victoria: Its walls, built of clinker bricks with inserts of narrow heeler-bricks, take on a tweedy texture, and the Tudor character is emphasized by steep roofs of shingle tiles, and half-timbered effects. The tall buttressed chimneys are notable.

wealthy, socially prominent clientele. His lush double-storeyed residences, such as Audley, Bangalla Street, Warrawee, built about 1935, displayed an extensive array of Classical features: porches on Corinthian columns, heavy Italianate balustrading, balconies railed with curvilinear wrought iron and windows that advanced far beyond the typical Georgian format, which were arched, set in recessed panels or combined in decorative multiples.

Gilling also introduced a complex geometry into his building designs, with curving bays, circular stairwells and oval dining-rooms. His sumptuous Burnham Thorpe, built in about 1937, now the Lady Gowrie Red Cross Home in Edward Street, Gordon, was a particularly lavish example which broke out into circular tower-like ends at its rear, joined together by a run of balustraded arcades. The facade displayed a multi-columned *porte-cochère*, ornamented quoins at each corner return and a variety of window forms, including an oriel, arrayed across an immense stuccoed facade.

Eryldene, Gordon, designed in 1912 by William Hardy Wilson, is an Australian version of the Georgian Revival. Its exquisite garden is the work of Wilson's client, the camellia expert, Professor E.G. Waterhouse.

The architect John D. Moore sought a simpler interpretation of the Georgian. In the house he designed with Laidley Dowling for Justice Sir Frederick and Lady Jordan, in Wentworth Avenue, Vaucluse, Sydney, he allied the eighteenth century to the modern era, hinting at Classical forms while he used modern materials and detailing. Built in about 1934, the house has now been altered. Originally its long cream brick facade was broken by bays into two sinuous curves at each level around the asymmetrically set front porch. The porch columns were slender unornamented steel pipes, painted cream, supporting a balcony with railings of simple wrought iron spokes. The balcony, against the normal tenets of the Classical styles, ran asymmetrically along one side only of the facade. There were two rows of square paned windows with cream painted shutters and the front door, with fanlight and paned sidelights, was painted jade green. At the rear, massive fluted concrete columns formed a pergola and supported a railed balcony set around a formal, green swarded courtyard. The interior continued the simplicity of the exterior. The walls were unpanelled, the internal sweep of the hall archway was simply reeded and the chimney breast in the main rooms was a curve topped by a shelf of black glass.

The entrance front of Greenway faces north, towards the sun and the angophoras in the garden. Upstairs, between the bedrooms, there are sleep-out porches designed for favourable weather. The house was designed by Professor Leslie Wilkinson in 1922.

The cross-vaulted loggia of Greenway, Vaucluse, shades the house from the western sun and links it to the small rear garden.

A Georgian influence was also to be found in the work of Leslie Wilkinson. The English-born Wilkinson came to Australia in 1918, to take up his appointment at Sydney University, the first Chair of Architecture in Australia. His architecture, based on the scale and harmonious proportion of the Georgian revival, also revealed the influence of the Mediterranean, which he had visited and sketched in his youthful travels. The two were combined with a view to practicality and elegance, and often with a playful wit which introduced whimsical decorative detailing, such as dragon-headed pergola beams to otherwise straightforward constructions.

Though many of his designs were compact, Wilkinson contrived elegant living spaces. His own house, Greenway, Vaucluse, 1922, was planned around a large living-room, opening to a verandah to one side and a courtyard to the other. He usually allowed double-storeyed hallways and main rooms that stepped down from the rest of the house, forming high ceilinged, grand spaces. Wilkinson's practical planning also ensured cool, airy, well-shaded houses designed for comfortable use, as well as elegance. He opposed the accepted practice that placed houses square on block, facing the street. Instead he looked for the best aspect of sun and wind, laid out his houses to encourage through breezes and protected his buildings by thick walls and loggias, pergolas, verandahs and overhanging balconies designed to let in the sun during winter and exclude it in summer.

Wilkinson used the Georgian revival as the basis for his individual architectural approach. William Hardy Wilson gave it a parochial form – establishing a Colonial Revival that looked back for inspiration to the Georgian buildings of colonial Australia. Convinced that architectural beauty lay in Australia's own heritage of buildings, he made an intensive study of early buildings that provided the details he was to use in his architecture and was later published as his magnum opus, *Old Colonial Buildings in New South Wales and Van Diemen's Land*.

The Colonial house Horsley, at Smithfield, based on an Indian bungalow, provided much of the inspiration for Wilson's work, with its hipped roof pitched low over a front verandah, and paired Doric columns at the entrance: details that were repeated over and over in Wilson's designs. Macquarie Cottage in Pymble, built in 1918, numerous speculative and holiday cottages designed prior to 1920, and the well-known Eryldene in Gordon, designed for Professor E.G. Waterhouse in 1913, bear this character.

Wilson's own house, Purulia, Warrawee, built in 1916, was modelled on the simple lines of William Cox's Clarendon, formerly near Richmond, New South Wales. It was a rectangular bungalow, with no verandah, having a long hipped roof and shuttered and multi-paned sash windows, around a central door. The door was panelled, with sidelights delicately subdivided into diamond panes. It is this graceful detailing, based on colonial prototypes, that distinguished Wilson's architecture. Internally the house was simply planned for 'servantless' living. The rooms were compact and rectangular, with living spaces along one length of the plan, and sleeping and functional areas along the other.

The surrounding garden was filled with complementary 'colonial' plantings, such as lavenders, box, rosemary and white plumbago, laid out with a neat geometry, reflecting that of the house. The integration of architecture, particularly architectural surfaces, with the less tangible effects of nature, such as light, moving reflections and shadows, preoccupied Wilson. In his article, 'Building Purulia' in *Domestic Architecture in Australia*, a special issue of *Art in Australia*, 1919, he wrote of light as the most beautiful quality seen at Purulia, especially:

the reflected light on the eaves. Along the sunny northern wall there are white flag-stones; the eaves are white plaster; and the wall is white too: a subtle white with grey and gold in it. The sunlight on the stones is reflected on the plaster and the wall lends a golden glow to the reflection.

At Eryldene, the garden was planned with its owner, who planted specimens of the camellias he was developing along its stone-flagged paths. Within the confined space the garden provided vistas terminated by architectural elements: a fountain, a dovecote, a summer house next to the tennis-court. The summer house, a dramatic Orient-inspired building, with upturned eaves and giant columns, marked Wilson's interest in Chinese architecture. Though Wilson was intrigued with the symbolism of Oriental art, his designs in this vein were, in the main, confined to paper and never built.

Wilson retired, disillusioned, from architectural practice at the age of 46, but his influence was strong. His house Purulia, reviled by his neighbours in 1916, who claimed it would lower property values, became the prototype for Colonial bungalows throughout Sydney's North Shore. His firm, Wilson, Neave and Berry continued work in a Colonial inspired manner, in designs for both commercial buildings (particularly country branches of the Bank of New South Wales, now Westpac), as well as domestic – notably the Flynn house, a large double-storeyed residence in Ginahgulla Road, Bellevue Hill. Wilson's friend and contemporary, Robin Dods, a Queenslander, also noted for his work in a Classical manner, revealed the influence of Wilson's Colonial preoccupation on his work in the design of his own house Fenton, Albert Street, Edgecliff, built in 1913.

Wilson also promoted an interest in eighteenth-century furniture. He brought a collection to Australia, much of which was given to the National Gallery of Victoria, and designed several pieces of furniture in an eighteenth-century manner, which were made up by his brother, David Wilson.

Furnishing: a mixture of styles

Georgian furniture, whether antique or reproduction, was in vogue from the early 1920s onwards. Highly polished pieces were displayed against a background of polished wooden floors, rugs, chintz-covered sofas and pelmeted curtains. It was the ideal style for a newly designed Georgian residence, but was not necessarily restricted to houses in that idiom.

Whatever the style expressed in the house exterior, the same character was not always echoed inside. Reproduction furniture, much of it of high quality, was available in styles ranging from darkened Jacobean to the ornate carvings of the Renaissance. Boomerang, for instance, was furnished in a variation of the Renaissance, complete with tapestries and hangings, but included Art Deco bathrooms.

The decorative arts were developing apace during this period, and furnishings and decoration often pre-empted architectural innovation. Many a dumpy, liver brick suburban cottage built in the mid-1920s to 1930s displayed links with the Jazz Age, once you passed through its front door. The clever geometry of the Art Deco style was found in zigzag plasterwork, angular doorhandles on

A shower screen of 1938 employing plate glass with a gravé, or sandblasted, design. The makers claimed that 'this design pervades its surroundings with freshness and beauty'.

a skyscraper silhouetted door-plate, windows glittering with geometrically-patterned glass, wooden chair backs carved with a rising sun, a cubic, walnut-veneered radiogram and a predominance of cream, brown and 'autumn colours' in the upholstery. Even the potentially glamorous Spanish Mission buildings of the late 1920s, with some notable exceptions, tended to follow this pattern, with roughly textured walls of an 'old parchment' colour, wall mirrors tinted amber or green, autumn-coloured upholstery and Futurist patterned carpets.

A Melbourne flat of 1933, pictured in the *Australian Home Beautiful*, illustrated the extremes of the Art Deco styled interior. Jazzy pelmets covered the windows, with

a geometric silhouette; stepped tables supported a statue of a dancing maiden; there were small triangular tables, a wildly angled clock case, a circular mirror and extraordinary armchairs, upholstered in abstract geometrically-patterned fabric, with backs that sloped sideways to form a sharp angle and arms to match, one built up much higher than the other.

Robin Boyd, in *Victorian Modern*, likened such stylism to the film *'The Cabinet of Dr Caligari*: the carefully insane distortion of familiar things ... when young it was so brave and new, so very much the smart, right thing to do'. However, few interiors in the normal run of suburban houses revealed such distinction. On the contrary, they usually appeared stuffy and conservative. Their jazz furniture maintained an uneasy truce with the barley-twist legs of a Jacobean table, while the rich colours of the Genoa velvet upholstery of a three-piece suite, combined with dark-coloured wallpapers and treacle-varnished timber, cast an air of dullness and gloom over the interior. Even the showy veneers of the 'Art Moderne' furniture later proved anathema to the houseproud, as they tended to split and inevitably peel.

High rise living

Despite the romance of period houses in suburbia, the city remained a major drawcard, the hub of commerce, entertainment and activity. Here were the office blocks, each a warren of wood panelling and tapping typewriters, slowly beginning to peek above the nineteenth century city skyline. Here were the glamorous hotels, the cocktail lounges, the mirror-walled basement restaurants, the dance palaces and the department stores – Myers, David Jones, Farmers, Buckley and Nunn's – with layer upon layer of desirable commodities, from women's costumes to stout trunks for sea voyages to England, had little competition from suburban shops.

For many it became a status symbol, 'chic' and 'terribly modern', to abandon suburban house and garden and move to the edge of the city for life in a flat. 'Life in flatdom is lived at a faster rate than life in a suburban house' advised the *Australian Home Beautiful* in November 1933, and such an existence was recommended for business couples, or women with outside interests, such as the avid golfer or bridge player. For others, flats were a welcome alternative to a room in a boarding-house, or they provided a first home for newlyweds. There was opposition, however, to flats as homes for children. Washing was always a 'battle', toys were always underfoot and the restrictions of a flat allowed no place for pets, uproarious games or gardening in a typical 'sardine box ... with two rooms and a kitchenette'.

Flat-building, however, introduced many innovations in domestic design and planning, as well as lifestyle. The Astor in Macquarie Street, Sydney, built in 1923 by Esplin and Mould, architects was renowned for its early concrete structure with large window areas, though the

Right: The Astor, Sydney, is an impressive block of city residential units built in 1923. Its style is a high-rise interpretation of the Italian palazzo form. The building is an early example of a reinforced-concrete frame used in a tall structure.

facade was traditional, resembling a square, Classical column with a decorative cornice. The Astor was built by a co-operative venture of prospective inhabitants, who each purchased shares in the proposed building.

The most luxuriously appointed flats, such as Burnham, in Toorak, Melbourne – 1933 by R.B. Hamilton – contained two bedrooms, a maid's room, a lounge, dining-room, kitchen, pantry, two bathrooms and an open verandah or sleepout. Generally a more compact layout was found; the dining-room was often reduced to an eating alcove, the kitchen and pantry to a kitchenette and two bathrooms to one. Flat dwellers were advised to

store, boiler house, drying-rooms and what must have been one of the earliest basement car parks for flats. It was provided with circular turntables to help manoeuvre cars in the confined space. At the top of the building were maids' quarters and a caretaker's residence – all in addition to a 20-metre high stained glass window, illuminating the stairwell, depicting Captain Cook, Governor Phillip and Australian wildflowers.

The design of flats revealed the ultimate in modern architectural fashion. Red texture brick towers with Art Deco patterned summit alternated with sleek, cement-rendered blocks, banded in curved glass and set off with

increase the illusion of size with simple decoration, a single prevailing scheme in light reflecting colours and wall-to-wall carpets. Built-in and multi-purpose furniture was recommended for efficient use of space.

Most flats built in the 1920s and 1930s were advantageously serviced with modern conveniences. Hot water, often still a luxury in the suburbs, was laid on. Electric refrigerators, bathrooms, built-in baths, fitted cupboards, porcelain or metal sinks, ventilated cupboards, rubbish chutes and service hatches were standard adjuncts to life in a confined space.

Hillside, a soaring, Gothic, towered skyscraper, in Edge-cliff, Sydney – 1936, Pitt and Bolot, architects – boasted an underground service centre, complete with a laundry,

Cairo bachelor flats, Fitzroy, 1935, form a broad U about the perimeter of an old garden.

metal railed balconies: the epitome of modern city living.

In 1934 in Sydney, Birtley Towers designed by architect Emil Sodersten, was the largest block of flats in the country. Towering over Elizabeth Bay, its vertical textured-brick tower burst into brick sunrays at the summit and over the arched *porte-cochère* at its base. The whole was topped by a multi-coloured mansard roof. The foyer, today, is still redolent of its original period, retaining its domed ceiling, a black glass mantel set over a radiator, a 'digitless' clock, metal finned windows, square shouldered armchairs and a golden-tinted mirror, etched bubbles and all, with a flowing fountain. Inside, each flat was luxuriously up-to-date, with central heating, a balcony and a compact kitchen, where the high tiled walls were crammed with built-in cupboards, easily cleaned benches and an 'Early Kooka' stove.

But even flats, seemingly compact and convenient when compared to a traditional house, could be further rationalized. The architect, Best Overend, returning in the early 1930s from working in England with Wells Coates, introduced his Minimalist theory, 'that the modern human had so little property that the smallest space necessary for living was the most convenient' and helped to popularize

doors, concrete balconies jutting out with a solid curve of concrete balustrade, and flying concrete stairs with pipe rail balustrades, cantilevering out in an athletic curve from the building.

The mixed metaphors of the era are well illustrated in another contemporary block of flats in Sydney Road, Parkville, Melbourne. Named 'King's Keepe', this block also included some Minimalist bachelor flats, with small bathroom, kitchenette and a fold-away bed. But true to their name, these apartments were set in a building of extreme medieval flavour with half-timbered gables, a castellated tower, leaded windows and flower boxes.

Birtley Towers, Elizabeth Bay, 1934 – dramatic Art Deco sky-scraper flats.

bachelor flats. His 1933 formula for a 'minimum flat with maximum comfort' comprised adjoining rectangular spaces, the larger for cooking, dining, eating and sleeping (the bed folded up into the wall when not in use); the smaller with a bathroom and dressing area with luxurious cupboards. Overend's Cairo Flats in Fitzroy, Melbourne built in 1935 – Taylor, Soilleux and Overend, architects – fitted twenty-eight bachelor flats based on this plan into a double-storey 'U' shaped block around a courtyard. The flats presented a minimally chic modern exterior as well, with their large squares of plate glass windows, portholed

Machines for living

By the mid-1930s, the suburban sprawl of Tudor manors, Georgian villas and countrified cottages had been infiltrated by a surprisingly innovative architectural form – one that had associations with modern ships.

Instead of a prow, the house had a jutting curved bay and a horizontal streamlined emphasis as if it were built for efficient action. Corners were rounded, even the glass was curved, and pipe railings and porthole windows completed the analogy. Flat roofs were desirable, but if local authorities did not permit this innovation, then high parapets were built to disguise a low-pitched roof behind. In addition to these tethered ships, there were squared

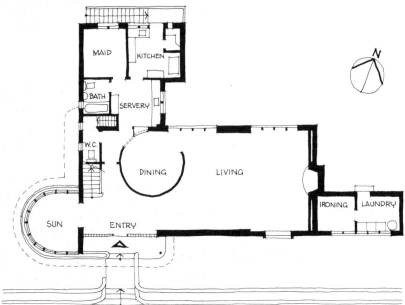

*The Prevost house, Bellevue Hill, by Sydney Ancher, 1937.
Top: The design was a precociously early example of the
International School in Australia. Above: The plan, however,
revealed Ancher's debt to the austere aesthetic of Le Corbusier
and Mies van der Rohe.*

blocky buildings, resembling miniature factories, with metal-framed windows, stark brick or cement rendered walls stripped of every vestige of traditional decoration, and overall design owing more to the imagery of technology, than to the familiar forms of 'home'.

The origins of this new architectural vocabulary can be traced directly to Europe, where since the early twentieth century, widespread attempts to bring architecture and design up-to-date, taxed leading architectural thinkers. In France for instance, the architect Le Corbusier described his houses as 'machines for living' and delighted in the functional imagery of ocean liners, aeroplanes and grain silos which he translated to an architectural idiom. The Dutch architect Dudok, the German Bauhaus design school headed in turn by Walter Gropius and Mies Van der Rohe, and later, English architects such as Wells Coates and Serge Chermayeff, were united in their attempts to create a functional architectural formula for contemporary living.

Their principles were based on the utilization of new domestic construction techniques such as the steel frame and concrete slab construction to allow a more flexible internal layout in a building and free houses from the restrictions of small rooms and passages. An efficiently functioning building was of prime importance and modern expression was to be achieved in the elimination of traditional ornament. The geometric arrangement of openings and projections on a plane wall surface and the use of the most avant-garde materials both inside and outside the building substituted for the more familiar shutters, panelled doors, decorative columns and steeply pitched roofs that had been prevalent in domestic design for centuries.

Such theories, and the buildings they produced, were gradually imported to Australia in contemporary journals and publications and through the direct overseas experience of many young architects during the Depression. Travel overseas was a more tempting alternative to the meagre supply of work and many, often assisted by travelling scholarships, left to seek jobs and inspiration in England, the United States and 'on the Continent'. Some, like the talented Raymond McGrath, a Sydney University graduate who in the late 1920s won both the Wentworth Travelling Fellow Award and the Australian Medallion, and was author of a definitive work on modern design, *Twentieth Century Houses*, set up practice abroad and never returned. But the fresh impact of modern architecture was felt in Australia through the work of others who returned inspired, such as Roy Grounds, Norman Seabrook, Arthur Baldwinson, Dudley Ward, Gerard MacDonell and Sydney Ancher.

A reflection of an overseas influence in Sydney Ancher's work is seen in the house he designed with his partner R.A. Prevost in Bellevue Hill, Sydney. Built in 1937, it was a sophisticated interpretation of nautical influences. Curved glass rounded off a corner topped by thin projecting concrete slabs and pipe railings. The entrance door, set in a wall of glass bricks, was framed in a geometric pattern reminiscent of the modern artist Mondrian. The rendered walls were coloured off-white, highlighted by scarlet columns and Wedgwood blue eaves. The interior was open-planned, with few corridors and the dining area was separated from the large living space by a semi-circular screen – a device used by Mies Van der Rohe in Tugendhat House at Brno, Czechoslovakia in 1930.

Despite its advocates, the development of a Modern style was punctuated by criticism, debate and a reluctance to accept changes from traditional forms. In the conservative Sydney-based *Building* Magazine, in January 1930, Le Corbusier's Modern work was denigrated as it 'outrages the normal intelligence . . . [and] lacks harmony, rhythm and general design', though by August 1935, the same journal in an article 'Modernism in Architecture, Where is it leading' admitted that it led to 'sunshine and light and healthier living'. A running debate in the *Australian Home Beautiful* in the same year over an article by Norman Seabrook on modern design, 'What is Modernism?', had as many proponents for the new style as it had antagonists, or defenders of traditionalism. Indeed, this debate has never been wholly resolved, for though innovative design has trickled through the pattern of domestic architecture of every ensuing era, traditional forms have retained a high place in architectural and popular fancy.

One of the most fashionable representations of the Modern Ship style was Burnham Beeches, a looming three-storey mansion built in 1933, in the Dandenongs, Victoria, for A.N. Nicholas. It was designed in reinforced concrete by the architect Harry Norris and described as a 'battleship' – an analogy that related to its sturdy construction, its bulky, built-up outline and long stretches of 'deck'. It was, however, one of the most luxuriously fitted residences of the era, the last word in modern convenience and decoration. Art Deco ornament was used to dramatize the extensive building mass. The iron balustrade of the deck zigzagged in a pattern of Art Deco chevrons. A run of horizontal lines was incised into the smooth rendered facade which was ornamented with diamond motifs and representations of Australian animals. And a wrought-iron bronze deer, a familiar Art Deco symbol, leapt across the massive entrance gates of the property.

Inside the house, planning was ship-like, with engine-room, stores and theatrette set in the basement. The main stair, outlined by the chrome band of its balustrade, rippled upwards through an elliptical stairwell and an adjacent lift ran through all floors to a lookout at the top of the house, where a loud-speaker, complete with radio antennae and receiver, broadcast the latest dance bands or the news, over the sleeping lawns below. Every major room had access to a deck and giant picture windows opened up to the view in all directions. The house was fitted out with the latest furniture, much of it made by the Melbourne firm Branchflower, and characterized by shiny veneers, streamlined curves or clever Chinese puzzle-like geometry. Some idea of the style of decoration throughout the house could be seen in the lounge-room, which was laid with a jade green carpet, had an embossed Art Deco patterned ceiling, ornamentation over the doors, striped curtains, ivory walls and Australian timber furniture upholstered in autumn tones.

The design of Wyldefel Gardens built in 1935–36 in Potts Point, Sydney, was imported more directly from

Burnham Beeches, designed by Harry Norris and built in 1933 near the Sherbrooke Forest area of Sassafras. Of concrete and metal, it is a large and lively example of the Ship style.

Germany. William Crowle, a noted Sydney connoisseur and collector, was inspired by a modern housing complex, fanning down a hillside, that he spied when motoring near Oberammergau. With photographs and the assistance of architect John R. Brogan, whose usual mode was Tudor revivals on Sydney's North Shore, Crowle's vision was re-created. Following the lines of a 'V', each unit formed a step down the hillside with a green turfed garden laid out on the roof of the flat below. It was a clever concept, enhanced by the modern lines of the building, with its cantilevered overhanging eaves, curved corners and sweeps of bent glass, opening to the view over the harbour.

The design of Wyldefel Gardens is remarkable not only as an innovative example of Modernism but also because Crowle had no trouble in having his radical and experimental concept accepted by building authorities. Twelve years later conservative attitudes to Modernism had become more rigid. Sydney Ancher had to instigate a lawsuit against Warringah Council in order to build a simple flat-roofed house at North Curl Curl in 1948.

Smaller scaled houses too, reflected the new 'International' Modernism. The architect Roy Grounds' house at Raneleagh, Mount Eliza, Victoria, designed in 1933 by Grounds and his partner Geoffrey Mewton, was a blocky, flat-roofed building, topped by a glassed-in sunroom and an upper deck, railed-in like a ship. A smattering of porthole windows continued the naval theme, but much of the interest in the house lay in its construction – an innovative combination of steel and asbestos cement sandwich sheets, echoing the current European interest in prefabrication and system building.

Grounds and Mewton also produced a scheme for a residence at Upper Beaconsfield, Victoria, for Mr Critchley Parker. The *Australian Home Beautiful* of January 1934, reported that the house, La Mabellion, was 'modern by circumstance'. Originally an 'adaptation of a South African Dutch Colonial type of residence' had been envisaged, but was discarded when the materials required for the ornate scheme had proved too costly. A flat, iron-roofed building decidedly Modern in appearance took its place.

It had a long central 'trunk' with rooms growing out like branches to either side, to capture views from every angle. The external walls were rendered and painted white, the frames of the long, horizontal windows were coloured rust red and the entrance defined by heavy feature brick piers, extending into window-boxes, with horizontal joints raked out to echo the low lines of the building. The

Top and centre above: The Californian bungalow was usually described as 'cosy, roomy and warm'. Top, an early example at Bowral; below it is Aldrea, an Adelaide bungalow with immensely wide, protective roofs providing open-air living areas.

Centre below: Wyldefel Gardens, Potts Point, was a German-inspired housing project designed by John R. Brogan in 1935.

A house by Sydney Archer at North Curl Curl, which was the subject of a 1948 lawsuit by the owner against Warringah Shire Council. The council claimed the design was ugly, and unsuccessfully insisted on a parapet to hide its flat roof.

interior followed the Modern theme, with walls lined in standard sized insulation boards, their horizontal joints emphasized. Windows and doors fitted flushly into the walls and no architraves, cornices or skirtings cluttered the sparse clean look. Some effort was made to link the outside environment with the interior, and brick-paved terraces and patios led off from every room. Indeed, La Mabellion predicted, in a naive way, the fascination that architects of the 1950s would show for integrating the environment with the house and creating an easy flow between the building inside and the outdoors.

appearance the house was low-key, its white painted brick walls with horizontally emphasized joints were topped by a low-pitched roof with blue eaves and a red fascia, with windows geometrically balanced around a brown brick porch. The interior was tightly planned to eliminate corridors and ally rooms in logical conjunctions. There was a well-fitted-out kitchen, planned around the tasks of meal preparation, and an open-plan living area, where the sitting could be divided from the dining area with a pull of a curtain. The interior was sparsely furnished with bare polished floors, long straight curtains at the windows and

Ship-style curves on a house near Bowral, about 1935.

A footnote in the development of architectural Modernism is the house of Norman Seabrook, the youthful progenitor of so much discussion about Modernism. His house, built in Hawthorn in 1935, was a small, two-bedroom residence. It was non-aggressively, almost unnoticeably Modern in appearance, illustrating his precepts that Modern architecture was not an applied style, but rather a logical approach to planning and arrangement of spaces, requiring the elimination of extraneous ornament and unwanted decoration from functional buildings. In

a minimal display of chrome-plated furniture that was to become synonymous with this Modern style.

More indicative perhaps of architectural trends were the buildings displayed in the Centenary Homes Exhibition in Melbourne in 1934 and the designs entered in the competition held in conjunction with it. The majority were overtly Modern; squared, flat-roofed, bunker-like buildings, with their metal-framed windows and unpanelled doors painted vermillion, emerald green or sky blue against the white of their rendered walls. Surprisingly, all the competitions were won by the one designer, Donald C. Ward, a young architect with the

Department of the Interior. No doubt the consistency of his Modern approach reassured the assessors that a new age of architecture had dawned. All his designs were built up from planes and each had a logical, almost predictable, plan with 'L'-shaped lounge and dining-room, service areas to one side and rooms placed around a central hall space, eliminating corridors. All the main rooms led out to concrete paved terraces.

Despite Norman Seabrook's assertion that Modern design was an attitude and approach, rather than an applied style, the marks of Modernism showed little variation in the last half of the 1930s, while its idiosyncracies were adopted with ease and became quite fashionable. In Sydney, for instance, F. Glynn Gilling created some remarkably adept translations of the Modern style for clients in Vaucluse who required curved corners and plate glass windows instead of his usual rendition of the lush Georgian. In Melbourne, Yuncken, Freeman and Freeman designed a massive Modernistic house for socially prominent clients, Dr and Mrs Geoffrey Smith in Hopetoun Road, Toorak in 1936. It had terraces paved in a concrete chequerboard of green and white, a built-in cocktail bar in the dining-room and a sweep of curved glass jutted out from one end of the living-room, encompassing the outdoors in its arc so that the garden 'seems . . . part of the room'.

Decorating the streamlined house

As Modernism was gradually accepted by both designer and home-maker, there was a corresponding increase in the use of modern building and decorating materials, as if innovative design relied on the latest technology. For instance, William Crowle, the owner of Wyldefell Gardens, installed plastic slabs instead of marble as mantlepieces in his ultra-modern house. The new materials – or revamped older ones – were all wonder materials, with scientific sounding names and qualities to match. 'Ligno lea' and 'linotex' were waterproof, easily cleaned, hard-wearing floor coverings, 'lagoline' and 'artona' were new paints with special ultra-glossy, never-fade properties, 'permaglaze' windows never leaked, 'cementone' coloured concrete retained its colour, 'staybrite' stainless steel benches, sinks and fittings never rusted and 'monel metal' a silvery nickel alloy, also rustproof, was widely used for glittering, long-lasting, decorative effects.

'Bakelite', 'ebonite' and 'vitrolite' were among the wonder plastics. Concrete and cement became favourite materials around the house, used to construct plant pots, crazily paved paths, edgings, fencing and goldfish pools – their hard-edged neatness complemented by the geometry of conical cypress trees, cacti and spiky shrubs like the bird of paradise or gladioli, beloved of the 1930s. Bright, gleaming chrome or highly polished metals were well used in fittings that ranged from door handles to spaceship-like lights. And, of course, it was the booming age for glass.

Sunlight and fresh air were deemed essential for modern healthy living and windows abounded in the newly designed houses. Curved glass, figured rolled glass, etched, sandblasted, coloured and intaglio glass, not only allowed the light to stream into the interior but was used as a

Stair halls walled with Australian-made glass bricks were featured in many houses from the mid-1930s onwards. This illustration appeared in the trade periodical Decoration and Glass *in 1936.*

decorative material to enliven the harsh lines of the building. The 'Agee' glass brick, named for the initials of Australian Glass, was also introduced in the mid-1930s, becoming immediately fashionable in curved glass brick stairwells or glass brick feature walls in houses of both modern or more traditional appearance. 'Gravé' glass shower screens were 'smart' for the bathroom, etched with a lithe nude or a marine scene with seaweed and bubble-blowing fish. Structural 'carrara' glass panels, in black, aqua or cream, trimmed with monel strips, outlined a fire surround and the same treatment was used to jazzily modernize shop fronts.

Peach-tinted mirror tiles, golden ray mirrors, large mirrors etched with a fountain, or small ones in geometric shapes, reflected the sunlight in every corner. A large circular mirror, hanging above the fireplace or framing cut flowers in the hall, was the ubiquitous symbol of Modern design, while a glass-fronted, mirror-backed cocktail cabinet that held all the ingredients for exotic mixed drinks, was the ultimate adjunct of modern living.

Bathrooms became a focus of the house – larger in size than ever before, efficiently organized, more conveniently located beside the bedrooms, and a paean to the vitreous china industry. The walls, tiled two metres or so high, often formed stepping skyscraper patterns, with contrasting border, above the terrazzo or mosaic floor. Matching sets of vitreous china soap dishes, toilet roll and toothbrush holders, towel rails, pedestal basins, plunge bath, shower and lavatory toned in the favourite bathroom shades of green or cream, or combined more astonishing colours such as shrimp pink and black, mauve and buttercup yellow or cornflower blue and peach. Hot water gushed from the gas or electric hot water service through chrome taps with dolphin-shaped spouts.

The kitchen also had developed through the interwar years to become the acme of efficiency, planned to aid the process-line motions of food preparation and service. Cupboards, drawers and benches were streamlined into built-in double decker units that lined the kitchen walls between the sink, stainless-steel draining-board, electric refrigerator and gas stove, the last a hefty enamelled unit with oven and burners combined, although the separate wall ovens appeared in the late 1930s. The more elaborate kitchens were fitted with special purpose cupboards for electrical equipment, with heated pipes for tea-towels, ventilated doors and adjustable shelves in a special cake cupboard for different-sized cakes. In some houses, the kitchen expanded to include an eating area, with built-in booths with table and benches, like those of contemporary milk bars. A special storage area might also be found with built-in broom cupboards and a fold-down ironing-board. The laundry, however, was often stuck like an afterthought underneath the house or on the back corner, closest to the clothes-line. In the many houses with household help, the kitchen formed part of a service area, with a maid's room, bathroom and laundry.

Modernist design envisaged the house interior as efficient, clean, functional and no doubt as sterile as a hospital ward. Skirtings, cornices and panelling on doors were stripped away to reveal hard surfaces and design based on shape and form, rather than overt decoration.

A bathroom of the late 1930s – a stylish arrangement of ceramic tiles, glass bricks and Art Deco curves.

Top: Convex window glass was an appealing material to home-builders of the 1930s. 'It can transform a house into a home', its makers claimed.

Flush-panelled doors fitted into the walls without an architrave. A tapestry brick fireplace surround encased a serviceable gas heater. Patterned wallpaper was eschewed for a textured wall surface, and home decorators were advised to use neutral colours, in cream and 'warm white' and textured weaves rather than patterns in their furnishings. As a result, rooms were often stark. The bareness of polished wood, linoleum or parquet flooring was relieved by a rug of abstract design or an Australian 'Llamba' sheepskin, featuring a sunburst. Shelves, tables and mantlepiece were swept clean of all save a vase, a small figurine or lamp, or perhaps an electric clock, in an 'Art Moderne' case, with a stepped design in figured wood.

A house by Harold Desbrowe Annear, built late in his career, in Toorak. Its detailing, Classical in manner, precise and elegant, was by then old-fashioned.

Far below: The Lippincott house, Heidelberg, by Walter Burley Griffin, 1917. A simple brick and tile design, recalling Griffin's earlier American work.

Furniture was limited to essentials, including a wireless. Tubular chrome tables, chairs and lamps, unashamedly copied from European originals, were made in Australia by Healings and Newton Bros. Chrome looked so shiny and so ostensibly modern – it was praised as labour saving, not requiring the 'elbow grease' of polishing to maintain. Timber furniture was more ostentatiously styled, with extravagent geometric forms, contrived 'streamlined' curved corners and a highly unlikely mirrored polish finish. Severe lines were in vogue, and incongruous items abounded: hefty dining-room tables with inlaid bands of ebony on stepped bases were more suited to skyscraper boardrooms than domesticity, and leather armchairs suited the clubhouse more than small-scale living. But not all pieces were stark: a dressing-table, by the Melbourne firm Branchflower, combined a circular mirror, drawers, table and round seat in a coil of shiny figured timber.

Built-in furniture was recommended for flats, where space was limited. In her 1937 Toorak apartment, Melbourne dress designer Mavis Ripper installed a built-in dining-table with sliding top to allow access to the built-in seat against the wall. A built-in sofa in the living-room broke into a bookshelf and table at one end and her bed was built against a mirror-tiled wall. The furniture was of Queensland maple and its adjuncts, such as brown and white check curtains, venetian blinds, tub chairs and shell wall vases for flowers, represented chic urban living, or 'Beauty in Simplicity' – the Modern catchcry.

Two mid-1930s Georgian Revival examples with a Mediterranean flavour. Below: Audley, at Warrawee, by F. Glynn Gilling, though more formal, shows the Mediterranean influence especially in its roof forms and textures. Far below: Twelve Trees at Killara was designed by E. L. Apperly, who, like many other architects, had had the direct Mediterranean experience which reinforced Professor Wilkinson's teaching.

Ironically, however, and in wry summary of the inter-war period, architecture and design were far from straightforward simplicity. Confusion in style, in design and in architectural interpretation reigned throughout the two decades and was hardly resolved by the end of the 1930s. For as one house rose up in the suburban landscape, stark and white and a monument to European Modernism, another would be built beside it commemorating the Georgian era, and there was no guarantee that the interior of either would reflect the tone of its exterior. The inter-war years represent a return to the precepts of the Victorian age, when abundant stylistic choice, confusion and a naive delight in technology, represented by Functionalism and Modernistic design notions, spread across the whole range of available housing.

THE SINGLE FAMILY detached house remained the preferred dwelling in Australia through the decades from the 1950s to the 1980s. Change was slight in some respects, such as materials and building methods, but in others, such as planning, changes have been considerable. Domestic design ideas alter because of many varied factors that range from financial consideration through to aesthetic preferences. Architects have designed only a small percentage of the houses built in Australia, but it is primarily through their work that the Australian house has progressed towards a more suitable form for the conditions and way of life in this country.

In the 1940s most Australians planning their house would have imagined having a timber or brick bungalow with a chimney stack, overhanging eaves, and front porch, standing in its own allotment of ground. The house would have had a 'front' with the entrance and principal rooms facing out over the tidy garden towards the street, a 'rear' with kitchen and other utility rooms opening on to a 'backyard', and nondescript 'sides', set the regulation distance from the neighbours. The lot would be fenced and, depending on economic circumstances, may or may not have contained a free-standing garage.

This dream was shattered by the realities of post-war

ports and garages found a place in most gardens. Within a decade they became incorporated into the house, with the 'double' garage sometimes appearing as the most dominant element of the design.

Stark simplicity

In Europe in the 1920s and 1930s the question of suitable housing for the twentieth century had been pursued by architects such as the Swiss, Le Corbusier, and the German, Walter Gropius. They had understood the extent of the problem of providing housing for the many from limited resources. They saw the increasing demands of the future being solved by technological means. But perhaps even more important, they considered that twentieth-century man's perception, vision of himself, social behaviour, and relationship with nature, differed radically from those of past generations. The dwellings they produced were intended to suggest the means to accommodate this changing physical and philosophical condition.

Their houses for the general market were based on efficiency and they utilized minimal floor areas and materials. To lighten the housewife's work the use of electrical equipment was encouraged. In order to make the spaces seem larger, interior individual 'rooms' became

BEYOND THE 1950s 6

shortages of skills, materials and equipment, the government restrictions of possible building areas and limited finance. The minimal war-service loan provided the total expenditure for the building of a large percentage of the houses of this time – and many houses were needed. The policies of both public and private development continued to encourage the construction of free-standing single family houses, and the Australian cities experienced their most extensive physical expansion in history. The suburbs grew with what were often inappropriate dwellings on quarter-acre allotments, arranged regularly along each side of the equally regular street patterns.

The design features that had made the bungalow such a suitable building type for the 1930s and 1940s could no longer be achieved under the restrictions. 'Luxuries' such as eaves, porches, verandahs, and fireplaces disappeared. In its stripped-down form the Australian house had few redeeming qualities. Further, the organization of the space of the house, which had admirably accommodated the earlier lifestyle was unsuitable and too restrictive for the increased social freedom of the mores of the new era.

The changes affected every social group. Servants, who were not uncommon in the more affluent homes of the pre-war years, were now few. Motor car ownership became more widespread in the years from 1950 and car-

The John Andrews house at Eugowra, built in 1981, interpreted the traditional homestead form using new and appropriate technology such as prefabrication and passive solar energy systems.

less strictly defined by walls, and extensive exterior glass panels were used to help increase the feeling of spaciousness within the dwelling. Although not built of factory-produced components, they aimed to demonstrate what machine-built houses would be like. Consequently, the buildings had crisp rectangular forms without the conventional craft-based details such as window sills and roof overhangs. To make a clear distinction between man-made and natural objects the houses were painted white, often elevated, and clearly differentiated from the surrounding terrain. Such architecture became known as that of the International style.

This house type was introduced to Australia in 1949 in its fully developed form by the Viennese architect, Harry Seidler, with the first of three houses he designed for a site in Clissold Road, Turramurra, Sydney. With these and subsequent dwellings of all types, including project houses and apartment blocks, Seidler was to make a major contribution to Australian house design.

The 1949 house was a masterly example of the use of the open-plan, and demonstrated that pleasant environments could be created out of minimal floor areas. Its living-rooms were orientated for the view rather than being focused on the street regardless of aspect. An open patio became an integral part of the living area of the house instead of an appendage. The building itself was an object to be seen in the round, and not a conglomerate of rooms behind a front 'facade'.

At first Seidler's houses were seen as too radical and not

sufficiently sympathetic to the conditions of Australia, and his early influence was less extensive than that of the Australian architect, Sydney Ancher. Ancher had lived in Europe between 1930 and 1936, and had been greatly impressed by what he saw as the more appropriate buildings of designers such as Gropius. In particular he was struck by the work of another German, Ludwig Mies van der Rohe. The houses Ancher built after 1946 in Maytone Avenue, Killara, Sydney, exemplify his translation of the European models for Australian trade practices and sites. His houses seek the same direction as Seidler's but they are not as 'pure' in their organization and forms and their less precise nature made them more acceptable to Australian architects. Ancher was one of the most influential architects of the time, but perhaps it was his personality rather than what he actually built that had such an impact on the following generation of Australian house designers. Nevertheless, Ancher's many houses, with their wide terraces and pergolas, generous open living and minimal bedroom areas, provided models to which the Australian house today is endebted.

In conservative Australia it was difficult to have these radically different houses accepted. The flat roof, which appears in both the Seidler and Ancher designs, was a particular point of contention, and clients and architects were forced to contest local councils' rulings against what were seen as aesthetically offending designs.

In the other states the influence of the new European architecture was taking its effect, though not as directly as in Sydney. One early example is the 1946 house at Poet's Road, Hobart, by Garfield Haslock. This was the first house in Tasmania to break with convention and to find a solution determined by modern lifestyle and the environment.

The architectural climate in Melbourne was distinct from that in the rest of Australia. Before the war architectural leadership had come from the Victorian architects – an adventurous group with the courage to extend technological and aesthetic frontiers. This continued to show in their houses of the 1950s and 1960s. Structural and functional efficiency were their predominant concerns, and these established the expression of the buildings. Inexpensive materials were used as a matter of principle. The houses of the architect-critic Robin Boyd are typical of this work. There is little consistency in his architecture as each commission opened up the possibility to explore some new idea. The spirit of Melbourne of the time is captured in his Richardson house of 1954: a small house, designed for utmost functional efficiency, built across a water culvert and given a startling architectural form through the exhibition of its bridge-like spanning structural system. Boyd was not alone. The Peter McIntyre house of 1955 shows a related image in the dramatic 'A' frame that supports the floors on different levels over a steep site. The double cantilevered truss structure was an exciting yet rational response to the flood conditions of the site. The emphasis on the steel frame is highlighted by the vivid colours of the infill panels. This was the new daring and expressive architecture of Melbourne. But these buildings led to overstated solutions, and a later obsession with geometry that derived principally from the houses of Sir Roy Grounds and denied the logical principles of the earlier designs. In the hands of less competent designers, the Melbourne architecture became simply a matter of stylistic devices.

Back to nature

The second significant development of the Australian house took place in the mid-1950s, again primarily in Sydney. This, contrary to the rationality of the International style, was a romantic movement and its inspiration came not from Europe, but from Japan and the United States of America. Rather than accepting high technological advancement as the panacea for the future, traditional Japanese philosophy taught of the need for a continuing communication between man and nature. Australian domestic design from the mid-1950s to the present has to a marked extent been conditioned by Japanese examples and ideals. They reached Australia directly from the East and through the work of the American, Frank Lloyd Wright, and other architects practising on the west coast of America.

Since the end of the nineteenth century Wright had been designing houses which integrated indoor and outdoor spaces, with projecting and therefore sheltering roofs, and what he called an 'organic' relationship between building and site. Wright believed that the furniture, fixtures, building and landscape should form an integrated and harmonious composition. The influence of Wright's work, however, did not have its full impact on the Australian house until it appeared in an assured manner in the houses of architects such as Peter Muller, Bruce Rickard, and Ian McKay. The first of the houses came from an individualistic designer, Peter Muller, who sought a dwelling of sheltered spaces in communion with nature for his own house at Palm Beach, built in 1955. He was more concerned with beauty than efficiency, and the cheap construction and materials of the house were simply the result of economic constraint.

With his use of warm-toned materials, and his respect for the natural features of the building site Muller designed houses that seemed to become a part of their surroundings. Most of the early buildings were small and unpretentious but there were exceptions including the Richardson house, Palm Beach, 1956. Clearly inspired by Wright's late work, the Richardson house is one of Muller's most accomplished buildings. Sited on a constrained allotment, the long narrow house clings to the rocks above a cliff face and at one point cascades down over the edge with an elevator shaft providing access to the waterfront below. The interior consists of a progression of spaces, partially defined by the interior sturdy round pillars, and sensitively, even quite magically, related to each other and the view beyond. The climax to the building was the living area roofed by a translucent copper-green fibreglass dome with solid white discs separated with small accent discs of red. Such poetic buildings by Muller were particularly convincing to the rising generation of designers in the architectural schools, and the influence of this early work was sustained through the following decades.

The Richardson house at Palm Beach, by Peter Muller.

An interior of the Rickard house, Wahroonga.

Right: The Adelaide house of Robert Dickson, 1950.

Bruce Rickard returned to Sydney, following a period in the United States, in 1957, and the 1959 and 1962 houses he built for his own family exemplify the lessons he had absorbed from seeing Wright's architecture. They are finely crafted, richly coloured buildings of deep brown and honey shades. Their long horizontal lines give a feeling of repose and shelter among their bushland settings. Rickard's houses were planned to spread over their sites and all rooms, even the small bedrooms, relate to the exterior. The main living-rooms have an uncommon sense of spaciousness as there is little division from room to room, and variation in ceiling height allows for light and the extension of space from above. His most developed and sophisticated house is the Curry house, Bayview, 1980, with the interior levels functionally arranged to step down from the entry to reveal the view of the ocean below – a striking and quite beautiful composition.

The houses of Ian McKay are more robust, often with heavy timber members that determine their char-

acter. They show daring attempts to explore the three-dimensional qualities of the interior spaces. Changing floor levels and steeply pitched roofs provide a dramatic yet 'earthy' architecture that responds to the rugged qualities of the Australian landscape. The David Moore house at Pretty Beach shows an imaginative use of standard timber framing with glazed trusses and asbestos sheet roofing. With its wild forms seemingly perched precariously on a high rocky outcrop the Moore house shows McKay at his most wilful. McKay remains one of the most creative of the romantic architects in Australia. His recent houses in northern New South Wales are primarily single space dwellings with exposed frames of heavy raw timbers and encompassing iron roofs. There is a primitive almost religious mood to this powerful rude architecture.

The attitude to domestic design as exemplified in the work of Muller, Rickard and McKay, was in some ways a backlash against the technological buildings that were altering the character of the inner cities. It was also a genuine attempt to design in accord with the nature of Australia. The influence of both directions established by the Sydney architects spread through Australia, and presented alternatives to the conventional house type inherited from the post-war years.

A third house type emerged midway between the two principal streams of thought. It lacked the cool excellence of Seidler's rational designs, and the passion and warmth of Muller and McKay, but took something of each to produce an inexpensive, sensible, and craft-based dwelling that provided a pleasant and easy-to-live-with setting. Typical of these houses are the Adelaide house of Robert Dickson, designed for his family in 1950, the 1959 house in Hobart of Barry McNeil, also for his own use, and the architect Russell Jack's house in Sydney of 1957.

These houses were usually flat-roofed and of simple rectangular plan. They often expressed their timber post-and-beam framing and were enclosed externally with exposed inexpensive materials such as chipboard, 'masonite' and asbestos-cement. They opened to the landscape with sliding glass doors protected by overhanging verandahs or pergolas. They were sited and planned for privacy, considerations of climate, and to take advantage of the positive qualities of their sites.

Housing in the heat

During the post-war years the distinctive and appropriate stump house of Queensland suffered a fate similar to that of the bungalows of the other states. With the restrictions, it also became an ungracious and uncomfortable dwelling. In what was virtually a time of abdication by the Queensland architects, the influence of the southern states increased when out-of-state practitioners, notably from Melbourne, established offices in Brisbane. The influence of firms such as Hayes and Scott and Ford, Hutton and Newell was positive and their houses responded to the Queensland setting. Unfortunately, many designers were less sympathetic and the suburbs of Brisbane began to resemble those of Sydney and Melbourne, with incongruous designs for a semitropical environment.

Brisbane also received a small number of the architects and future architects who migrated from England during

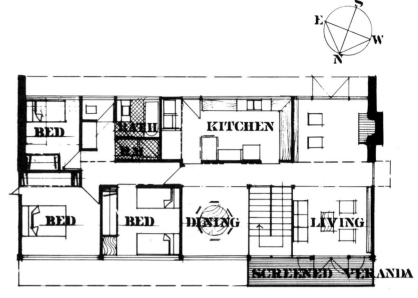

Two houses by John Dalton in Brisbane. Top: The floor plan of the Graham house. Above: The Musgrave house, 1973.

the 1950s. Outstanding among these was John Dalton. From Dalton came the first signs of a genuine re-emergence of sensible thought about the Queensland house. His own house of 1959 is related to Ancher's designs with its simple pavilion form and direct access from inside to the verandah and the garden. But the type was adapted for Queensland conditions. The roof is fitted with a water spray to cool its surface under extreme conditions and has a central clerestory vent to allow hot air to escape from the interior spaces. External adjustable blinds shade the verandah and glass walls. Dalton's later houses became more complex with sharply raking roofs and fractured plan forms determined by considerations of sun, shade and breezes, and the natural beauty of the sites. Into his houses he introduced raised floors, breezeways, wall vents and ceiling fans. Dark timber and white bagged masonry walls characterize his houses of the 1960s and 1970s. They are relaxing buildings with verandahs, courtyards and patios, and they are enlivened by the design for light and shadow patterns across their walls.

The architect Robin Boyd's own house, South Yarra, a radical rectilinear design with a tensile roof, built in 1959.

The 'Growth House', a project design by Cocks and Carmichael, in Melbourne.

Centre: One of the many designs produced in the 1950s by the Age Small Homes Service, directed by Robin Boyd in conjunction with the Royal Australian Institute of Architects.

Common concepts

Despite philosophical differences, the architect-designed houses of the late 1950s shared common characteristics. Most were unobtrusive buildings, more concerned with comfort and convenience than with outward show. Their sites were commonly 'battle-axe' blocks or out-of-the-way pockets of land. One of the greatest differences between these houses and their predecessors lay in the minimal use of interior partitions, and the resulting interconnections of many of the rooms. Because of this open-planning, privacy levels within the house lowered, and much of the organization of the houses was based on zoning in relation to the activities that were to take place. Separation was achieved by distance or by differing floor levels. One of the clearest examples of these concepts appeared in the Robin Boyd house at South Yarra, Melbourne, in 1959. In this house a covered courtyard acts as a spatial barrier between the children's and adults' areas. Within each section changes of level, rather than walls, divide the house into general use and private zones. While the Boyd house is a somewhat radical example, the principle of zoning has conditioned much of the distribution of space in the open-planned house. These houses represented a different attitude to domestic design to that of the pre-war years – the Australian house had gone through a metamorphosis.

Developers and design

Developers throughout Australia, however, were blind to the new designs, and the house that was available to the average buyer had few of the advantages brought about by the planning changes. Architectural journals, and magazines with a more broadly based readership, such as the *Australian Women's Weekly*, published the new work and attempted to promote the ideas. The Royal Australian Institute of Architects' Small Home Service fulfilled a useful role in assisting individual home owners, but had little effect on the general market. It was not until the collaboration of the architect and developer occurred with the first project houses that the public became aware of the possibilities of housing available to them.

Changes in house design usually permeate into the general market, but with a considerable time lag. Through project houses and exhibition villages the transference of architectural ideas to the market place is now more immediate. The architect prepares project house designs for the developer, monitored to the front edge of public acceptance. In an exhibition village the buyer can experience the various proposals and select a design for construction on his own site.

The first project houses were built in Melbourne, but it was the 1961 Carlingford Demonstration Village in Sydney by Lend Lease that established the project house as a marketing alternative. At Carlingford, houses by many of Sydney's leading architects were displayed, each in its own way opening up a new option. Project housing proved successful and resulted in a high standard of domestic design for the average Australian buyer. The aims of the project builder varied from company to company and from state to state. In Sydney companies such as Pettit and Sevitt, with designer Ken Woolley, and in

Melbourne Merchant Builders, with designer Graeme Gunn, produced high quality designs that could be modified to individual requirements. In Adelaide, with a different market situation, Brian Snowden for Martins and Marshall, and Turner and Wood with designer John Chappel produced less expensive and less flexible houses.

Providing options for clients with limited funds is a challenge faced by architects and developers alike. In Brisbane, Edwin Codd has been working towards a 'system' design based on light steel framing and various infill panels. Terry Dorrough for Merchant Builders, and Cocks and Carmichael for Civic Construction have also

who were to play a major role in domestic design returned to Australia from England. With its war-damaged cities England faced an acute housing problem and highly motivated architects, such as those of the London County Council, were attempting to arrive at a practical and socially successful solution. In order to lower costs and to give what they described as 'integrity' to the architecture, buildings began to appear without linings and finishes. Structure and services were exposed, and the materials were used with the surfaces they arrived with from the manufacturers. The philosophy came again from Le Corbusier, but now it followed the concepts represented

The Lowline House, a project design by Ken Woolley for Pettit & Sevitt in 1961.

been investigating the possibilities of adaptable systems to widen the options of buyers. The 'Growth House' by Cocks and Carmichael, which can be planned by a purchaser on the basic grid, provides a flexible system that also allows the selection of 'extras'. While the economic downturn of the mid-1970s severely affected the project house developer, the early 1960s idea of the project house remains a viable concept for better design.

The beginning of the project house was closely related to architects developing an increased sense of social responsibility. Towards the end of the 1950s several architects

by his later brick and concrete buildings. His *Maison Jaoul*, outside Paris, was particularly influential.

The basic house

Again, it was first in Sydney that these ideas took root. Tony Moore, an architect who had studied and worked in London, built a house for his family on a steep site in North Sydney in 1961. This house most clearly exemplifies these concepts. It is of cheap brick construction with a sloping roof and projecting timber balconies and has minimal floor area with rooms on several levels arranged around a narrow central stair. But the most significant aspect of the building is the handling of its materials and services – timber and bricks were used in a raw funda-

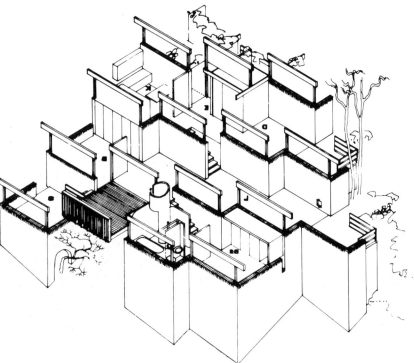

The Woolley house, Mosman, 1962, was a deliberate attempt to create an Australian style. The integration of the house and the site, and the use of cheap and natural materials, were the primary ingredients. The trend became known as the 'Sydney School'. The house won the Wilkinson Award for 1962.

mental manner and plumbing, wiring, chimney flues and the like are all clearly evident. It was intentionally as basic a house as Moore could provide.

Similar in spirit is the house by David Saunders in Parkville, built in 1963 when he was a lecturer in architecture at Melbourne University. The house is related, without stylist copying, to the row of nineteenth-century terraces in which it stands. Again, it is a fundamental building of exterior concrete block, with reused handmade bricks for the interior lining. The trusses of the double skillion roof are exposed on the upper level and the roof is lined simply with its foil-back insulation. The plan was equally straightforward, with what amounted to two rooms on the lower and two rooms on the upper level. The spaces were multipurpose and beds were folded away and screened by curtains during the day. The informal nature of these buildings was sympathetic to a casual family lifestyle. There was much to be learned from them.

Boyd remained one of the most innovative house designers in Melbourne throughout the 1960s. The Kaye house, 1967, and the McClune house, 1969, both in the Frankston area, are typical of his later work – in this he uses natural timbers and simple verandahs, often supported by diagonal props. Vestiges of the features of his houses reappear in Melbourne work a decade later.

Low cost, practicality, and suitable design for local trade practices was only part of the story. Of equal importance was the conscious aim to produce a domestic architecture, which by responding to local conditions, would have a recognizable Australian identity. It was the architects, building on the steep bush and sandstone sites of Sydney's northern suburbs, who gave this work its full sophisticated expression. Among the earliest examples are the Ken Woolley house, 1962, and the Peter Johnson house, 1963. This too, was a romantic movement with the blending of building and site being a prime consideration.

Rough textured bricks, such as the then cheap clinker rejects, gave a rugged appearance to these multi-levelled houses. The bricks were exposed internally, and floors kept uncarpeted. Loose rugs allowed their floor timbers and quarry-tiled paving to be seen. Dark roof tiles and the stained off-saw timbers added to the mood, and successfully related the buildings to their equally rough environment. The form of the houses, with the raking roofs that followed the terrain also contributed to this integration. Sites were left as much as possible in their natural state.

This was a distinct regional architecture that grew out of a positive response to the climate and conditions of Australia. The suitability of these houses was recognized and for more than a decade the attitudes that they represented have conditioned domestic design throughout Australia. This 'Sydney School' architecture proved suitable for project house design, and today speculative builders are offering dwellings with some of the visual attributes but little of the logic of the prototypes.

Some of the finest houses in this idiom were designed in Adelaide by Dickson and Platten. The Draper and Warburton houses of 1966 are typical of this work. The houses are planned to take full advantage of their sites for outlook, privacy, and the use of outdoor areas for informal living. Exposed brickwork, off-saw timber cladding, straw ceilings and expressed timber frames impart a warm casual mood. They are finely crafted buildings with a level of refinement rarely found, with the exception of Rickard, in Sydney work. Particularly noteworthy was the example provided by a pair of town houses for North Adelaide, also of 1966. Special permission from the Council was required for this scheme, and the solution demonstrated the advantages of the joint development of the site. The houses have different setbacks and their internal arrangement shows variation within a shared concept. The handsome landscape of native species by Allan Correy enhances the site for the owners' use and contributes further to the streetscape.

In Queensland similar concerns brought about a quite different architectural solution. Timber and corrugated iron were used rather than brick and tile, and the houses exhibit a casual unpretentious character. In Brisbane, the house by Rex Addison stands on stilts over a sloping rough site. Its main living area is reached by a small timber bridge from the road. The dominant sweeping pitched roof extends over the outdoor decks uniting the enclosed and open spaces of the dwelling. Like the Tony Moore house, this building rejoices in its obvious low cost and the talent of the architect to create places that 'feel good to be in' out of limited resources. Akin, but less consciously frugal, is the 1973 house by John Mobbs at Burleigh Heads. Again, contrary to the Sydney examples that were firmly based on the ground, the Mobbs house is elevated over its steep site in a projecting timber frame. The simple single space that is contained under the straight raking skillion roof is of two levels at the higher point of the site. The plane of the roof is fully exposed within, and projects well beyond the walls. The house is sited high in the hills with views over the ocean, and the openness of the building with the raised light timber verandahs gives a feeling of freedom in empathy with its setting. These two houses were for their architect's own use. Queensland developers continue to follow designs from the southern cities, however, and it would appear that the example of architects, building appropriately for the north, has gone unheeded.

Landscaping and land division

In the 1960s there was an increased appreciation of Australia's flora. Attune with the regional character of the houses, surrounding landscapes were retained or planted with native species. The hardy nature and low maintenance requirements of the indigenous plants increased their level of appeal. Landscape designers, in Sydney Bruce McKenzie, and in Melbourne Ellis Stones, played a major role in developing an Australian landscape tradition.

But many of the disadvantages of the Australian house came from the standard subdivision of the land on which it was placed. In America grouped and mixed-density housing related to shared open space was common, but in Australia it proved difficult to alter by-laws to allow for such planning. In the Canberra area the Swinger Hill scheme by Ian McKay brought together single-family dwellings in an arrangement of attached cottages. The considerable publicity accorded this scheme drew attention to the possibilities of the greater density and amenity such land usage provided, but the lessons were rarely

The Johnson house of 1963 was a distinctive addition to the Sydney School idiom. Its site remained almost totally natural and the materials used – clinker bricks and off-saw timber – were also used in their natural state. The house is fitted to its sloping site by having several floor levels.

followed. The idea of 'cluster' housing was championed in Melbourne by David Yencken of Merchant Builders. In cluster housing the individual dwellings, with their own small gardens, are related to an overall plan of shared open space. Winter Park, by Graeme Gunn for Merchant Builders, 1970, provides an excellent example of the greater amenities made possible by such subdivision. The houses are carefully related to each other for outlook and beneficial orientation. Privacy was well protected and outside the individual lot is the sympathetically landscaped areas of the shared parkland. The most recent scheme for grouped housing from that office appears in the Waitara village design for an adult community in Sydney. With its structured planning and Picturesque cottage details it contrasts with the loose casual nature of the earlier developments in Melbourne. Thanks to the success of Winter Park, cluster housing is becoming more readily available, yet the majority of development subdivisions remain those of the traditional pattern. Much has to be achieved in order to free the dwelling from the constraint of the standard allotment.

Housing developments

The Housing Commissions and Trusts in the various states, with their extensive programmes, have the opportunity to explore new and better ways of living. One

A low-rise, medium-density residential development at Little Bay, designed by John Andrews for the Housing Commission of New South Wales. As well as the shared open space, each dwelling has a small individual garden.

of the more progressive bodies is the South Australian Housing Trust. Their 1950s town plan for Elizabeth was one of the most extensive undertaken in this country, but Elizabeth, laid out on conservative lines, has not proved a success socially. More promising is the cluster development at Westlakes, 1971, where extensive playing fields containing the local school are surrounded by mixed housing types approached by paths through small parks between blocks of rows of houses. Each individual house has, in addition, its own front and rear garden.

Unfortunately, land available for new low-income housing is often on the outskirts of the cities, increasing the transportation problems and costs of the occupants. The New South Wales Housing Commission is attempting to find alternative higher density solutions for the inner cities, without resorting to the high-rise tower. The Little Bay Scheme in Sydney of 1975, by John Andrews' firm, is one such example – dwellings are stacked and interlocked to give individual open space to each unit, with shared play areas between the fingers of the dwellings that branch up from the street.

The Seidler house, Killara, 1966 – 67, is a classic manifestation of the International style. It is a sophisticated combination of reinforced concrete, masonry and glass, complementing the rugged complexity of its stony bush site.

The palette of materials

In its use of materials domestic design in Australia is still conservative. Masonry and timber remain the major building materials despite advances in the performance of steel, concrete and synthetic materials.

The Harry Seidler house at Killara, 1966, is the most accomplished and expressive concrete house of the time. Seidler's work continued to run counter to the mainstream of Australian architecture, though the influence of his experience of building in this climate is evident. By the 1960s his practice had become involved primarily with large projects, but the occasional house also appears.

The Seidler house dramatically contrasts with, yet responds to, its sloping site with projecting strong cantilevered horizontal forms. As in all of Seidler's work there is a logic in the structural order of the composition. Internally, the spaces on the various levels are interlocked, and the strong horizontal lines of the house visually extend the interior space across the terraces to the surrounding terrain. In addition, the overlapping of the floor planes allows views into the spaces above and below giving a continuous vertical dimension to the building. Stone, timber, and precise off-form boarded concrete are used without additional finishes, but handled with a quality of refinement that contrasts with the rougher finishes of the 'Sydney School' work.

Another immigrant, Enrico Taglietti, from Italy, has produced noteworthy houses of concrete construction for both Sydney and Canberra. Taglietti's use of concrete contrasts with that of Seidler. He uses the material in a free manner to create wilful, emotive forms rather than following rational structural determinants. Taglietti shapes his buildings around the emotional as well as practical needs of his clients. In some respects his architecture is related to the post-war Japanese concrete buildings. From the exterior the houses such as the Paterson house, Canberra, 1965 and the Smith house, Sydney, 1971 are vigorous and visually demanding with their sometimes eccentric shapes. They take control over their sites in a fortress-like manner and make a strong architectural union between inside and outside. Internally, with the Smith house in particular, clear functional planning combines with the drama of highly sculptural spaces and elements. But the costs associated with in situ concrete construction, and an apparent lack of interest by the industry in prefabrication for domestic use have restricted the use of this material in houses.

Prosperity continued through the 1960s and into the 1970s. It was not until the early 1970s that Australia's conscience was aroused about the state of its cities. Boyd had remained the major spokesman against the destruction of the environment, but Boyd had directed attention primarily towards social attitudes, what he called 'featurism' in buildings, and the poor design of artifacts such as billboards, telephone poles and the like. The effects of the large-scale urban changes took most by surprise.

Two major offshoots in housing came from the new

A house on Scotland Island by Morrice Shaw, with a light steel frame, and curvilinear cladding of corrugated metal, plywood and glass.

attitudes of the 1970s. A search for alternate lifestyles focused attention on the owner-builder and the use of recycled and unconventional materials. While the majority of owner-builder houses are of conservative design, many of the new community dwellings were not. Books on inexpensive and easily erected shelters were available from other countries that had experienced the social crisis before Australia and provided a stimulus for adventurous solutions in low cost design.

Age-old materials, such as adobe and mud-brick, re-

appeared in domestic work. To Eltham, Victoria, mud-construction was not new. In the 1930s Justus Jorgenson had started an artists' colony in the area, with buildings of *pisé de terre* (rammed earth) and this tradition has continued under the guidance of the builder, Alistair Knox. There is a socially moral and conservationist attitude towards building in this community. The material is readily available, it can be used without machinery and it is amenable to expressive use by the individual. The craft basis of the work is taken seriously, and finely conceived and executed details in parts such as paving, timber joinery, and metal work make the finest of these dwellings galleries of ingenuity.

Among the most sensitive and artistic of the mud-brick dwellings is the house at Cottlesbridge by the architect Morrice Shaw. Shaw, who came from Poland as a child, is a whimsical and lyrical designer and his work is conditioned by his passion for music. He is more concerned with the spiritual and emotional needs of his clients than with the structural rationality or even the convenience of the designs. He often works on the building site as a labourer and the design evolves during the process of construction. Each house is original and his designs range from the steel and glass of the Scotland Island house to the mud-brick at Cottlesbridge. Yet his attitudes are consistent. The Cottlesbridge house offers both cave-like shelter and expansive openness. The interior enclosed area is of free-form curving sculptured walls. The continuity of the building and the surrounding bushland is established by the splaying timber roof that dips in parts towards ground level and the flowing wavelike patterns of the paved floor. Beer bottles set in the mud walls transmit a warm amber glow to the exterior at night. This mystical building was developed to harmonize with the personality of the client.

Shaw's own house in Glebe is a further outcome of his unique feelings about design. It is a renovated nineteenth-century single storey terrace house that Shaw has transformed by exploiting the deficiencies to create a refreshingly different domestic environment. Cracked plaster has been chipped away and fashioned to expose curving abstract patterns of the underlying handmade bricks. Rotten floor-boards removed from the living-room suggested a garden in the middle of the house, this in turn led to an overhead roof light that transmits rays of sunlight and a sprinkler system that gives light falling 'rain' within the room.

The Scotland Island house is a poetic construction with curving blue corrugated iron sweeping down a steep site towards the water and a silhouette that echoes the rolls of the waves. Banded blue and white plywood follows the curves of the roof, internally reinforcing the sense of motion in the building. The light steel frame is enclosed with sheets of glass. Shaw's houses are idiosyncratic. Their influence will come from his example that given imagina-

Right above: The Peter Glass house, Eltham, an adobe and timber design by Alistair Knox, 1954.

Right: A mud-brick house at Cottlesbridge by Morrice Shaw, built in 1968.

tion new and exciting solutions for domestic design can be explored.

The work of Richard Le Plastrier is unique in Australia. His sensitive, beautifully tooled houses are mostly to be found in the northern beaches area of Sydney. Le Plastrier works alone and, like Shaw, is often involved in the building operation itself. His meticulous attention to all aspects of architecture is evident throughout – showing most clearly in the relationships, joining, and finishes of materials. Le Plastrier's architecture is influenced by Japanese philosophy and building techniques, but while the spatial arrangement and gentle siting of the buildings relates to traditional Japanese work, with skilful adaptation of these concepts to Australian conditions, he has created an original and special architecture. His philosophical tendencies are somewhat esoteric but in other

Low-income infill housing by Philip Cox, part of the comprehensive Housing Commission rehabilitation of Woolloomooloo in the 1970s.

respects Le Plastrier is a pragmatist and the planning, particularly in his later houses, is clearly and functionally organized. The house at Bayview, 1975, is ordered along the circulation spine. Minimal service areas are linked along the spine on the approach side of the building, allowing the main rooms to face the splendid view. In the Bayview house concrete, timber and steel are used with an articulated order, and structure, function and mood are in harmony. In the exquisite Bilgola house, 1974, the house and walled garden of magnificent old cabbage-tree palms become one. For the most part enclosure is minimal but there are some small contained areas, allowing framed views. Contact with nature is paramount and the canvas vault of the main living area folds back to allow the sun and stars to provide the canopy overhead. Le Plastrier's houses show a subtle balance of the East and Australia, and of romanticism and rationality.

The low-technology position, as exemplified by mud-brick construction, received further emphasis with the growing awareness of the potential crisis in world energy supplies. In a climate like Australia's it is surprising that further advances have not been made towards environmental comfort with low energy consumption. Experimental buildings, such as the alternative-technology house of the Architecture Department of Sydney University, have probed for new answers using wind driven generators, solar collectors, heat absorption and storage beds, recyclable waste systems, and orientation for climatic benefits. In practice, little has affected the consumption of power in the average house. The exception is solar heating collectors that too often are visually destructive with their ungainly placement and lack of integration even in new houses. There is small consolation in their presence when the houses on which they are perched are usually climatically unsound in design.

Understanding the past

The second important development from the raised consciousness of the early 1970s was a reappraisal of the inner-city areas. This heralded a change in both public and private housing concepts. Conservationalists decried the destruction of the nineteenth century inner-city housing belts, and the house purchaser found the drive to the outer suburbs less appealing.

The tower block solution for urban public housing came under increasing criticism and the possibility of upgrading and renovating old cottages was considered. In Paddington in Sydney, and Carlton, in Melbourne, private enterprise had already demonstrated the suitability of old terrace houses for present lifestyles. Two major government supported schemes were initiated in Sydney in the mid-1970s. The Glebe Project is involved with the rehabilitation of workers' cottages for government-assisted housing. That of Woolloomooloo, also for low income groups, is more ambitious with its combination of new and old town houses and medium-sized multi-level units. Here new work has been sympathetically designed to relate to the scale and order of its neighbours. In particular the Forbes Street housing group by Philip Cox shows the possibilities of pleasant living environments with handsome urban architecture. Town housing as an alternative to suburban living had been reintroduced to Australian cities in the 1960s, but never at a scale comparable to the Woolloomooloo scheme.

Private town house developments have generally been of groups of eight to ten houses with varied relationships to each other and to the commonly shared access paths and roads. Peter Overman, who came to Australia from Holland in 1955, has designed several pleasing groups of town houses for South Perth. These schemes have a Mediterranean character that comes from their light ochre washed walls, narrow alleys, and the treatment of the gardens. Details such as striped entry canopies and pergolas add to the particular charm of these houses. Overman is unusually aware of the beauty of shadow patterns on plain wall surfaces and his houses are full of light and sunshine. These qualities appear in his individual dwellings, such as his own house of 1978 with its subtle relationships of horizontal and vertical space.

Many fine examples of town houses are found in the Sydney area, notably those by the firms of Ancher, Mortlock, Murray and Woolley, and Allen, Jack and Cottier. One of the main achievements of many of these schemes has been the way in which Sydney's sloping sites have been exploited to take advantage of the panoramic views and to bring sunshine to the buildings despite the higher density. This type of house, which has many of the advantages and few of the disadvantages of the detached dwelling, must become a more prevalent form of accommodation in the future.

The renewed interest in the Australian architectural heritage was not restricted to housing in the cities. Writers, such as Philip Cox, drew attention to the old buildings of Australia, and the time-proved means of design for the conditions of Australia came under reappraisal. He was one of the first to demonstrate an understanding of traditional principles. Cox, who had been in partnership with Ian McKay, established his own practice in 1967. His houses for the Sydney region have demonstrated his sensitivity and talent for restful and harmonious design. The first houses were primarily of timber and brick with an integral association between building and site. With his admiration of old architecture of country areas and his belief in the need for an architecture for Australia free from international plagiarism, it is not surprising that Cox instigated a new direction in Australian housing. The house for a horse stud at Kellyville, 1972, is clearly based on the traditional homestead plan of rooms surrounding a courtyard, and then in turn, encircled by verandah. The planning is appropriate for a modern busy household, while the building relates to its surrounding with the ease and compatability seen in early farmhouses.

The Kellyville house evolved from a search for an Australian identity in domestic design in the late 1970s. Unlike the Sydney School houses that sought a regional image from the direct response to the conditions of climate and site, this later attitude was more historical. The architects turned to traditional plans and materials, not merely for the sensible solutions they provided but also for their associative value. There was an effort to forge links with the unselfconscious tradition of Australia's vernacular buildings.

At Shoreham, in Victoria, architect Daryl Jackson built a complex of buildings for his family's horse stud in 1979. The old slab timber and corrugated iron house on the property suggested the use of the same materials for the new buildings. The house steps in several levels down the slope of a hill and the raking plane of the corrugated iron roof emphasizes the nature of the land form. The house is separated into two principal sections with the family living area at the top of the site set apart from the main bedroom unit by a covered courtyard. Construction is of intentional rough timber framing and slab cladding with a character akin to early rude dwellings.

In Queensland, after years of neglect, the old style timber raised house once more became appreciated for its rational planning and the beauty of its form and details. The Schubert house, designed in 1973 by Gabriel Poole, recaptures these qualities. The house stands on a fine raised

A house at Kellyville by Philip Cox, 1972. A traditional homestead plan type, complete with courtyard and verandah.

The Jackson house, Shoreham, 1979, a clearly modern house built of rough timber frame and slabs to capture the character of the past.

site in the pasture land of a small farm outside Yandina. Its traditional roof forms and verandahs impart a sense of belonging to its setting. The established character of the house is furthered by Poole's sensible and sensitive use of old patterns of lattice-work and verandah railings.

The country house generally has been neglected. As with the Queensland house, the vernacular farmhouse has been replaced by inappropriate urban bungalows. John Andrews' house at Eugowra, built in 1981, is directed towards this problem. The house is based on the traditional homestead, but in the design Andrews has retained the positive qualities and introduced quite radical changes in tune with today's technology and lifestyles. The house is of light steel frame construction of units prefabricated in Sydney. It is clad and roofed with easily transportable corrugated-iron sheeting. It aims to demonstrate the use of passive energy systems in difficult climatic conditions, as well as establishing an appropriate technology and form for rural settings. The vertical energy tower, the wide sheltering roof, and the visually striking water collection tanks make it a highly symbolic as well as practical solution. It is a formal design that projects a dramatic, regional image. Andrews is developing a prototype from

A country house at Mount Irvine, by Glenn Murcutt: a new expression of comfort and simplicity using the traditional materials of timber and iron.

this building for a rural house that can be ordered from catalogues in a manner similar to that available today for haysheds and barns.

Among the principal proponents of an architecture in sympathy with the Australian culture and environment is Glenn Murcutt. Murcutt's city and country houses are distinguished by their thoughtful planning, meticulous detailing and construction, and simplicity. They combine a rational order and structure, related to the early work of Mies van de Rohe, with an Australian romanticism. The farmhouse at Kempsey, built in 1975, echoes the theme of the barns and haysheds of Australian rural areas. Its twin gabled roofs of corrugated iron sit lightly on the timber frame. Murcutt uses iron sheeting in many of his buildings as he sees it as a logical and inexpensive material which can be freely shaped into pleasing profiles. He employs readily available low-cost standard units, such as glass louvres, in a highly imaginative manner. Perhaps his greatest achievement lies in the handling of the clear light

An interior view of Glenn Murcutt's Mount Irvine house, showing its simple geometrical forms.

and sun of Australia. The Murcutt houses are always alive with the patterns of light introduced through walls and roofs. At the same time the houses are environmentally protected by shading overhangs and well placed blinds and louvres. This aspect of his work is well illustrated by the pair of country houses at Mount Irvine. These small pavilion houses of timber and iron are beautifully related to their setting. They have an essential simplicity, rationality, and a subtle poetry of form. Murcutt's architecture has many features that can contribute to a more delightful and comfortable Australian house.

Concern for the character of residential streetscapes has brought about fine examples of infill design that provide lessons for the use of the pinched narrow sites of nineteenth-century areas. Cox's urban work is as assured as his rural and suburban houses. The David Moore town house, Sydney, 1978, is an infill building in a row of low terraced cottages. From the street the house is unobtrusive but underivative – plain surfaces of ochre bagged brickwork give an abstract sculptural expression of the building.

The site is well utilized with an internal open courtyard providing light to the spaces of this long narrow house.

The architect Don Gazzard's own house at Paddington is an impressive building of contemporary design related to an old setting. It is a confident concrete structure with the open-planning of its multi-level spaces opening at the rear to a grand portico that overlooks the garden. The handling of the materials and organization of the house is related to that of Seidler, with whom Gazzard worked before establishing his own practice. In its alternative day and night use of some interior spaces it is also indebted to traditional Japanese design. It is a fine demonstration of the possibility of creating an uncommon sense of spaciousness on a restricted site by the use of the open-plan and layered floor levels.

The Gazzard house stands on a double allotment but on narrower sites the courtyard is the more favoured solution. The Redlich house, 1979, by Graeme Gunn in Melbourne is a sophisticated urban house with a double level unit facing the street and a long narrow wing placed along the length of the block. The remainder of the site provides a generous rectangular courtyard space covered by a pergola of deciduous vines. The result is a delightful,

quiet and private house and garden in a busy inner-city location. His Scroggie house, 1978, has a related design but with the courtyard forming the central focus of the house. Set in a landscape of white daisies the house shimmers with light that passes through its transparent walls and reflects off its white walls and white polished floors.

A further variation on the courtyard plan can be seen in the Chappel house in Burnside, Adelaide, 1979, by architect John Chappel. Enclosed and open spaces are layered in alternating bands across the narrow allotment and each roofed area becomes a pavilion in a garden. The structure is simple with 'glulam' beams spanning the cross dimensions. The flat roofs and the beams of the pergolas give the house an intimate scale yet a feeling of generous space as one looks from one courtyard, through the glazed walls of the rooms, to the courtyard beyond.

Blending buildings and sites

Highly significant for the Melbourne area were the houses of Kevin Borland. Borland, with a distaste for architectural fashion, believes that architecture should generate directly from Australian condition. His first houses, notably the Rice house at Eltham of 1960, show evidence of the influence of Roy Grounds. The Rice house, with its sweeping curved roofs, is original and ingenious, but bears the mark of the formalism and structural expression of the earlier Melbourne School. His houses of the 1970s, however, are distinctly his own. Their rough timber, casual detailing, and spontaneous spirit clearly relate to the Australian bush vernacular buildings. But there is a consciousness and artistic flair in the houses that sets them apart from the fundamental quality of rude rural buildings. This shows most clearly in his use of the forty-five degree diagonal that appears in both plan and construction. Its use is not arbitrary — by breaking up a preconceived way of seeing things Borland has introduced a new and dynamic quality into his houses. The forty-five degree diagonal also has allowed him to wrap his houses around the fine features of the site, and to bring light into the interior in a most dramatic manner. These are loosely related, complex buildings with a distinct character that comes from Borland's personality and his response to the nature of the country.

The Paton house at Portsea, built in 1970, expressed the Borland spirit. It is an informal beach house on a flat site, containing a fine stand of ti-trees. Borland was able to give full reign to his love for the natural timbers that clad the building externally and internally. Spaces are stacked vertically with a second level, sleeping loft, and double height living area arranged casually under the steeply pitched roofs. More dramatic and provocative is the Marshall house, perched on a rough steep site with extensive ocean views. The disjointed forms, and what appear as impromptu structural solutions, give this house a make-shift character attune with a holiday atmosphere.

Related in mood, but more sophisticated in concept, is the Yencken house, Merimbula by Graeme Gunn. This is a pole house that sits like part of the forest on a site overlooking extensive views. The broken forms and the strong rhythm of the uprights of the pole construction make for an arresting, romantic building. But the Yencken house

Left: The Gazzard house, Paddington, 1975, a pristine steel and concrete structure. The interior character is reminiscent of Japanese design.

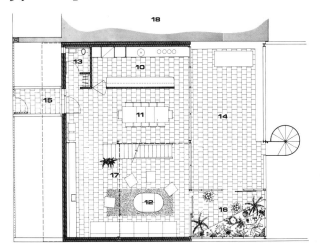

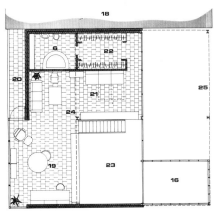

Top and centre: Floor plans of the Gazzard house, built on a double terrace-house allotment in Paddington.

Below: The Redlich house, Melbourne, by Graeme Gunn, 1979. A quiet courtyard house in a busy inner-city area.

has a sense of order and resolution not found in Borland's more spontaneous designs.

A similar attitude towards the blending of buildings with sites through fractured forms and natural materials appeared in the 1960s on the west coast of America. Most influential among these buildings was the group of condominiums called 'Sea Ranch' by architect Charles Moore. While the Australian work sprang from a genuine response to the native landscape and informal way of life, the American work demonstrated ways in which intriguing yet harmonious results could be produced. These lessons had most effect in Melbourne.

The Rattle house, Harkaway, by Max May, 1972, is a most successful and accomplished house that relates to this direction. It is built of a pine frame with a corrugated-iron roof and straw ceiling. Diagonal planking laid in opposing directions on either side of the walls stiffens the frame. Its outstanding characteristic is the sense of movement of the building and the constantly changing nature of the light that enters through unexpected openings. Bedrooms on the second level open on to timber decks that interrupt the roof planes. The angular plan and diagonal boarded siding, and the wing wall that moves into the building and rises over the fireplace, contribute to the air of vitality.

Towards the end of the 1970s notable differences occurred in this distinctively Melbourne work. Even Borland's houses became more reserved, but the changes can be seen most clearly in the buildings of two younger architects, Greg Burgess and Peter Crone. Their houses demonstrate their debt to Borland. Burgess' work shows the same casual irresolution. His Stutterd house at Eltham stands on a sloping timbered site, and the stepped forms, vertical timber siding and the rhythm of pergolas and posts relate the house to the natural features of its setting. The house projects a different character to each side and is more self-consciously formalized than the Borland houses. Contrasting shapes, such as the curved corner of the stair with its half-circle window, are used to generate visual interest. Here, internally, dynamism is replaced by restful spaces. The open plan persists and the principal living areas are separated by gradual changes of level down the slope.

Crone's houses are meticulous and refined. His beach and country houses, however, retain the diagonal lines and natural timbers of the previous Melbourne work. Planning is often based around a solid spine of service rooms, flanked by well lit, pleasant and interesting corridors. The main rooms are then freely and openly arranged around this core. Crone has a fine sense of form and space and the architecture is restful and resolved. Among his finest houses is the Porritt beach house at Mt Martha, 1979. Both the house and its site are tranquil. The silver grey of the weathered cedar siding, the low angled forms, and the large openings suggest a group of aged farm buildings. In plan it folds forwards and embraces a sheltered lawn area. The house, however, is a far cry from bush carpentry. It is a highly studied composition, meticulously designed. In case any doubt remains, Crone has made a strictly Formalist gesture by placing a painted grey-green cutout projecting wall at the focal point of the main elevation. This accomplished building marks the mature phase of a regional design development.

Signs of the future

Architecture is in a state of transition and the directions being explored for the future are many and varied in Australia and throughout the world.

The influence of new movements from abroad, particularly from the United States, are being seen in the southern states of Australia. The white geometric houses of Robert Nation and Michael Viney, in Hobart, are clearly based on the revival and further exploration in New York of Le Corbusier's early houses. The colour, large expanses of glass, the absence of projections, and the emphasis on tight sculptural form place this work in strong contrast to previous Australian domestic design.

Norman Day's work in Melbourne with its use of vibrant colour and its juxtapositions of forms and specific details relates to the daring Melbourne architecture of the immediate post-war period. It reacts in an aggressive manner to its surroundings by appearing to pay lip-service to their tone, but instead transforms derived elements and creates ironic contrasts. Examples are provided by the overblown elements and the clashing colours of the renovations of the Pizzley house, and the extension to the rear of the Rozens' house which is in the form of an enlarged bay window echoing those at the front.

A further direction can be seen in the Abrahams house, Brighton, by Daryl Jackson. The house stands on the beach front facing west. It is constructed from silver timbers of weathered cedar that relate it to old boat buildings along the waterfront. Through the use of devices such as timber screens to protect the interior from sun, salt and wind, Jackson has created a complex layering of the skin of the building. The overall form of the house is compact and ordered – this emphasizes the broken pattern of the wall planes. With its transparency, multi-layered enclosure and constantly changing patterns of light and shadow, the Abrahams house introduces a new spatial dimension into Australian domestic architecture.

Equally revolutionary is the large house at Toorak, by Max May, 1980. This splendidly romantic house of apricot bagged masonry has no precedent in Australian domestic design. The house is of two levels with the main rooms a double storey height of 6 metres. Despite this, interior spaces are not overwhelming as there is a careful balance of floor area and height. A courtyard is enclosed on three sides and has a raised tennis-court to the east. The remarkable qualities of the house are its transparency, the quality of light, and the balance of the solids and voids. The architecture is that of an enclosing wall that wraps around the glass pavilion of the house. The wall passes across the front of the site as a visual barrier, becomes the wall of the building itself and then crumbles down into a pool near to where it commenced. The house is saved from aggrandizement by the whimsey and humour shared by architect and client. Corinthian columns in the front garden mark out a private space, and plants suggesting age grow over a rusticated brick room, which is a room within a room within the enclosing wall. There is a fine

Frame and masonry. Right above: The Lachlan house, Lorne, by Robin Blume. Right: The Abrahams house, Brighton, by Daryl Jackson, 1977.

Below and right: The Hackford house, Traralgon, by Gregory Burgess, 1982. Instead of building a wide-verandahed bungalow-type of country house, Burgess created a complicated sculptural structure of steel and timber around a staircase core. The house is in two parts – one an entry and garage and the other the house proper – linked by a timber bridge which crosses a small pool and watercourse. The large site has been carefully landscaped; sundecks overlook the garden and lake, and a look-out tower caps the design. In its complexity and geometry this house is comparable with Harold Desbrowe Annear's historic house at Eaglemont, 1902.

Legend

1 Porte cochere
2 Water tanks
3 Walled garden
4 Entry
5 Vestibule
6 Guest room
7 Family
8 Kitchen
9 Sitting room
10 Dining
11 Fernery

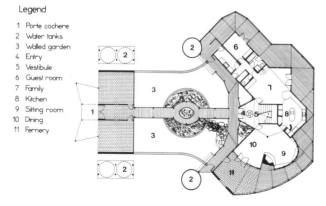

balance between splendour and slapstick in this striking house, the grand dimensions of which have not inhibited its use for casual family living.

These Melbourne works are too recent to be able to predict their effect on the general housing market. In the early 1980s a geometric order appeared again in domestic design by Sydney architects. The recent house by Harry Seidler at Castle Cove, and the Murphy house at Rockhampton, Queensland, by Don Gazzard are both based

Murcutt houses – indicates a break from the Picturesque casual design that was dominant in the preceding decades.

Present and future problems

Australia has one of the highest standards of domestic design in the world, but there are unresolved problems. Despite the attention of many concerned and dedicated people, housing for the Aboriginal groups has been unsuccessful. Generally house design for all living in the

on the geometry of the arc. In the house by Seidler the arc opens up the house to an 180 degree view. In contrast, in the Murphy house, the arcs fold around to enclose a courtyard which is the pivot of the building. The house by Gazzard is designed for tropical conditions. A colonnade with sheltering lattices and screens surrounds the building. Breezes are induced into the house, across the pond in the courtyard, and released through high lights on the perimeter of the opposing segment. The integral composition embraces the entry, garage, pool house and connecting walkway. Such formal balance in design is uncommon in Australian domestic architecture. The self-conscious formalism of the southern cities and the classicism from Sydney – including the Andrews and

harsh conditions of the north and inland of the continent lacks commonsense and initiative. But the major cause for dissatisfaction lies with developer housing for the middle- and lower-income groups in the suburbs. Over the last thirty years the Australian house has been liberated from the limitations of the immediate post-war bungalow. It has become more attuned to Australian conditions and more sympathetic to Australian lifestyles. But all around us, where financial gain is the only motive, we still find the erection of new housing that exhibits few of the advances that have occurred. Land is poorly subdivided, trees are destroyed and houses are badly planned and orientated with little regard for comfort or amenity. There can be no excuse. We know better.

IN ANCIENT GREECE the Delphic oracle predicted future events. Today, without the oracular powers of the priestess, we can only extrapolate from statistics, assuming that current trends will continue and that no earth-shattering discoveries will intervene to modify the forecast. The predictions that emerge are frightening. At the present rate of increase (now exceeding 2 per cent) there will be a doubling of the present world population by the year 2010[1]; land and energy, so long taken for granted, will be in critically short supply.

For 10,000 years human beings have built and occupied permanent dwellings exploiting the earth's food and material resources; now we are warned that these resources will be exhausted within the next century. Consequently, a discussion on housing of the future must, of necessity, begin with a consideration of these problems.

Even if we believe that technological developments can save us, the least we can do is to give support to those schemes that decentralize all facets of society. This would reduce the distances to places of work, increase planning densities, encourage multiple land use, and advance the design of buildings that permit urbanized populations to live around centres of work and learning. As well, we can support the research and development of schemes that

servation can entirely change their most pessimistic conclusions.[3] In the past no constraints have been imposed upon the designer effectively to use the heat and mechanical waste or 'left-over' energy, which has been lost to our atmosphere and drainage systems, continuously polluting air, land and water. Designers must be involved in socially responsible decisions for all future buildings. State and federal government encouragement could stimulate private experiments by injecting far more funds than are allocated now into energy conservation research. To date the conservation of existing energy resources has been the Cinderella of energy alternatives.

A number of United States owner-occupier companies have invested in buildings which minimize long-term costs by providing for low energy consumption, but developers still prefer the past practice of quick yield and return. This attitude must be rethought by the owner-financier and the building consultant team, so that both can survive in a future when new economic and social conditions will prevail.

There are signs of a new morality and aesthetic being expressed by a more educated public than existed a decade ago. Some of them now judge whether buildings are appropriate for future conditions. New standards en-

FUTURE DIRECTIONS 7

provide urban centres of moderate population numbers that are virtually self-contained and autonomous.

Energy alternatives

Reliable forecasts of an impending dearth of energy now make it imperative to advance new options that will satisfy the future needs of society. We need to concentrate upon the development of innovative technologies, such as small-scale power sources from the sun, wind and water, the conversion of solar energy directly into electrical or motive power, and the utilization of energy from photosynthesis and plant alcohol. Vast sums of money and decades are needed for the research and development of these alternative energy sources. In the meantime, sensationalist speculations and 'prophesies of doom' aside, architects and engineers must come to grips with the challenge of extending present resources while the technologies for energy alternatives are developed.[2] It is daunting to consider vast areas of land surface covered with solar collectors, and mountains and ridges spattered with giant windmills. This presents an aspect of landscape pollution, and makes it clear that research should concentrate upon energy sources that are non-polluting in both the physical and visual senses.

It is agreed by most economists that recycling and con-

A mud-brick house sited snugly in a bush setting at Mount Riverview, New South Wales, designed by owner-builder Roderick Yates.

quire: does a building use materials wastefully? How much energy will it consume to heat and cool? Will it add to pollution?[4] Ultimately, all architects must face these questions. The Royal Institute of British Architects has reported that architects are responsible for buildings that use 70 per cent of all energy produced in the United Kingdom.[5] If professionals do not adjust their philosophies to these new conditions, they will deserve the criticism and condemnation that will follow.

Using the land

The pressures upon land use are another problem which has to be faced. Development is inundating the land surface, and life-giving soil is being lost beneath the hard crust of buildings, concrete and bitumen. Open space for vegetation and recreation is fast disappearing, and is being replaced by sterilized, unusable left-over land. As residual natural areas continue to be threatened, we should remember that each year 150 square metres of leaf surface per person – equivalent to some 30 to 40 square metres of trees, shrubs, plants and grass – are needed to replace the carbon dioxide breathed out by one family of three people. We depend upon this air-cleansing property of vegetation. For example, the air quality along roads with treed verges has been found to be 300 to 400 per cent purer compared to treeless roads in the same district.[6] Yet we forget that vegetation disappears when buildings are erected and ground surface is paved over.

A desirable minimum of one part of polluted air to 3,000

parts of relatively pure air increases to one to 1,000 along many highways and requires a kilometre-wide green-belt each side of the expressway to provide the necessary oxygenation and gaseous dilution to counteract the effect of its vehicles.[7] The same principle applies to the use of trees around industrial zones. This is understandable, for not only do shelter belts of trees modify wind effects, but the particles of pollution carried by the wind 'drop out' of the airstream as a fall in air-pressure occurs within the belt. Not only do the trees function as filters of particles; they are also gas-exchangers. For example in a very large tree, the total intercellular leaf-surface area available for converting noxious gases into oxygen is equivalent to the combined areas of 160 large suburban blocks of land.

As hard surfaces replace natural vegetation the range of scenarios for the future housing of populations on the coast of Australia is wide. At one extreme (already found in the United States of America) there is the potential of forming a megalopolis out of the metropolis of a region such as that stretching between Newcastle-Sydney-Wollongong – a city spread flat.[8] At the other extreme there are compact 'megastructure' cities such as those designed by Paolo Soleri. From his Macrosanti with 531 persons per hectare, to his Arcvillage or Arcoindian cliff-dwelling, with 1,754 persons per hectare, these are cities condensed into a single envelope of 'high-technology' materials.[9]

Soleri's philosophical content for his 'arcology' (ecology plus architecture) is rambling and interesting.[10] These revolutionary prototypes of proposed future cities, most of which have been designed as part of canyons, cliffs and mountains, dominate their natural environments – a process that began some 10,000 years ago. It is appalling to stand on the rim of a desert canyon in Arizona and contemplate the final scale of Soleri's partially-constructed Arcosanti. This will be a city with vast glass flanks spilling down the scarps to the valley floor: a technological assault upon a fragile desert environment. This intensive investment of resources and technology is a good example of the rift that exists between the abstract thought and metaphysics of Soleri and the buildings that result.

Another alternative has been presented: that of far-flung networks of small autonomous towns and villages existing at an energy-deprived near-medieval level of living which some experts forecast to be our future housing. And between the extremes of megalopolis and megastructure there is the spectre of the traditional blocks of alienated populations separated by neutralized open space – belonging to a 'Modernism' of the past – which are still occupying the planning schemes of traditionalist statutory authorities and planners of the present.

The design problem

It is difficult to find architecture that honestly interprets human requirements without recourse to displays of architectural vanity. A new so-called 'Post-Modern' architecture attempts to extend 'the language of architecture in many different ways into the vernacular, towards tradition and the commercial slang of the street'.[11] Modernism,

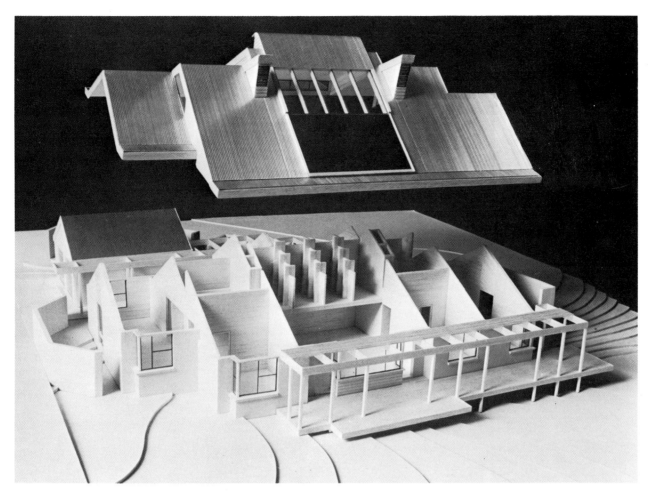

A model of the 'Integrated House' prototype developed at the University of New South Wales by Johnson, Judd and Lesueur. The design is a zoned arrangement of rooms around a central core which includes the 'communal' family areas. Above the kitchen part of the core there is a 'thermal attic' of vertical brick fins which store heat entering through the north-facing roof light.

with its purist connotations and rationalist substitutes for traditional social patterns, influences and affects the behaviour of the occupants of its buildings by imposing upon its users the concepts of designers who consider they know what the public needs because they have been 'trained to know'. Fortunately there is an increasing trend away from this arrogance towards the use of sociologist-consultants, with surveys being undertaken to find out what people need and how they want to use the buildings they are given. This may be seen in the work of several Australian architects and, for example, in the research of Paul-Alan Johnson, Dr Bruce Judd and Geoffrey Lesueur, whose experimental 'Integrated House' will be built at the University of New South Wales. This research project will explore flexibility in interior design to accommodate changing patterns in leisure and education that are linked to changing technology and domestic patterns.[12]

In fact, Modernism has created adverse reactions to its clinical, esoteric aesthetic. When people say 'that house looks like a service station' or 'that school looks like a factory', these are justifiable and potent criticisms. If such similes are inappropriate to the architect's concepts, this is just too bad. The people have made their judgement and the designer has been found wanting.

Future prospects for house design

Houses should be designed for the needs and wants of both society and the individual and yet produce a result that fulfils professional aesthetic criteria. Eventually, the principal criteria for assessing the social responsibility of house designs will be whether such designs minimize the use of resources as well as conservatively utilizing primary, secondary and tertiary energy in the production of the building materials and in the final construction process. Adobe, *pisé*, stabilized earth-wall and other similar wall construction methods have these attributes, and are justifiably becoming popular. This is because, at last, we are beginning to feel the economic pressures imposed by our 'high-technology' building industry.

If enough people create a demand for simple, low-cost goods, industry would adapt; it is really up to all of us to be conservative and simple in our use of resources, and in our needs and wants.[13] The main trends in residential architecture are listed. All of these tend ideally towards the completely autonomous house which, however, is still beyond us because of the cost of initial installation and maintenance. Yet this ideal should be our goal.

These alternatives could be considered as indicators of future trends in conservation, and would be improved by the addition of energy-effective design principles in both architecture and landscape architecture. It is possible to combine some of these alternatives to produce results that are more effective than each in isolation. (The very 'high-tech' alternatives of outer-space and underwater housing have not been included because of the disproportionate amount of resources involved in their implementation.)

The options of conservation housing

Utilization of natural resources

Future research and development

Solar design and construction

High initial cost and, generally, still uses solar-collector 'high-technology' (low entropy) with high energy demands on natural resources. Some materials used deteriorate quickly. Solar design may be *passive* (collecting and storing thermal energy without the introduction of significant amounts of energy external to the system) or *active* (requiring extra energy from outside – whether from natural or artificial energy systems). Hybrid systems (combining both active and passive principles) are often used, together with solar screen devices.[14]

Soil and vegetation are 'lost' over full building area. Conserves energy in heating and sometimes in cooling.

Further research is needed into:
a low technology materials (high entropy);
b conversion of solar energy directly to electrical/mechanical energy;
c solar air-conditioning;
d high thermal mass materials at low cost.

Houses at Bonnyrigg Solar Village, designed in 1981 for the Housing Commission of New South Wales by Solarch to publicize and test passive solar design principles.

Greenhouse design and construction

Often used as an adjunct to solar and other types of housing. This is a cold-climate concept for heating (as well as growing exotic vegetation), and is sometimes misused in temperate and hot climates. Often built of glass and aluminium materials that are high in energy to produce. Soil and vegetation are usually 'lost' over full building area.

Careful control of incoming solar radiation and solar heat gain is essential. Very limited future use in Australia.

Earth-wall design and construction

Many attractive examples exist in adobe and *pisé*. Low materials cost; high labour input that may be offset by owner-builder labour being used. Problems of night heat build-up and shading of sun-exposed high thermal mass walls require careful study (sleeping quarters can be timber-framed for speedy cooling at night). Soil and vegetation are 'lost' over full building area.

Present uses indicate future limitations. Compressive strength of mud brick or stabilized earth is low; however this is increased with cement-stabilizing. This form of building provides the greatest potential for the home owner to design and build, without the degree of input from professional consultants required by the other forms.

Utilization of natural resources	Future research and development

Pole-house design and construction

Permits economic use of steeply sloping sites and uses a replaceable resource, timber. Vulnerable to bushfire. Much soil and vegetation retained.

Present method of termite control indicates possible limitations (there is doubt about certain health safety aspects of treated timber poles if licked or burnt).

Underground housing 'Geotecture' design and construction

Conserves thermal energy and land surface. Permits increases in total populations without a corresponding increase in population density or loss of open-space and visual amenity. Can be designed to be bushfire-proof. Although the ecosystem is changed, it has less long-term impact than other types because soil and vegetation is fully retained over almost the complete building area.

Lithotecture of the 1840s. Miners' dugouts in the banks of a dried-up creek bed at Burra, South Australia.

Earth-covered housing 'terratecture'
Currently uses 'high-technology', although materials now exist that may make it possible to integrate this with earth-wall construction. Timber construction, often used in the United States, is not recommended in Australia.

Research into low technology methods is needed, such as frictional-fill, stabilized mudbrick with increased compressive strength.

Rock-enclosed housing 'lithotecture'
Use is limited to the incidence of appropriate geological formations (self-supporting rock and soil).

Potential for 'vertical sites' – the cliff-dwellings of tomorrow.

Integrated systems

Design and construction emphasize the utilization of waste heat, energy sources available on-site (for example sun and wind), and waste water to be utilized. Generally integrated systems use only one energy source. 'High-technology': therefore demands upon natural resources are high.

Present trends are encouraging; these are based upon the integration of one energy source, with another as 'back-up'. They depend upon the type of energy storage used that is compatible with the output required, for example storage by chemical means (batteries, hydrogen production), mechanical means (flywheels), biological means (energy extraction from methane digester, algae production), and thermal mass (water, rock, concrete, earth).

Trends towards the completely autonomous house are clearly discernible. This ideal, however, requires a high level of resources because of its extensive technological content, and it is well outside the budget of most home owners. The first building constructed in Australia that used various alternative technologies to form an integrated system was the house erected in 1982 for M. and J. Bos at Pearcedale, Victoria, by Cocks and Carmichael, architects – its cost assisted by various public authorities and government grants.[15] It was designed to obtain all its energy requirements from renewable resources.

In all conservation housing the site must be planned to take advantage of its natural resources including climate and vegetation. Space should be used economically through good design and materials should be used that insulate, give high thermal mass storage, allow accelerated heat loss to occur where necessary, and recycle heat for

A passive-active solar house at Forest Range, near Adelaide, designed by Leon Byass Architects. This view shows the 'sunspace' with its 'skylids', which give the house good summer comfort conditions.

re-use such as in heat-exchangers for cooling. Thermal energy should be conserved so that solar heat is gained for winter conditions, and heat gain is prevented during hot weather by sun-control devices and landscaping.

Each of the conservation architecture technologies listed is available now, although none has yet become widely accepted. They would all, however, provide society with a means of bridging the fifteen- to fifty-year gap between the perfection of alternative energy sources and the near-exhaustion of non-renewable energy forecast.

Of these options for alternative building, underground or earth-covered housing can provide the most direct form of passive utilization of solar energy, and also can be adapted to the use of solar collectors, greenhouse technology, and possibly eventually to low technology construction. It will most effectively enable Australian communities to live in natural surroundings without the excessive impacts and conflicts of the past – including

bushfire – and must be a major direction of Australian housing in the next century.

Living underground

Underground or earth-covered housing frees the soil surface for the growth of vegetation and, in underdeveloped areas where flat land is scarce, for the raising of food crops. Surface land can be recycled back to nature, enclosing the building in a material having a high thermal mass, and hence the capacity to store and save thermal energy. The savings involved have been established as ranging from 40 to 90 per cent in the short term. Long-term life cycle and running costs are as yet unproven, but are estimated as being approximately 50 per cent less than a conventional above-ground house on the same site.

This is a conservation-based method of building, one that conserves land-surface, thermal energy and maintenance to exterior finishes. It may also have an application to urban settlements; for as fuel for private vehicles becomes more expensive, the aggregation of people around centres of work and learning – this has already begun – and the fragmentation of workplaces by decentralization will increase. Because of these population density shifts, the availability of land around urban centres is already becoming increasingly scarce. Any planning option – such as the one suggested here – permitting the dual, or multiple use of land, could help to ease some of the attendant social and economic pressures. By leaving the ground surface available for gardens or recreation the protection of natural environments, such as National Parks, and the use of land for agriculture and permaculture becomes possible.[16] To better understand this scenario of the coming century, it is useful to look into the past use that Australians have made of the underground space.

Caves and rock shelters

Whereas in Europe the earliest known cave occupation is dated approximately 600,000 years ago, Aboriginal Australians are said generally to have avoided the use of underground space;[17] there are notable exceptions to this such as the surprising evidence of the use of a deep cave by Aborigines at Koonalda in South Australia, where a collapsed doline cavern was once used to mine flint nodules, and probably to conduct some form of religious ceremony, some 16,000 years ago.[18] Authorities vary on whether Aborigines used underground space in prehistoric times, and the available evidence is often contradictory. However, it appears that although some tribes may have avoided the use of deep caverns, most Pleistocene sites comprised either caves or rock shelters[19] while cave occupation at Devil's Lair, Western Australia, dates back to between 25,400 to 23,800 years ago. An example of a shallow cave is located at Buchan, Victoria where, although nearby deep limestone caverns showed no occupation evidence, a small but impressive single-chambered cave exists (known as East Buchan II), with an occupation date of 2,300 years ago.

Right: Two views of Groundhous, an earth-covered house at Yungaburra. The architect-owner-builder was Robert Mair.

A pole-frame residence at Clontarf utilizes a renewable resource—timber poles, impregnated with preservative to protect the material from insect and fungus attack. The architect-owner is P. Y. Koo.

A passive-solar earth-covered house in the Hunter Valley conserves both thermal energy and land surface. Architects, ECA Space Design Pty Ltd.

Dugout dwellings

With European occupation of the arid region that began in 1829 (the first explorers entering from the comparatively newly settled areas of New South Wales), the use of underground space in Australia changed from the occupation of naturally occurring rock cavities to the underground architecture of Burra and Coober Pedy, in South Australia, and of White Cliffs, in New South Wales.

By the early 1860s most of the arid region had been explored while the pastoral and mining potential of the inland was also being realized. From the port of Adelaide, South Australia, streams of immigrants disembarked in the 1840s. They were mainly Austrian and Welsh smelters, and Cornish miners journeying to a newly opened copper mine located in the township of Burra Burra, situated 156 kilometres north-east of Adelaide.[20] While others built conventional houses, only the Cornishmen excavated and constructed dugouts within the banks of the creek. Coming from a homeland where underground housing had been in existence for over four millennia, and with centuries of mining tradition behind them, the Cornishmen created 'dugouts' of self-supporting earth with deep soil cover on top; these were cool in the summer heat and warm in the chilling nights of winter.

Two partially restored, but derelict, dugouts are all that still exist of this community of underground dwellings that once accommodated 1,500 miners and their families – probably the earliest occupied lithotecture in Australia. In 1851, a disastrous flood occurred, and the miners were forced to leave their dugouts. When a dam was constructed across the creek to prevent further flooding, the trickle of water left in the creek-bed became the source of a disastrous typhoid epidemic. Finally, the mine management refused to employ those miners who persisted in living in their dugout homes, and it is recorded that, as a consequence, they unwillingly yielded to management demands and moved into still extant, sturdy row-houses.[21] Later this tradition of underground housing was to become a distinctive Australian mining-town style of dwelling that may be seen in White Cliffs, New South Wales and Coober Pedy, South Australia.

It is difficult to imagine the small settlement of present-day White Cliffs, with its floating population of approximately ninety-five, housing 3,000 people as it did in 1902. At that time, enormous quantities of white seam-opal were being won, and in the ensuing development of the town six hotels were built, together with a miners' club and two newspaper printing offices. After its reserves became depleted, the town never recovered from a slump in the German-controlled opal-market that occurred during World War I.[22]

Today there is only one hotel, a general store, post office, hospital and a small school. Water no longer has to be carted 96 kilometres from the Darling River by bullock teams, as there is now a large government bore on the outskirts of the town. Opal is extracted using hand-held tools because mechanized tunnelling machines are not permitted. The dugouts in which most of the residents live provide comfortable interior conditions while outside temperatures range from well above 45 degrees celsius to freezing.[23] To shelter from the harsh climate, as well as from winds that blow almost constantly, the early miners first occupied the portals of their mines. The construction of dugouts solely as dwellings was a later development that continues to the present day.

Following the settlement of White Cliffs, opal was discovered at Lightning Ridge, New South Wales and in the Stuart Ranges of South Australia; however in the former case the geology was unsuitable for dugout dwellings. Upon discovering the area where opal was later found in 1915, John McDouall Stuart had recorded in 1858: 'it looks as though the land has dropped almost straight down about 100 feet along a line running N.N.W. and S.S.E. for many miles'. He was describing the 'breakaway' country, a landscape that forms the background to present-day Coober Pedy, 943 kilometres north-west of

Lithotecture at Coober Pedy. Crocodile Harry's 'dugout', formerly an opal mine.

Adelaide. The name of the town was derived from the Aboriginal Araba tribal words *kupa piti* meaning 'boy's waterhole', and not 'white man in a hole' or 'white fellow burrow', as is often mistakenly recorded.[24]

Stuart's words described the low caprock tableland with softer underlying beds eroded away by flash flooding where characteristic 'J' profile gulleys remained. It was into these plateau-scarps that the first dugouts were excavated once the opal fields were developed by the 'gougers' as they were called, when returned servicemen from World War I poured into Coober Pedy in 1919.

Although initially the dugout was part of the mine it served, eventually it became a dwelling in its own right with interesting, often sculptural, interior spatial effects. Half the Coober Pedy community of 1903 persons[25] (with a floating population that can more than double this size) resides in some form of underground dwellings, sharing a style of housing that has common roots with the rock-cut dwellings of the tens of millions who have adopted this underground lifestyle throughout the world

Left: Lithotecture in Central Cappadocia, Turkey. For two millennia the volcanic tuffaceous rock of Goreme has been used for underground towns and villages.

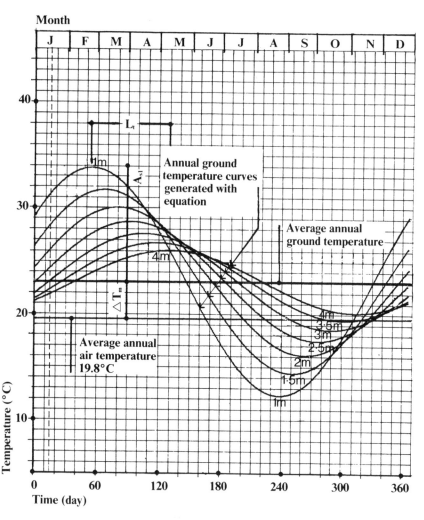

in China, Tunisia, Turkey, and many other countries.[26]

The earth-covered dwelling is a form of housing that presents a totally different approach to problems associated with designing for arid region habitats, one that is the antithesis of the often unsuitable but very common conventional type of house that was designed for temperate climates and modified in piecemeal attempts to provide tolerable conditions of comfort.

Advantages of earth-covered buildings

Given the same plan and standard of finish, an earth-covered house will cost about the same to build as an architect-designed, custom-built, passive-solar, double-brick and terracotta tile above-ground house on the same site.[27] The question of its appropriateness for mass housing in Australia has also been investigated, and at least one urban project of earth-covered houses has proved to be cheaper that its above-ground equivalent. Designed by ECAspace Design Pty Ltd, the project contains twenty-seven pensioner units in quiet garden surroundings, backing on to an expressway.

Over a period of fifty years, the earth-covered house will cost almost half the amount of its above-ground counterpart on the same site because of the following factors:

Thermal comfort conditions. Although not a particularly good insulator, earth in sufficient depth has a significant insulation effect. Heat also takes a considerable – although variable – time to travel through the soil. By covering a building with a depth of earth appropriate to the climatic conditions of its site, and incorporating passive-solar principles, it is possible to make substantial savings on heating and cooling costs (up to 80 per cent). This is because the temperature within remains almost constantly stable, producing comfortable internal conditions in both summer and winter – due to the thermal inertia effect of the earth, and phase-lag in the annual ground temperature wave, also known as 'season lag' when the delay equals one season. This means that by integrating a building with its site, the enveloping earth acts as a massive accumulator of thermal energy, gradually storing heat in the summer months to warm the building in winter when it is needed. The reverse happens in summer when the stored winter-cold serves to cool the interior of the building. Provided all the major sources of heat concentration, such as stove and bath, are exhausted directly to atmosphere, the correctly-designed, properly managed earth-covered dwelling should provide the equivalent to air-conditioned levels of comfort, while requiring little energy for heating and cooling. This effect

Above: Lithotecture in Northern Shaanxi, China. Forty million people live in these 'dragon-caves', houses cut in the rock.

Graph showing that ground temperatures are more stable below the surface. The curves plot readings at depths of from 1 to 4 metres. A_{sl} is the amplitude of the curve at 1 metre below the ground surface. L_t is the time-lag, in days, associated with the phase shift in the ground temperature wave as heat transfers from 1-metre depth to 4-metres depth. ΔT_m is a temperature differential (in Kelvin) that varies with the geographic location of sites.

Two views of a model of an Australian design for twenty-seven home units beneath an urban garden park. Architects, ECA Space Design Pty Ltd.

Earth-covered building is feasible even at the scale of medium-density residential development. City slum land can become garden apartments, with roof 'commons' for recreation.

is a function of depth below ground surface, vegetation cover, and the thermal characteristics of the soil.

Consider an earth-covered house sited in a blocky, shale or clay soil with a roof-cover of 1.5 metres and a floor level 3.9 metres below the ground surface. A graph predicting ground temperatures throughout the year can be used in the thermal design of such a house. In the case cited, the summer air maximum of early December takes approximately sixty-five days to reach the roof (1.5 metres below) and 100 days to reach the soil at floor level. For this house, the seasonal range in temperatures in the earth around floor level is a maximum of 5 degrees celsius, while the seasonal difference in the outside air temperature is 42 degrees celsius.

Energy efficiency. When properly designed, earth-covered structures are the most efficient of all passive-solar, energy-effective, building types. Such buildings, when correctly orientated and constructed, permit sunshine to enter the interior during winter when solar heat-gain is desired, but exclude it during summer. As all habitable rooms have windows, and because they are designed using correct solar and daylighting principles, many of these buildings provide better conditions of natural light and ventilation than are found in above-ground buildings. Atria, or internal courtyards, are often used for this purpose.

Minimal maintenance requirements. Most of the outside of an earth-covered building is protected from the damaging effects of ultra-violet radiation from the sun, environmental pollution, and weather conditions. In addition to this, external building components such as gutters, downpipes and most external finishes are eliminated; hence, the time and costs involved in maintenance are negligible. Properly designed roof-gardens complete this low maintenance aspect of earth-covered structures.

Mass production adaptability. The design of many housing developments is visually monotonous, reflecting similarities of interior layouts. Yet in earth-covered housing, interior planning can afford to be repetitive, thereby making it possible to suppress costs. The cost of a single dwelling in a mass housing project is significantly cheaper with this type of house than its above-ground equivalent. The problem of the sameness of exterior appearances of dwellings would be overcome by a scheme to unify all the houses into attractive street landscaping.

Other advantages

Earth-covered buildings not only provide comfortable interior conditions because of the almost stable year-round temperatures, but other factors were also commented upon by residents.

An improvement in health was found because most of the pathways by which dust enters a building are eliminated and obvious benefits accrue from the reduction of interior maintenance and dust-related illnesses that affect the health of occupants. Stress related to high noise levels is also minimized.

Noise is reduced. The earth-covering to an 'underground' building, and the general mass of the structure, effectively reduces airborne noise, making such buildings extremely suitable for developments in industrial areas, near main roads, under aircraft flight paths, and anywhere where noise levels, which would normally make occupancy difficult, exist. The advantages for inner city projects with any of these problems are self-evident.

As the roof and walls are not exposed, earth-covered structures provide increased security against vandalism as well as from external threats such as storms, cyclones, lightning strike and bushfires.

By the incorporation of specially-designed shutters, it is possible to design buildings that are virtually bushfire-proof. The addition of such shutters over the glazed areas will also enhance security.

All occupants of both terratecture and lithotecture who were interviewed stated that they had an increased sense of security associated with physical safety. Also many people remarked upon an intangible sense of comfort they felt because they were within a building that was enclosed by the earth. Earth-covered buildings can be sited almost anywhere that above-ground structures can be located, from hills to flat terrain. It is not necessary to have either a large block of land or a rural setting.

Although the short-term environmental impact of an earth-covered structure is possibly greater than the above-ground house, the long-term impact is far less. This is significant especially in areas of natural beauty, historical importance, and in the regeneration of areas despoiled by mining operations, industry or freeways. Earth-covered buildings also help restore some of the natural ground-water seepage patterns, by reducing a sheet runoff during storms and decreasing the load on stormwater drainage channels and the damage caused by erosion.

Earth-covered buildings enable greater land use than any other form of building. In inner-city development, earth-covering should make possible the reduction of the minimum lot size or an increase in the permissible plot ratio and the site-coverage ratio.

The earth-covered building is the most efficient passive-solar building form. In all Australian climates – from the snow country, through temperate regions to the deserts – the correctly designed passive-solar earth-covered building will produce a more thermal energy-efficient result than any other type.[28] With snow, cold and heat, this becomes a question of if and where to use insulation, and what depth of earth-cover is required. In temperate climates, solar design works with most buildings, but the earth-covered building is chosen because it preserves the scenic quality of a site. In terrain where bedrock outcrops or is near the surface, the bermed type of building provides a good solution. All slopes can be catered for with the possible exception of steep south slopes (facing away from the sun). Yet with such an aspect and on that type of site any passive solar building would present difficulties and the bermed type of building will improve on this.

Disadvantages of earth cover

The advantages of earth-covered buildings outweigh problems such as:

Rainwater Collection. Each site has to be studied for its rainwater collection potential and for the possibility of using alternatives like bore water or dams. Rainwater for sites not connected to a town supply is normally collected from roofs. Often this technique can be utilized for earth-covered projects if there are outbuildings, garages or carports. Another method is to collect runoff from paved areas and purify it, or to use the motorized retractable awnings now on the market.

Future extensions. Specific allowances should be made for additions during the planning and construction stages, as unplanned alterations or additions are more difficult (although not impossible) than they are in above-ground housing.

Adverse psychological reaction. Some people in the community reject the concept of earth-covered living, often before understanding what the words mean – however, such attitudes exist among very few.

Solid-borne noise transmission. Solid-borne noise, as opposed to airborne noise, can present a potential problem, although it is possible to damp such noise with commercially-available materials.

Constructing for Australian conditions

It is important that an appropriate depth of soil roof cover is used for each site under consideration, otherwise uncomfortable interior conditions could easily eventuate. Recent research has shown that there is only one small area on the whole North American continent with a climate similar to any in Australia – in California. In Australia, the ground climate varies substantially in the first 2 metres of depth, and the amplitude of the ground temperature wave also varies considerably with different soil types and vegetation cover. Not only is the Australian climate unique, but also Australian vegetation is quite different from that of Europe and the Americas in its effect upon soil temperature. Consequently, a house built using inappropriate northern hemisphere information to establish the depth of earth-cover could perform worse than an uninsulated, above-ground building on the same site. Inappropriate use of northern-hemisphere design techniques has been made in several earth-covered and earth-bermed projects in Australia, providing disappointing thermal results. The depth of earth-cover should be calculated for individual home-sites, using specific Australian information.

Many United States construction and detailing aspects are quite different from those required in Australia where soils do not freeze. In Australia, government and commercial standards vary from those existing in the United States of America, and local conditions create unique situations that do not have parallels there – Australia's

Right above: Lithotecture at White Cliffs, New South Wales. A rock-enclosed house designed and built by Lindsay White. A swimming-pool terrace, looking towards the dugout entrance.

Right: Inside the exhibition area of 'Cosanti', a residential complex in Arizona designed by Paolo Soleri in the 1950s. The gentle principles of 'arcology' expressed here were later extended, in the revolutionary city of 'Arcosanti'.

fungus and termite problems, for example, virtually eliminate the use of timber in earth-covered building construction. Also, many materials used in the United States are either not available or applicable in Australia.

The earth-covered building could represent a way for both nature and humanity to coexist in ecological balance. By adopting the concept in low- to medium-density residential development, 'recycling' city slum land to become garden apartments with garden roofs and 'commons' for play and passive recreation, by undergrounding transit systems and industrial complexes,[29] and by requiring every development proposal to provide some 90 per cent of its site area in gardens or natural landscapes,

A mud-brick house in a bush setting in Sydney. Top: The interior, showing access to a loft space. At left is the central load-bearing column for this part of the house. Above: The eastern elevation.

the next century would be entered with responsibility for the stewardship of nature's resources. Apart from high-technology, outer-space and undersea architecture, geotecture is the only serious departure from the traditional that the twentieth century has seen. Yet it is the most traditional of all styles. The Chinese architects of Shaanxi province, for example, have adapted the rock dwellings of the past to the earth-covered housing of the present; experimental earth-covered buildings are now being designed and built on the terraces of the hills, incorporating modern principles of energy conservation, with roof gardens for agriculture.[30]

In the conclusion of their book *Dimensions*, Moore and Allen wrote: 'so buildings speak to us in many voices – soft and loud, sober and silly, important and modest.

Blessed especially are the modest for they will shortly cover the earth'.[31] It is to the modest, gentle earth-covered buildings of the future to which we may look for restoration of an inner psychic balance and a lost relationship with nature.

In the words of Paul Ehrlich:

There is no technological panacea for the complex of problems comprising the population-food-environment crisis, although technology properly applied ... can provide massive assistance. The basic solutions involve change in human attitudes especially those relating to reproductive behaviour, economic growth, technology, the environment and conflict resolution.

Society has always had its visionaries who talked of love, beauty, peace and plenty. But somehow the 'practical' men have always been there to praise the smog as a sign of progress ... It must be one of the greatest ironies of the history of the human species that the only salvation for the practical men now lies in what they think of as the dreams of idealists. The question now is: can the 'realists' be persuaded to face reality in time?[32]

Today's visions become tomorrow's realities, and the potential for the passive use of nature's energies to provide for all the systems needed to house future generations is immense. Combined with life-cycle economies and utilizing low-grade heat conversion and other energy conservation strategies, designing, building and using earth-covered housing from now into the next millenium will be exciting and satisfying for us all.

A house based on the portable Mongolian yurt form, and now available as an Australian design in kit form. The lightweight timber modules can be handled and positioned by one person alone. Top: An interior. Above: An exterior of another version. Designer, Mike Shepherd.

ARCHITECTURE IS MADE by people using materials to fashion spaces for living in. This part of the book discusses some of the distinctly Australian approaches to the ways living spaces are made. It has been said that there is nothing that makes the Australian house unique, but this claim ignores the unique environment, the characteristic materials, and the way of life. If the Australian homestead is not unique, for example, it is certainly inimitable, and there are many other house forms which are special to this part of the world. Australian variations on the world-wide house theme are full of interest for the observer with eyes to see them.

In building construction, for instance, things which we now take for granted – light-weight timber framing, the brick cavity wall and brick veneer – are methods developed particularly to suit Australian conditions. Almost every traditional way of building has distinctive variations demonstrating local ingenuity or character.

Australian house design has almost always tended to be looser, less formal, more relaxed, than European or American. Our towns are more open and have lower densities than European ones. Our cities have extensive suburbs, with dwellings of two main types – the villa and the terrace. The villa form has nearly always been conceived as a

cernible. Distance, not so tyrannical now, has modified design.

The first part of this book dealt with what Shakespeare called the glass of fashion. This part, as though to complete the bard's quote, deals with the mould of form.

An ensemble of materials that fit nicely in the environment: hardwood, mud-brick and glass. The Le Gallienne house, Eltham, by Alistair Knox, built in the 1950s.

ASPECTS OF DESIGN PART TWO

bungalow form – its very name evocative of a sub-tropical ambience – while our terraces, similar to Britain's in general, have always displayed local characteristics. In Australian cities, apart from their dense and limited centres, flats and home units are a minority and high-density living is unusual. Yet 'semis' – those ubiquitous pairs of joined houses – have been built for well over a hundred years.

In a country as big as Australia there are bound to be considerable regional differences in house types. Responses to climate produce dwellings as varied as the dugouts of the Red Centre, the stilt-houses of the tropical north, the cyclone-resistant structures of Darwin, and the skillioned shelters of the Sydney School. Differences in natural resources, such as timber species, impart subtle but obvious variety to domestic design.

Population changes have been evidenced not only by the growth of the cities and their suburbs, but also in the kinds of houses that have been available. In times of rapid early development prefabricated houses flooded in, while more recent population increase has advanced the concepts of the project house and the owner-builder. All of these trends have had their peculiar Australian character.

There has, nevertheless, always been a dichotomy about the Australian house, whether stylish or merely functional, contrived or vernacular. It results from the facts that our historical roots are in Britain but our environment is our own, and that American, and more recently, European and Asian-Pacific influences have become dis-

WALLS ARE THE VISIBLE garments of buildings. They are to a house what clothes are to their wearer, giving protection, comfort, privacy and adornment. Some words that describe clothing can be applied just as readily to the walls of a building: material, fabric, cladding, covering, decoration. As the choice of materials for a garment says a lot about the personality of the one who wears it, so the choice of walling materials establishes, more than anything else does, the character of a house and the people who built it.

Walls enclose the living spaces needed by people, and must be stable to support other parts of the house such as roofs and floors. The roof also is visually important, in the same way as a hat which crowns a stylish ensemble; but its contribution to architectural character is generally constrained by the rigorous job of protecting everything beneath it. Walls are not so limited; for them, except in the meanest of houses, appearance has always been nearly as important as efficiency.

Columned or continuous walls

There are two kinds of walls, and they express the two structural systems which are basic to all buildings: mass construction and frame construction. In mass construc-

steel and concrete, more usual for larger structures, have appeared also in domestic work. For sheeting over the frames, or filling the spaces between, the materials used are very diverse; as well as wattle-and-daub and weatherboards there have been slabs, logs, tiles, shingles, masonry and plaster. More recently, particularly since it has become possible to construct frames with great accuracy, such claddings as asbestos-cement, sheet metals, glass and plastics have from time to time been in vogue. The transparency and lightness which glass can bring to a framed house is a truly twentieth-century characteristic.

In the long history of houses, walling materials have been commonly used in their natural state, but where greater weather protection was desirable they were often covered. It became customary in the Regency period, for reasons of fashion, to conceal commonplace or even poor materials under coatings of plaster and paint, often decorating them to simulate more refined or fashionable finishes. The Victorian period inherited this practice which, because it coincided with Australia's greatest growth, was absorbed into its domestic architecture. Thus stucco was formed and coloured to look like stone, plaster was coloured and lined to look like marble, plain walling was painted to resemble panelling, and cheap

MOSTLY ABOUT WALLS

tion the loads imposed by roofs, floors and inhabitants are borne by continuous walls, which also provide environmental protection for the activities within. In frame construction the loading from roofs, floors and inhabitants is borne by a framework which transfers the forces to the foundation through such devices as columns or posts. The walls, which then no longer have to carry the loads, may become mere weather-protective screens between the posts, or may be made altogether independent of the posts. Both mass construction and frame construction have been used for houses since the beginning of building, and throughout history there have been many variants and hybrid forms. A solid brick house is an example of mass construction, while a weatherboarded house has walls of frame construction. Brick veneer is a modern hybrid: the walls are timber framed, while an external skin of brickwork gives the appearance of mass construction. A much older hybrid was wattle-and-daub, the earliest recorded walling type in Australia, where massive panels of 'daub' were constructed in a framework of timber posts.

The materials used for mass construction have been stone, brick, earth and, in recent years, concrete. Frame construction traditionally employed timber, but iron,

Walls are the most evident parts of houses, supporting the structure and excluding the weather. But walls may also be handsomely textured, modelled and coloured, as in this example at Ashfield.

timbers were stained to imitate exotics.

Walls depend for their stability upon a sound foundation and strong connections. Because houses are not very massive buildings, most foundations are more than adequate to support them. But some soils, such as the shrinkable clays of South Australia, change seasonally, making the house move slightly up and down – usually unevenly – as the clay layer on which it is founded swells and shrinks, and this movement makes walls crack. Only in recent years has the problem of shrinkable clay been overcome by constructing houses with stronger footings and basework.

A wall of mass construction has no obvious connectors. Masonry comprises separate pieces of stone or brick, which must be made stable by interlocking or 'bonding' them, and if they are also mortared into place the wall is made still stronger. Walls of fluid materials such as *pisé* and concrete need to be supported by 'formwork' until they harden and become homogenious. On the other hand, the separate pieces of frame construction may be connected by using any of an amazing range of fixing devices. Usually in traditional house frames the members were mortised and tenoned together, while in the modern stud frame nails are the most common connectors.

In so many ways, walls are of the essence of architecture, and it is helpful in developing an understanding of the history and the character of a house to consider the materials, techniques, functions and fashions that have made its walls what they are.

Stone masonry

Stone is the aristocrat of building materials,[1] the most traditional and symbolic. The mysteries of the masonic crafts go back to the first permanent structures ever made – those of ancient Egypt. In every age people have regarded stone buildings as the strongest, longest-lasting and most handsome.

Stone has been available in the majority of Australian settlements for the building of walls, though it has not always been used as hindsight might expect. It was the favoured building material for public buildings and was considered prestigious for houses. But it was also the first of the versatile materials, and consequently was used not only for walling but also for paving, kerbs, guttering and drains, for hitching posts and mounting-steps, for fences and fountains, for bridges and piers, and for all kinds of civic monuments.

Australian architecture has been enriched by the great variety of stone used across the country. Sydney had the good fortune to be founded on a great bed of Triassic rock called Hawkesbury sandstone. Because it was easy to cut out and work into building blocks it was immediately called 'freestone', and the early settlers likened it to Portland stone, England's best freestone. The first government quarry was opened in 1802 in what is now the West Rocks area of Sydney, and from then on masonry dwellings of good quality could be erected by all those who could afford them. The famous quarry at Pyrmont was one of the busiest of the Victorian period. The popularity of Hawkesbury stone has never waned, even though now only one or two quarries can provide it.

The same distinctive golden-brown colour and sandy texture of sandstone is common also in Tasmania. The stone character of the buildings in Hobart and Launceston is different from that of Sydney's buildings, however, because there are fewer verandahs and thus less shadow to hide the texture of the stone and its architectural embellishment. As in New South Wales, sandstone walls were often dressed, or finished, with a pick – a pointed steel tool struck with a mallet. Stones so dressed are often described as 'sparrow-picked'.

Adelaide's freestone, from quarries such as Teatree Gully, is similar in texture but slightly darker and more bland in colour. It was also more expensive, and was therefore usually chosen for detailed work such as plinths, quoins, string-courses and cornices.[2] More common for domestic stone walling was the thick dark blue-grey or blue-brown slate, quarried at locations such as Glen Osmond, and known in South Australia as 'bluestone'. This did not lend itself to cutting and squaring into

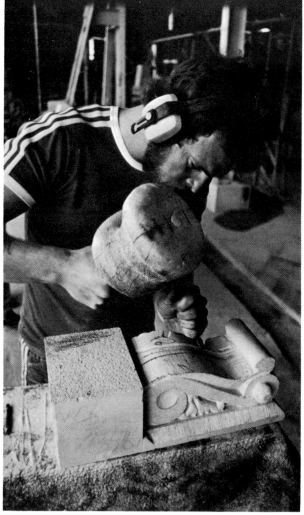

Above: Finely-finished ashlar work of Barrabool sandstone – a window detail in Werribee Park, Werribee.

Left: A craftsman carving a console bracket similar to the one at Werribee, in a mason's lodge.

Right: A domestic tower in Perth, built about 1900 from the distinctive coastal limestone of the west.

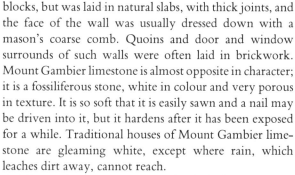

Stone walling built of interlocking blocks laid with joints of mortar. Left: A house of roughly coursed basalt. Above: Basalt has a coarse, tough texture.

blocks, but was laid in natural slabs, with thick joints, and the face of the wall was usually dressed down with a mason's coarse comb. Quoins and door and window surrounds of such walls were often laid in brickwork. Mount Gambier limestone is almost opposite in character; it is a fossiliferous stone, white in colour and very porous in texture. It is so soft that it is easily sawn and a nail may be driven into it, but it hardens after it has been exposed for a while. Traditional houses of Mount Gambier limestone are gleaming white, except where rain, which leaches dirt away, cannot reach.

Melbourne's native stone was the dark, hard volcanic basalt which Victorians – like the South Australians with their different stone – have always called bluestone because of its blue-grey colour. It was first quarried in what is now Fitzroy Gardens,[3] and it became so popular that scores of quarries were needed in southern Victoria to meet the demand. Its toughness and durability made it ideal for road pitchers and engineering works such as jetties and railway viaducts, but its intractability made it very expensive to work. Consequently bluestone walling

was usually laid in rough rubble, with only details such as corners and jambs being dressed, while carved decoration was rare. The coarse and honeycombed texture of basalt is caused by its rapid cooling as volcanic lava. It contrasted with the softer and more colourful building stones like the greenish-brown Barrabool Hills sandstone from near Geelong, or the fine-grained Stawell sandstone from the Grampians, both of which were used more frequently in public buildings.

Queensland is so rich in other materials, particularly timber, that no tradition of stone domestic building really developed. Few examples may be found as good as Oakwall, a sandstone house built in Windsor, outside Brisbane, in about 1858. Sandstone was used in the Brisbane area for public buildings, and it varied in colour from almost white to red-brown, and in texture from coarse schist to very fine-grained freestone.

Sandstone. Above: Sparrow-picked in courses or rows of squared blocks. Right: Sandstone ashlar, fine-chiselled to a vermiculated ('worm-eaten') surface and laid in courses.

The indigenous walling material of Perth and Fremantle was the so-called coastal limestone, a porous, creamy-coloured dune limestone. Its pleasant pastel hue and luminous texture gave great beauty to early houses. It also influenced the later use of concrete, cement render and paint, for these more modern materials have often been modified to harmonize with or even imitate limestone.

Hundreds of other locally-quarried stones have been used in houses, inside as well as out, often to show an owner's wealth or prestige. There were granites, from quarries like Moruya or Harcourt or Dromana, which could be intricately carved and polished. Figured marbles of intriguing beauty came from numerous quarries such as Angaston or Buchan. The slates of Bangor, near Launceston, and Bacchus Marsh, in Victoria, were split for covering roofs. There were also, of course, the many imported varieties, used particularly in interior design for decorative effect. Chimney-pieces, for example, were commonly fabricated from exotic imported stones. But the handful of Australian building stones – sandstones, limestones and basalt – were by far the most widespread, typifying the regional differences in architecture.

Stones were laid in walls in very diverse ways. The best, and therefore the costliest, was called ashlar, which consisted of accurately squared and dressed blocks, closely fitted with thin mortar joints. The opposite of ashlar was walling of random rubble, in which the stones were used almost as found, with a minimum of shaping, roughly assembled with thick and irregular mortar joints, so that the wall took on a very rough texture. In between these two extremes the variations were numerous and, where two or more different masonry materials were combined, almost limitless. The exposed surfaces of the stones could be dressed, if desired, to achieve either plain or decorative finishes, using a range of steel tools, from the rough axe to the fine chisel, to the claw or 'comb', and the pick or 'point'. Rubbed and polished surfaces added even further possibilities to stone walling and detailing.

Brickwork

Brickmaking consists essentially of heating a shaped lump of clay until it becomes permanently hard.[4] The brick, like bread, is one of man's most historic substances. Unfired or 'green' bricks need, like flour, only cooking to make them perfect.[5] This basically simple process, the combination of clay and fire, dispersed brickmaking and brickwork far more widely that stone quarrying, because suitable clay could be found almost anywhere. The clay available to one brickyard tended to be different from that of another, and one brickmaker's method was usually slightly different from another's. These differences, and the kinds of mechanization the brickmakers were able to employ, meant that there were great variations in the quality and appearance of bricks throughout Australia during the nineteenth century.

The earliest bricks were sandstocks, so called because they were made by throwing a lump of prepared clay, called 'pug', into a box-like timber mould. This mould had no top or bottom, but was placed over a base board called the 'stock' which was fixed to the surface of the moulder's bench. Before the mould was positioned over the stock, both were dusted with sand (the same as a cake tin is dusted with flour) to prevent the plastic clay from sticking. The lump was pressed well into the bottom corners, and the excess clay was removed by scraping a small wetted board called a 'strike' across the top of the mould. Then the mould, containing the clay, was lifted off the stock, tipped over on to a pallet, and slid upwards off the moulded brick. The pallet was then used to carry the 'green' brick away to be stacked for drying. After a few days of air-drying the green bricks were re-stacked in the kiln, leaving ample spaces between them for the heat to circulate, and fired.

Bricks made by this early process were well-formed and, although of adequate strength, were porous and not very hard. They had a distinctly sandy texture, and their colour varied according to the source of the clay and the heat of the kiln. Bricks tended to be light in colour because temperatures generated by wood in these simple kilns were not very high. Bricks from Sydney, yellowish-pink or salmon-coloured, were called 'samels'; those from Parramatta were brownish-pink.

Improved techniques

As brickyards spread throughout the colonies, techniques improved. When coal replaced wood as a kiln fuel bricks became denser, and then, from about 1815, some brick-

Top right: A brickmaker at his moulding bench, right foreground, and bricks being stacked to dry before firing, left. In the background brick clay is being prepared.

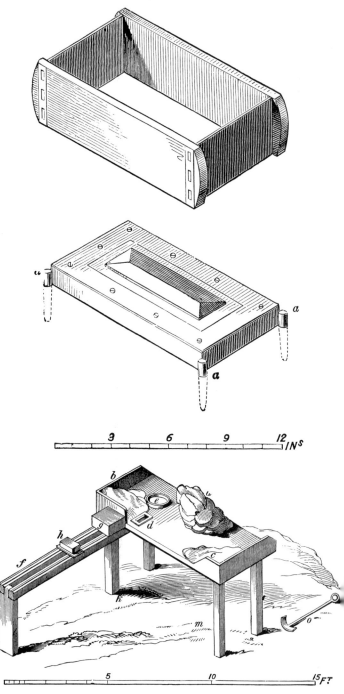

Making a brick. Centre: A brickmaker's mould and stock. Right: The moulder's bench with the stock, d, ready for moulding a brick. A brick has been made, h, and is ready for carrying on its pallet to the drying stack.

makers added cinders ('breeze') to the pug, which gave the bricks a mottled colour with black or brown specks. About 1820 the arrow, a sign of government property, appeared on bricks; it was an indented mark made by a raised symbol attached to the moulder's stock. From the 1830s other symbols made their marks, such as the initials of a property or its owner's surname. Such indentations became known by about mid-century as 'frogs' (though no one knows the origin of the term) and they appeared in great variety. Diamond and heart shapes were the most familiar, though bricks without frogs were made still. The rectangular frog was first used at Boyd Town in 1843, and by the 1860s was commonplace.

The texture of bricks improved and their density increased with the introduction in New South Wales of pug-mills from the 1820s. A pug-mill was a man-powered or horse-powered machine for mixing and kneading clay more efficiently. One of the mills used was shaped like a large barrel and loaded with brick-earth from the top. It had a vertical shaft, to which metal blades and spikes were fixed. As the shaft rotated, the blades milled the clay pug and ejected it through an opening at the base, ready for moulding. Later pug-mills were steam-operated, and ground the pug by means of rollers before kneading it. In the 1850s there were both American and English machines in Australia which did even more than this; they could grind, mix, knead and extrude the plastic clay into a continuous band that was then cut into separate bricks of appropriate size, the whole process being almost automatic.

This was matched a little later by the introduction of the Hoffmann kiln, which fired bricks, continuously, in great numbers, cheaply and uniformly. The first local Hoffmann company began operations in 1870. These were typical of the many rapid developments that occurred during the second half of the nineteenth century. One of the most influential was the dry-pressed brick, the material for which was not pugged at all, but granulated, dampened, and packed into the mould under great steam pressure. This process allowed the use of shales as well as clays. Dry-press bricks were potentially so hard that they reached their intended strength at a lower kiln temperature. It was also discovered that longer controlled firing could produce a different-coloured brick from the same material – by carefully controlled burning a wide range of brick colours, from cream, through reds to dark brown, was possible. Additions like iron filings and sawdust also were used in the clay mixture to make unusual colours when fired. All of these developments made polychrome brickwork popular; indeed, multicoloured brick houses became a phenomenon of the Victorian period. Incidentally, most of the new machinery was designed for

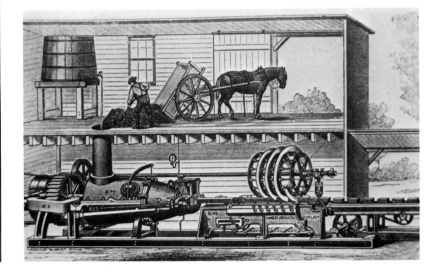

Above: A girl brick-labourer wheeling her hack-barrow. There is a pugmill in the distance.

Centre: Sandstock bricks with distinctive arrow frogs, the sign of government property.

Below: A semi-automatic brick-making machine of the nineteenth century.

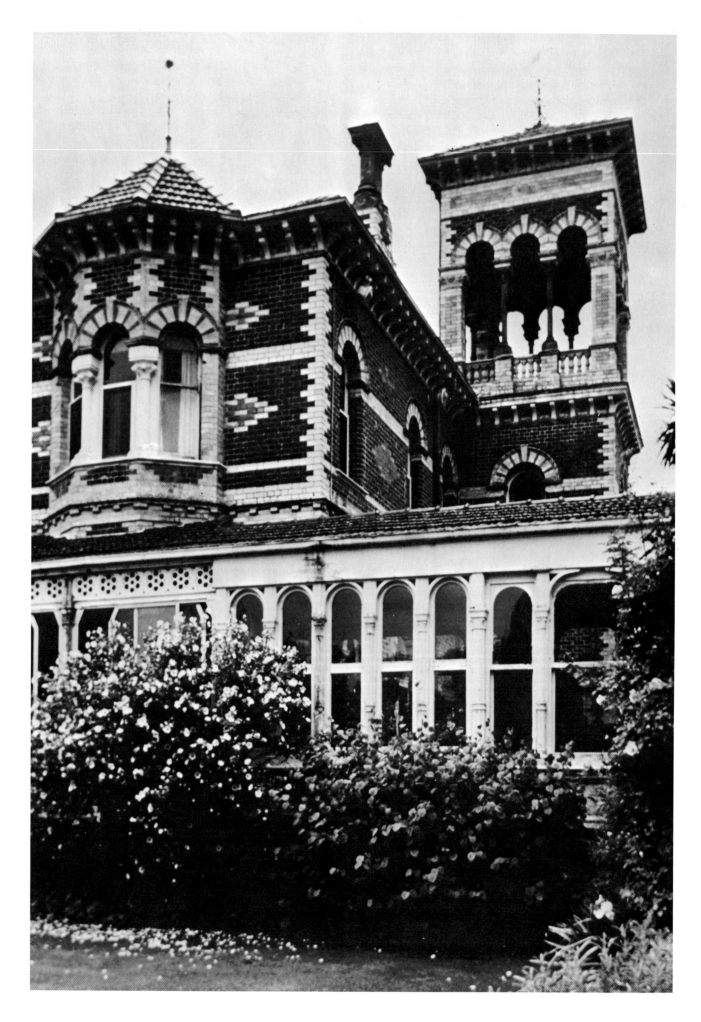

making the so-called 'German-sized' brick which, at about 230 millimetres by 115 millimetres by 75 millimetres, was larger than the earlier sandstock brick, made from Macquarie's time in a fairly standard size of about 200 millimetres by 100 millimetres by 60 millimetres.

By the 1880s regional variations became more distinctive. Near the cities, extruded wire-cut and dry-pressed bricks in many colours were available, while in country areas those who could not afford to bring these in could use sandstocks, which were still locally available. Among the most notable of all bricks were the dark browns of Melbourne and Geelong (called 'Hawthorn blacks' in Melbourne), Castlemaine's patent pressed reds, the orange-reds of Bathurst and Goulburn, the metallic greys of Armidale, the rose-reds of Hobart, and the wonderful dichromatic decorative brickwork of Sydney and Melbourne, in creams and reds.

made, and fitted together in a wall so well, that the mortar joints between them could be made thinner. Pointing is the name given to the way brick joints are finished off. In tuck-pointing, the joints were made with mortar coloured to match the bricks and trowelled flush with the wall-face. Using special tuck-pointers' tools each joint was then scored with a groove 2 or 3 millimetres wide, and into this was pressed a flat narrow ribbon of lime-putty, which was then carefully trimmed. The effect produced was a greatly esteemed super-fine jointing.

The distinctive 'bonds' of brickwork resulted from the ways that the bricks were overlapped and interlocked in a wall to give it adequate strength. The proportion of the brick (length twice the width) was an important factor in bonding. In solid walls of any quality two traditional bonds were common. English bond employed alternating courses of headers (bricks having their ends to the wall-

Examples of colourful versatility in nineteenth-century brickwork. Left: Rippon Lea, Melbourne, with polychrome walling. Above: Smith House, Armidale, New South Wales, with dichromatic work in greys and creams. Right: Government House, Perth, the walls of which are laid in Flemish bond, with headers selected from bricks which were well burnt in the kiln.

face) and stretchers (bricks having their sides to the wall-face). In Flemish bond each course comprised alternating headers and stretchers. Flemish was considered more decorative, but this was true only if it was well laid. Sometimes houses had their front walls laid in Flemish bond and the others in English. Occasionally, as in Perth, bricks for Flemish bond were carefully sorted so that all the headers were slightly darker in colour than the stretchers – the resulting pattern from this was much favoured in the nineteenth century. Both Flemish and English bonds were simplified – and also weakened – by reducing the number of headers, to make bricklaying easier or quicker. These simpler, cruder patterns were frequently used; they were called 'garden wall' or 'colonial' bonds.

From about this time, bricks moulded to special shapes were used extensively to obtain particular decorative effects. Bullnose, splay, ovolo, scotia and ogee were some of the brick shapes that contributed to the amazing versatility of nineteenth-century brick walling.

At the end of the century, and especially after the 1893 depression, there was a return to simpler houses, and people preferred plain good quality red brickwork rather than the ostentation of stucco or polychrome. This Federation period was the heyday of the good bricklayer, whose hallmarks were accuracy and fine jointing, tuck-pointing, and cavity walls. Bricks were now so accurately

The problem of moisture

The walls of traditional brick houses were of solid construction, usually with a thickness equal to one-and-a-half bricks (about 350 millimetres) or one brick (about 200 or

230 millimetres). Such walls always tended to allow moisture to enter, particularly if they were facing the weather or unprotected by stucco. Dampness got into walls either upwards from the ground, or through the wall from the outside. Rising damp was prevented by building a 'damp-proof course' into the wall just above the ground. The earliest such barrier, used from about the middle of the nineteenth century, was a layer or two of thin slates. Soon after this sheet lead was used; it was most effective but very costly. Then followed asphalt, spread while hot over the basework before the wall proceeded upward. At the end of the century bitumen-impregnated felt, an American importation, was tried, and in more recent years barriers such as bitumen-coated aluminium, and mortar additives such as stearic acid, have been tried. Knowing the kind of damp-proof course helps to determine the age of a house.

Through most of the nineteenth century, whenever surface penetration of moisture became a problem, a coating of lime-wash or plaster was applied. This was sometimes tinted; as early as 1806 Governor Bligh ordered that yellow ochre be added to the lime-wash for painting government buildings. Stucco became fashionable not only because it could imitate stone but also because it protected porous brickwork from driving rain. The removal of stucco from an old house thus not only destroys the integrity of its appearance but also exposes vulnerable brick walling to the weather. In the third quarter of the nineteenth century a very different kind of moisture barrier was devised. It was the technique of making walls in two skins, each half a brick thick, separated by a cavity, the total thickness being only 280 millimetres. Cavity walls are now the standard method for brick; they are laid without headers, and display stretcher bond. It is easy to understand the overwhelming popularity of brick walls for houses of the Federation period, for by then brickwork was supremely efficient, permanent and handsome.

Bricks of this century

Developments in brickmaking and brick use since federation have been steady but unexciting. The output of the yards has been dramatically increased by new massive extrusion equipment, improved wire cutting machines, and electrically-fired tunnel kilns of vast capacity. But the bricks that result are bland and uninteresting by comparison with those of former years. Sydney's bold liver-coloured bricks, for instance, cheap and popular about the time of World War I, and a vital ingredient of the California bungalow style, were no longer available after World War II.

Among the brick types that the new extruders and cutters made in millions were heelers (thin bricks, for laying in narrow courses) and texture bricks (called 'tapestries' in Victoria). These gave new character to brick walling in the inter-war years, and played a large part in the Georgian Revival of that time. As well, some architects developed a liking for clinkers, those overburnt and hitherto rejected

Some brick bonds. Above: Sandstocks roughly laid in Flemish bond. Centre: Sandstocks finely laid in English Colonial bond. Left: A tuck-pointed wall of English Colonial bond.

bricks, which innovative designers began to use for adding strong colour and textural emphasis cheaply to walls. After World War II clinker bricks became an important part of the design vocabulary of the Sydney School.

One distinctly twentieth-century innovation was brick veneer construction, consisting of a single half-brick skin protecting a stud frame. This seems to have been used first in Melbourne in 1915 to give the status of a brick house to one that was really a timber frame designed for extensive plywood panelling in the main rooms.[6] It was not until about 1930 that the system was considered sound enough for a bank to approve a building loan,[7] but by 1936 brick veneer (so named by a Melbourne estate agent) was recognized as a standard domestic construction. In the 1960s it accounted for about half of all houses built in Victoria.

Walls of earth

Consolidated unbaked earth is one of the oldest building materials known to man. It is also the only one, apart from concrete, that can form a homogenious mass – all the others rely upon the skill by which separate pieces are put together to make a structure.[8] The abundance and ease of construction of earth has been responsible for making it one of the great 'do-it-yourself' materials, the very stuff of vernacular building style.

The golden rule of earth wall building is to keep moisture out. A traditional English saying is that all an earth wall wants is 'a good hat and a good pair of shoes'[9], in other words a dry base and a roof overhead. Without these things an earth house will quickly disintegrate, as many decayed ruins testify. It has always been the custom to protect mud walls by means of rendering or lime-wash or plaster, which conceals as well as protects the construction. Unbaked earth is also one of the least-documented of materials, probably because of its vernacular or humble nature. People who built with earth simply did not write about it, as processed or manufactured materials were written about. These three factors – rapid decay, covering up, and lack of written record – indicate that there were many more houses of earth than are presently recognized.

Five earth techniques have been used in Australian houses: *pisé*, adobe, sods, cob and daub. A couple of these age-old techniques still flourish today, and some striking new Australian houses proudly utilize the cheapest and most ancient of materials. Daub, probably the most varied of the five, has always been an adjunct to wooden construction and will be considered when timber is discussed.

Pisé de terre

Pisé, or *pisé de terre*, is rammed earth. A wall is made by ramming loam mud into timber formwork, which is moved both along the wall section by section, and upwards layer by layer, as the wall hardens. It is also called 'pisa' and 'pisey' in the eastern states, and 'jim-jam' in Western Australia.[10]

Above: Adobes being laid as infill panels between the heavy posts of a timber frame.

Below: Diagram of a pisé wall under construction.

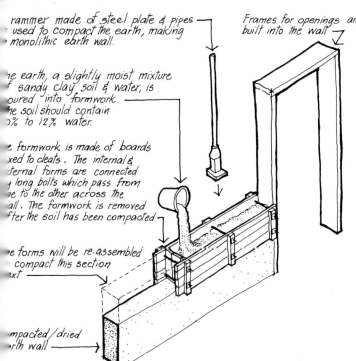

rammer made of steel plate & pipes — is used to compact the earth, making a monolithic earth wall.

The earth, a slightly moist mixture of sandy clay soil & water, is poured into formwork. The soil should contain 0% to 12% water.

The formwork is made of boards fixed to cleats. The internal & external forms are connected by long bolts which pass from one to the other across the wall. The formwork is removed after the soil has been compacted —

The forms will be re-assembled to compact this section next.

compacted/dried earth wall —

A nineteenth-century house with pisé *walls at Jemmalong.*

Walls of *pisé* are thick and stable, and have good insulating qualities that suit Australian climates. It seems that the system was first used in New South Wales and Van Diemen's Land in the 1820s, and there is evidence also of its early use by settlers in Victoria and South Australia. The earliest known survivor is a two-storey house, Wanstead Park, near Campbell Town, Tasmania, which was erected in 1827, and is still in use. Wanstead Park was built on a stone base, as was common in Europe, but most Australian *pisé* buildings were built straight on the ground. Verandahs or wide roof eaves were always considered desirable to protect the walls from driving rain and for preventing erosion from splashing water at ground level. Not all soils are suitable for *pisé*; the best is the red-brown earth of the premier wheat-growing areas of eastern and southern Australia, and most of the known rammed-earth houses were erected in these districts.[11]

In 1823 the *Sydney Gazette* published a translation of a French description of *pisé* construction, in the hope that it would prove useful 'on the settlement of Bathurst, and other parts of the country which may be thinly wooded'.[12] The soil of the Bathurst region indeed proved to be satisfactory for *pisé*, though little is known of its early use. An eight-roomed, two-storeyed house, built in the town of Bathurst in 1854 was admired years later:

In Bathurst all brick buildings generally crack a few months after they are put up; but the building to which we refer is now as sound as the day it was finished . . .[13]

Pisé was never common in urban areas because the earth needed for making walls had to be excavated nearby. In country areas, however, mud was often more readily available than stone or brick or timber. In 1870 at Mylong, in the Riverina, a selector dug a dam by machine and used the excavated material to build a *pisé* house. This combination of dam-making and wall-building was considered to be the sign of a bright future for *pisé* as a rural material.[14] The Corowa architect A.C. Macknight designed *pisé* homestead buildings that were constructed well into the twentieth century and, according to Peter Freeman, in *The Homestead: A Riverina Anthology*, they stand as testimony to this technique.[15]

Bricks of mud

Adobe is the Spanish-Mexican term for sun-dried brick. The English call it clay lump, which is clay puddled with chopped straw and formed into the shape of a large brick in a mould, then left to dry. In wall building these blocks, or adobes, are laid in courses using mud for mortar, the adobes of each course overlapping the joints of the course below in the same way as brickwork laid in stretcher bond. The age-old methods of clay-lump making and walling may have originated in North Africa, but by the early nineteenth century they were widespread; influences came to Australia from Britain, Mexico and Germany.

Alistair Knox's own house of adobe at Eltham, built in stages between 1962 and 1970.

The English influence came from settlers – particularly those from areas like East Anglia where clay-lump building was common – and from instruction books such as C.B. Allen's *Cottage Building or Hints for Improving the Dwellings of Working Men and Labourers*, published in London in 1886. According to Allen:

The clay to be used is first freed from all large stones, and soaked with as much water as it will absorb; it is then well beaten, and a quantity of short old straw added, and the whole well and thoroughly mixed up together. The mixing should be continued by the treading of horses ... till the clay becomes thoroughly beaten, and of about the consistence of mortar: it is then put into moulds, 18" long, 12" wide, and 6" deep, without a bottom and moulded in the same manner as bricks. These lumps are then dried in the sun, and laid in the usual manner with mortar.

The adobe size recommended by Allen (about 450 by 300 by 150 millimetres) remained fairly consistent in all traditional earth masonry.

The German influence was seen in South Australia and in the Wimmera district of Victoria, and in a few other places where Germans settled in the nineteenth century. There are some mud-brick houses at Newcastle, New South Wales, where significantly they are described as 'German brick' houses.[16]

The Mexican influence is revealed by the particular instances of the Birkbeck house, Strathmore,[17] and Glenmore homestead,[18] both near Rockhampton, Queensland, built in the 1860s with Mexican labour; and also by most adobe construction in Australia following the Mexican tradition of starting walls at ground level instead of having brick or stone basework as was usually the case in England.[19]

Although they are found in many areas where suitable clayey soil was available, adobe houses were never as common in Australia as those of *pisé*. Nevertheless advice about building in sun-dried unburnt bricks was still being published as late as 1911 in the official New South Wales *Farmers' Handbook*; and good examples survive in all the south-eastern states.

Perhaps the most interesting aspect of adobe is its rediscovery, which has grown hand-in-hand with the environmental movements of the past half century. Alistair Knox, of Eltham, Victoria, is the man most closely associated with the earth-wall revival, and according to him it began at Eltham in 1934, when Justus Jorgenson established the alternative settlement called Montsalvat. Knox became involved with earth construction and environmental design in 1947, when post-war austerity frustrated ordinary house building. 'Earth was free and available', he wrote, 'and combined perfectly with other natural materials which were mostly cheap – being held in low esteem by those who thought the new age meant new

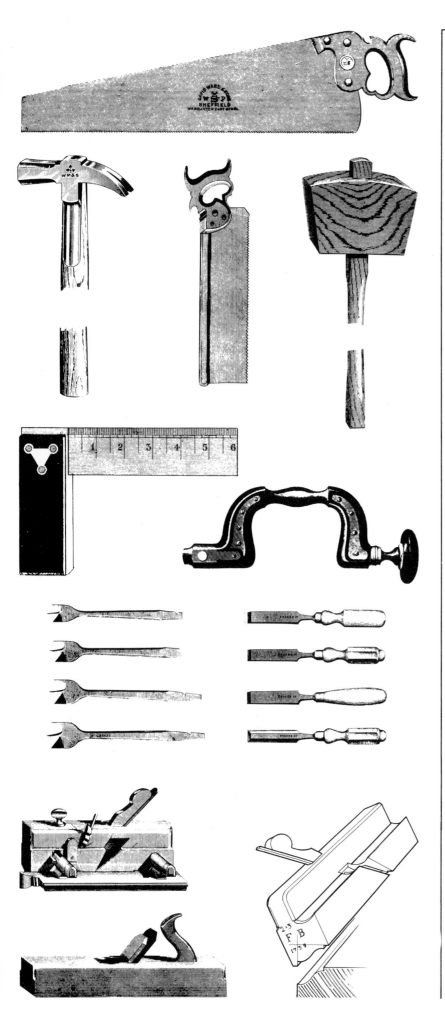

materials rather than good ones.'[20] Eltham became almost synonymous with adobe simply because Eltham was the only municipality that would issue a building permit for an earth building in those early days. The many houses designed and built by Alistair Knox since then perfectly suit the beautiful and natural landscape of the Yarra Valley. Now, as more municipal councils discover the efficacy of earth for building, notable houses are appearing in many other areas of Victoria, and earth-wall co-operatives have formed in other states.

Earth-wall building, particularly in *pisé* and adobe, became the subject of scientific investigation by Australia's Experimental Building Station, where the traditional methods were tested. The resulting publications, particularly some of the *Notes on the Science of Building*, and G. F. Middleton's E.B.S. Bulletin No. 5, *Earth Wall Construction*, all of which are still current, have done a great deal to spread the knowledge of the simplest and most satisfying of all house building crafts.

Soft blocks of clay

Cob was used extensively in England, but authenticated examples in Australia are few. In cob walling, rough blocks of clay, rather like soft adobes, were piled in thick layers without any forms or moulds. After the outline of the wall had been marked on the ground, a layer of cob was placed, using long-tined forks, and then 'flayed' or beaten down and compacted. Successive layers were forked on and flayed until the wall was built to its full height. Then a specially-shaped cutting tool called a paring iron was used to trim the wall true and straight. Openings for doors and windows were either made as the wall proceeded by using arch-like supports for the plastic cob, or they were cut out of the completed wall after the work was dry.[21]

The best known cob building in Australia is Bear's Castle at Yan Yean, Victoria, erected about 1847 by Thomas Bear's overseer and subsequently used for a shepherd's quarters. It was a square structure of about 6.5 metres, with rounded and, formerly, castellated corner turrets, and a thatched roof. It has now been altered.[22] Middleton's Bulletin *Earth Wall Construction* refers also to an example of cob construction built as recently as 1946.

Lumps of turf

Sod walling is a building technique of which little physical evidence remains in Australia. It is very simply a method of piling up lumps of turf into the form of a wall, sometimes in combination with other materials such as layers of stone. It is believed that the first buildings of the Port Phillip settlement had walls of sod or turves, and by 1837 there were three sod pubs and a sod lock-up as well. There are records of earlier sod-wall houses, with thatched roofs, in Van Diemen's Land. To the west of Sydney there is a settlement called Sodwalls where the technique is thought to have been common, but virtually no trace is visible today.

Sod construction, for roofs as well as walls, was common in other parts of the world, including Ireland. One Irish roofing method, which was brought to Australia at the end of last century, was to lay turves over a spread of branches and twigs supported on purlins or rafters, and then to fix wheat-straw thatch over the turf. New layers of turf and thatch were added as the roof developed leaks, which was every few years. This incredible system, rounded and elephantine in appearance, is still in evidence in farm buildings at Parwan in Victoria,[23] Cudal in New South Wales, and a handful of other rural stations in south-east Australia.

Constructing with wood

Almost all of Australia's settlements were founded where forest resources were plentiful – a major factor behind the colonization of Australia had been Britain's world-wide search for quality timbers not only for naval purposes but for all kinds of building.[24] Wood became the most used of all materials, and a house without timber in its construction or finish is virtually impossible, even today. It is not surprising that timber has had a profound influence in the progress of domestic design and detail.

The peculiar and challenging qualities of the indigenous Australian forests made themselves quickly known to the early colonists, but it took considerably longer to develop the tools and technology to deal adequately with them.[25] Working in isolation or in small groups, settlers built with wood more-or-less as they found it: logs, saplings, split slabs and bark. A house of logs and slabs was an ingenious response to the shortage of labour and tools in the harsh bush life. The settler felled the trees for the building himself, helped perhaps by a wife or a son. From trunks of about 250 millimetres diameter he made the frame, which was assembled with very simple joints cut by saw and axe. The bark, removed with the axe, was kept for covering the sapling roof. From larger trunks, cut into lengths with a cross-cut saw where the tree fell, he split the wall-slabs. This was done by driving in a series of steel wedges in order to part the fibres of the wood along the length of the log, and clearing away the splinters afterwards with the axe. This basic dwelling could be built with axe and saw, wedges, mallet, and a few iron spikes.

As communities grew it became common for building timber to be supplied by tradesmen – timber fellers, splitters, broad-axe men, adzers, and sawyers. An itinerant axe man could, with the broad-axe, readily convert a round sapling to a squared post, and, with the help of wedges and mallet, convert a bigger tree-trunk into squared posts and wall-slabs. The higher 'finish' imparted by adzing and pit-sawing made wrought timber more desirable, and marked one of the early differences between 'bush work' and town house carpentry.

The properties that made trees eminently exploitable can be indicated by a short list of species and some of their initial uses. The *Angophora*, impossible to work into building timber, was used to make wheel naves, and burned to make potash, an ingredient in early whitewash. The *Casuarina* species, such as sheoak, were called 'the pine of this country', for they were easy to saw for making house frames, to split for making roof shingles, and to dress for furniture and turnery. The versatile cabbage-palm was cut into billets and split for log walling, its fruit was used to feed stock, and its leaves were made into hats. Wattle

Pit-sawing cedar in the Minnamurra area of New South Wales in the nineteenth century. The man standing on the large half-log is the top-notcher, who is responsible for guiding the two-man saw along its straight line. The pit-man below helps to keep the saw cutting plumb and true.

The residence of Dr Smith, somewhere in the Victorian gold-fields. Its roof, walls and chimney are made of bark sheets.

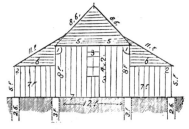 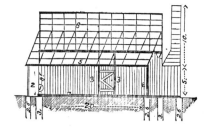

Summer campers at a drop-log snow hut, built in the 1930s beside the Snowy River.

Centre: Part of the instructions for building a four-roomed house of vertical slabs, published in The Australian Enquiry Book *in the 1890s.*

got its name from its pliability – its thin branches could be woven into panels called 'wattles', which were set between posts and 'daubed' or plastered with mud to form house walls. The long fronds of the yellow-gum tree (*Xanthorrhoea*, called 'blackboy' because of its black trunk) were used for roof thatching, while its gum was used as a medicine. Tea-tree was useful for joinery, and its leaves made a beverage. The bark of the kurrajong was used to make cordage.

The east coast eucalypts were logged and processed to the limited extent that the settlers' resources would allow. Stringybark, found west of Parramatta, was cut for general construction and its bark, relatively easy to remove, was used for roofing and walling. The toughness of the ironbarks restricted their use at first, but they split into excellent shingles. Blackbutt, turpentine, tallow wood, the mahoganies and the boxes were some of the other eucalypt species whose potentials were quickly realized; but their hardness blunted English axes and saws, and their refusal to float made transport almost impossible. The one tree which grew tall and straight, and converted to timber light enough for reasonable handling, was *Cedrela*, called red cedar because of the bright colour of its spring growth. From 1790, when it was first logged in the Hawkesbury area, the east coast as far as north Queensland was steadily and ruthlessly harvested for the red cedar which, for a century, was extensively used for wall and roof framing, cladding, joinery and furniture.[26]

In the early nineteenth century the conversion of forest wood to building timber was fraught with difficulty. Early writers often remarked about the density of the bush and the immensity and toughness of the trees. But almost nothing is told about felling, or about bringing the logs to the saw-pits. For example the English felling axe, large, straight and light, must have been frustrating to use on Australian hardwoods. It was the so-called American wedge-axe, introduced in the middle of the century, that successfully cut the big trees. It had a smaller but heavier head, with swollen sides, and a long, curved, shock-absorbing handle of hickory.[27] The American axe was swung wide and thrown into the wood, its fat cheeks making it easier to extricate the head when wedged tight in the cut. Once felled and its branches lopped, the trunk was cross-cut sawn into long lengths. The transporting of these logs to the saw-pit, manhandled on stout jinkers unless draught animals were available, was attended by great danger. There were many disasters like that which overtook poor William Collins, a labourer who, in 1804, was crushed to death by 'a log of immense size and weight' which got out of control as a team of sawyers were rolling it on to a saw-pit at Isaac Nichols's timber yard in Sydney.[28]

A good team of pit-sawyers could cut logs into building timber with great skill and accuracy, but the work was arduous and slow. The largest sawn members were called flitches; next came scantlings (smaller squared timbers such as rafters), battens (strips for holding shingles) and then boards (thin pieces such as flooring). A house could be framed and covered entirely from scantlings and boards, only the roofing – of shingles or 'tin' – not coming from the saw-pit.

A re-creation of the Pendlebury house at Forbes, built with pisé walls and a traditional tin roof at Forbes in 1974.

The Le Gallienne house at Eltham, designed by Alistair Knox in the 1950s. Its ground floor walls are built of adobe blocks and the top floor is of timber.

Left: The enormous living-room of Alistair Knox's own house in Eltham. There are several chimneys of brick, and the walls are made of adobe blocks smoothed by hand and colour-washed. The refectory table is made of solid eucalypt.

A few dwellings built this way still survive, in areas formerly richly forested. One is Millbank, at Terrara, New South Wales, a house of the 1830s, framed and weatherboarded in cedar and with its original cedar ceilings made of beautifully pit-sawn boards about 250 millimetres wide and barely 12 millimetres thick. Here, as in many other houses of the period, the wall studs were tenoned into a 'vermin' plate at floor level, and into a top plate at ceiling level. The vermin plate was supported on floor joists which in turn rested on bearers, and these were supported by timber blocks made of billets of tree-trunks or of flitches. The top plate supported the ceiling joists and also, around the perimeter of the house, the roof rafters, which were 'birds-mouthed', or notched in order to seat tightly on the plate. Panels of brickwork or 'noggings' – acting both as insulation and as a base for interior wall plastering – were laid between the studs. Boards, butted together as closely as possible, were nailed over the floor joists. Battens were nailed to the top surfaces of the rafters at intervals of about 100 millimetres, and shingles were nailed to the battens after the shingles were bored. Apart from the brick-nogging only the fireplaces and chimneys were brick-built.

There were several variations of this constructional theme.

If there was no brick-nogging, split laths were used instead, nailed across the interior faces of the studs, room by room, to support the plaster. The same method was applied where the ceilings were plastered. If slates were used on the roof, side-butted sawn boarding sometimes substituted for battens, and when corrugated roofing sheets were available, the battens were spaced more widely because the metal was strong enough for greater spans. Sometimes brick perimeter walls and piers supported the bearers instead of sub-floor blocks, and often the frame was of hardwood instead of cedar. But throughout the carpentry work, the standard connection was the mortise-and-tenon joint.

Houses with masonry walls still needed scantlings, battens and boards for their floors, roofs and ceilings. Throughout the first half of the nineteenth century practically all of these members, in both town and country, were made manually at a saw-pit. Furthermore all the joinery elements, unless they were imported, were also made by hand. Doors, windows, staircases, chimney-pieces, and trimwork such as skirting-boards and architraves, usually began as pit-sawn pieces which were subsequently hand-wrought at a workshop bench by the use of an array of joiner's tools – the development of which

Some houses built with timber slabs. Above: A handsome vertical-slab cottage at Scone. Far left: A wall detail at Scone showing the round-back eucalypt slabs chamfered to fit the frame. Left: McCrae Cottage, near Frankston, was built about 1845 with walls of short horizontal slabs dropped down into grooves in the posts. The edges of the slabs were adzed to ensure a tight fit.

reached its climax at the time of Australia's expansion. As well as bench saws, try-square, rule, mallet and hammer, the joiner's basic cabinet of tools included chisels (for accurate cutting of joints such as mortises) and a brace and bits (for boring, as in dowelled joints). But the key tools were the planes, for smoothing and shaping timber. A window sash, for example, was prepared for glazing by using a rebating plane to make the groove – which held the glass and putty – and a moulding plane to shape the interior edges of the sash components.

With the spread of settlement all over Australia, the various properties of regional timbers became known and exploited. In Western Australia jarrah and karri, two of the finest of the eucalypt species, were found. Jarrah's strength, durability, and its handsome red colour, made it the principal timber of Western Australia, where it was used for all building purposes, even shingles. Karri was the giant tree of the west; its timber resembled jarrah in colour, but was even stronger, though not as durable. Victoria's eucalypt forests yielded the so-called mountain ash, tallest of all Australian trees. Its timber was straight-grained, strong and easy to work although, even more than most hardwoods, the shrinkage and warping that took place after it was cut made it unpredictable until a satisfactory process of steam seasoning was introduced in 1911.[29] Mountain ash then became the most favoured building timber in Victoria. Another eucalypt, called peppermint, was used in Van Diemen's Land for splitting the especially long shingles which gave old roofs a distinctively Tasmanian texture. Of the non-eucalypt timbers, cypress pine, with its unusual sweet odour, was one of the most widespread in inland areas. When large trees were available, cypress was used for house framing and cladding, including shingles. With their depletion smaller trees were milled which, because of their many branches, produced timber that was very knotty but not very strong. Queensland's special figured timbers, kauri, maple and walnut, came into widespread use for joinery and cabinet-making in the second half of the nineteenth century.

The land was so richly endowed that fine woods which today are scarce and costly fulfilled the most ordinary of purposes. As early as 1825 one observer wrote:

But this is New Holland ... where the humblest house is fitted up with cedar ...; where the fields are fenced with mahogany ... and myrtle trees ... are burnt for firewood.[30]

Machine milling

The traditions of hand craftsmanship in timber building began their decline when machinery made its appearance in the 1830s. A great population expansion made house-building an urgent need, and the discovery of forest resources in vast new areas provided the potential to satisfy it. But though saw-pits abounded and bush-building methods continued to thrive, they were far from adequate for the changing conditions, especially in the new areas and towns. It was the mechanized saw that started the building revolution by making timber available quickly and in suitable quantities.

Daniel Dering Mathew, Australia's first trained architect, who arrived in 1812 and was the designer of the

Judge-Advocate's Sydney house in 1814, is believed to have established the first large-scale colonial sawmill. By 1825, on his land grant called Clanville (now Roseville), Mathew had set up the Cowan Saw Mill, a remarkable bullock-powered operation employing a circular saw for converting cedar logs from the central coast into building timber for the Sydney market. Mathew advertised in 1828 for '20 good BULLOCKS', indicating that at least four beasts at a time worked the capstan which provided the driving power for the blade.[31] In importing and setting up a circular saw, Mathew was an innovator. In other coun-

drive a flour mill instead.[33] The first steam-powered mills for sawing timber appeared in the 1830s and were at once a great success. An indication of their potential is given by W.G. Gard & Co.'s advertisement for the Australian Saw Mills, in Bathurst Street, Sydney, in the *Sydney Herald* of 31 October 1838:

Cedar plank on Sale ... $\frac{3}{8}$ inch, $2\frac{1}{4}$d per foot, under 24 inches wide ... $\frac{1}{2}$, $\frac{3}{4}$, 1, $1\frac{1}{4}$, $1\frac{1}{2}$, 2, $2\frac{1}{2}$ inches, up to 7d per foot ... Shipping can be supplied in any quantity not exceeding four thousand feet, in twenty-four hours notice, cut to any dimensions required ...

Handcarved decoration at Hawthorn Park, Buninyong.

Left: Machined weatherboarding moulded to imitate stone, on a nineteenth-century house at Alphington.

tries machine sawmilling seems to have developed from the intermittent up-and-down saw (a kind of mechanized pit-saw) which had been invented three or four centuries earlier and was traditionally powered by water-wheel.

Water-powered sawmills had existed in Australia from at least 1834, when Captain J.G. Collins operated a water-wheel on the Minnamurra River at Kiama to drive both flour-milling and timber-milling machinery for his Woodstock Mill. It was converted to steam in 1838.[32]

John Dickson announced in 1813 that he intended 'to erect a saw mill in the neighborhood of Sydney', but he did not do so. Dickson imported the first steam engine about that time, and installed it beside Darling Harbour to

William Gard's sawmill had three frames carrying twenty reciprocating saws, and a powered wood-turning lathe.

Francis Girard claimed in about 1834 to have operated the first steam sawmill in Sydney, by adding sawmilling to an existing flour mill. In 1840 his mill, in Kent Street, had a circular saw as well as an up-and-down saw.[34]

From then on – except for the effects of the depression that were first felt in 1840 – woodworking by steam power burgeoned in Australia and, as new machines were introduced, more and more of the processes previously dependent upon hand-tooling were mechanized. The gang-saw combined several blades and, in a single pass through the machine a log or large flitch could be cut into six or seven scantlings or boards. The powered drill simplified the boring of holes for dowelled, pegged or bolted connections, and the mortise-drill, which could bore a square hole, made mortise-and-tenon joints easier and quicker. The mechanical planer superseded the adze and made it easy to smooth large surfaces; the thicknesser

By the end of the nineteenth century foreign building timbers, mostly softwoods, were being imported in appreciable quantities. The principal of these were Oregon and redwood from North America, Baltic pine from Europe, and kauri from New Zealand. This also helped to make timber one of the most important components of the housing industry by the beginning of the twentieth century.

Other factors helped to popularize timber. It was 'dry' construction, which meant that it was both cleaner and quicker than 'wet' trades like bricklaying. It was light and

A small house with walls of notched logs, at Swan Hill Folk Museum. The tapered chimney, made with logs of diminishing sizes, is notable.

produced planed members of uniform sizes; and the introduction of moulding machines, employing a rotating cutter fixed to a spindle, made it possible to prefabricate elements such as skirting boards and architraves without hand-planes. Veneering machines skimmed thin layers of figured wood off a billet for use in joinery panels and repetitive cabinet-making, and also led to the development of plywood. As machines became more efficient, timber prices went down.

therefore easy to transport to almost any house site, especially as roads and vehicles improved. Structural testing and scientific analysis increased the predictability of a timber's strength. Most importantly, joining pieces of timber together was greatly simplified by the availability of mass-produced cheap wire nails – the nailed joint became one of the most tenacious of all timber fixings.

These developments did not change timber construction suddenly, or everywhere. The old customs of hand-craftsmanship continued until about the time of World War I, particularly in remote regions. A wall, for example, would still often have studs 120 millimetres wide and 75 millimetres thick spaced up to 600 milli-

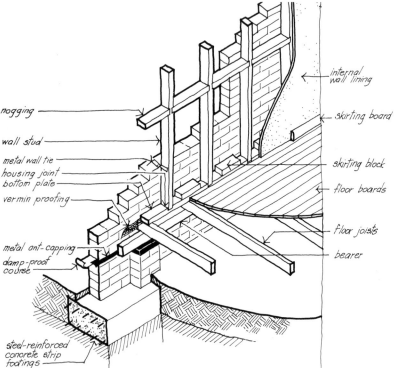

nogging

wall stud
metal wall tie
housing joint
bottom plate
vermin proofing

metal ant-capping
damp-proof
course

steel-reinforced
concrete strip
footings

internal
wall lining

skirting board

skirting block

floor boards

floor joists

bearer

metres apart, and carefully tenoned into mortises in the top and bottom plates.

But, in general, timber buildings in Australia became lighter than ever before, and more consistently light-weight than anywhere else in the world. Machine milling and the nailed joint made this lightness possible, while the mild climate, which did not demand the insulation of heavy construction, made it acceptable. Thus walls comprised studs only 100 millimetres wide and 38 millimetres thick spaced at 450 millimetre intervals, connected to the plates with a 'housed' joint (a very simple cut to fit the ends of the studs) held by two 'skew-nails' (nails driven on an angle from the stud into the plates). Light cross-bracing was nailed over the frame to stabilize it. The American equivalent of this system was called the 'balloon frame', to highlight its light weight, but the term was not applied in Australia until the twentieth century.[35] A sheeting of thin machine-sawn weatherboards was sufficient external protection, while thin laths, nailed to the studs, supported the inside wall-plaster. Towards the end of the century it was common for laths to be of machine-sawn imported Oregon instead of hand-split Australian hardwood.

Roofs also became lighter and easier to erect with the widespread acceptance of galvanized corrugated-iron sheeting (often simply called 'tin'). 'Tin' grew in popularity in rural areas long after it had been ousted in the cities by the more fashionable Marseilles-pattern terra-cotta tiles. Wherever it was available in the outback – and its light weight made for easy transportation – the versatile, cheap and durable metal sheeting was preferred even to wood shingles. And it was used surprisingly often for wall cladding, giving currency to a new name – 'tin and timber' architecture.

Infilling techniques

Timber framing has always allowed experimentation with infilling and covering materials and techniques. Plywood, an early example of interior sheeting, has already been mentioned in connection with brick veneer walling. Subsequent developments such as waterproof glues have made plywood available in the form of huge membranes which may be used externally as well as internally, to impart great strength and beauty to light framed walls. For traditional wet plastered surfaces wood lathing was first supplemented by other kinds of lathing – such as wire mesh and perforated sheet metal – and then, in the Federation period, superseded altogether by fibrous plaster, which was in turn banished by cardboard-faced gypsum sheets. Fibrous plaster and gypsum sheets eliminated wet plastering and allowed room surfaces to be nailed directly to framed walls, needing no further work than jointing. Asbestos-cement sheets became popular between the wars. William Spriggs of Sydney claimed to be the first to import the material – which was also called fibro-cement – from Italy in about 1930.[36] Soon it was being made in Australia, and its heyday was the period just before and just after World War II. A large range of natural and synthetic sheeting materials – from 'soft-boards' and 'hardboards' to plastics and metals – has developed for use with framed construction, particularly since World War II. One of the most notable is glass, which has been used dramatically as an infill sheeting, especially where the structural members have been exposed as joinery elements, and the frame becomes a 'window-wall', with mullions instead of studs.

A great vernacular technique

Wattle-and-daub has been left until last because of its importance as a low-technology infill in timber-framed construction. In its Australian history many modifications and some name changes have revealed its adaptability. The first examples were recorded early in 1788, when huts around Sydney Cove were built with posts and plates of sheoak, and the spaces between them were 'wattled with slight twigs, and plaistered with clay'.[37] This technique was a very old English one, requiring supple wood like willow or hazel. In Sydney the tree used is thought to have been the *Callicoma* or black-wattle, which got its name from the basket-weave panels made from its twigs. The English method was to cut thin, straight branches and spring them vertically into grooves cut in the horizontal members of the frame. Between these, thinner twigs were woven to form a mat. The mud plaster was daubed thickly over the inside and the outside of the core panels, filling the spaces, and then whitewashed. In Australia this early wattle-and-daub, without a binding ingredient such as lime or even bullock-dung, was hardly durable in the autumn rains. No examples of this method are known to have survived in New South Wales, but there are some 1840s panels remaining near Melbourne.[38]

A later variation of the system, current in gold-rush days, has been described as 'sapling-and-mud', although it is still called wattle-and-daub in the Bathurst region of New South Wales where numerous examples may still be found.[39] In this the 'frame' consisted of posts and top plates, usually made of round logs. There was rarely a bottom plate. Over the outside faces of the posts, long thin straight saplings were nailed from the ground up at intervals of about 120 millimetres. The same was done over the inside faces. The space between the saplings was packed with earth, dug from the site or nearby and lightly pugged to make mud, without much effort to remove stones. The filling was struck off flush with the outer faces of the saplings, and after partial drying was given a coat or two of render which included lime if available, or, in some cases, cement. The earliest example of this mud method was used in the building of the first 'Government House' at Adelaide in 1837, and some later examples are found at French Island, Victoria.[40]

Other variants utilized short saplings, laths or narrow planks nailed across the posts, or even chicken-wire instead of wood strips to retain the mud, so that the panels before plastering were reminiscent of *pisé* construction. A German method, used in South Australia, comprised wall panels made by coating pointed wooden stakes with mud-saturated straw and then standing them together in prepared holes in the frame. These sausage-like forms, called 'Dutch biscuits', were then smoothed over with more mud to make a flat surface.[41] Wattle-and-daub, a bridge between mass and frame walling, has been one of the great vernacular techniques, answering the needs of many different times and places.

Left above: Decorative fibrous plaster work in the living-room at Burnham Beeches, Sassafras, done in 1933. The material was factory-cast in sections, nailed to light timber framing, and flush-jointed with plaster of Paris.

A small wattle-and-daub cottage built at the Facchini property, Warrandyte, in 1979. The only departure from the traditional sapling-and-mud technique was that the daub of the external corners of the house was rounded off.

Left below: Diagram of brick veneer construction. A thin skin of brickwork is fixed to the studs by means of metal wall-ties.

IF WE COULD HEAR the cries and whispers of pieces of furniture in Australian homes for the first hundred years of white settlement we would hear many plaintive moans. Like their owners, for the most part they were out of place in their adopted land. Lamentations for lost companions, past certainties, former grandeur and familiar users could well have wafted up from buttoned satin chaise, floated from Chinese vases and risen in chorus from Georgian dining-chairs, sentenced to transportation for no other crime than that they were part of the eighteenth-century paraphernalia of living.

How the Reverend Mr Broderick's fine carriage must have wailed when it arrived on the shores of the Swan River in 1830, vainly expecting a neat town with paved roads! Marooned on a sandy waste of untamed land, it witnessed the dramatic chasm between the dreams and the reality of settling in Australia. Just as surely as the pioneers, whose letters and diaries are strewn with the pain of comparing their rough lives with the security of their past ordered existences, the furniture in the early days was forced to acclimatize.

Lists of goods packed by settlers show their anxiety to take civilization with them. Many took their entire household possessions on the voyage. Georgiana McCrae, in

lines, and so limited was the knowledge of alternatives, that the brave and beloved items were placed in houses based, in design and finish, on what was built 'At Home'; little houses complete with thatched roofs, looking for all the world as if they had been lifted bodily from the British Isles. Inside and out, little understanding of the weather of the Australian continent was shown. Rather, the British attitude prevailed; to keep the heat in rather than out, to build compactly and to open doors directly to the outside. Some settlers, however, inspired by the Aboriginal mia-mia, used wide bands of bark for the walls and roof of their houses. And with the innovation of the versatile verandah by ex-Indian settlers, an indelible contribution to Australian design was made. In Queensland especially, the verandah became an extension of the interior and was furnished with an easy spread of tables and chairs.

The first European house built in Australia was Government House, 'an elegant brick house' constructed in 1788. It had three rooms upstairs and enjoyed the great distinction of having walls cemented with lime mortar. Investigation in 1983 of its remains, which had been buried beneath a site on the corner of Phillip and Bridge streets, Sydney, revealed many as yet unsorted fragments including peach-coloured plaster. Perhaps this was the wall

INTERIORS AND DECORATION 9

1840, took the bathtub as well as the dining-room table and chairs, paintings, books, china, bedsteads and linen, all of which had to nestle into a home built on a gritty mix of nostalgia and determination. But determination often gave way to desperation as crisis upon crisis rocked the confidence of settlers. Eliza Shaw bravely wrote from the embryonic Swan River settlement:

Here we are under our tents, set down close to the sea beach, higgledy-piggledy up to our ankles in sand. Our sofa serves Shaw, myself and George and sometimes Mary for a bedstead![1]

Think of Georgiana McCrae's staid, spindly 'table for my cabin, with folding leaf and borders',[2] finding its way by bullock-wagon to the modest slab home built on the fringe of Port Phillip Bay by the McCraes. Imagine similar possessions wrenched from the bosom of British domestic perfection to be set among the queer mix of makeshift furniture in a hard-won home. In most cases a desperate struggle was being staged to uphold the dignity of the household. An early visitor to the Port Phillip District observed that 'Mahogany displays itself in the sofa and table, although both wear a kind of reckless air, as if inured by long usage to the hard knocks of a roving life'.[3]

So powerful was the desire to build anew but on old

The rich vigour of Victorian interiors is well illustrated in these two comfortably cluttered rooms of an unidentified house of the late nineteenth century in Geelong. The upper view shows a dining-room, and the lower one a sitting-room.

colour for the first governor's drawing-room. But we have not kept such precious information about our earliest, most significant rooms. Basic furniture for the residence was brought out with the First Fleet – again records are meagre.

Modest huts or cottages were built to house the various personnel in the colony. Most were timber-framed with wattle-and-daub or log infill and inside they must have been crudely furnished. A man able to make a table, chair or bedstead, would be well ahead of his less talented contemporaries. Decoration (it seems) was, like the white cliffs of Dover, far out of reach. Pressing needs for basic shelter and food came first.[4]

Pioneer expediency

The pattern of pioneer beginnings was repeated over and over again in the colony's first hundred years. And stories of building the first house were similar: find a good site, preferably close to water, clear the land around, cut timbers for the main posts, build the chimney of stone and fill in the walls with the best offering local material. Bert Facey, in his delightful memoirs, tells how it was done:

Our next job was to build a decent home. We selected a spot and I suggested that we build the house out of bush timber with a galvanised, corrugated iron roof. My plan was for a structure with two ten-feet by twelve-feet rooms with nine-foot ceilings, a large kitchen twelve feet by twenty-four feet, making the overall size of the house twenty-four feet by twenty-two feet. The walls on the south and east sides were to be bush timber, and hessian whitewashed with a mixture of pipe-clay and lime with two percent English cement mixed with water. The north and west sides were to be made of iron because all the rough weather came from those directions.[5]

In Queensland, half a century earlier, the problems were much the same and the shortages of materials a fact of life. Rachel Henning wrote:

We took up our quarters at Biddulph's old house, a very comfortable sort of abode ... There is no glass in the windows and certainly there are interstices between the logs, but they are not very wide and the climate is wonderful.[6]

As late as 1895, in a newly opened up area of Western Australia, the same steps were being taken to provide shelter for a large family. Comfort and privacy were the only reasons for such things as curtains; decoration was an unheard of luxury:

Uncle Archie and my brothers were busy building a house. I suppose it would be called a humpy. They cut the poles about twelve feet long, and six inches thick at one end and about three to four inches thick at the other. They cut hundreds of them and carted them to where they intended to build the humpy ... Then Uncle and the boys dug a trench at each end and put poles in them in the same way, joining the two fifty foot walls together. Then they put up two dividing walls, making a twelve by twelve room at each end of the structure and leaving a living and dining-room in the centre, twenty-six feet by twelve. They then put a timbered roof over the three rooms and thatched it with blackboy spines ...

Uncle Archie and Aunt Alice had one of the twelve-foot rooms for their bedroom and Grandma and the girls the other. We boys slept in tents outside. Uncle made a door frame for the big room out of bush timber, and sewed kangaroo skins on to it to keep out the cold weather and water. The doorways leading into the bedrooms had only curtains over them. When the building and thatching were finished, Uncle and the boys dug out clay from the creek which ran through the property, and after making it very wet and soft, they pushed it into the cracks of the poles that made the walls. When it was dry it made the place nice and weather-proof.[7]

Internal walls were rough. Improvements were made by degrees as time and money allowed. Plastering was sometimes done in one or more rooms, especially if the house was built to last, with solid walls. These rooms could then be painted or papered. In the early years, settlers from higher stations in life, anxious to lift the appearances of the house to a respectable level as soon as possible, tended to cover ceiling rafters with sail cloth. This gave a neater look and also helped to exclude rats and draughts.

For the same kinds of reasons, hessian found its way on to walls later in the century; bringing about an improvement in appearances and in comfort. If, later, the cottage was made more permanent, then the walls could be papered.

Some of the pride in putting together a house in the colonial days emerges from the 1855 letter of Biddulph Henning about his dwelling near Bulli Mountain:

I put up a small place at first in 1855, which was afterwards used as a kitchen, men's room, etc., and later built a nice cottage with one large sitting-room with French lights and four bedrooms, with a veranda in front with a splendid view of the district and ocean. The timber was cut on the ground and the cottage was put up by a runaway ship's carpenter. It was floored and lined with sassafras, and doors costing £1 and windows 30s. made of cedar. The cedar from a small tree I found on my land. The sitting-room had a stone chimney, which was built for me by a man who had been convicted by my grandfather, John Henning, of Poxwell, Dorset. He did not tell me the nature of his offence. I think the whole building only cost me £60.[8]

He points proudly to his expediency, his practicality, and his taste ('the French lights'), but there is no mention of decoration as such. Later on in 1863, however, when his sister has taken his outback Queensland household in hand, she writes glowingly:

The house was being floored when Biddulph returned but now he has had the sitting-room enlarged by taking a bedroom which used to be behind into it. It makes quite a pretty shaped room ... Last evening the services of the whole station were pressed in to sew together the long lengths of 'osnaburg' for the lining over which the paper is to be pasted.

With a triumphant note she reports three months later:

We have got the room papered at last. We finished it yesterday, Biddulph and I and Annie and Mr Hedgeland. We did about half each, and it really looks very well considering that it is extremely difficult to paper over strained canvas, much more so than over a good, firm plastered wall. The paper is an extremely pretty one, a very light green ground with a small white pattern of wild roses and ivy-leaves on it. I am afraid it is the true arsenic green, but in this airy abode I do not think we are likely to be poisoned. It is the greatest improvement to the house and sitting-room. There is paper enough for all the rooms, but I do not think we are likely to undertake any more at present. Our room is lined with white calico, and Biddulph does not care about doing his own or the rest.

The house is so comfortable now that it is all floored and lined. We have a chest of drawers, too, in our room, which is a great convenience. You hardly know how much till you have had some months' experience of 'rooting' in boxes for your things. Four looking-glasses have likewise been set up in the different rooms. We have a large one with a marble stand wherein I have discovered the interesting fact that I look very ancient and Annie more so under the influence of the hot climate, though it agrees so well with me.

Biddulph is and looks very well. I think he is pleased to have the house and place so pretty and comfortable. It is the exception, too, in the bush. The furniture was rather damaged in coming up, but one of the carpenters here is a cabinetmaker also, and he has put everything into capital order, mended sideboard, tables, looking-glasses, drawers and chairs.[9]

As the settlers were dependent on England for the supply of all kinds of hardware and furnishings, lights, door furniture, nails, mirrors, carpets, wallpapers, linoleum, matting and so on, the acquisition of items was often costly and slow. It followed that improvements were eagerly anticipated for months and years. Much excitement attended every step forward and little bits and pieces were treasured until they were put to use. Resourcefulness and ingenuity sifted the successful from the failed. Rachel Taylor (Henning) made blinds for the sitting-room while her husband made numerous pieces of furniture. She describes their first house in 1866:

There are four rooms inside. The sitting-room where I am now writing is remarkably bright and pleasant. On my right is a large fireplace wherein a wood fire is burning, for though the sun is still hot the mornings and evenings are cold up here. On each

Monsieur Henri Noufflard's house, Sydney, early 1850s. The drawing-room has a relaxed Oriental flavour, and its happy combination of random objects makes this a highly individual interior.

Left: The servants' quarters in the attic of The Grove, George-town, Tasmania, built about 1827. Servants often fitted into 'left-over' roof spaces such as this.

Three Federation interiors. Left: The entrance hall of Pastoria, near Kyneton, 1892, is a reminder of Morris's dictum, 'have nothing in your house which you do not know to be useful or believe to be beautiful'. Top: Art Nouveau detail in a Fitzroy dining-room of 1905. Above: The entrance hall of Tahara, Deloraine, was 'modernized' about 1910.

side of the fireplace is a window, a real glass window with nine large panes in it. These windows look into the garden on the side of the house, and beyond the garden paling into the forest and the path from the village that winds down between the trees. In front of me is another window looking into the veranda, and from it I can see as I sit a rose-tree covered with blossom, and then down the paddocks to the river, lying dark and still under the trees on the opposite bank. The blacks have an encampment there now, and I can see them moving about their boats, which are moored to the bank.

Next to the window is a very nice cedar bookcase made by Mr. Taylor [her husband] wherein are arranged all my books. They have not seen the light before since they left Bristol. The cedar table at which I am writing and a side-table that is under the window are also of Mr. Taylor's manufacture. The rest of the furniture consists of a mahogany chiffonier, some mahogany cane-seated chairs, an American chair (mine), a hearth-rug, some strips of India matting, a green damask table cloth, and buff blinds to the windows. These last are my making, and I am rather proud the way they roll up with a lath.[10]

The India matting to which she refers is what we would call coir matting. It was very popular as a hard-wearing and quite pleasing-looking material. Strangely enough it seems to have been dropped from the fashionable repertoire by the end of the century.

An interior is not complete without the small items. In a modest house these are seldom noteworthy but a personal account of them is always intriguing, partly because it shows their origins but mainly because it shows which were most valued and for what reasons; clearly sentiment plays a big part, but the guiding hand of fashion shows itself everywhere. Splashes of colour electrify the scene.

Mrs. Hirst gave me a very pretty green and drab tablecloth, which at present adorns the table, and in the centre stands the red vase upon a crimson and white mat knitted by Emily Tucker. The luncheon or dinner table looks quite smart with all the things that were given to me. A very handsome cruet stand from Biddulph stands in the centre, the teapot, sugar basin and cream jug were Annie's gift, and the jam or honey always appears in a pretty ground-glass dish which Emily Tucker gave us. Mrs. Tucker gave us a set of dinner mats made of strips of white and dark wood fixed on a lining so that they roll up. You know the sort . . .

Although we spent so little about furnishing, the place looks very snug and comfortable. The sofa Mr. Taylor made is a great success. I almost always sit there to work, and it is adorned with an antimacassar I sent for to Sydney, a black net darned with flowers; at least it is a woven one in imitation of those darned ones you used to make.[11]

The busy housewife in 1866 is delighted to avail herself of the fruits of mechanization and is just as happy with the woven article as she was with the handmade one. A sign of the times indeed.

English style transferred

While the resourceful rustics toiled away, the prosperous few made their contribution. For most there was a short painful period of adjustment, of getting things in order, and thereafter life went on much as it had in their places of

Interiors at the Plough Inn, Stanley, Tasmania, built as a terrace in about 1840, and now a small house museum. Above: One of the attic bedrooms. Below: The living-room.

origin. Arriving in the colony with complete households – children, nurses, governesses, grooms, and the rest – as well as complete housefuls of furniture, it was only a matter of time before they could establish a suitable foothold for themselves from which they could create little modules of English life; in short to make the Australian colonies the 'new Britannia in another world'[12] that Wentworth had prophesied. Never daunted, it seems, by any thought of incongruity, never lacking in competitive spirit or determination, they built houses in the early nineteenth century that would have been a credit to any man building a grand house in the well-groomed grounds of his estate in England or Europe.

Fitzwilliam Wentworth's small room in the upstairs hall of Vaucluse House, Sydney. The checkered 'floorcloth' is a replica.

Captain Piper's marvellous Henrietta Villa built between 1816 and 1822 at what is now Point Piper, Sydney, was described by architect and author Clive Lucas as a most 'avant-garde and romantic classical villa'.[13] It brought European architecture to the Australian colonies in a single leap. Dominating the design which was detailed in the Greek style were two magnificent domed pavilions. The interiors of these pavilions are highly suggestive of Sir John Soane's work and a strong comparison can be made with the latter's Bank Stock Office at the Bank of England, built in 1792–93. Fortunately, we are left with an evocative drawing by Frederick Garling of the interior of one of the pavilions at Henrietta Villa. Beautifully peopled, with ladies in silks brandishing fans

Private Drawing Room

14 Arm Chairs, Cane bottoms and Backs
1 Sofa.
1 Grate.

Governor's Bed Room.

1 Bedstead (Rose Wood, carved &c) no-
        bedding or furniture).
Fire Irons, Fender and Grate.
3 Plain common Chests of Drawers, made
       in this Colony. –
1 Do. Cloathes Press –Do. –Do.
1 Wall Mirror –and 1 Swing looking Glass

Dressing Room. –

1 Dressing Table. –

Passage

1 Handsome Linen Press.

Large Dining Room.

2 Small Tables. –
4 Imitation Marble Side board Tables
1 Sideboard. –
2 Cane bottomed Sofas. –
28 Chairs. –
2 Fenders, 2 Grates, & 2 Sets of fire
    Irons.

Drawing Room.

2 Card Tables. –
3 Sofas. –
38 Chairs. –
2 Large Arm Chairs. –
2 Grates, 2 Fenders and 2 Sets of fire Irons

Hall

1 Carpet Press.
2 Tables Do. for Spare Leaves. –

Front Hall.

12 Hall Chairs. –
1 Large Dining Table. –

Little Dining Room.

3 Dining Tables.
2 Do. Ends and Spare Leaves. –
2 Card Tables –old.
12 Chairs.
1 Grate, 1 Fender and 1 Set of Fire Irons.

Governor's Office.

4 Small Chests of Drawers for books & papers
1 Office Table.
1 Sofa. –
1 Large Book Case. –
18 Chairs.
1 Grate, 1 Fender, & 1 Set of Fire Irons.

Small Bed Room up Stairs.

1 Small Dressing Table.
4 Window Seats. 12 Chairs. –
1 Grate, 1 Fender, & 1 Sett of Fire Irons

in the best ballroom style and gentlemen posturing perfectly in their military outfits, the drawing gives a colourful taste of colonial splendour. The impact of the building and the life contained within it must have been enormous. The artist Joseph Lycett described it in 1824:

The interior of the Villa is fitted up a style that combines elegance with comfort. The principal apartments are a spacious dining room, a banqueting room and a drawing room; all furnished in the most tasteful manner. This Naval Villa may be considered the most superb residence in the colony, having cost, according to general report, at least ten thousand pounds.[14]

It is altogether a staggering achievement when one considers the difficulty of obtaining building supplies and presumably also, skilled tradesmen. Perhaps the real hallmark of Australian style is determination; a desire never to be outdone or left behind because of circumstances.

Other members of the wealthy military coterie and their friends in government circles showed similar style. The Macarthurs, of legendary assertiveness, established a reputation of being up-to-the-minute in their English tastes and lifestyle. Visiting them in 1845 at Camden Park, the French artist Eugene Delessert admired:

a drawing room with the latest albums from London and Paris, an excellent piano, bookcases stocked with the best works and, on the mantel piece of local marble, a beautiful Renaissance-style Parisian clock and a selection of ornaments arranged with taste by Mrs James MacArthur. When one thinks that all this exists in a part of the world so far removed from Europe, in the interior of a country where communications are so difficult, one is all the more staggered by these luxuries and comforts.[15]

There were many other fine houses built by the elite in the colonial period. John Verge, who designed the Macarthurs' house, also designed a string of impressive buildings for other people. Like many other high-minded architects of his day practising in Australia, Verge espoused Classical ideals of good proportion, clean-cut lines, simple Greek detailing and good craftsmanship which are evident in the interior as well as the exterior of his buildings. He made a major statement of quality and style in the entry hall, especially in the case of Elizabeth Bay House, the saloon of which ascends to the pinnacle of architectural success. In a less spectacular house though, the entry hall would still be handsomely broad, entered through a gracious fanlighted doorway, and possess some niche or pediment and plaster-work or other detailing of Classical design.

Frequently a fine geometric stairway would rise delicately from one side, the first of these having appeared around 1815. Walls would often be painted in imitation of a rich Sienna marble, while the floor would be either polished hardwood or flagged stone.

Early nineteenth century elegance. Left: An 1821 inventory of the furniture at Government House, Sydney. Right above: Captain John Piper's domed ballroom, Point Piper, built about 1820.

Entrance halls. Right: Part of the entrance hall at The Vineyard, Rydalmere, 1833. Far right: Barwon Park, Winchelsea, by Davidson and Henderson, 1869. The view up the stairs from the entrance hall.

Withdrawing and dining in luxury

Other impressive treatments would be reserved for the drawing-room. Rich silk or satin drapes, probably in a crimson or a deep blue, gold or green would be at the windows; walls would be painted perhaps a rich cream, a soft peach colour or blue, and a strong moulded plaster cornice and concentric ceiling rose painted in off-white or pastel shades would crown the room. A central chandelier would hang delicately and the marble chimney-piece would lend the room added dignity. The drawing-room at Lyndhurst, Glebe, an 1830s house, was painted Wedgwood blue – a bold choice, against which rosewood furniture, upholstered in drab and blue, was placed on a white-ground Brussels carpet. Another brilliant scheme can be seen in a portrait of the prosperous Sydney merchant Robert Campbell. It shows him in 1834 against the backdrop of his dark green drawing-room walls, rich red upholstery and coloured geometric floor covering.

We are fortunate to be able to experience still the superb rich reds and yellows in the drawing-room at Elizabeth Bay House. They are radiant, yet absorbed by the body of coloured carpet on which the room visually rests, and by the bland grey walls which are a sturdy foil. Upholstery at this time was sumptuous and expensive.

The Louis XIV style found its way into an Australian drawing-room in the 1847 creation of part of Vaucluse House, Sydney. There a richly carved marble chimney-piece is the centre of a lovely room, the walls of which have been arranged into panels with flowered borders in the French style. Recent restoration is bringing this room closer to its original feeling.

Diaper wallpaper on a white ground hangs on the walls in the earliest photo of Sydney's second Government House which was finished in 1845. The simple strong cornice is painted in a drab shade, and the ceiling is darker than the walls. A lofty Baroque mirror, or chimney glass as it was called, spans the great space from mantel to cornice. A number of rosewood pieces including several chairs, a settee, a sofa, a centre ottoman and two stools, all upholstered in the same patterned fabric, a glowing amber tambouret, congregate in the lower level of the room. Surprisingly soft for such a room are the lace drapes which are drawn across the vast Gothic window.

Burdekin House, an extraordinary house of the 1840s which lingered on into the 1930s, was a Macquarie Street mansion built in the Neo-Greek style but with a splashy Louis XIV interior. A surviving photograph shows that it was as complete an expression as could be found of the Louis style – including France! Walls and ceilings carry oval and elliptical painted panels of such designs as pairs of cherubs cavorting on cloud tops. There is no surface not covered by some scroll or garland or swirl.

According to contemporary illustrations, both in England and Australia, furniture could be wonderfully varied and splendidly colourful. Regency taste favoured Neoclassical styles, but the worldliness of the age admitted Chinese and other exotic items. It was said that Captain Piper had 'curiously painted vases and jars and a pair of mandarins with moveable heads', in his mansion Henrietta Villa.[16] Comfortable chintz-covered chairs stood side by side with light mahogany ones, French settees and

chairs; a cloth-covered table carried a book or two and ladies' hand-work, while items of special interest such as vases, porcelain, pot-pourri holders and small statues were displayed on a pretty French-style table. A piano or lamp might fill a corner of the room. Altogether the pieces would be spread elegantly, not oppressively, across the room over a colourful patterned carpet. An air of comfort and pleasure pervaded the best rooms of the time.

Joinery in this and other rooms might remain natural timber and polished, as in Elizabeth Bay House, or it may be painted in pastel shades, or even wood-grained. Wood-graining was a virtuoso treatment in Georgian and Regency times, and a feature of a room – as English illustrations such as of the drawing-room of Meesdenbury in Hertfordshire, England, painted about 1840, clearly show. Marbling, its companion skill, was also found in green in the Elizabeth Bay House saloon, and a fragment on a chimney-piece in a modest house in remote Port Arthur, Tasmania. But not all rooms were painted – wallpapers were available in the 1840s and 1850s.

As early as 1830, in Tasmania, a magnificent wallpaper was used to decorate the walls of a house, Clairville, near Launceston. It was of the very special breed of papers, known now as panoramic papers, or 'papiers peints'. They were the province of the French makers such as Zuber et Cie, whose artists worked for many months on a single paper or panorama, sometimes painting it with over a hundred colours. Their subjects were scenes of a Classical or an historical nature such as *Les Vues du Brèsil* designed in 1829, or *L'Hindoustan* designed in 1807. The panorama at Clairville shows the arrival of a fleet somewhere in the Middle East with local dignitaries arriving in entourage to greet the visitors. Architecture and vegetation as well as crowds of people are all depicted in detail.

Other papers were perhaps milder, using pastel shades in pretty patterns to ornament walls. These papers were of course hand blocked. Many had a vertical or geometric basis to their design, either in the suggestion of columns of flowers or in trellis shapes and diapers.

The dining-room in the colonial house was also a most significant room. Just as luxurious upholstery and *objets d'art* were lavished on the drawing-room, so were handsome timbers and the art of the cabinet-maker shown to excellence in the dining-room. Camden Park's dining-room with its stately air of quality is a good example. John Verge's Doric colonnade harbouring the sideboard in cedar at the far end is a fine gesture which emphasises the large table and good-looking chairs that are constructed from rich timbers with symmetry and balance.

Ox-blood red is magnificent in the dining-room of Elizabeth Bay House, giving great warmth and strength to the already powerful room. Other likely colours for a dining-room would be green, ochre, or blue.

The dining-room at Woolmers, Longford, Tasmania, was built in 1843 and was decorated in 1859 as we see it today. It possesses a compelling richness, from the warmth of its Italianate design, but perhaps also from the wonderful red flock wallpaper which is such a rare survivor from this time. The mahogany furniture was made for the room and does much to enhance it. Spread above the table is a branched kerosene light – another rarity.

Left above: The main hall at Clarendon, Tasmania, built for James Cox in 1838. It is divided by pilasters into five bays, with a doorway in each.

The warm and opulent dining-room of Woolmers, Tasmania, decorated in 1868. The wallpaper is rich red flock, and the central light device is a counterbalanced five-branched fitting of kerosene lamps.

Left: The dining-room alcove at Camden Park House, Menangle, 1831. It has plaster vaulting supported by nicely-detailed Doric columns.

The sumptuous drawing-room of Werribee Park, 1876. The silk damask drapes and gold-leaf accents contribute to its French flavour.

Vigour and richness

By the 1860s we see the emergence of Victorian pride – the Great Exhibition of 1851 had set the wheels in motion and British industry was out of Victoria Station and roaring round the countryside. Before long it had touched down at every town, village and hamlet brushing them with the transforming wave of mechanization. Old processes were made swifter and new goods were released. Engineering and artistic skills were harnessed in the great industrial cities making carpets, china, fabrics, furniture, cutlery and a thousand and one items for the home.

The drawing-room was the first room to feel this injection of vigour. A number of impressive specimens came to life in Tasmania, Victoria, New South Wales and South Australia. Mona Vale in Tasmania still has its original elegant diamond-patterned white and gold wallpaper of this time, as well as the basic elements of the room. Its original dining-room wallpaper was royal blue, grey and white and included a frieze of classical figures.

As we come a little closer to the fat ornate body of Victorian decoration we see an interesting emergence of late Colonial sparkle. French merchant M. Henri Noufflard, in his residence in Bligh Street, Sydney, shows a charming use of mixed items. The drawing-room, though modest, has a large rectangular table like a dining-table in the centre, which dwarfs the sofa beside it. The room may have doubled as a dining-room. Over-size vases flank the chimney-piece on either side. The Oriental flavour increases with four pieces of dark lacquer-ware: a bureau, a cabinet in front of the fireplace, a chest and a cabinet. The walls are hung with a small geometric paper in blue. Several water-colours and a gaily overloaded mantelpiece give the room its easy air. Its happy combination of random objects helps to dispel any idea of colonial rooms following a hard and fast formula. Indeed it seems that they rejoiced in the unpredictable!

The 1870s saw a quickening of the pace. More large new houses were built, and many more smaller ones. The cities were filling up and the suburbs expanding. In the typical pattern, a family such as the Chirnsides, who had started out with a large holding in the 1850s, consolidated it in the next two decades living at first very simply in a hut, then in a solid small house, and finally by 1876 built their own mansion, Werribee Park. It was hardly an 'avant-garde' building but its interior is full of indicators of the taste and materials of the time. The entry hall's wide, grand space is flanked by Corinthian pilasters and culminates in a sweeping divided staircase. Underfoot is the clink of the cool quality of marble, while on either side there are busts of the Chirnsides. Walls are coloured in soft green and detailing is rich with gold, cream and brown.

Luxurious blue silk damask, encumbered by weighty tassles, swathes the blue-walled drawing-room and again

This room in a late-Victorian house at Geelong has the expected cosiness and variegation, but the animal portraits impart an additional air of individuality.

gold leaf is plentiful. Beside the marble chimney-piece are placed two glistening gilt mirrors. The room is dotted with sumptuous spongy members of a nine-piece suite, an ottoman in the centre, several chairs, a settee and arm-chairs – all straight-legged and in good French style. A cheeky ebonized cabinet has crept in – a taste of the mixtures that were becoming fashionable. Cosiness ema-nates from the fluffy hearthrug sitting snugly over the richly swirling 'body and border' carpet.

Across the hallway, the library stands suitably solid – a room that has not experienced a rustle of silk or a child's footstep. Portraits hold one in their gaze. A magnificent bronzed gasolier is suspended from a ceiling rose.

The dining-room is suitably masculine – not excessively, but just enough to convey all the right impressions – with oak furniture providing the key note. A massive table, sturdy chairs from John Taylor & Co. of Edinburgh, and a mighty sideboard groaning with weighty silver give weight to the room. The chimney-piece is dark and burly: just right for the centre clock and pair of figures on either side to rest upon. Again the bronzed light fitting is a powerful element in the room. The morning-room is also in its way a capsule of Victorian style. Establishment style it was, a far cry from that of the masses, but Victorian indeed.

The masculine billiard-room is another prototype. The

buttoned leather seats raised on a platform suggest many hours spent in jolly sporting company and stag heads and animal portraits give the room atmosphere. Each of the bedrooms has its own individuality and interest. In gen-eral they show Victorian decoration and furnishings in their most restrained, English form. Light coloured bed-room suites predominate, along with diaper wallpapers on pastel grounds – nothing so fussy as a frieze or a dado.

It was not interiors such as these that aroused the ire of Richard Twopeny, an English upper-crust visitor and short-time resident of Australia. His writing in *Town Life in Australia*, published in 1883, gives us an image of the ludicrous extent to which British fashions were carried to the colonies. He complained that 'The frowzy carpets and heavy solid chairs of England's cold and foggy climate reign supreme beneath the Austral sun.'[17]

Nor would Mandeville Hall, in Toorak, the home of Joseph Clarke, have been his target. It was too individual and truly artistic to be included in his broad sweeps at the local mediocrity. In securing the services of architect Charles Webb and the firm of English decorators, Gillow and Co., Joseph Clarke achieved a house of singular impact. The quality of materials – silk and velvet and embroided hangings in the drawing-room, and the paintwork in the dining-room and entry hall, particularly of the friezes – was second to none in its period. However it was in the use of these riches and talents that the real success of the building lay, in the creation of stylish, delicate, crisp and altogether memorable interiors.

A handful of other individuals took the trouble to establish houses which were distinctive, not just in the extent to which they followed fashions. Relatively unknown English designers such as Pugin and William Morris had a house or two furnished in Australia to hint at their vastly more important reputations in Britain. Morris furnished a drawing-room at Torrens Park in Adelaide by proxy. Pugin's sphere of influence was largely in the Catholic churches built by his admirer, William Wardell. Two excellent examples of his Gothic-inspired designs survive in Melbourne: St Patrick's Cathedral and St Mary's Church in Caulfield. They display vast areas of tile-work and stencilled designs. One of Wardell's builders, John Young, was inspired to build a Gothic house for himself and his family at Annandale, Sydney, and built a small row of them, his own being the only one to survive intact today. It is a house of many marvels and exquisite workmanship. Some of the pieces of furniture in the Gothic style are of interest, especially the sideboard and the cast-iron chimney-piece which is reminiscent of a cathedral.

Other historical revivals were to be found in the suburbs and the country; houses which aped the Norman castle, the Elizabethan manor, and even the Moorish palace. It was a time when the rich felt free to express their most far-fetched dreams in architectural terms – with interiors as magical as exteriors, though the two were not necessarily of the same fanciful design.

On the whole, however, the trend-setters and local suppliers of furnishings were one and the same. Entrepreneurs like W.D. Rocke promoted their styles with booklets and expansive showrooms. They gave detailed instructions on combinations of furniture upholstery and the like – which had the effect of standardizing 'taste' and increasing sales! For instance Rocke comments:

The next striking feature of the room is the carpet (which is a 'Brussels'). The chosen pattern is as new as it is striking and picturesque. Its prevailing colour is French grey blended with oak, and minute touches of blue ... The coverings of the furniture are of cretonne – the admirable cotton cloth that has cast almost all the ordinary chintzes into the cold shades of unfashionableness.[18]

Heaven forbid that the householder should enter the cold shades! Better to endure the ridicule of Twopeny:

Whilst the ambition of the wealthy colonist not infrequently finds vent in building a large house, he has generally been brought up in too rough a school to care to furnish it even decently.[19]

Furthermore he jibes at the incongruity of certain favourite items such as the piano: 'A piano, tune immaterial, is a *sine qua non* in every middle class house.'[20]

A house of ornament

The typical house of the 1880s, so distasteful to visitors such as Twopeny, was a house of appearances. Facades, surfaces, materials all had to be titivated to achieve the best appearance. The nature of the intrinsic materials – whether they were worthy and solid – was less important. The aim was to enhance, to ornament.

The house was entered through an imposing – frequently wood-grained – doorway, where panes of col-

oured glass cast shafts of tinted light into the entry hall. A lantern gasolier of similar glass hung centrally. Bright encaustic tiles in geometric pattern covered the floor, unless their place was taken by a carpet runner on a pine floor. Walls were divided into three decorated zones – the dado, filling, and frieze and, if not painted or stencilled, these were recipients of a growth of subdued wallpaper, probably varnished for protection. The ceiling was framed in an elaborate crusty cornice richly coloured in browns and greens. It might be papered in a lustre geometric paper or fancifully stencilled. Conventionally, a hall stand stood on the right side of the entry hall, with a solid timber carved hall chair on either side and a hall table opposite. In order to separate the entry hall from the domestic traffic areas beyond, a heavy drape was often hung from behind the archway.

The predictable elements in the drawing-room were its white marble fireplace and gilt overmantel mirror, its suite of walnut, or perhaps rosewood chairs of curvacious style, its *de rigueur* piano, its elaborately decorated walls, and its patterned and perhaps unmatched carpet. Other items such as paintings, vases, statuettes, knick-knacks, were wildy variable in one sense, but in their general conglomeration, embarrassingly predictable. And the critics of Victorian sentimentalia, memorabilia, and ornamentalia had a heyday – the 1880s gave them a target in every street. Yallum Park in South Australia, Rouse Hill House in New South Wales, Wardlow in Victoria, Ralahyne in Queensland: all are vivid extant examples of Victorian decorative enthusiasm. It was not difficult for Twopeny to lampoon the unimaginative choice of chairs:

As for the make of the chairs, they are to be found in plenty of English middle-class drawing-rooms even now. The shape may be named the 'deformed'. The back is carved out into various contortions of a horse shoe, with a bar across the middle which just catches you in the small of the back...[21]

In the dining-room certain items were perhaps chosen in 'slavish imitation of what prevails in the "old country" '[22], rather than in response to their Australian environment. The heavy chairs and table, the gilt-framed oil paintings, the sombre chimney-piece, the mighty sideboard, and the pervasive air of deepness and solidity were somewhat retrospective. How could it be otherwise when 95 per cent of the population at the time were of British origin? Mass-produced items available at the furniture stores tended to boast constantly of English and French antecedents, which compounded the problem. Wallpapers found an eager market in the building boom of the 1880s, and many a wall became a mural of burgeoning garden-like blooms from dado to cornice, or a mosaic of Japanesque geometry, or even a tooled masterpiece of imitation leather far from its Spanish ancestors.

Other rooms paralleled this carefree embrace with wondrous worldly goods. Libraries were 'wardrobes of

Decorative ceilings. Right above: A detail of the lively frieze in the dining-room of Villa Alba, Kew, decorated in 1883. Right and far right: Swirling Art Nouveau ceiling motifs in painted pressed metal, in a late-Victorian house updated in 1905. The nearer picture shows the dining-room, and the further one the entry hall.

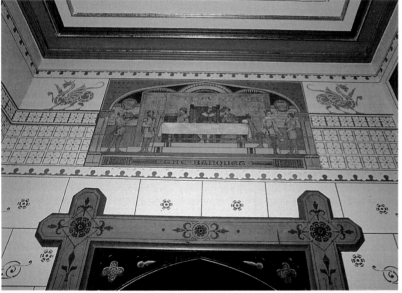

A painted wall panel 'The Banquet', above the dining-room doorway at The Abbey, Annandale, 1881–82.

Top and right: Two drawing-rooms which suggest the new fashions of the late nineteenth century – pastel tones, timber fretwork. Top, Glenhope, Sydney, 1895; right, a house in Kew.

thought' with cases of books impressively displayed. Master bedrooms were bowers of luxury, with elaborately papered walls enveloping draped bedspreads, a richly upholstered *chaise-longue*, and an array of similar pieces. Lesser bedrooms displayed a range of treatments from the comfortable to the frugal.

All in all, the Australian home of the 1880s, while it reflected the circumstances and to some extent the personality of its occupants, was a concoction of commercial opportunism made possible by the brilliant technical prowess of Victorian England, and fanned by the optimism and expansion of Australia at that time.

Despite the dominating impact of machine-made goods, the skills of craftsmen in the design and execution of decorative items from wallpaper dadoes to stencilled ceilings, and including the arts of the colourist, the upholsterer, the draper, the carpet designer and the stained-glass maker, were essential to the Victorian interior. The impressiveness of their accumulated talents in a surviving interior such as Labassa or Mandeville Hall or Villa Alba is in itself sufficient reason to justify the retention of such interiors for posterity, as they represent a standard hardly likely to be reached again.

Art Nouveau and the Aesthetic movement

The Aesthetic movement, or 'Art Movement', missed its prime target in the Australian colonies, but it was the basis for a shift in decorative taste. Ideas that germinated in the intellectual ferment of England in the 1870s were overlooked or misunderstood in Australia – the notion of bringing a new artistic sense into the heavy and static interiors of the 1860s was lost. The colonists, however, were impressed by the swirling chrysanthemums and other floating vegetable-based paraphernalia associated, at its most accessible level, with the movement. Bamboo, pampas and feathers made their entry while Louis XV suites made their exit. The radiant, cheerful sunflower symbolized the aesthetic ideals and became a regular motif in decoration from the 1880s. Mandeville Hall's drawing-room shows the repeated use of it in many beautiful forms, painted on the door panels, on the ceiling, and carved on the chimney-piece. Decoration by rote gave way to decoration by whim; staidness was discouraged while a dignified informality became desirable.

Anything which gave a supposedly refreshing tang to a room was included – bringing about an unchecked rush towards all things exotic, Japanese in particular. Rooms based on a tradition of decoration and furnishing were subjected to turnabouts, updates, revamps and repapering. Nothing fundamental changed except in the rarest of houses (such as Mandeville Hall) but the effect was one of added garnishing and busyness.

Eventually embellishment could go no further. Every surface had been used to its limits as a vehicle for decorative inventiveness. Even quite simple rooms 'could end up as rich as an Aladdin's cave'.[23] Dadoes had crept higher and higher while chimney-pieces grew more gross. Cornices were havens for lurking bands of colours, while ceiling roses threatened to collapse under increasing loads of larger-than-life fruit, flowers and frills.

Back in England, much concern was voiced in the 1870s over the loss of status and welfare of the older-type artist and craftsman, and this concern culminated in the emergence of the Arts and Crafts movement, led by William Morris. Its direct impact in Australia was negligible, but an indirect effect came from Morris's emphasis on the essential beauty or usefulness of an object, expressed in his saying, 'have nothing in your houses which you do not know to be useful or believe to be beautiful', which eventually cleansed the twentieth-century interior of much of its redundant flimflam of contents. His fervid and eloquently-expressed beliefs in the integrity of true individual craftsmanship was like a white light shining through the last years of the nineteenth century to illuminate the passage of Art Nouveau into the twentieth century. His ideals had a cosiness and an intellectual vigour that made an irresistible impact, which was made even greater by his colossal talent as a designer and his romantic image.

The sinuous threads of his richly-hued wallpapers found their way into the soul of Art Nouveau. The spin-off of the infatuation with Japanese design also led naturally to the simplicity and refinement which characterized the new style. The debris, as it were, of late nineteenth-century interiors was cleared by the two clean-sweeping brooms of Morris on the one hand, with his heartfelt attachment to basic quality, and the fresh, incisive, exotic thrust of Japanese art on the other. The actual mix of ingredients seems to emerge from the architectural hand of Victor Horta in Belgium, in his curvilinear masterpiece, the auditorium of the *Maison du Peuple*.

The acceptance of Art Nouveau as a style in Europe, America and Australia was made the more rapid by the highly-developed network of periodicals which promoted the notion of a 'new art'. Well-subscribed international periodicals such as *Studio* and, locally, the *Australasian Decorator and Painter*, were enthusiastic in their adoption of an original style that was not just building another layer on the previous layers of the nineteenth century. It was the answer to everybody's prayer, the firm rock for which intellectuals and entrepreneurs alike had been grasping in the closing years of Victoria's reign. They could set their teeth into it, and champion its purity – emblazoning the characteristic flowing tendrils and wavy lines on to plaster, brass, copper, timber, glass, and all other materials.

The tenuous lines and drooping tulips slid into the new houses of the new century, like an insignia of membership of a fashion-followers club, and ousted items in the older houses of those who had lost their Victorian nerve. As people lifted themselves out of the gloom of the 1890s depression they no longer viewed their Victorian baubles (if they had any left) with joy. Instead they were persuaded to an acceptance of paleness and simplicity. Ochres, greens, creams and oranges had their place but on the whole the new century ushered in a sea of off-white furniture, emasculated wallpapers and pastel walls.

The twentieth century eschewed the stratified order of things Victorian as well as their crowded ornate rooms. The Edwardians traded the tyranny of nineteenth-century status seeking for the freedom of cool caves of contemplation in houses deserted by romance. The demise of the

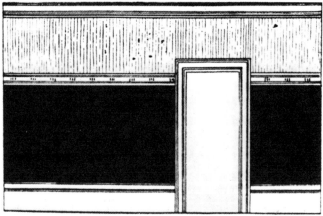

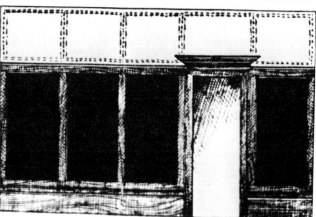

'A few suggested schemes for rooms', published in a Melbourne journal of 1906. Ornate and crowded surfaces were no longer in vogue; the typical Federation interior seems simple and austere by comparison with those of earlier years.

Victorian interior is best evoked by the contemporary poem *Peaceful Furniture*.

> He lived in a riot of painting,
>   Of carpets that screamed their surprise.
> His guests were oft carried out fainting
>   Through the strength of the wallpaper's cries.
>
> His curtains were rowdy and blatant,
>   His mats had a hooligan air;
> His chairs, it was brutally patent,
>   Were designed for the raising of hair.
>
> From couches came horrible moaning,
>   Occasional tables ran mad.
> And ever the sideboard kept groaning
>   In a way that was bitterly bad.
>
> His heated brain seethed like a crater;
>   He anguished for quiet and peace,
> Till he called in a Skilled Decorator,
>   Who said, 'All the tumult shall cease;
>
> 'Your pictures must be without color,
>   Your curtains resemble a pall,
> The scheme of your carpets grow duller
>   In fact, why a carpet at all?
>
> 'I shall strip you wallpaper of passion,
>   In its place you shall have neutral grey;
> An artic freize [*sic*] quiet in fashion
>   Shall solace your eyes night and day.
>
> 'As to sideboard, chairs, couches, and tables,
>   And objects that litter your floor,
> Consign them to outhouse or stables
>   And list to their ravings no more.'
>
> The householder dumbly assented,
>   And now he's as merry as May,
> For he sits at his ease, undemented,
>   In a solitude vasty and grey.
>
>   LJ McQ[24]

The Federation interior

The interior which took shape in the twentieth century was a reflection of its exterior. The suburban Federation house, in the Queen Anne vogue, consists largely of thousands of red bricks, capped with an ornamental tiled and turreted roof. Windows, often leadlighted, hide under deep eaves. A staunch front portico links the outside with the inside. Entering the portals is like entering a dark, spreading cave, with shafts of light coming from windows in the distance. There is a sense of space, accented with heavy timbers, dark floors, and very deliberately-styled doors and door furniture.

Openings to right or left may be through double doors to a drawing-room which is not askew, but nearly so, with a fireplace and ingle-nook on one wall and perhaps a cosy corner or bay window on another, creating an interesting tension. A fretwork screen, painted cream, is fetching inside the opening to the cosy corner. The ceiling looks vast, with its off-white plaster area divided into square panels, each one ribbed, or the whole made into Jacobean swirls. Or there may be a softly-tinted Wunderlich pressed-metal panel ceiling. A deep, deep frieze is of a lugubrious tawny and pastel design, and the top of a low picture-rail takes in the architrave. Flat-framed pictures hang from the rails, the subjects including the usual flowers, watercolours and scenes, with an occasional filmy portrait. Pale yellow textured paper covers the main part of the walls.

From the centre of the ceiling, unannounced, hangs a sculptural brass and copper branched cluster of electric lamps – the electrolier – with glistening shades. This is probably the most striking item in the room. Alternatively, in celebration of clean electric power, there might hang a voluptuous waisted and gathered silk central light, dangling like some blowsy Edwardian lady in suspended animation. The room's light is augmented with a standard lamp and brackets of similar bent.

An odd but again quite stylish assortment of chairs, some polished, some painted, some wicker, as well as tables, armchairs and sofas, sprawl easily about the room, not filling it by any means, not covering half of the Persian-styled carpet mat. The chintz-covered upholstered items dominate the room, and there are numerous cushions, vases, aspidistras, palms and other bric-a-brac added to lift the room. Somehow, though, the heavy fireplace and mirrored overmantel conspire to hold it down. Nevertheless, comfort is there, and the ideals of Art Nouveau simplicity are not altogether lost.

Other rooms such as the dining-room, library, billiard-room and bedrooms bring few surprises, except that again there is a break away from symmetry. If anything, the billiard-room and dining-room have overworked the theme of masculine evocation with their tendency to mock-Elizabethan timber panelling and heavy furniture such as were found at Tudor, in Elizabeth Bay, Sydney. The colour-scheme barometer seldom rises above the pastels except in a library or some such deeper-toned room, which might incorporate a new landscape frieze complete with russet hills and gum-trees – such a room can be seen at Boree Cabonne, in Cudal in New South Wales. Wallpaper and colours were not the *pièce de résistance* they were in the nineteenth-century home.

Australian motifs

Australian nationalism is not strongly evident in this stream of design. In the first hundred years or so, any conscious nationalistic efflorescence would have been quashed in favour of the more estimable British ones. On the unconscious level, however, the expressions were there from the start, in the materials and in their soulful combinations: the bark, the mud, the brush, the bricks and the indigenous timbers worked into habitations. The great struggle to get on top of the unwilling land shows through in our early interiors. But it took almost a hundred years for the settlers to espouse the brilliant waratah instead of the primrose. Joseph Clark's 'Four Seasons' at Mandeville Hall in 1878 was strictly British, with winter snow and the rest, although he was born in Tasmania some fifty years earlier. In 1888, however, the Mayor of Adelaide, Sir Edwin Smith, interspersed some splendid Australian flowers, including the Sturt Desert Pea, as part of his Japanese-style dado in The Acacias, Marryatville. More flowers and birds came to the fore from about that

The dining-room of a house in North Fitzroy which was redecorated in 1905 by Swan & Co. The ceiling is of tinted Wunderlich pressed-metal panels, and there is a striking central pendant light fitting.

time, both in exterior decoration, such as cast iron, and in painted glass. In 1890 French designer Lucien Henri designed an interior featuring superb Franco-Australian lyre-bird chairs. In other media, such as glass, the waratah, the kookaburra, the kangaroo and other native symbols were taken up.

By the first decade of the twentieth century Australia's interiors had at last come of age and reflected an acknowledgement of the new country. Overall the decorative offspring of the twentieth century looks different from her bulky, busy parents, but it is not in shape or weight that the telling difference lies. It is in the way her eyes are set openly in the direction of the future rather than to the past.

BETWEEN THE TIME of the first settlement of Australia and the beginning of the twentieth century – from First Fleet to federation – dramatic developments took place in domestic kitchen design. At the outset the kitchen, in common with traditional kitchens everywhere, was like an isolated and austere slave house, burning a dirty fire fifteen hours or more every day to feed and sustain its dependants. By the end of the century it was a sophisticated food factory, largely freed from filth by the gas stove and plumbing, integrated into the house plan, and ready for the even greater things that the introduction of electricity promised.

For many centuries a fire in the hearth was a source of great comfort to the human race. In Australia, it not only provided the pioneer with a limited supply of hot water and a means of cooking but it was the heart of the dwelling, where the social activities of the household centred about its warmth and brightness. The teapot was usually to be found ready at the fireside, and the first thing a stranger would do, upon entering a hut was 'to help himself to a pannikin of tea'.[1]

Cooking methods and equipment reflect a community's development and customs. This was aptly described by Mistress Margaret Dods in the introduction to *The Cook*

The fire in the hearth

Camp-fire cooking was brought inside as soon as the first rough huts were constructed. Sometimes, the fire was made in the centre of the earth floor and smoke was left to filter out of the doorway or 'a hole in the wall' in whatever way it could.[6] The central hearth was used in the great halls of England to the end of the medieval period[7] and was still in use in a primitive Highland cottage in 1803 which Dorothy Wordsworth described in her *Recollections of a Tour Made in Scotland*.[8]

These simple huts quickly developed a large chimney with a huge opening at floor level for a fire, which usually dominated one end of a multi-purpose room. This open fireplace against a wall – called a down hearth – became the basis of traditional cooking. The down-hearth system survives in some isolated areas where wood is plentiful.

Australian settlers did their best to re-create the familiar cottage and manorial kitchens and to produce the closest possible resemblances to an English cuisine. A curtain or rough partition might sometimes divide the space within the hut, but more often than not the kitchen was the whole house.

The available make-shift materials caused certain problems. The highly inflammable nature of the grass, bark or

THE COLONIAL KITCHEN

10

and Housewife's Manual, 1826, when she recorded a speech at the conclusion of a sumptuous Scottish feast:

Man is a cooking animal; and in whatever situation he is found, it may be assumed as an axiom, that his progress in civilization has kept exact pace with the degree of refinement he may have attained in the science of gastronomy.[2]

The nineteenth-century kitchen was one of the domestic areas least influenced by fashions and decorative styles, where cooking techniques evolved slowly according to the dictates of supply, function and inventiveness. Generally speaking, early settlers in Australia arrived with a background of English, Irish and Scottish cookery, based on the traditional skills of past generations, and they attempted to continue to use these culinary techniques in the new country. Almost nothing was learned from the Aborigines in spite of the knowledge and skill which enabled them to survive in such a harsh land. Elsewhere in the world, for example in India, British colonists absorbed some of the local cuisine into their diets. In desperation, Governor Phillip tried to find native vegetables to bolster dwindling supplies in New South Wales,[3] but until the settlements developed their farms and crops, it was commonplace to have a monotonous diet of 'mutton, tea and damper three times a day ... from year's end to year's end',[4] or in other areas pork and kangaroo.[5]

The sparse, stone-flagged kitchen of the Sydney house of M. Henri Noufflard, a wool merchant in the 1850s.

reeds used for roofing sometimes made it necessary to build the chimney as a free-standing structure, well clear of the roof. Another solution was to plaster the thatch with clay on the outside to prevent sparks from the chimney igniting the roof.[9]

Bark, sod, wattle-and-daub and timber slabs were all used to build the first chimneys. Many ingenious methods were tried to help reduce the area of the flue in order to improve the 'draw'. William Howitt described the chimneys at the Bendigo gold-fields as 'extraordinary pieces of architecture' built of slabs and covered with bark or sheets of tin from packages. 'A considerable number are surmounted by dry casks – American flour-barrels – which make the upper shaft of the chimney.'[10] Such unorthodox methods were not confined to the gold-fields. In 1831, William Tanner wrote from Swan River colony where his partly finished house was served by a kitchen that was 'a mere makeshift being only a piece of canvas strained on 2 poles as a roof and having a turf chimney topped with an empty cask'.[11]

If the chimney flue stood clear of the wall of the kitchen building, an advantage could be gained by forming a gutter between the flue and the wall, to run towards a barrel standing on the ground. This collected the rainwater and provided a modest water supply conveniently placed near the kitchen door.

Where stone was available, a slab chimney might be lined with stones bedded in a sand mortar to a height of about a metre above the hearth.[12] Alternatively, a slab hut

233

Traditional down-hearth fireplace of a farmhouse in central Victoria, regularly whitened with pipeclay.

might have a stone chimney 'mortared together with mud'.[13] In the 1840s, a young Irish wife living at Yandoit, Victoria, is said to have been so dissatisfied with her Australian-type, slab chimney, that she carried the stones from a creek and built a large, square, 'proper' chimney like those of Ireland, which still stands in the 1980s.[14]

The fireplace was built broad and deep – some were like small rooms similar to traditional ingle-nooks. These were prevalent in the north-eastern area of Victoria. A story is told of the Beechworth area where a huge log would be fed continuously through a hole in the wall into the hearth of one of these massive kitchen fireplaces.[15]

Henry Lawson created a vivid picture of social life around an outback fireside:

It was a very cold night, enough to cut the face an' hands off yer, so we had a roarin' fire in the big bark-an-slab kitchen where the darncin' was. It was one of them big, old-fashioned, clay-lined fireplaces that goes right acrost the end of the room, with a twenty-five foot slab-an-tin chimbly outside.[16]

There were problems with these big, wide chimneys; sometimes the rain splashed down and put out the fire![17] However, it was necessary for the fireplace to have a considerable height and width to enable the cook to manoeuvre the equipment required for down-hearth cooking. The slightly raised hearth, normally about ten centimetres above the floor, helped to make cooking more convenient and cleaner than if built at floor level. At the same time, this assisted in providing a draught which was a constant problem, but on the other hand, if the chimney drew too well, the heat for cooking purposes was reduced.[18]

Last thing at night the fire was made safe by raking the live coals to the centre and covering it all with fine ashes. In the morning it usually came instantly alight with the addition of a little kindling wood. In colonial America the same system was known as 'raking up the fire'[19] but in Australia, this way of making the fire safe without letting it go out was called 'damping' a fire. This in turn gave the name to damper, the traditional Australian bread which was cooked in hot coals.[20] It was possible for a complete range of cooking skills to be carried out over the fire or within its embers. By using the down-hearth method the cook was able to bake, grill, boil, stew or brown.

The bread oven

The ideal addition to the down-hearth fireplace was a brick bread oven, based on the centuries-old principles used in medieval bakehouses, eighteenth- and nineteenth-

McCrae Cottage, in Victoria. A covered way was intended to link the detached kitchen to the back door's little gable.

century English farmhouses[21] and American colonial cottages.[22] Some were built outside the kitchen, as at McCrae Cottage, Port Phillip, built in 1845; some were placed in a verandah or semi-external situation as at Heronswood, Dromana, Victoria, built in 1870; occasionally a larger establishment might warrant a separate bake-house, but most commonly the bread oven was adjacent to the main kitchen fireplace. Countless examples can still be found throughout the country – in cottages and farms as well as in more substantial houses such as Wanstead Park, built in Tasmania in 1827; Franklin House, Tasmania, 1838; Como, Port Phillip, 1846; The Springs, New South Wales, 1867 and in the late 1850s' kitchen of Reedy Creek homestead at Broadford, Victoria.

Since each bread oven was built on the site there were slight variations in size. They were placed about a metre above floor level – a comfortable height to operate when standing. The oven door, which was smaller than the brickwork opening, was recessed and had a brick sill. The opening usually had a camber to the top formed by a soldier course of bricks. The cast-iron doors were about 350 millimetres high by 400 millimetres wide and the earlier designs tended to be a simple rectangle with plain

T-hinges. The blacksmiths, however, had an opportunity to shown their skill by often making these doors with a curved top, parallel to the arched opening, and with elegantly scrolled hinges and Norfolk latch.

The oven was built entirely of brick with a height of about 450 millimetres from the floor to the domed top. It was not less than one metre in depth and 600 millimetres in internal width, and had a smooth, flat floor. When the door was shut the oven was completely sealed.

It took considerable skill to have the dough ready and the oven hot, all at the right moment. Heat was provided by burning a quick fire of well-dried light wood and the door was left slightly open to provide the draught. Most bread ovens had a small flue which led into the main chimney-stack from the arched brickwork in front of the metal door. This allowed the smoke to escape without filling the kitchen.

The fuel was thrust into the oven with a long-handled fork kept specially for the purpose. This fork was also used to stir up the embers until they burned completely out, leaving no smoke at all. It took an hour for a brick-oven to become properly heated for the dough. The bricks would change in colour from black to red as they got hotter; and when a handful of flour, thrown lightly against the side of the oven, burned up with a blaze of sparks, the housewife knew that her oven was hot enough for baking.[23]

An old lady described watching her grandmother bake bread in her kitchen at Ovens Vale, Victoria:

The bread oven was always perfectly cleaned out before the bread was baked. She used a long handled garden hoe to scrape out the ashes and then swept it clean with some sort of whisk broom before the bread was placed on the floor of the oven. This would be done every week.[24]

The actual cooking was done entirely by the heat stored in the masonry and with the door tightly shut. After the bread was finished, pound cakes which required slower cooking would use up the remaining heat.[25]

Sometimes there was a space provided in the brickwork below the oven for the storage of ash. One unusual design had an opening in the sill in front of the door which must have enabled the ashes to be swept straight into a receptacle in the recess below.[26]

The fuel stove revolution

A dramatic change in cooking techniques was brought about by the manufactured stove. For the wealthy householders of England, kitchen ranges began to appear in the late eighteenth and early nineteenth centuries. Compared with an open fireplace the convenience must have seemed miraculous, but for the Australian market the range or kitchener as it was sometimes called had the great disadvantage of consuming vast quantities of coal.[27] Firewood was the normal fuel in Australia and the new equipment was slowly accepted. A few cooking stoves were made in Australia during the early 1850s but the price 'precluded all but the very wealthy from purchasing them'.[28]

Vaucluse House had a 'Russels patent fire range and stove' in 1853.[29] It may well have been similar to the very latest in cooking equipment which had been displayed at the Great Exhibition of 1851, generally still adopting the spit system for roasting over a wide grate, with hot water tanks, warming cupboards and ovens at each side. The water tanks had to be filled by hand but still provided a great advance in home comfort. Flavel's kitchener, shown at the same exhibition, had double ovens at each side of a central open fire-box[30] but it was not until about 1860 that the range became commonplace in the English home.[31] Mrs Beeton only touched on the subject of ranges in the first edition of her *Book of Household Management* in 1861 but the advantages and care of various patent fuel ranges were discussed in detail in the 1890 edition.

In Australia, many people who could afford to do so adapted their large kitchen fireplaces to accommodate a colonial oven. The portable American cooking stove also made its appearance in the mid-century. Alfred Joyce wrote that 'the kitchen labour is abridged as much as it can well be'[32] by the addition of an American stove, but it appears that the colonial oven was by far the most popular. It could be set into the existing fireplace 'with each end resting on a hob so that the fire could be placed underneath it. The smoke and flames were also to be drawn up at the back of the oven while another fire was lit on the flat top',[33] thus suggesting its alternative name of 'two-fire' stove. Bars rested across the top fire to provide a place to heat pots, pans and kettles and a popular blacksmiths' design was in the shape of a giant hairpin which allowed

The colonial oven, almost unchanged for sixty years. Illustration from a catalogue of Foy and Gibson Pty Ltd, Melbourne.

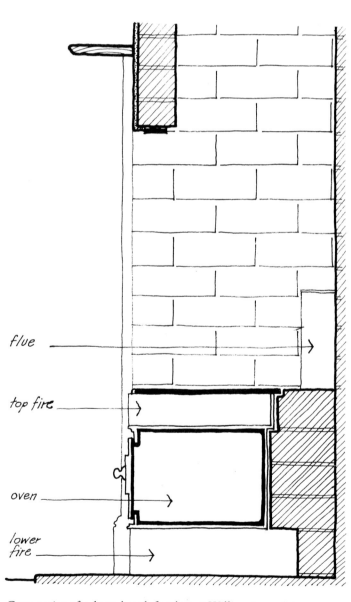

flue

top fire

oven

lower fire

Cross section of a down-hearth fireplace at Williamstown, into which a colonial oven was installed in about 1860.

the large pots to stand at the wide end while the smaller vessels could be supported safely at the narrow end.

The colonial oven had many advantages for outback households. Constructed of sheet steel it was lighter to transport and less expensive than the cast-iron kitcheners developed in England. In addition, it had the great advantage of being designed to burn firewood rather than coal. Richard Twopeny summed it up:

The kitchen is ordinarily very poorly provided with utensils. Ranges and stoves are only found in the wealthier houses, the usual cooking apparatus being a colonial oven – a sort of box with fire above and below, which is very convenient for burning wood, the usual fuel throughout Australia.[34]

Some people expressed much more enthusiasm. Ellison Westgarth was so pleased with the improvement in her household that she included the following comment in a letter dated 9 March 1855: 'Jane makes a capital cook and is anxious to try everything, and now since we have a cooking stove her powers are not so cramped'.[35]

The colonial oven proved itself by its performance and economy, although some people still preferred the camp oven for cooking despite the fact that it was so heavy to handle.[36] Colonial ovens were on the market for a considerable number of years. They were on display in the Intercolonial Exhibition of 1866–67[37] and were available in fourteen different sizes from F. Lassetter & Co. Ltd, Universal Providers of Sydney, at the end of the nineteenth century.[38] By 1911 they could still be purchased from Lassetters in eight sizes.[39] Around 1930, John Danks & Son Pty Ltd included an 'Old Style Colonial Oven' in their catalogue, available in four sizes.[40]

In 1888, Metters Bros, Range Setters and Plumbers of Melbourne, advertised an 'improved oven' in three sizes, stressing the fact that only one fire was required to roast, bake or heat the hot plate. This was its big advantage over the two-fire colonial oven. The one-fire stove was adaptable – it could be installed with or without brickwork and if desired a high-pressure hot-water boiler could be fixed at nominal cost. This close fire range, which was recommended for its economy of fuel and cleanliness by Mrs Beeton, was extremely suitable to Australian conditions. The closed fire-box could burn wood and there was less fire risk than was associated with the earlier, open coal burning fire-box.

In its 1870's catalogue, James McEwan & Sons of Melbourne showed large, imported, English type cast-iron kitchen ranges suitable for big households.[41] The range which exists today at Como is similar and demonstrates the changes that had taken place in many kitchens. The original bread oven is present but the down-hearth fireplace had been adapted to take a large, high quality wood fuel range built by E. Pullinger of Melbourne.

Designs changed slowly. There was no pandering to the dictates of fashion. The Superior Leamington Ranges advertised by F. Lassetter & Co., Limited, of Sydney, in about 1896 and 1911, were remarkably similar to James McEwan & Co.'s Improved Kitchen Range of the 1870s. The Dover Cooking Stove, manufactured by Metters of New South Wales appears almost unchanged in Lassetter's c. 1896 and 1911 catalogues, the catalogue of John Keep &

Lake View, Chiltern, built about 1870, was Henry Handel Richardson's house. It was a brick bungalow, with a separate brick kitchen.

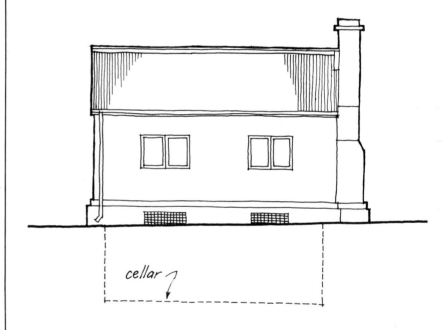

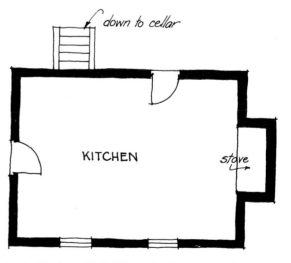

The simple detached kitchen of Lake View. An American-made colonial oven was built into the fireplace. The celler underneath is unusual.

Sons Ltd, Sydney in 1904,[42] and Metters' catalogue of 1926.[43] This stove was designed on the American style, free-standing on legs and not requiring a brickwork base.

It was necessary to specify whether wood or coal would be burnt when ordering a stove. Careful directions were given to the bricklayer for excluding unwanted draughts and arranging the damper correctly. If the installation was slightly complicated, with perhaps several ovens and a hot water boiler for the bathroom, a special fitter usually carried out the work. It was possible to order spare stove parts to replace any that burnt out over the years.

Keeping up the wood supply was no mean task. The job often fell to one of the sons in the family. Around 1908, A.B. Facey cut the firewood to oven-size lengths and it took about one and a half hours to fill the woodbox each morning with 75 millimetre-thick pieces cut into 300 millimetre lengths. The thicker pieces were split down to 50 or 75 millimetre strips and then cut into lengths to fit the oven![44]

Twentieth-century wood fuel stoves tended to become reduced in overall size although they were equipped with a larger, more efficient fire-box – probably the result of a widening market to supply smaller families and house-holds. The principle of placing the fire-box above the oven with the hot plates directly over the fire, which had been adopted years before by Metters Bros and some other suppliers, became the usual one-fire stove design for small kitchens. A downward opening hinged door or two doors sliding from the centre opened and closed the fire-box. This system was far more suitable for wood fires than was the smaller fire-box which had developed from the coal-burning fire-boxes used in England. These models had a plainer, more up-to-date appearance than the earlier designs which continued to be manufactured with central fire-box between ovens or at the side against a single oven. There was usually a plate-warming compartment below and sometimes the doors were curved at the top, reminiscent of the old bread oven.[45]

Kitchen equipment and implements

The contrast between the ruggedness and simplicity of the basic kitchen and the array of equipment available for use in food preparation and cooking was marked. Most kitchen tools came from overseas, and the quantity and variety of implements and utensils in a kitchen were considered by some to be a mark of status. But not all tools were imported. There was much ingenuity displayed by local makers too, and many items were designed, adapted and wrought by colonial blacksmiths.

The first requirement was a simple metal bar, embedded into each side of the chimney, usually well over a metre above the fire. From the bar hung a variety of pots and cauldrons on adjustable trammels, chains and hooks. The crane was a more efficient arrangement. The crane's vertical arm was hinged on one side of the fireplace, so that the pots which hung from the horizontal arm could be swung out, away from the fire, to enable the cook to deal with them in a more comfortable way.

In some of the grander kitchens, the cooking equipment could be lifted or lowered by adjustments to the crane. The old kitchen fireplace at Woolmers, built at Longford, Tasmania, in 1819, was over 2 metres wide and was ingeniously fitted with two cranes of different design – one was notched along the top edge, probably to ensure that there was no risk of the pots slipping and upsetting their contents! These cranes were hinged, one each side of the fireplace, and swung in and out from the centre. On the wall above, roasting spits were stored on brackets. They were probably supported on special racks or fire-irons while the meat cooked in the fire, and would be turned by hand unless one of the complicated mechanically- or dog-driven wheels was used, as in some of the great English kitchens.

Some of the grand house designs of Australia incorpo-

Changes in solid fuel stoves. Left: A 1908 model with a door reminiscent of a bread oven. Below: A 1920s model with a two-door oven.

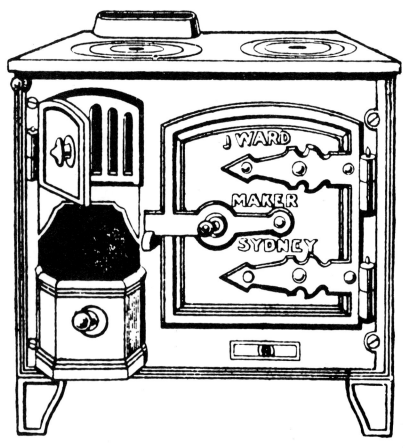

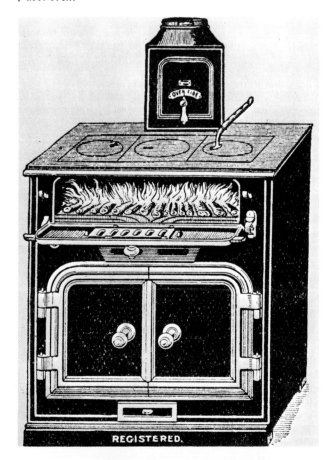

rated reproductions of the basement and semi-basement late Georgian English kitchens. Such examples are Elizabeth Bay House in Sydney, designed by John Verge and commenced in 1835; Clarendon at Evandale, Tasmania, built during the years 1834 to 1838 and Killymoon built between 1842 and 1848 at Fingal, Tasmania. In 1872, William Wardell adopted the same practice at Government House, Melbourne.

In these kitchens, the cooking principles were the same as those used in the humble farms and huts, but the degree of sophistication was expressed by the array of copper utensils, the roasting spits, the coffee roaster, kettle tilter and other such ingenious aids. These beautiful kitchens, with their flagged floors, vast dressers and ancillary storerooms, usually had a brick bread oven which provided a relatively efficient means of baking. The cooks who had to use simpler, more primitive kitchens, however, had no alternative but to bake in the ubiquitous camp oven – unless they made use of an outdoor clay oven.

Used throughout the world and sometimes called by names such as camp oven, the 'three-legged iron pot is the origin of the term "to take pot luck"'.[46] A similar vessel was used in colonial America, in England and especially in Cork and Limerick until well into the twentieth century where glowing peat sods were placed on top of the lid to ensure an even heat. In Ireland, it was called a bastable oven which gave the name of 'bastable cake' to the traditional soda bread.[47] The flexibility of the camp oven was remarkable. It could be lowered or raised over the fire by chain or trammel or it could be moved to the side to stand among the coals. The rimmed edge to the domed lid enabled coals to be heaped on top, thus providing oven conditions within. The handle was close to the pot at each side so that it could stand upright in the air to prevent overheating.

Compact and comprehensive. Right: The Dover stove was an American design burning wood or coal. Below: The 'improved' one-fire Metters model of 1888.

Some women found the camp oven impossibly difficult and heavy to manage. Jane Isabella Watts, who lived on Kangaroo Island in 1837 before settling in Adelaide was one of these. 'Of all the perverse, iron-hearted culinary utensils that were ever invented a camp oven is the worst.'[48] On the other hand, the wife of the overlander John Hepburn 'learned the art of camp-oven cookery, the grinding of flour and porridge meal, the making of bread and damper . . . Most pioneer women, and especially the Scots pioneer women, could produce a savoury meal out of almost nothing'.[49]

Alfred Joyce confirmed the versatility of the camp oven while hut keeping at his Port Phillip run, Plaistow, on Joyce's Creek during the 1840s. He first used it as a mixing bowl for his damper dough and his 'next cooking operation was to clean out the three-legged pot and put in the joint of mutton for boiling over the restored fire for the evening meal, and a kettle of boiling tea completed the bill of fare'.[50]

Even when Mrs John Pendergast had a brick oven built at Pender's Court in the Omeo District, she still preferred to make what was locally called a 'cartwheel' of bread in her huge camp oven. One was always ready for the men when they set off for a long trip in the bullock dray.[51]

Years after their childhood, people have reminisced about their mothers' wonderful camp oven cookery.

How we enjoyed hot, home-cooked bread soaked with butter! We used to argue over who should have the 'kissing crust' – the soft crust where the loaves were broken apart. For special treats we had leatherjacks (thin pieces of dough cooked on the camp-oven lid), beggars-on-the-coals (tiny loaves baked on the hearth), and 'pufftaloons' (fried bread dough).[52]

There are variations on these names such as leather-jacket and devil-on-coals – the word leather thought to be appropriate for something so tough![53]

These kitchens must have been a fascinating sight. Around the mantelpiece hung an array of long-handled implements made of brass, copper, cast iron and tin. Close at hand was a selection of forks, spoons, ladles, strainers,

skimmers, pans, slices and the salamander, girdle plate, gridiron and bottle jack. Sir Walter Scott described such a kitchen fireplace in *Marmion*:

> The chimney arch projected wide,
> Above, around it, and beside,
> Were tools for housewife's hand.

Many early settlers brought to Australia the equipment they considered necessary to run a household. John Moffat included two fluted gridirons in his list of goods which were shipped in 1859 from England, via Geelong, to Hopkins Hill on the edge of the Western Plains of Victoria.[54] The gridiron, used for grilling meat in an open fire dated back to medieval times. The nineteenth-century version had a handle and four short feet; the meat

tory included one in 1872[57] and Mrs Beeton's famous illustration of an Australian kitchen in her *Book of Household Management* of 1890 shows the joint being cooked in this way with a pan below to catch the drippings.

Frying-pans were often made with a semicircular handle and a swivel ring at the top with which they could be suspended from a hook. An alternative design had a very long handle which enabled the cook to stand well back from the fire while the pan stood on a brandreth or baking-iron, similar to a trivet.[58]

The salamander was used to brown dishes of potatoes or pastry. It was a circular metal plate at the end of a long handle which was placed in the fire until red hot. It was then held just above the crust which quickly browned by the radiated heat. This was an old English tradition and

rested on channelled bars allowing the gravy and fat to be collected in a small trough at the end.

Iron cauldrons, not unlike those in use since the Bronze Age stood on short legs in the fire or were suspended on chains, S-hooks or adjustable trammels which were raised or lowered by simple ratchet or hook and eye systems. The household's hot water supply normally came from a cast-iron fountain with lid and brass tap. This would be hung permanently at one side of the fireplace, unless there were two – then they were placed at each side of the fire.[55]

The bottle jack, operated by a clockwork mechanism, was developed for the late Georgian kitchen.[56] The meat to be roasted was hung below the jack which rotated backwards and forwards in front of the fire while clamped to the centre of the mantelpiece. This device was used for a considerable time in Australia. The Hopkins Hill inven-

A capacious rubble-stone ingle-nook provided a source of warmth as well as cooking for this old couple.

the blacksmith did the job for the villagers if they had no salamander of their own.[59] This fascinating piece of equipment was included in the James McEwan & Sons furnishing lists of its *Illustrated Catalogue* of about 1870 and in the *Catalogue of Kitchen Utensils, Etc.* published by F. Lassetter & Co. Ltd of Sydney, in about 1896.

Hard-working Scotswomen brought with them their flat, circular griddle or girdle irons. Common to all Celtic countries it is one of the oldest cooking utensils. 'The word probably comes from the Old French, *grédil*, meaning grid-iron, although the hot stones used for baking by the early Gaels were called greadeal.'[60] The griddle is used still in parts of Scotland for cooking bread, bannocks or scones. Sometimes, the flat cast-iron plate had a semi-circular handle with which it was hung from a crane or placed vertically at the back of a small fireplace when not in use.[61] Those which had a handle at the side stood on the brandreth during cooking. William Westgarth described a meal with 'brither Scots' at Dunmore Station.

Janet from the kitchen, too, sent us the best oatcakes and other Scotch fare. I always fancy now that such cooks must be called Janet, from lively remembrance of the savoury hotch-pot and sheeps' head of another Janet at old Robert Sutherland's.[62]

The kitchen in the house plan

The early Australian kitchen varied not only in size, quality and quantity of equipment and the range of its ancillary rooms, but it also varied in its location within the

was an old slab-and-shingle place, one room deep, and about eight rooms long, with a row of skillions at the back; the place was used for kitchen, laundry and servants' rooms. This was the old homestead before the new house was built. There was a wide, old-fashioned brick-floored verandah in front ...[64]

Some kitchens were built as detached rooms without even a covered way to connect them to the main house. Lawson spoke of 'the usual weatherboard box with a galvanised-iron top – four rooms and a passage, and a detached kitchen and a wash-house at the back'.[65] He observed a kitchen which was even bigger than the house it served. 'The two-roomed house is built of round timber, slabs and stringy-bark, and floored with split slabs. A big bark kitchen, standing at one end is larger than the house itself, veranda included.'[66]

An early cottage at Bathurst with its separate kitchen connected by skillion-roofed verandahs.

house. There was a strong custom for external kitchens, particularly in rural areas – a practice not unique to Australia. *A Manual of Domestic Economy* published in London in 1857 stated that the kitchen is usually 'within the area of the house, though in country houses the contrary is often the case'.[63] It appears that the early settlers were already familiar with the external kitchen.

The placement of the kitchen and service areas varied considerably – depending largely on social and economic factors. The original small hut frequently became a separate detached kitchen when a homestead was built at a later date, just as Henry Lawson described:

a two-storey brick house with wide verandas all round, and a double row of pines down to the front gate. Parallel at the back

There was only a garden path between the house and kitchen built in 1839 for C.J. La Trobe, superintendent of the Port Phillip district,[67] while in 1844 Georgiana McCrae indicated a covered way between the house and kitchen at Arthur's Seat to give some minimum protection from bad weather. However, her later sketches suggest that this was never built.[68]

A good example of the detached kitchen connected by a covered way is shown in the ground plan of Limekilns built in about 1870, near Mansfield, Victoria – a property which burnt and supplied lime for buildings in the surrounding area. The 'Indian Room' off the kitchen was given its name because Indian hawkers were given a bed there when in the district![69]

However, where a comprehensive selection of building materials was available to people of affluence, the kitchen was sometimes included within the building. In 1855,

Alfred Joyce wrote from his Leonard Terry designed home, Norwood, at Maryborough, Victoria, proudly describing his kitchen as being 'in the house'.[70] When Robert Russell designed the elegant Yarra Cottage in 1839, he included a large kitchen with internal access.

In England, it was considered to be good house planning to isolate domestic noise and smells from the inhabitants of the public rooms, while saving 'our domestics from unnecessary and fatiguing labour'. As an alternative to the basement kitchen which could even be supplied with a food lift to the dining-room above, as at Pleasant Banks, Evandale, Tasmania, 1838, the solution was to place 'all the working apartments completely at the back and isolating them by a door at the end of the hall or lobby'.[71] Richard Twopeny found the most common layout in Australia and the favourite in Adelaide was:

an oblong block bisected by a three to eight foot passage. The first door on one side as you go in is the drawing room, on the other the dining room. Then follow the bedrooms, etc., with the kitchen and scullery at the end of the passage, or sometimes in a lean-to at right angles to the hinder part of the house proper.[72]

In Australia a verandah usually provided the communicating link – perhaps because of the added problems of flies and fire risk, and a less rigorous climate. In all parts of the land the verandah was used to connect the kitchen to the house proper. When Corio Villa was built from its cast-iron component parts at Geelong in 1856, the large kitchen, store and pantry had access from a rear verandah – all a considerable distance from the dining-room. The limestone house, Wallcliffe, built by Alfred Bussell in 1865 at the mouth of the Margaret River, Western Australia, has many of the characteristics of an English country house – its generous kitchen with immense fireplace, however, was connected to the main rooms by a small verandah. Franklin House, built in 1838 in Launceston, has a rear verandah which provided access from the 'Offices' to the Georgian living-rooms. Connecting and covered ways fitted into the Queensland vernacular of surrounding verandahs such as at Canning Downs, 1846.

Another planning device extensively used was the kitchen courtyard, where the service rooms formed wings around an enclosed area which often contained a well below the ground and a hand-operated pump. Lady Casey remembered Stony Park – her grandparents' home which was rebuilt in the 1880s after fire devastation:

Far from the dining room was the kitchen. One passed through a large pantry lined with cupboards of glass and the finest pale wood into a courtyard that led to a separate building where the cooking was done. In all the houses I knew in my youth the kitchen was as far as possible from the place where one ate. It seemed that people preferred to eat tepid dishes, delivered with difficulty from a distance, to the awful risk of smelling food as it cooked and of hearing the laughter and mutterings of the cook and her helpers.[73]

Vaucluse House in Sydney has a beautiful courtyard with covered way which leads to kitchen, scullery and cellars – its elegance, with Classical columns and Georgian details, probably unmatched in Australia.

It the latter part of the nineteenth century some Victorian households became much more elaborate; the kitchen staff had to service large numbers of people through a variety of culinary routines, necessitating a scullery, larders, pantries and servery in larger houses. The kitchen was large and well lit; one of the best surviving examples in England is at Lannydrock, built in 1881, and described as 'the offspring of a college hall'.[74] In Australia, up-to-date architects provided their clients with a similar range of domestic offices. Horbury Hunt designed extensions to Havilah in the Mudgee district in 1884 with a white painted, bagged-brick walled kitchen 'in general concept and size ... roughly equivalent to a chapel in one of the smaller Oxford Colleges'.[75]

By this time the domestic area was more frequently within the house itself. Thos Watts & Sons' design for Davies' Folly (so called because the Hon. J.M. Davies, MLC, was not sufficiently affluent to live in the completed house), shows the extent of a ground floor kitchen wing of a grand house of 1891, complete with servants' rooms, pantries, scullery and stores. The servery or serving pantry was conveniently placed off the dining-room. Here the dishes used in the dining-room were washed up and the door position and swing were carefully arranged so that those dining had no view into the service area.

At about the same time smaller houses often included a scullery for food preparation and dish washing. The kitchen became a more comfortable room for a modest household. Here children would often be fed and the housewife would spend a considerable part of the day, perhaps with the assistance of one maid. Twopeny described it as a merciful fashion 'the cook preparing the dishes and doing all that does not require the presence of a fire in a large back-kitchen'.[76]

Recommendations for the kitchen varied little in basic plan and furnishing. The room tended to be almost square; an area of 5.4 metres by 4.8 metres was suggested to provide an adequate farmhouse kitchen to serve a property in England of up to 250 hectares. It required a large dresser, one or two tables depending on space, and good access to scullery and fuel storage.[77]

Storage in the heat

The fast deterioration of food in a hot climate presented a major problem to the housewife in her efforts to feed the family. Before refrigeration, milk, for example, could be preserved only in the form of cheese. Meats could be held over only by salting or smoking. Fruit could be kept as jellies or jams, but the high cost of sugar made these a luxury. Other methods of preservation included pickling and drying. Vegetables, except for root crops such as potatoes and onions, were completely seasonal.

The problem of storage is a reminder that the kitchen was often the 'processing centre' of a network of facilities, especially in the complex of structures that comprised a homestead: smokehouse, meat-house, bakehouse, dairy, cellar, scullery, laundry, chicken-coop, wood-pile. But food storage was given special consideration because of heat and flies. In 1852 it was 'usual to keep all provisions in a wood safe, with a perforated zinc door, to prevent flies, ants, and other vermin entering'.[78] Kitchen safes – prevalent until the widespread use of the ice-chest – varied greatly in appearance. Some were made to look elegant while others comprised a few pantry shelves which were adapted for the purpose. Hanging safes were used in cellars, pantries or on the verandah. The unique one was the Coolgardie safe, used extensively in Coolgardie, Western Australia, although the origin is not known. It was a hessian-covered timber frame 'with a tray of water on top from which the moisture percolated over the sides to keep the contents cool and safe from flies'.[79] The legs often stood in tins of water to discourage ants and it was usually placed on the verandah or somewhere shady near the kitchen door.

Sets of metal dish-covers, both with and without fly-wire, hung in a row along the wall or were stored on high shelves. The cellar provided admirable cool storage for meat and dairy produce and it is surprising that they were not universal in Victorian houses. Some cellars could be entered from the kitchen, but many had external access or opened into a hall or lobby. By 1893 Dr Philip Muskett was adamant that the ice-chest was 'an essential for every house and was within the means of nearly all'.[80] This heralded a new era of food preparation and eating habits.

Kitchen furniture

Examination of early settlers' inventories shows that many brought cooking equipment but not kitchen furniture. Solid, country-made tables and dressers, often built of local timber, graced the kitchens of most Australian country houses. The quality varied from those described by Lawson in *The Selector's Daughter*: 'A plank-table, supported on stakes driven into the ground, stood in the middle of the room, and two slab benches were fixtures on each side' to the Wonnangatta Station where 'an old photograph reveals a blackwood table in the kitchen with a sheen that glistens although it was polished with nothing but a smear of kerosene'.[81]

The table was the main work space for almost all houses and therefore had to be firm and strong. Sarah Midgley's mother made forty-eight dozen candles in four days of wet May weather in 1858, which illustrates the magnitude of some of the kitchen tasks.[82] Since good access to the table was necessary, it was not normally surrounded by chairs: two Windsor-type chairs plus a long form or stools which did not cause obstruction were usual.

Deal was generally recommended for the table top 'and this must be kept white with constant scrubbing; while the cookery is going on a thin piece of oil baize might be laid over it. Pearson's carbolic sand soap will remove any grease spots very quickly; the paste board and rolling pin can also be kept white in the same way'.[83] So plentiful was the supply of timber in the nineteenth century that the top was frequently made of a single plank, while a depth of three centimetres was considered essential for stability.[84] There were local variations when the legs were made from blackwood or red gum.

Wood turning became fashionable in the late Victorian era and some tables were supported on legs of turned cedar. Apart from the fact that a stool could be tucked out of the way, under the table, there was a good reason for its use: 'On the low stool one was free from the smoke, which, when it reached a certain height, wandered at its own sweet will and escaped as best it might...'[85]

The kitchen yard at Crail, near Singleton, showing the underground well, into which roof water flowed, and from which all house water was pumped.

A wooden dresser, built in 1907, continues to provide essential kitchen storage more than seventy-five years later.

Improvised or 'knocked together' furniture was commonplace in small, outback households. A woman remembered her mother's jam cupboard 'made of kerosene cases, flat on their sides, one on top of another, with a curtain tacked neatly to disguise the boxes. It was one of the many storage shelves which any resourceful country woman could and did make for herself inexpensively and without having to depend on busy menfolk.'[86] There were stick-legged stools and forms, and sometimes a 'rough gin-case cradle' for the baby.[87] In primitive cottages simple shelves were used for storage and covered with newspaper if nothing better was available.[88]

The traditional dresser, a direct import from the 'Old Country' appeared in almost every house of any substance. It varied in design, although there were always open shelves in the top section, but the storage space in the lower part, generally below flat drawers, could be open or behind hinged or sliding doors. Glass doors, and the built-in dresser beside the fireplace, appear later.

Lighting was important and many of the simplest, detached kitchens had two windows, whereas other rooms might only have one. Skylights sometimes were seen although they appeared to be a late Victorian innovation and were found usually in architect-designed houses. Dr Holbrook recommended a 'light, well ventilated, cheerful' kitchen; 'pretty pictures should adorn the wall, and comfort reign'.[89] Texts were popular. Hal Porter remembered those in the kitchen of his childhood: '*The beloved of the Lord*, states one text encircled in mock orange, *shall dwell in safety*. The other, interlaced with jasmine, states, *without me ye can do nothing*.'[90]

The American-style 'steeple' clock was a decorative and commonly seen centre-piece above the stove, with flowers or scenes painted on the glass below the clock face. Lawson described an 'old-fashioned spired wooden clock (the brass disk of the pendulum moving ghost-like through a scarred and scratched marine scene – Margate in England – on the glass that covered the lower half) that stood alone on the slab shelf over the fireplace'.[91] Baskets for eggs and fruit, stone jars for storage and wooden boxes for knives, salt and candles all added their own utilitarian beauty to a room full of scrubbed and polished surfaces.

The kitchen sink

There is no doubt that improvements in plumbing must have revolutionized the way of living for cooks and housewives, but they were slow in coming. In 1852 it was said that 'there is not a single drain or sewer in all Melbourne'.[92] Alfred Joyce wrote in 1855 that 'our kitchen is quite an uncommon affair'. It was 'fitted up with every convenience, a sink, plate rack and complete dresser, clean water led inside with a pipe and tap' and he intended to have another pipe to carry away the dirty water into a covered drain. Few households had any improvement on 'water in a cask outside or standing in a pail'.[93]

A few kitchens of the large houses had sinks hewn from stone as in the Georgian kitchens of England; there was the occasional brick sink but often the water had to be tipped in by bucket! Although major cities began piping water in the mid-nineteenth century it was not generally reticulated to every household until the early twentieth

Gas stoves. Above: Traditional in appearance but advanced in performance, this Galliers & Klaerr vertical gas stove of 1887 had a simmering burner on the top and grilling, toasting and browning burner in the oven. Top: An early gas stove advertised in 1881 by S. Jeans of St Kilda, which derived its appearance and door details from earlier models such as the colonial oven.

century.[94] Rectangular earthenware sinks began to appear in the corner of the scullery, to be followed by enamelled cast iron or plain, painted and stamped steel sinks. A woman described one of these, which had existed in her childhood home, as 'a terrible dark tin sink'![95] Accompanying the sink, there would sometimes be a timber plate rack on the wall where the dishes would drain.

Mr Mansfield, a plumber from Kew, was piping water to sinks in the 1870s and more frequently during the next decade. Far more often he appeared to repair water pumps and replace their leather washers.[96] Only cold water was supplied; hot water came from the tank incorporated in the stove or as in Hal Porter's childhood home 'from an enormous iron boiler with a brass tap which sits perpetually murmuring on the perpetually lit wood-fire stove, and contains a marble which has a practical reason but which I believe is there to make the boiler sing'.[97]

Finally, the kauri draining-board was placed beside the sink; a refinement of this was to place the timber above the sink which was fitted directly underneath a rectangular opening cut out of the draining-board. This became a regular part of kitchen equipment in the early twentieth century as the scullery began to lose favour. In country areas, a tap sometimes supplied water to the kitchen from the rain water tank outside – the tap was placed at the level of the bottom of the tank. One family was 'proud of having water "laid on" to the kitchen, and thought nothing of the tap being low...' There was no sink. The enamel dish and big, strong oblong tray for draining the dishes were used on the table.[98]

Cooking with gas

Running parallel with the expanded use of the one-fire stove was the increased use of gas for cooking. Gas was an established success for lighting, but gas stoves only appeared after the invention of the bunsen burner in 1855 and were found in England in custom-made form around 1860. The 1870s saw gas stoves enter the Australian market. At the Intercolonial Exhibition of 1875, five local manufacturers exhibited gas cookers.[99]

Despite occasional accounts of the unreliability or breakdown of imported gas stoves, and the continued popularity of colonial ovens,[100] it soon became known that gas cooking eliminated chopping wood and cleaning filthy flues. The kitchen could become a different room.

At first local firms assembled imported components for gas stoves and firms such as Galliers & Klaerr manufactured under licence, but once the Metropolitan Gas Company in Melbourne established a department for selling stoves in 1880, gas became increasingly popular.[101]

Jeans' patent gas cooking stove, advertised in 1881, was designed with a water heater at the side, griller and a door that looked exactly like a colonial oven with elaborately scrolled hinges and latch.[102] Galliers and Klaerr registered a gas stove design in 1887 which still retained the old world character on the door although, overall, it was very similar to the vertical gas stoves which were commonplace until the mid-twentieth century.[103] About the same time, the Metropolitan Gas Company advertised that 'STOVES CAN BE HAD ON HIRE (for not less than 12 months) from 2s. per month and upwards'[104] but apparently

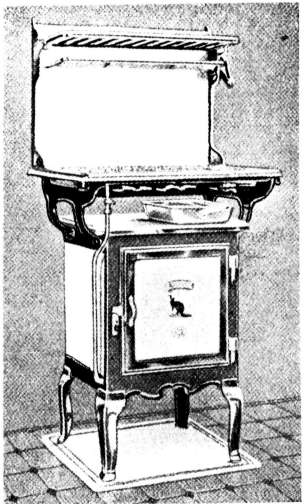

A gas stove of the 1920s, for installation, free standing, in a fireplace recess. The enamelled door has a kangaroo motif.

Top: A solid-fuel range for the wealthy of the 1870s. It had a boiler 'arranged to convey hot water' to baths.

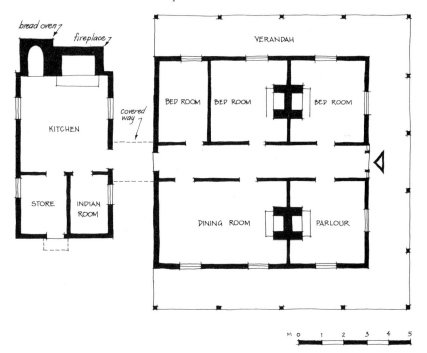

Plan of Lime Kilns, Mansfield, about 1870. It is a good example of a country homestead with a detached kitchen, connected by covered way to the main house.

A plan from the book of conservative designs produced by the State Savings Bank of Victoria in 1936. The kitchen is now included under the main roof, and serves also as a dining-room. Its wide fireplace will take both solid fuel and gas stoves. A minimal sink is in one corner.

many of these were returned during the bad economic period of the 1890s.[105]

At the same time, F. Lassetter & Co. Ltd advertised small stoves for grilling and boiling as well as gas rings, one of which was described as 'practically indestructible. It will boil water in a light kettle at the rate of over 2 quarts in 12 minutes'.[106] These were designed to use in conjunction with a range, to provide some flexibility in quick heating and hot weather cooking. Similar designs were selling some thirty years later – reflecting a very slow change in kitchen equipment.[107]

The traditional brick chimney recess remained for many more years, even though the gas stoves did not need to be built in. Perhaps there was some mistrust of gas, for it was common practice for houses in Melbourne to have both wood fire and gas stoves up to the 1930s.[108]

Kerosene arrived in Australia during the 1860s and was used for a cooking fuel within the following two decades.[109] Primus hot plates and kerosene stoves were available but were used mainly in country areas for summer cooking or for quick heat when the fire was out.

Surface finishes

The main characteristic of the traditional Australian kitchen was one of spartan simplicity – it was primarily a room for work. There were no fixed fashions relating to its decoration. People who lived in inaccessible areas and had no money to spare on their houses did the best they could. The walls were 'whitewashed if possible; dark in their native bark or split slabs if not whitened'.[110] Others lined their kitchens with hessian and newspaper.[111] At Wonnangatta, 'when the homestead was first built all the walls were covered with wall paper; the paper in the kitchen being a gold and green design . . . but as it aged and the paper wore through it was repaired with pages from papers and fashion magazines'.[112]

More substantial brick buildings often had whitewashed or plaster walls. Mrs Beeton recommended wallpaper only if above a timber dado and varnished, so that it would be washable.[113] She also maintained that pale blue, cream or white varnished paper on the ceiling was a requirement for good light reflection. Blue seems to have been the choice in many outback kitchens. Several bushmen have reiterated the belief that pale blue is a deterrent to flies, and many kitchens, when scraped back, have revealed a pale duck-egg blue as the first coat. Late Victorians were more sombre: dados of dull greens and browns were often painted to a height of not less than a metre. This trend continued well into the Edwardian era.

Floor finishes ranged from the beautiful flagstones in the grand Georgian and early Victorian kitchens to earth floors still in use well into the twentieth century. The timber floor at the Wonnangatta station was smooth and shining with its daily wash of soap and water.[114] Dr Muskett considered that:

Deal boards well scrubbed look nicer than anything else, but to keep them spotless involves a lot of labour, and as this is not always to be had, perhaps the wisest plan is to cover it with oilcloth or linoleum . . . By the way, it should not be washed but only rubbed with a damp cloth first and then with a piece of flannel dipped in oil, soda and scrubbing will ruin it very quickly.[115]

Mrs Beeton, however, suggested that boards should be varnished so that they could merely be wiped over in the same way as linoleum. She insisted that all finishes in the kitchen should be varnished, whether painted or natural.[116] Edwardian kitchens continued these principles and changed little in basic concept, except that the gas stove normally stood beside the fuel stove in areas where gas was available. It was not until the era between the two world wars that changes began to appear in kitchen planning. Then it became a place to prepare meals relatively quickly, but not to carry out the range of domestic skills of the past. Mary Gilmore, as she recollected an old kitchen with drying herbs hanging from the ceiling, understood when she said 'the habits of older countries, less prodigal and hospitable than this, still governed the habits of the people who first came here'.[117]

The simplified kitchen

During this eventful century developments in kitchen design matched those in building, transport, communications and social change. At the beginning of the nineteenth century, when transport was slow, unreliable and costly, people had to try to keep large stocks of everything that would keep. Cooking depended upon solid fuel, so a supply of firewood had to be kept close by, and a main stock of wood also had to be stored not far away. Fuel was consumed throughout the day and evening, making the simple task of fuelling very demanding.

In such conditions the kitchen became hot, and smoke and dust, though they may have been controllable, nevertheless penetrated everything. One result of this was that the kitchen was made as large as possible, not only so that its occupants could get away from the fire but also to accommodate the variety of cooking and living operations. Another result was that decoration, such as painted walls, had to be either easily re-done or easily cleaned.

The early kitchen was merely the most important link in the chain of food preparation; just one room in a suite of spaces for storing, cooking, eating, and cleaning up. But by the beginning of the twentieth century the kitchen was a much more specialized room, now an integral part of a house plan in which most of the rooms were specialized spaces – for eating, sleeping, sitting and bathing as well as for cooking. Tradesmen of every sort came regularly, bringing supplies of milk, butter, flour and vegetables. With the coming of the telephone such provisioning was made even easier. It was generally no longer necessary, except in the remoter country areas, to store large quantities of supplies. And as gas became the standard fuel – soon to be supplemented by electricity – cooking became not only easier but quicker, and cooler.

The image of the kitchen – clean, efficient and specialized – was transformed even more as lighting improved, better paints became available, and sleek finishes such as tiles became cheaper. And, particularly in the cities, the idea of 'designing' a kitchen made economy of function and space important: the room became more business-like. The story of the nineteenth-century kitchen ran parallel to the development of the Australian house.

In this 1883 Melbourne cartoon the lady of the house is working in the kitchen with the maid. The open-grate range is large, and there is a gas wall-light.

A cartoon of the World War I period. Traditional elements continue to be used: the large preparation table, a dresser, and cooking implements hanging beside the built-in solid-fuel stove. Notice the gas bracket light and the text above the fireplace, and the kerosene lamp.

GARDENING IS AN Australian activity that is as old as the First Fleet. Captain Watkin Tench declared in 1788 that 'the rare and beautiful flowering shrubs, which abound in every part, deserve the highest admiration', while Surgeon-General John White reported that on one occasion 'we picked up, in the distance of about half a mile, twenty-five flowers of plants and shrubs of different genera and species'. George Worgan, another First Fleet surgeon, wrote:

The Woods are decorated with a Variety of prettily coloured Flowers, but there is not above 2 or 3 kinds that have any Fragrance ... The spots of ground that we have cultivated for Gardens, have brought forth most of the Seeds that we put in soon after our Arrival here, and besides the common culinary Plants, Indigo, Coffee, Ginger, Castor Nut Oranges, Lemons, & Limes, Firs and Oaks, have vegetated from Seed ...[1]

Plant propagation has always been a pastime of the British, particularly in their colonies.

Gardening in relation to buildings also has been evidenced since the earliest times. A great many of Australias historic houses are tied to their landscape setting; without it, their importance would be greatly diminished.[2] Just as buildings are enhanced by their gardens, so the beauty of gardens is increased by their association with architecture.

Taming the landscape

In *A History of Garden Design* Derek Clifford has noted:

All gardens are the product of leisure. It is no good looking for gardens in a society which needs all its energies to survive. As soon as a society has time and energy to spare, some of the excess is devoted to enjoying the residual aspects of enclosure, of cultivation, and of humanized landscape. The way in which that residue is shaped to give pleasure depends partly upon the physical opportunities, but far more upon man's spiritual needs.[3]

Clifford's remarks clearly put the gardens of pioneers into perspective. If he had been writing from the frontiers of Australian development throughout its first 100 years he would more likely have said that 'All gardens are products of survival'. It is nevertheless astonishing to see the vast scale and horticultural variety in the planting of many early gardens, even in the most remote areas. The desire to tame the landscape around a house was clearly strong.

To understand the beginnings of Australia's domestic gardens we need to know something of the gardens familiar to the early immigrants before they set sail for Australia, and something of their attitude to their new and unfamiliar environment. But we know relatively little about either. Much has been written of the great

ABOUT AUSTRALIAN GARDENS   11

But a garden is subject to constant change. Unlike a building a garden is made up of organic material, growing, decaying and dying, and because most Australian gardens throughout the nineteenth century lacked the formal and architectural elements which would have been more likely to endure, sadly, they have often vanished without trace.

It is possible, however, to re-create a picture of certain early Australian gardens. The skeletal outlines of some remain, and there are sketches and paintings of others – even a few dating from the end of the eighteenth century. Others are known from descriptions, although the frequently extravagant prose of the nineteenth century makes it difficult to extract an exact image of the garden.

Very little, however, is known of the ways the early colonists and settlers viewed their landscape. Despite considerable research, the designers of even the larger early gardens remain shrouded in mystery. Even less is known about the smaller, simpler gardens made by ordinary folk, though a few of these are tenderly depicted in early paintings. There is much more to be pieced together before a consecutive narrative of the development of Australian gardens can tell a truthful story.

Cruden Farm, Langwarrin, designed originally by Edna Walling for Mrs Syme, and owned and re-created by Dame Elisabeth Murdoch. A drive of local grey gravel is lined with lemon-scented gums.

eighteenth-century aristocratic parklands of Capability Brown and his protogees. But his work, important and extensive though it was, made little impact on any but the wealthiest parts of British society and therefore had minimal result in Australia. The early colonists instead would have been familiar with the small gardens of the city and country labouring classes – while a few, like Mrs Macquarie and Mrs Macarthur, would have known the gardens of the minor gentry and the clergy. But little has been written about these gardens, though John Harris, in a recent article, has noted 'that the formal tradition [of the seventeenth and early eighteenth centuries] survived well into the 1770's, if not later ...'.[4] Certainly there is evidence that many gardens followed the simple and traditional geometric pattern of earlier times.

What must those first settlers have thought when they arrived at Sydney Cove? To some the whole country was a garden. Arthur Bowes, the First Fleet surgeon who clearly had an eye for the picturesque, wrote of:

the finest terraces, lawns and grottos with distinct plantations of the tallest and most stately trees I ever saw in any nobleman's grounds in England, cannot excel in beauty those w'h nature now presented to our view.[5]

But not everyone viewed the landscape with such enchantment. Most of the population was more concerned with survival than with the aesthetics of their new surroundings – that would come in time. Their gardens were simple, rectangular and geometric, with an emphasis on subsistence crops, especially vegetables. Such a regular

Right top: Part of the garden at Panshanger, near Cressy, including the fish pond and water tower.

Right centre: The ubiquitous Aracauria tree, signal of an early homestead – Burrundulla, Mudgee, 1864.

Garden rectangles and circles. Top: A pioneer's home, on a cattle station in Queensland, with the home paddock set out in geometric plant beds. Above: A surgeon's house at Sydney Hospital about 1793, with a front garden laid out in beds of vegetables.

Right: The entrance to Fernhill, Mulgoa, 1840, the centre of an English-style garden using indigenous plant material.

pattern no doubt gave some sense of comfort, of control over the natural environment, but it was also practical. The layout of vegetable gardens has changed little today.

Oline Richards, writing of the colonial gardens of Western Australia, has said that:

as a symbol of aspirations ... they are important and their function as a reinforcement of a preferred way of life cannot be disregarded. The convention of the garden was one way of confirming that the ideals were being achieved, whether the gardens were at the same order as the images was of less importance.

Richards suggests that this 'can explain why even the most primitive gardens were worth having.'[6]

Early views of Government Houses in both Sydney and Parramatta show that even the vice-regal residences followed the squared geometric formula. Indeed most illustrations of the first gardens around any house in a newly opened frontier are similar. Not until the necessities for survival had been taken care of, whether in 1788 or 1890, did other considerations achieve any importance.

In 1794 John Macarthur wrote that his house, Elizabeth Farm, Parramatta, was 'surrounded by a vineyard and garden of about 3 acres, the former full of vines and fruit trees and the latter abounding with most excellent vegetables'.[7] Within a short time his wife Elizabeth was engaged in more decorative gardening, and her description of the garden would seem to indicate more attention being given to Picturesque rather than culinary qualities. The Macarthurs had found their fortune early, and this, combined with Elizabeth Macarthur's genteel background, produced an early interest in decorative gardening.

The Picturesque ideal

By 1830, when Augustus Earle painted Government House, Sydney, the earlier straight lines and formal design had given way to a more relaxed 'natural' design of curving paths and informal planting. Not that such a process was universal. Both Elizabeth Macarthur and some of the governors and their associates had more 'taste' than the majority. Their gardens, like their houses, reflected their relative wealth, interests and education.

Alexander Macleay, the colonial secretary and owner of Elizabeth Bay House, had an immense garden of some 20 hectares. His great interest in scientific pursuits – he had been secretary of the Linnean Society for over twenty years prior to coming to Australia – was reflected in the garden at Elizabeth Bay. Sir Joseph Hooker wrote of it after a visit in about 1841:

My surprise was unbounded at the natural beauties of the spot, the inimitable taste with which the grounds were laid out, and the number and rarity of the plants ...[8]

Mrs Macquarie, wife of the governor, was more interested in the Picturesque than with botany and horticulture. She and her husband found the scenery around Sydney ideal to indulge their taste for Gothick buildings – the combination of a dramatic landscape and the powers of an autocratic ruler was too good to resist.

Her Gothick buildings were meant to be seen as objects in a great landscape garden, and Lord Bathurst had some justification in resenting the fact that the British Government was footing the bill for these expensive ornaments – especially when the garden was a whole colony.[9]

But it did not prevent the Macquaries from ornamenting the Sydney area with forts, towers and other structures.

Others, too, took the broader view. Thomas Shepherd, though in some respects fifty years behind the times, advised, in his series of *Lectures on Landscape Gardening in Australia* published in 1836, that advantage be taken of 'the pastoral nature of this country' where 'sheep might feed on our lawns and parks, adding the pleasure of seeing living objects enjoy the benefits of improved scenery'.[10] In a few instances such advice was taken. Whether or not he was assisted by Shepherd is not known, but Edward Cox certainly employed such principles when he created a landscaped parkland around his house, Fernhill, 50 kilometres west of Sydney in 1840. By thinning out and removing some of the native trees he was able to enjoy a ready-made park. Joseph Archer also seems to have sited his house – Panshanger in Tasmania, built in 1834 – and landscaped the grounds according to Picturesque theories. Near Hamilton, in Victoria, Samuel Winter settled on the Wannon River in 1837 and the transformed landscape around his now much enlarged house, Murndal, owes more to the eighteenth than the nineteenth century. Avenues of enormous exotic trees extend from the house into the landscape and many hectares of contrived parkland have been created.

But as Shepherd noted in his lectures of 1836:

With very few exceptions, Landscape Gardening has been totally neglected. The wants of the early Colonists were objects of too much consideration to permit them to devote much of their time to embellishment. They were contented with large crops; and had scarcely any other object in view than the attainment of a steady independence, which must be secured before the objects of the Landscape Gardener can make much impression on the mind of the Settler. We have a few orchards it is true, and some romantically situated country residences, mostly embellished within the last few years, where attention seems to have been paid to this delightful art, by gentlemen of taste and capital.[11]

The gardens created at Government House, and by the Coxes, Macleays, the Archers in Tasmania, and the Winters in Victoria, however, were just as exceptional in Australia as the great aristocratic estates were in eighteenth-century England.

The geometric garden

But what of the gardens of the ordinary settlers – for whom the aesthetic differences of the sublime and the Picturesque were as remote as their mother country? They seem to have been simple, geometric and practical – vernacular gardens to complement vernacular architecture.

Like the houses which grew from practical requirements and the materials at hand, so did the gardens surrounding them. Split-paling fences, earthen paths and split-timber plinths or local stones to contain raised beds formed the 'bones' of these gardens. But, like the imported lace at the windows of their cottages, there were imported vegetables and flowers in the garden.

Few, if any, of these early settlers would have read the advice of J.C. Loudon, the new garden doyen of the first

half of the nineteenth century, when in 1839 he advocated 'the suitableness of a Geometric Style for a country in a wild state' because of 'the contrast which its clearly defined lines and forms offer to the irregularity of the surrounding scenery'.[12] The geometric style was adopted, more for its convenience than for any more consciously aesthetic reason.

The garden at Rouse Hill House, west of Sydney, though relatively large, is the earliest surviving garden in Australia of this type. Its rather awkwardly shaped oval carriage turnabout at the front of the house (probably a later addition) contrasts with the remaining garden laid out in large rectangles defined by wide brick-lined gravel paths. Most geometric gardens were much smaller.

Generally gardens of this sort became small oases, blocking out the surrounding landscape. Occasionally though, there seemed to be a conscious effort to embrace the wider landscape such as at Alexander Riley's house, Burwood Villa. This is not surprising considering the great interest in the nineteenth century about Australia's landscape and scenery and its extraordinary flora. There are many records of plants being dug from the bush to be nurtured in both country and city gardens. Writing in her diary in 1841, Anne Drysdale, who lived on a remote property on the Barwon River in Victoria, noted that:

the ladies again rode after dinner. While they were away I was employed with the children bringing home roots of flowers from the bush to plant in the garden.[13]

No exotic flowers are mentioned, though there was a wide variety of fruit and vegetables. The emphasis throughout the Australian colonies, however, was still on exotic plants, and seeds and cuttings of precious roses, geraniums and other flowers were purchased, swapped and propogated and soon spread across the country.

The geometry of these early gardens varied greatly. At their simplest they consisted of little more than a split paling fence enclosing a space in front of the house, with a straight path to the verandah and front door of the house. Furthest from the house could be fruit trees, then vegetables, and immediately in front of the cottage an area might be devoted to flowers. This small flower garden was often more decoratively laid out and the straight central path might divide around a series of circular diamond or squared flower-beds. Even in the heady days of Hill End when most were scrambling for gold, Holtermann photographed numerous examples of such gardens.

In towns and cities across the continent this form of garden persisted well into the twentieth century, though the front garden had shrunk in size and the vegetables had been banished to a yard at the rear. What remained was the decorative geometric flower garden in its thousands of combinations of geometric shapes. By the 1860s clipped box hedging was becoming popular and was used to define the pattern. At the same time decorative terracotta edging tiles appeared and were used for the same purpose. The split paling fence, too, was gradually replaced by more decorative picket and cast-iron fences, often backed by a clipped evergreen hedge of pittosporum, laurel or coprosma. Like these simple gardens in front of the unpretentious villas, the gardens in front of terrace houses followed a similar pattern with a central circle of planting surrounded by a narrow circular pathway seeming to be most popular. Barcelona Terrace, Melbourne, built in 1881, is probably the best surviving example.

The geometric garden – sometimes symmetrical, sometimes not – was repeated thousands of times across Australia in front of the small brick and timber terraces and cottages of the working classes. But it could be found also with more substantial dwellings. Summerhome and Rouseville, both in Hobart, and Mount Boningong at Scotsburn, Victoria, still have large geometric box-hedged gardens in front of their houses.

Crammed in rich confusion

By the 1850s when substantial gardens were being made in some quantity in Australia, the entire British Empire was being swamped by the products of a new age. As the century wore on so too did the quantity and elaborateness of the new features. Houses, whether large or small, were decorated on the outside and inside with a range of 'off the shelf' ornaments, and the passion for decoration produced multicoloured and multipatterned interiors overflowing with equally rich furniture and bric-a-brac. Gardens did not escape the passion for embellishment, and urns, fountains, conservatories, summer-houses and other fancies vied for attention among the colourful ribbon border plantings. The tiniest front garden could be stuffed with half a dozen urns and other ornamentation.

This all coincided with rapid growth in Australia and with an expanding upper and middle class. As a result whole suburbs such as Toorak and Elsternwick in Melbourne were dominated by hundreds of mansions and their enormous gardens, of which Rippon Lea in Elsternwick is one of the few to survive. Though remarkable for its size and complexity even in its heyday, it nevertheless gives an indication of the scale and intensity of gardening in the late nineteenth century.

The ready availability of horticultural and gardening journals encouraged a wide interest in garden activities, and horticultural societies, patronized by both rich and poor, flourished. With information readily accessible from the journals and societies, and with shops piled high with garden decorations, it was not difficult for anyone with some imagination to put together a garden. The results were sometimes astonishing.

Large gardens were not confined to the cities. The great pastoral mansions that sprang up from the 1850s onwards also developed gardens that reflected the new wealth of their owners – though, on the whole, these gardens were less busy and more restrained. By the 1870s some embraced the wider landscape with views sweeping across shaved lawns and over ha-ha walls into parklands beyond. Mount Noorat and Glenormiston at Noorat in Victoria are among the best surviving examples.

Some of the greatest horticultural extravaganzas were to be found in the hill station gardens. These had begun to develop in the 1870s, perhaps partly influenced by the

Landscape interacting with building. Right above: The parterre at Werribee Park. Right: A Tasmanian homestead. Far right: The boat jetty at Rippon Lea.

The shady vegetation embracing Gracemere, Rockhampton. Bougainvillaea is a mainstay in many tropical gardens.

Top: Bolobek, Macedon, is a Federation-period garden, recently further developed — a lush tapestry of green — by Lady Law Smith. In this view the closely spaced trees of the Poplar Avenue begin to give way to natural bushland.

The front fence of timber pickets at Camelot, near Camden, separates the house garden from the access roadway.

The picturesque tree-framed lawn at Withycombe, Mount Wilson. Like Mount Macedon and Mount Lofty, this area was founded by wealthy individualists as a retreat from the heat of the Australian summer. The garden at Withycombe was started by George Henry Cox.

Left: The organic style of John Horbury Hunt links the architecture of Camelot to its landscape. The prospect of its service garden takes in the chimney, which typically marks the kitchen of a Hunt homestead, while in the distance are the stables and the smokehouse block.

numbers of men formerly associated with the Indian army and the East India Company who settled in Australia from the 1830s on. At Mount Macedon near Melbourne, the Mount Lofty Ranges of South Australia, Mount Wilson in the New South Wales Blue Mountains, Kalamunda in Western Australia and Toowoomba in Queensland, the wealthy escaped the scorching summer heat of the coastal plains. With cooler climates, rich loamy soils and adequate supplies of water and cash, their owners created huge shady paradise gardens around their summer bungalows. As if to state the origin of such retreats many gave them names like Kirami, Darjeeling, Kuranda and Bungl'hi (all these are at Mount Macedon). The author Rolf Boldrewood, whose father had been an East India Company man, described Mount Macedon as 'that Simla of Victoria'.[14] The gardens often relied more on horticultural virtuosity than good design, and their owners imported crateloads of plants from around the world which were stuffed into every available space. Beneath the towering forest trees, imported from the northern hemisphere, the more tender plants were crammed in a rich confusion. Many of these gardens, sometimes consciously, were able to achieve a happy blending with the native forest.

From Picturesque to Gardenesque

The grand landscaped estates envisioned by Shepherd were, on the whole, not developed in Australia. By the 1840s they were old-fashioned as well. Loudon's books on horticulture and design, on the other hand, brought the vanguard of Victorian gardening taste to Australia. Where the Picturesque style featured an ornament or an architectural device to compose and focus each view in the garden, Loudon stated that the plants were themselves features. Each botanically and visually distinctive plant now assisted in the pictorial effect. Loudon wrote:

According to the Gardenesque School all the trees and shrubs planted are arranged in regard to their kinds and dimensions; and they are planted at first at, or as they grow, thinned out to, such distances apart as may best display the natural form and habit of each: while, at the same time, in a general point of view, unity of expression and character are aimed at, and attained, as effectually as they were under any other school. In short, the aim of the Gardenesque is to add, to the acknowledged charms of the Repton School, all those which the sciences of gardening and botany in their present advanced state, are capable of producing ... It has been more or less adopted in various country residences, from the anxious wish of gardeners and botanical amateurs to display their trees and plants to the greatest advantage ... it may be said to have always existed in botanic gardens[15]

From this emphasis there followed the widespread fashion, known as 'carpet bedding', of intricately formed and planted flower-beds. The Gardenesque thus resulted in self-conscious design, with tightly-curving paths, neatly edged and spotted along their lengths with urns, statues, or 'horticultural episodes'.[16]

The garden of Summerhome, above Hobart, features

The rustic bridge and summerhouse in the garden of Rippon Lea, Elsternwick. In grand gardens like this, water was an important element. The cast iron of the structures simulates wood.

Gardenesque ideas; it has a giant oval parterre with clipped box hedging, massed planting, garden vistas, and distant views. Springfield and Kippilaw, both in Goulburn, are two other examples.

Gardens were often contrived to reflect the architectural features of the houses they surrounded. Sometimes the flower-beds and lawn shapes echoed a building's formal elements, as was often the case with a house in the Italianate taste. Such gardens were found at Redleaf, Retford Hall and Cranbrook, all in Sydney; that at Leura, in Toorak, was even grander. An 1876 newspaper described:

ten acres of ground ... laid out as a garden ... Immediately in front of the house there is a broad gravel walk and then a sloping lawn extending for about 100 yards, at the bottom of which there are a number of regular shaped small beds planted in the ribbon style with very good effect ... A well-kept evergreen

The wistaria walk at Belltrees, Scone; part of the garden created by Henry White after 1907.

privet hedge shelters the ribbon beds from westerly winds, and divides the ornamental portion of the grounds from [the] cut flowers, orchard and vegetable gardens.[17]

By the end of the nineteenth century a reaction against the excesses of gardening had developed in both Britain and Australia. William Guilfoyle, in his private gardens in Victoria and more particularly in Melbourne's Botanic Gardens, devised a style which incorporated the best of the Picturesque and Gardenesque styles into an harmonious arrangement, where gardens flowed with curving beds and paths. Others, such as the architect and garden designer Walter Butler, preferred a more controlled and architectural approach where the garden became an extension of the house, divided, like rooms, into different compartments, each with a different character.

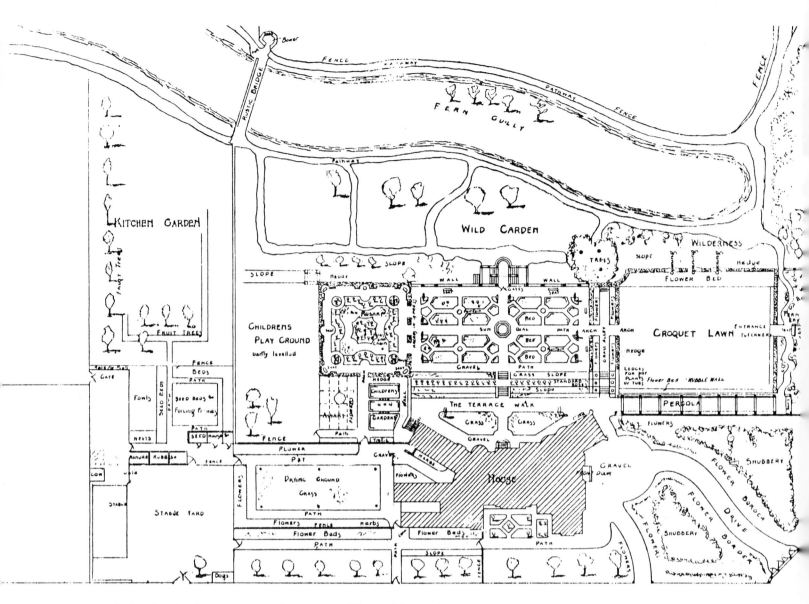

The main garden of Warrawee, Toorak, built in 1910, was a series of 'outdoor rooms', each having a different character and function.

Both styles, however, were the preserve of the wealthy, and, like the simple workman's cottage which remained relatively unchanged in form through the second half of the nineteenth century, so the gardens altered only little.

An invention of the late nineteenth century that considerably changed the nature of the small garden was the lawn-mower. It first appeared in Australia in the 1870s and, within a decade, the 'amateur's lawn-mower' as it was called, had become popular and cheap. Now, without the toil of scything or hand-clipping, the small-householder could cultivate a finely-finished lawn. Hardy buffalo grass became standard for lawns in the coastal cities. Flower-beds shrank in size in the humbler gardens to embrace and outline larger areas of mown grass which set off the fronts of suburban houses.

Other developments that made gardening easier were better water supply and reticulation, the rubber hose, and mass-produced fencing of wooden pickets and iron railings. As well, H.A. James's large work, the *Handbook of Australian Horticulture*, available in the 1890s, continued as a considerable influence into the new century.

The twentieth century

The nationalism evident in architecture around the turn of the century did not extend so naturally to gardens.

Australian trees were favoured less than English and foreign specimens, not because of their appearance, but because exotics were seen as real-estate 'improvements'.

Having in mind always the asset which his home represented, the owner was keen to effect as many improvements as possible. Improvements of course had nothing to do with improving the appearance or comfort of the property. The term could best be defined as changes from nature, for better or for worse. Every native tree chopped down made a simple but spectacular change from nature, and thus represented money in some hypothetical future bank. An English tree, on the other hand, was less natural and could almost be considered an improvement. A trimmed hedge or cypress cut into a kangaroo shape also qualified.[18]

The Guilfoylean style, albeit on a smaller scale, found some expression in the new middle-class Arts-and-Crafts-inspired houses of the early part of the twentieth century. These red tiled and turreted asymmetrical houses were surrounded by equally asymmetrical gardens – with beds, paths and driveways sometimes of tortured shapes. The more geometric style was refined to perfection by Edna Walling in the 1920s and 1930s. Walling managed to

A small and almost hidden courtyard garden in Sydney, by Ross Thorne.

Right: A Melbourne garden of the 1960s, formed with boulders surrounding a little pool, by Ellis ('Rocky') Stones.

synthesize the formal and natural styles by adopting a strong geometric and architectural form and overlaying it with a wild, though controlled, planting arrangement.

The California bungalow became immensely popular in the 1920s; its appropriateness for the Australian climate was its byword. Interestingly, its counterpart in the small suburban garden was the cultivation of Australian native plants and the encouragement of the natural look.

The straight line returned to garden designs of the 1930s, and the emphasis upon shrubs that had been so evident in the 1920s now disappeared. The suburban front garden often became a kind of public exhibit, with lawns, straight paths, and 'display borders' inside the front fence, and a 'nature strip' outside. In some areas, notably the residential suburbs of Perth, house owners removed their front fences altogether as a gesture of public spiritedness, promoting the idea of community space. With the opening-up of the front garden, private outdoor space was concentrated behind the house, with lawns, flower-beds and fruit trees located nearer to the building, and vegetable plots at the very rear of the site.

The Gardenesque tradition lingers on in some present-day landscape design but the pointers for the future are elsewhere. The influences which the early settlers brought to Australia are gradually being discarded and in today's gardens the virtues of indigenous plants are now recognized and valued more and more. Not only are Australian plants varied and subtly beautiful, they are also eminently suitable for the rigours of the climate, and, in the hands of a skilled designer, they integrate well into modern design.

Australians are now much more aware of the necessity to identify historic gardens and to see that they are conserved in the most appropriate ways. But major gardens such as Bolobek at Macedon, Victoria, are still being created; and a host of small, hidden examples show that the design of compact gardens is still a living art.

Not all gardens are great, nor can they be, but all efforts towards the creation of beauty merit appreciation. The fact that few gardens, and only a handful of great designers, have appeared so far in the short history of Australia, need not revive today the pessimism of R.E. Twopeny in 1883, when he wrote that 'the love of gardening is not at all common here; it is not a sufficiently exciting occupation'.[19]

THE STORY OF THE Australian terrace house is not about architects, and contains very little about styles or theories. The terrace houses must have had designers, some of them architects, but no architect is particularly associated with them, and few names have been discovered. The archives of the Blackets, in Sydney, and Bates Peebles & Smart in Melbourne (the best recorded nineteenth-century practices in Australia) contain a terrace group or two, but they are of no significance in their work.

A few well-known terraces, so far anonymous, deserve close attention as individual examples. For instance, Rochester Terrace in St Vincent's Place, South Melbourne; 90–112 Powlett Street, East Melbourne; Royal Terrace, Nicholson Street, Fitzroy; and Paddington, Potts Point and East Sydney, in Sydney.

But the chief interest in this form of housing is not in the excellence of individual houses. The terrace house represents an aspect of urban life which in its day everyone took for granted, but which today is an item of history, with modern comparisons to make but no direct modern equivalent. It was circumscribed by interesting practical limitations, but within those the range was considerable and it can be seen that the possibilities were thoroughly explored. It is an urban vernacular, important to Aus-

in about 1900, the prevalence of joined houses came to an end, leaving free-standing houses as the universal choice. The choice was, in those days, sharp and simple, with no other options considered. Apartment blocks were unknown, to be tentatively introduced for certain wealthy groups a generation later. Other forms of joined housing, the clusters and rows of recent times, the 'units' were not yet contemplated.

In that period terrace houses became almost extinct – their construction was an unpopular investment and not favoured by councils, some of which prohibited them. To some extent, this was a backlash from unhappy tenant-landlord experiences during the depression (severest in Melbourne) of the 1890s. To some extent it was the victory of the newly emerged movement for Garden Cities and Garden Suburbs and the change in living patterns that came with the emergence of the family car. Today, however, the old terraces are again popular, and new row housing of a similar theme is occasionally built.

The term 'Terrace'

'Terrace' is a term hard-worked in Australian speech, being used for all old joined (or abutting) houses, small and large, from a grandly coherent row design – there are

THE AUSTRALIAN TERRACE 12

tralian social history and important to design history.

Joined houses had always had some acceptance in town centres and became the custom for nearby suburbs of Sydney and Melbourne with the rapid population growth which, in the 1860s, followed the gold-rush. They were still the mode when the even more vigorous housing boom of the 1870s, 1880s and, in Sydney, the 1890s ensued. There is a strong possibility that there was a time in Melbourne, perhaps also in Sydney, about 1890, when the majority of people lived in terrace housing. What are now seen as the old and the inner suburbs then comprised almost the sum total of those cities. The developed areas were, with a few notable exceptions, such as South Yarra and Hunters Hill, terrace-house suburbs.

Hobart, almost as old as Sydney, was far from the gold rushes and hardly participated in the subsequent population growth. Adelaide, the same age as Melbourne, and for a short time copper-rich, lost population to the gold states. Perth, Brisbane, Launceston and Newcastle are more essentially cities of the Edwardian era and later; terraces exist in each, but they are uncharacteristic. In country towns, terraces are rare but not unknown – where they did exist they were usually simple workmen's cottages.

During an abrupt transition in housing habits, however,

a few – to a collection of individual houses having almost nothing in common. The idea of terrace house districts having 'special' characteristics is Australian by nature – though it could also be North American, another nation where the terrace (town house) was well established in some locations, unknown in others.

In Britain the tendency is reversed, at least when speaking of old residential areas; houses of these kinds need no adjective, they are just houses. The others are the ones in need of distinguishing – the villa, the semi-detached and the bungalow. The Australian still has a moment's surprise when his house, his plain, ordinary, no-other-name-needed house, is, by an Englishman, called a bungalow.

In Europe, and even in Scotland, a different situation again exists, for the apartment block became the norm once the joined or butting houses within old walled cities were superseded. In Europe, books about row houses were needed, to explain them to a population which never had houses like those of eighteenth- and nineteenth-century England. The first book about London's terraces, *London, the Unique City* – still without rival for a broad understanding of this kind of house in England – was by a Dane, Steen Eiler Rasmussen.

'Terrace' could, with some support from most dictionaries, be confined to the cases where a row is obviously designed as a whole, as a piece of street design, in an effort to give a little grandeur to a group of houses. That was the formal use of the word when these terraces were built. It would have been regarded as pretentious to

Two out-of-the-ordinary terrace groups. Left above: A provincial city terrace in Goulburn. Left: Brent Terrace, King's Cross, urbane, opulent and five-storeyed.

say 'terrace' for some of the cases where it is now applied. An even more restricted use of the word would be for a formal row on display in some elevated location, as with the famous terraces of Bath, in England. It is doubtful that 'terrace' could then find a single Australian application.

Flats of another era

In some respects terrace houses were the flats of another era. Like flats (at least, until the relatively recent strata title ownership) they were the products of the process of investment in housing for rent-income. They were built in groups, sharing plumbing and vehicle access (in the form of back lanes). They used to share a common postal address, such as Royal Terrace, Nicholson Street, No. 3 as, in later days, there would be a Flat 3. In one more respect there is a resemblance – their distorted reputation.

country towns. There is a striking difference between a street of detached houses and one whose houses are butting or joined which clearly sets apart those old districts. There are some localities which are just as old, but have free-standing cottages or villas and their age may not immediately be understood – but the 'terraced' streets are instantly recognized.

The 'terraced' suburbs contain many variations but have an overall distinctive character that comes mainly from their street facades. Upright, continuous fronts in groups and rows and streets are very rare in later suburbs but here they are the rule. Their visible gardens are diminutive or completely absent. The doors of houses are usually a few steps from the public footpath, and in the little garden which that permits there are not many trees, only a few flowers or shrubs or just paving. There is, as a result, more

Flat-life is now sometimes given a generalized stigma derived from the problems of multi-storey public-housing – ignoring highly prized apartments such as those near the water's edge of Sydney Harbour. In a similar way terrace houses fell into disrepute and it seemed forgotten that they were entirely satisfactory and that some were large, generously appointed, even luxurious homes.

In other respects, terraces were never like flats. There are two quite vital differences. The first is that a terrace has an individual, personal, front door, reached directly from the street. The other is that it has its own garden, or at least a yard. A terrace house stands on the ground, not upon another dwelling, as most flats do. The terrace is a house, not an apartment.

Street architecture

Most of the old, inner suburbs of Melbourne and Sydney have a street character quite different from the character of the familiar streets of other Australian suburbs, or of

Royal Terrace, Melbourne, is a fine gold-rush Regency terrace of 1854, attributed to John Gill, architect. It was designed for upper-middle-class residents.

visual importance in the garden fence or wall or hedge. Also distinctive are the relatively narrow house frontages, with their frequent gateways and repeated patterns of dividing fences.

The iron picket fences come in a variety of designs, with gate posts of iron or of plastered brick or occasionally of stone – their quick succession along the street measuring the rhythm of the frontages. The fences dividing one front garden from the next, seen one behind the other along the street, are all the more prominent if the front path rises to the doorway. That is especially true where they are brick or plastered walls, their tops sometimes curved to provide the rise.

The eye accustomed to the Garden Suburb, the district of detached houses with gardens and driveways and 'nature strips', is immediately struck by this environment, which is so much more enclosed and architectural. Even the least coherent, and meanest, examples of these 'terraced' streets have a stimulating impact; they may be appreciated or disliked, but they are not easy to ignore. The streets which hold the best houses are memorable streets. Those possessing unified rows and delightful ornament, whose front gardens have bold walls or fine fences, are streets which hold the affections of almost everyone who sees them. Some of the streets have the further asset of splendid street trees, or of public Squares.

It is easy to argue that a district of that character is in many ways superior to most of the Garden Suburbs. There is the social advantage of more people in sight and a greater sense of community provided by the numerous doors. There are more local shops supported by the closer

Because in these districts it is not far from the street, it is also more likely to function, and be seen functioning, as a place to sit where a person – especially the elderly – may feel in touch with the outside world. The balcony is an even better place to be for anyone who wishes to watch the street. Street architecture is another reason for the verandahs and balconies of terrace houses. One of the simpler ways to provide the unified appearance to a row and the 'touch of class' which developers sought for their properties, was to add the iron-decorated or the stucco-crusted verandahs and balconies.

Some of the generalizations made about verandahs and balconies are contradicted rather than reinforced by their application to terrace houses. For instance, it is assumed that they were built to shelter windows from the sun, but terraces face all ways, determined by land-subdivision,

These terraces in Waterloo, now part of the City of Sydney, are smaller and less grand. They were designed as workers' rental accommodation in the 1870s. The rhythmical parapets and fire walls result from nineteenth-century building regulations.

population, there are activities of children, of elderly people, of car owners, taking place in the streets which, in Garden Suburbs, are concealed and unnecessarily private.

These advantages for the terraced suburbs were, for several generations, lost from view. Wide appreciation returned in the 1960s, and continues to reflect in the real estate values of Paddington and Balmain, Carlton and Fitzroy and many others in the old and inner suburbs.

Viewing the street

Verandahs and balconies are strongly associated with terrace houses. The verandah is an enlarged porch. If the entrance door is to be sheltered, then on a narrow house that shelter might as well go right across the front.

made with no thought (it would usually seem) for desirable orientation of houses. Balconies do not only appear on north-facing terraces; there are no design modifications for the more difficult aspects of east and west; and they are not absent from the southern frontages. Balconies very rarely appear on the back of a house, as they might do with great practical effect, as shelter or as a place to sit. Whatever advantages they offered some of the houses, balconies were applied widely for one reason above all – it was a fashionable, admired part of that house-cum-street architecture which the terrace houses provided for a district. Those with them were evidently admired, preferred and more readily rented and purchased.

Roofs may or may not be much in view, because a concealing parapet is common, and that parapet is another location for street rhythm and for decoration. A minority of roofs, the oldest ones more particularly, project over the front door with a display of eaves (and their rafters or their brackets). A few roofs display gable ends, which

This tiny two-storey residence was squeezed between its neighbours on a left-over allotment in Enmore. The side windows of
the house on the right prevented No. 43½ from being wider.
The five-panel front door and the tiled stair-risers are typical of
Sydney houses of the late nineteenth century.

makes a very different appearance from all the rest —
usually early examples, probably of the 1850s.

The decorative cast iron is the workshop-product of a
foundry. It was delivered in parts, such as balustrade
panels, column capitals or brackets, and overhead friezes,
and fitted to the wooden posts or beams or handrails, or to
the iron columns. The patterns were advertised in newspapers and distributed in catalogues, and they could easily
be ordered, by mail if necessary, to fit the particular
frontage of the house.

Window surrounds may be quite plain, or Classically
architraved, or more lavishly decorated. When balconies
do not conceal them they provide the main rhythm for
upper floors. Another element, the pattern of which may
repeat through the street, is a protruding party-wall.
Walls, window surrounds and party-walls, along with
parapets, were commonly plastered, though both the
1860s and the 1890s showed a fondness for the colour of
brickwork. When plastered, and if embellished, the walls,
window surround, party-walls and parapets are found
with simple mouldings or with patterns pressed into the
plaster, or with applied items of stucco decoration.

The decorative stucco items had a lot in common with
the ironwork — both were products of plasterers' work-
shops and were similarly advertised and distributed, but
the stucco was secured in place by the bricklayer rather
than the carpenter. The stucco items are found as gatepost
tops, party-wall brackets and faces, archway and parapet
decorations, date plaques and crowning features such as
urns. The iron and the stucco are especially characteristic
of the building boom period of the 1880s. They are by no
means confined to terraces, or even to houses, but upon
terraces their most concentrated use is seen.

Nothing appears on terrace houses which is unique to
them, but the repetition along a street, and the variations
upon a theme which can be observed in a brief walk,
bring them into prominence. The glazed tiles, for instance, employed in some districts on the risers of front
steps — The Glebe is particularly rich in these — or the
encaustic tiles, when they appear on front paths or, more
commonly, as the verandah floor. They are found in
greater quantity and richer variety in villas, mansions and
public buildings, but it is among terrace houses that people
are likely first to notice them.

Terrace houses further embrace their street by accentu-
ating its shape. A row of houses kept close to the street
front, or right upon it, reflects the street's form: if a street
curves, the house fronts curve, as a street rises the houses
rise. The stepping upwards of many of Paddington's
houses is one of its clearest images. Where streets lie along
the contours of a hill the adaptation of the houses to its
slopes can be very apparent, because of steps or bridges.
These are all the more noticeable for being numerous
within a single view.

*Right top: Kent House and Sussex House, a fine terrace pair
in South Melbourne, with faceted ground-floor bay windows.*

*Right: Two views showing part of the splendid group called
Rochester Terrace, also in South Melbourne. The end house
'turns the corner' gracefully.*

Urban history aspects

The advantages of terrace living and those of a Garden Suburb strongly vie with each other. The space of the suburb allows for the pleasure of gardens and the needs of children and the hazard of fire, but those are in their way satisfied in terraced districts with slightly different life styles. Privacy is also not confined to separated houses – the acoustic privacy provided by a stout party-wall is very good, for most purposes better than that provided by a gap with windows facing each other.

One circumstance, however, diminished the arguments in favour of terrace housing – the advent of the family car. Accommodation for the car, or cars, is very easily achieved in a Garden Suburb site – there is space to park, to clean and to unload into a backyard store (the garage). The car also undermined a major reason for continuing the old tradition of joined houses. This was the desirability of locating residential streets as close as possible to workplaces, railway stations, trams and shops.

The distinction between the terraced areas and the equally old suburbs of free-standing villas was one of wealth. These villas (such as Point Piper or South Yarra) belonged to the people who had carriages and grooms and coachmen, and, of course, where they existed there were already maids and butlers and governesses. The terraced districts were not without servants, but a sign of much greater wealth was the presence of stables in the garden of a house. A personal vehicle was then a considerable distinction. When cars, mass produced, came within the reach of so many, the urban fabric was changing.

Paddington is a particularly interesting example. Its history began in the 1820s with an era of villas constructed for people of substance, which personal transport placed beyond the confines of pedestrian Sydney. Then in about 1870 Paddington began to be transformed into a district of terraces, many of them built upon the gardens of the former villas as the land around them was speculatively subdivided. Earlier landholders like Underwood and Cooper are commemorated in the names of streets made to give access to such subdivisions. Some estates were broken up more than once, the allotments decreasing in width and therefore increasing in number with each successive speculation, the houses eventually built upon them making a dense and rich residential mosaic. The construction of these terraces went hand in hand with the development of public transport.

Maps of nineteenth-century residential areas show very clearly the tight association between transport and development. After the family car, suburban housing played

Left above: Three houses in Annandale which, although separate, have the character of a terrace.

Left: A two-storey sandstone group from the 1840s in Darlinghurst.

Right above: Plan of a part of a terrace showing the rear spaces between them which gave currency to the term 'tunnel-backs'.

Right: Map of part of Glebe, largely a high-density nineteenth-century terrace-house suburb of Sydney.

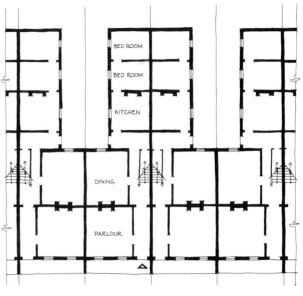

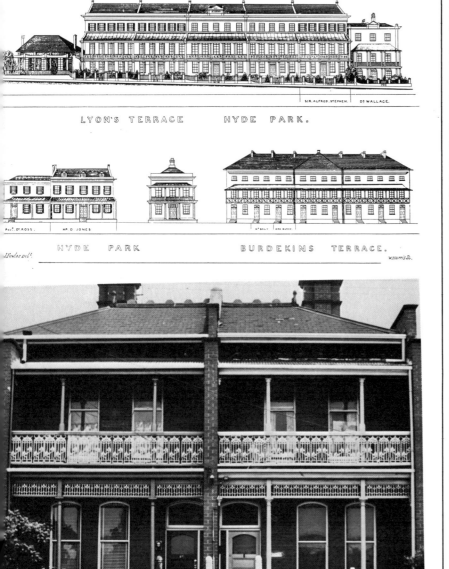

Two elegant Sydney terraces, Lyons and Burdekin, as drawn by Joseph Fowles in Sydney *in 1848. It was common to leave the top storey unverandahed, but far less common for the first floor balcony to be cantilevered, as in Burdekin Terrace.*

SYDNEY.

LYON'S TERRACE   HYDE PARK.

HYDE PARK   BURDEKINS TERRACE.

A Federation-period terrace pair in Preston, Victoria, with tall front windows. The cast-iron balcony and frieze panels feature the Art Nouveau tulip-bud motif.

a new game, a kind of hide-and-seek, pressing outward in much less predictable directions as land became available. A new liberty existed.

In the late stages of the old situation, terrace houses were every now and then located near outer railway stations, but they were never to expand into districts and suburbs of terraces like the inner suburbs. They looked forlorn and alien as the Garden Suburbs grew around them, at locations like Box Hill or Strathfield.

Frontage sizes

Terrace houses did not seem to grow with arbitrary dimensions – there are a few very common sizes, and variations away from these were the products of local circumstances. This regularity came both from land subdivision and from commonsense about the size of rooms.

Early Melbourne displayed street regularity much more than did Sydney, because it was a planned city whose early roads were regularly spaced. They were planned in a government office in Sydney, apparently following an ancient colonial experience in which surveyor-planners, living in the interesting muddle of a city which was not preplanned, are apt to impose with fervour a rectangular grid of regular streets.

Both the preferred widths for streets, and the preferred lengths for blocks were multiples of the measure called a chain, which was 20 metres. A common street width was one chain, a broad avenue was 3 chains. Four chains or 80 metres, was a common street-block depth (one frontage through to another frontage, that is two house-lots, front-to-back, along with whatever lanes were inserted). Finally, common street-block lengths were either 8 chains, or 12 chains.

A house frontage would, therefore, very likely be a subdivision of a chain, and indeed two very common terrace house widths are 6.7 metres, one-third of a chain, and 5 metres, one-quarter of a chain. The latter is about minimum for a readily marketable house, for after passage and wall thicknesses are accounted for, its main front room is about 3.35 metres.

Rear access

The modern suburbanite is perplexed about how people in a terrace house manage to reach the backyard with objects offensive to the hall carpets, or to leave by the front with the rubbish. Motor bikes are sometimes taken through the passage and push-bikes very often are. Garden hoses are all very well if rolled up, but if dripping after use they are problematic. When a wheelbarrow task occasionally arises, newspapers or a polythene runner will be pressed into service. The pram or the pusher can be almost as troublesome to a carpet. Children must be educated to take muddy shoes off at the front door and carry them to a workplace at the rear.

Such problems occur because a terrace house is a house, not a flat. People living in a flat amend their ways. People in a terrace live so close to 'normal' house life that they may be slower to change, and the occasional problem might be cursed rather than cured.

The back lane is usually there to solve almost any such problem if the extra distance can be faced. People living on the ends of the rows are obviously more fortunate than those in the middle.

The lanes were there, almost without fail, for the collection of 'night soil' – in other words, the dunny cans. The lanes needed entrance and exit, for horses could not be asked to reverse and a turning circle for horse and cart would be a foolish use of land in a pattern of houses deliberately compressed.

Some lanes retain outhouses to this day, against the back fences or incorporated within the back walls. The small low doors, for removing the cans without entering the yard, were removed and the openings were bricked up and the toilets became WCs whenever sewerage reached the district, probably not very long after 1890. Subsequently almost all WCs moved indoors.

Most blocks, it so happened, accommodated a car parked at an angle. Today, as a result, a back fence car port is the most likely thing to stand in the place from which those outhouses were taken. On the narrower blocks they have more commonly lingered.

Inside the terrace house

Terrace houses range from very small up to very large, in floor area and in volume – from a two-room cottage with 3.35-metre frontage whose area is about 22.3 square metres up to a three-storey house of twice that frontage or more, holding twenty rooms (examples in East Melbourne) and a floor area of 404.1 square metres. Those with more than three storeys could be larger.

Ceiling heights and therefore volumes varied from house to house. They followed the fashions shared by villas and became taller as the nineteenth century progressed. In some cases late in the century the room heights were awkwardly tall for rooms of lesser area, apparently governed by a desire for at least one very grand room. There were also variations between front and back rooms, and (to a lesser extent) ground floor and upper floors.

A fundamental feature of a terrace house that rules its internal planning is the existence of blind side walls. The two side walls upon the boundaries of the block can have no windows and are party-walls shared with the neighbours, or else they are butting against matching walls belonging to the neighbours. The exception, of course, is a house at the end of a street, a corner house, which has one of its side walls liberated.

This restriction of the blind side walls is in the nature of all joined housing. It belongs to the largest and the smallest, the wide frontage or the narrow. And it has the consequence that two rooms deep is the limit for the main part of the house. Front rooms have windows to the street, back rooms to a yard or garden, and no normal rooms with exterior windows can occur in between.

The possibility exists of an interior court or light-well for more rooms but these are very uncommon, except where additions and alterations have occurred over the years. It was misleading of Robin Boyd in *Australia's Home* to show only one plan (and provide no discussion at all) for a terrace house and to choose one with an internal light-well – and to inform the reader that it was a typical plan for workmen's cottages. It was not, and the implication that terraces existed only for workmen and in inferior

A group of bluestone and stucco houses in Collingwood, given a Classical treatment by a heavy cornice, window surrounds, and quoins.

Avenue Terrace, Stanmore, 1897. A symmetrical grouping of five asymmetrical houses, whose faceted bays and balconies give the terrace a gently Italianate cast.

forms was a blemish in an otherwise splendid book.

Light-wells require no further discussion, but an alternative certainly exists – the so-called tunnel-back plan which was used for a very high proportion of Australian terraces. The tunnel-back plan was one of the remaining options available to a designer when considering how to increase the size of a house plan beyond a basic few rooms.

The 'tunnel-back' is the side space where narrower back rooms are placed behind the main rooms – the space where back rooms do not fill the width of the site. One of the back rooms' side walls is then released from being on the boundary and can therefore have windows.

'Tunnel-back' is a severe term, for its nature was not often tunnel-like. Mean widths in tall houses made it so, but better circumstances usually prevailed.

The other basic options for the designer wishing to increase the number of rooms are these: to choose 'double fronted' rather than 'single fronted' (that is two rooms in width rather than one) or to have more storeys.

A double-fronted terrace is, however, in any city, much less common than the single-fronted. At first this seems surprising, for a double-fronted house not only looks grander but its entrance door is central rather than against one side – an obvious improvement.

Several things militate against them. One is that the tunnel-back and the central passage do not easily mix. The entrance to the room added to the back has to be through the initial room or through a passage. A passage must be placed against a party-wall, not the wall which has the windows. If the front passage, the one leading from the front door, is central rather than at the side, the two just cannot join directly, indeed they cannot join without

A 1901 Sydney photograph showing some of the 'mean terraces' of the Rocks area, on pocket-handkerchief allotments.

blocking off one of the main rooms.

To that must be added that the smallness of the rooms found at the back in the tunnel-back arrangement was convenient. They were the servants' rooms and the small-by-nature rooms – kitchen, bathroom, nursery and storage. Their location, distinct and separate from the main rooms, was also very acceptable.

This attitude towards the back rooms seems to have been emphasized strongly in Australia. English houses of comparable middle-class size usually had a well-worked basement, or semi-basement, containing the kitchen, along with coal-storage and other service rooms and a servant's quarters. North American houses put even greater emphasis on the basement because of the need to accommodate the heating system, and their houses, terraced or otherwise, still often are elevated by many steps to gain good light for that basement. Australians were relatively reluctant to provide a basement unless a slope in the land offered obvious opportunities. So, out into that appendage along the tunnel-back went those kinds of functions.

Short and narrow

Other points also weighed against the wider frontages. The fundamental aim was a compact residential area with streets not too stretched away from station or tramway. Making houses deeper rather than wider suited that purpose. Moreover, the taxation system was keeping it that way, for Council rates were calculated upon frontages, rather than upon site areas.

The grand Tasma Terrace, Eastern Hill, Melbourne, designed in 1878 by Charles Webb. It has unusual cast-iron decoration.

The Australian reluctance to provide a basement seems to have mirrored a reluctance to go high. In London and other major cities of England, houses were very commonly built three storeys (in addition to basement) and not infrequently four, or by way of attics, five. In Sydney and Melbourne, among terrace houses two storeys is by far the most common, and single-storeyed ones not infrequent. Three, in that environment, looks rather grand, and since it is exceptional was often the grand one, tall in ceilings as well as storeys and therefore all the more prominent. The headquarters of the National Trust in Victoria now reside in Parliament Place, Melbourne, in a three-storey terrace. Not far from that, in Collins Street and nearby streets, there were several splendid groups which were three storeys, and in a rare case or two, four. Outside the central city of Melbourne only a handful with three storeys were ever to be found, unless attics or lower-ground floors in sloping sites, are counted. Royal Terrace, Nicholson Street, is a good example, prominent and well-known because of its location. Round the corner from it, in Gertrude Street, there used to be Granite Terrace, also three storeys. Occasionally a portion of a terrace goes higher, for architectural emphasis, with towers. Those are found in Middle Park and St Kilda.

In Sydney, the most interesting locality for three-storey terrace houses is Potts Point, especially in Challis Avenue and part of Victoria Street. They have existed in the past in Sydney's central city streets, as in Melbourne. A few, of rather routine design, linger on in Phillip Street.

The entrance of light

The location of the windows – the admission of sunshine, daylight and ventilation – was the potential problem in terrace house design. The main windows of the terrace house face forward or backward, always in opposing directions, be it east and west, north and south, or some other points of the compass. A modern, garden-loving and energy-conscious viewpoint is likely to favour most the back windows facing north, associated with the more private, or perhaps the only, garden. Nineteenth-century obedience to those points seems to have been infrequent, although understood, and explained in the house-designer's text of the day, by Robert Kerr, *The Gentleman's House. . .* , concerned with villas rather than terraces.

Its other windows were in many cases all in the tunnel, but one potential location remained: the very back wall, that is the rear of the last room. Those backmost rooms were often the brightest rooms of all the house, yet were devoted usually to the laundry below and maid above.

But the term 'tunnel' is severe. Inside the ground-floor windows in a standard two-storey tunnel-back, the sky might not be seen but the light which reaches them is not ungenerous. Most terraces were adequately designed and many have splendid light – superior to so many of the later separate houses.

The location for the stair was, more often than not, straight ahead from the front door, in the passage and alongside the second room, rising in the same direction as the passage was going, towards the rear of the house. The width of the passage at the front door often was not sufficient to accommodate the stair and allow people to pass, so the passage widened after the first room.

The designer's alternative to that location was that the stair should lie across the house rather than in the direction of its depth. It was then placed immediately behind a front room, where it lacked a window making a roof light of some sort necessary.

The presence of tunnel-back rooms influenced the choice of stair location. A stair ascending towards the rear of the house suited tunnel-back rooms. Because these appended rooms were narrow, and in function service rooms, a lower ceiling was accepted, and so the rooms above them had floor levels lower than the main upper rooms. By means of a landing about two-thirds of the way up, the staircase gave easy access to this split-level first floor arrangement.

Where there were no tunnel-back rooms, light for the stair was easily gained, for it occupied a portion of the rear wall of the house. A window could be contrived above the roof of the appended rooms giving light to the stair, provided the difference in height between the main house and back rooms was sufficient. The intermediate case is a favourable one, where there is actually one less storey of tunnel-back than there is of main house.

Often where there was a straight-ahead stair in a tunnel-back house, no such window upon the stair was arranged, and the stair had to depend upon one or all of three remaining possibilities for its light. The simplest and least satisfactory was to depend on whatever windows were contained in the front doorcase, and that was usually one rectangular light above the door. The uppermost steps were never satisfactorily lit from there. The second possibility was that on the upper floor a passage returned to the front of the house, where it had a window, or a glazed door on to a balcony. The third option was a roof light.

The roof-light solution was capable of bringing a very satisfactory flood of light down upon the stair. Once chosen, it needed to be well designed and positioned: to make sure that it did not bring with it an equal flood of unwanted heat; to fit within the ceiling in such a way that it was not a strangely tall shaft rising up to a roof high above; and to be a part of the roof where its construction against rain would remain satisfactory over a long period of low maintenance. The same solutions for light apply to the passage, or passages. Where the plan did not permit them their own windows, there had to be dependence upon roof lights or upon doorcases. If they were well designed the result could be totally satisfactory, not only for lighting but also for ventilation.

Party wall

People who have lived only in a free-standing house, and have never experienced the party-wall of joined housing or of a flat of equivalent construction, are probably prone to distrust its ability to isolate sounds. Terrace houses were

Right above: Alfred Terrace, Sydney, illustrates the streetscape quality of modest houses joined to form a unified group.

Plans. Right: Floor plans of Horbury Terrace, Sydney, a simple 1840s terrace of which only two survive. The kitchen was located in the cellar. Far right: Plan and section of a typical split-level terrace house.

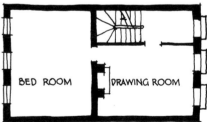

FIRST FLOOR

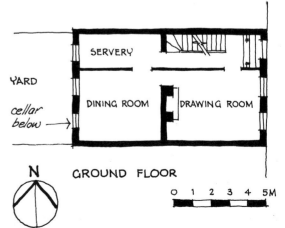

GROUND FLOOR

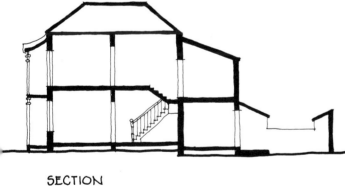

SECTION

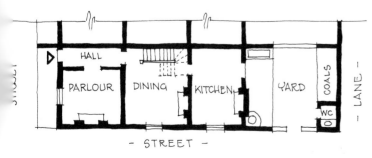

GROUND FLOOR PLAN

separated from neighbours by at least 230 millimetres of brickwork, almost always plastered on both sides. That describes a shared or party-wall. Some houses were constructed with their own walls, so that two thicknesses of 230 millimetres came between neighbours. Even the single wall is effective. Only in the quietest of circumstances is a normal sound noticed, unless it is a knock directly upon the wall, and that is quite muffled. Flats have often been constructed with concrete walls of less thickness which are less effective. Houses with gaps between and windows facing across the gaps are generally inferior to the brick party-wall, and must depend on thoughtful planning, so that bathroom faces bathroom, rather than, for instance, room-with-television facing bedroom.

The primary function for a party-wall is to confine any outbreak of fire. This is less often discussed, and far less often tested, but the thickness and the form of the side walls of a terrace house are determined by the intention to keep any house fire within the house where it started.

This discussion of party-walls leads back to the topic raised early in the chapter, the street architecture created by terrace housing. The design of the walls changed over the years, and by the time of the housing boom of the 1880s they were more elaborate, in a more strenuous effort to isolate fires. By then the regulations in most municipalities (there were no uniform, State-wide regulations then) insisted upon party-walls or boundary walls protruding in all directions beyond the house walls, roof and eaves, forwards, backwards and upwards. A row of houses built under those rules has that distinctive toast-rack appearance, with every house clearly defined. It is quite different from the long communal appearance which many older terraces have. If this insistent rhythm of the fire walls did not please the designer, the introduction of front parapets to conceal the roof, and of verandahs with balconies which incorporated the front protrusions, could be used. Other reasons to do with style – an increasing desire for elaborateness – made them acceptable devices. But even in that arrangement, the fire rules show up, where the wood of the balcony roof and of the balcony floor had to be isolated from the neighbour's similar wooden parts, by protruding brickwork. The corbelling to support those protrusions is distinctive.

New popularity

The interest of the terrace house lies in it being an urban vernacular. It is a house form circumscribed by practical considerations, but by constantly repeated experience over many decades it established a number of interesting variations upon the basic arrangement, from which the designers could choose in confidence. The best examples have an air of rightnness. In their day they suited the investors, the landlords, the occupants and the community. Their period of disfavour showed that circumstances had changed, rather than that designs were flawed.

Today's popularity for the old terraces is a product of a cycle in circumstances. Advantages of terrace living are now seen, along with some disenchantment with the options which were tried in the meantime, the Garden Suburb of detached houses, on the one hand, and on the other hand multi-storey blocks of flats.

IN THE LONG HISTORY of prefabrication there can have been no more productive period than the middle nineteenth century, about 1830–65. In this period Britain was the major prefabricator and Australia the largest importer. Prefabrication – as opposed to mass production, modular building, and the manufacture of specialized elements off-site – makes sense economically when labour is cheaper at the point of origin than at the point of destination. Conditions are particularly propitious when the recipient market is already importing building materials, so that labour and know-how simply need to be added to the existing package.

The first European house in Australia, that of Governor Arthur Phillip in 1788, had been of patent oilcloth, on a timber frame, imported from the London manufacturers Smith & Baber.[1] There may have been one or two others imported, such as Denbigh, Narellan, NSW, of about 1818, which is clad in weatherboards. It was built for Charles Hook, a partner in Campbell & Co., and brought from India through their mercantile connections.[2] But labour was cheap in a convict colony, and there was not much scope for more imports of this sort – on the contrary Sydney was soon to become an exporter in a small way. As early as 1804 buildings were made in Sydney to be sent

interchangeable, and the whole house – or at least the main frame of it – was built at the point of origin before being numbered and dismantled.

Prefabrication for the free settlements

The first documented attempt at system buiding, in which components were sufficiently standardized to be interchangeable and in which the whole frame was not necessarily assembled at the manufactory, was made in response to a new facet of the Australian market. The Sydney-made buildings were generally the work of the Royal Engineers and were intended for settlements dependent on Sydney. The Swan River settlement in Western Australia was mounted and equipped direct from England in 1829. One of the settlers had a father, John Manning, who was a carpenter and builder in London, and he began making what in that period were normally referred to as portable houses. They were probably at first still conventional structures, but apart from being brought from England to the site of erection, it was intended that they might also be dismantled after a time and moved to a new site – a great advantage in the early days of colonies with confusing and changeable conditions of land tenure. This offered a real incentive for the

THE PORTABLE HOUSE

to the subsidiary settlements at Newcastle and Van Diemen's Land. In 1832 a house of substance was designed by John Verge (later modified by Ambrose Hallen) to be taken to New Zealand by James Busby, who had been appointed the first British Resident. In 1836 the Royal Engineers at Sydney were called upon once more for a house for Captain William Lonsdale, first commandant of the settlement at Melbourne, and some components of this building still survive.[3] Next, houses were sent in 1838 to Port Essington in the Northern Territory, where they rotted.[4]

The wooden buildings made in Australia were made by the government and, it seems, were made in traditional carpenter's fashion. A mortised and tenoned box frame is quite suited to prefabrication because it has relatively few joints and these are pegged or dowelled, which allows them to be taken apart and put together. These early houses differed little from conventional construction, except that the components tended to have numbers cut into them to show the correct order of assembly. But even this practice occurred to some extent in conventional buildings. The question of the right order was important, for no special attempt was made to make the members

Left above: Lonsdale's cottage, Melbourne, prefabricated in Sydney by the Royal Engineers, 1837. Watercolour by W.F.E. Liardet.

Left: Vale Farm, Walkerville, South Australia, made by John Manning of London. Watercolour by S.T. Gill, about 1850.

development of a more flexible system of building, and Manning had developed one based upon panel construction at least by 1833, when he had made many houses, including some on the new system, for the Swan River Perth (and for other colonies).[5]

In Adelaide Manning's success was notable. Not only did he make a very large proportion of the buildings for the colony – one account suggests the majority[6] – but he was patronized by all the notabilities from Governor John Hindmarsh down.[7] He also made two houses in 1839 for C.J. La Trobe, Superintendent of the Port Phillip District and one for the Governor of New Zealand, William Hobson, in 1840.[8] La Trobe's houses give some idea of Manning's *modus operandi*. The first was a small panelled house which La Trobe was able to bring with him because it was essentially a package of standard components which Manning held in stock. The second was a larger Gothic house, not panelized, which could not be ready immediately and was sent out some months later. La Trobe, however, found his financial burdens so formidable that he sold the larger house without ever putting it up, and he lived in the smaller panelized cottage, which survived and has been moved to a new site and restored by the National Trust.[9]

Manning's system of panelization was based on units of a uniform size, about 0.9 by 2.25 metres: these contained a door and its frame, or a window with solid panels below and above, or simply solid panels. Each unit fitted between slotted posts. The journal of Samuel Vaughan, who

Mona Cottage, Perth, probably by John Manning of London, imported in the 1830s. Photograph by A.H. Stone, 1861.

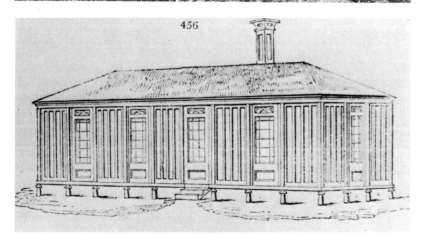

456

A portable cottage by John Manning, from Loudon's En-cyclopaedia, 1833.

Centre: A photograph of the Manning house erected for Super-intendent La Trobe at Jolimont, taken some years after it was vacated by the La Trobe family.

brought a Manning house to Melbourne in 1853, gives the instructions for assembling it:

First look out the ground plates or cills and knock them to-gether, take care to bring the corners together as they are marked – next place the corner posts according to their respective marks into the bottom plates + put the nuts on screws from the underside + screw them tightly up – next put in the middle posts those that are fastened with screws + screw them from the underside very firmly; next knock the top plates together ac-cording as they are marked (these plates are grooved the bottom are not) + lift them up bodily + place the same upon the top of posts already screwed in. then screw the top plates down to the posts but not close down at first until you get all the panelled framings + posts in all round which you must do by first plac-ing in a framing then a post and the last (when you come to close the last two) must be sprung in thus (*sketch*). You must take care to place the doors and windows in the places where you want them to be *before* you screw down the top plates *firmly* + put in the cross partitions – i.e. in a similar way to the external in-closures. the cross plates are marked at each end which you must be particular in looking to. having got all properly down screw up all the nuts very firmly – next put in the Rafters + nail two or three braces across the underside of the Rafters to keep them in their places – then nail on Board covering for the Roof – *and last of all* put down the Floor Boards.
The gable Enclosures are put in similarly to the Panell'd framing. Note. the Bottom plates are painted *Black*.[10]

Just as some of Manning's grandest houses were built conventionally, other manufacturers also were making timber houses in a less systematic way than by compiling panelled units. The most prominent after Manning was Peter Thompson, an eccentric character whose career embraced bookselling, art forgery, a pioneering experi-ment in building with hollow terracotta blocks, and, by the 1860s, attempts to promote the use of concrete con-struction.[11] Thompson may well have been responsible for thirty-five pairs of semi-detached cottages sent to Adelaide in 1836 by the South Australian Company to serve as an emigrant depot,[12] for he was making houses of this sort a few years later.[13] Certainly he was advertising in guides for emigrants to South Australia in 1839, and gives some idea of his constructional methods:

Emigrants' Houses are prepared complete, with Outside and Inside Boarding on Studwork Framing, Boarded Floors on Joists, and Boarded Ceilings, at once rendering them impervious to the heat and cold, and excluding all sounds and drafts. Houses for families are fitted up with Bedsteads, Wash-stands, and every convenience calculated for the comfort of a Dwelling House.[14]

Like Manning, Thompson sent houses to New Zealand, where the Chief Justice had one.[15] A similar house which survives and is documented as one of Thompson's is Woodlands, Tullamarine, near Melbourne, built in 1843. The house is in a U-plan, with a transverse service wing at the rear completing the enclosure of a central courtyard. Some changes were made to the design and possibly some materials were added from other sources, quite apart from the granite-piered twentieth-century verandah and other alterations. Yet there is much of technical interest: cast-iron casement sashes in one of the rear wings; the original 630 millimetre square diagonally-placed zinc tiles surviv-ing under the present roofing; lightweight trusses (or perhaps, as they are not triangulated, better described as tied rafters with the rafters strutted off the ties) spaced from 475 to 545 millimetres apart; and floors of grooved boarding with loose tongues.[16]

Manning and Thompson were only the most prominent among a very large number of portable house builders, for every carpenter was potentially a manufacturer. Not all their houses were well designed or adequately documented for easy re-erection. In South Australia, John (later Sir John) Morphett advised a friend in 1837:

only be sure you see it put up on the premises of the maker, and when taken to pieces, carefully packed, marked, and numbered, keeping a list, that you may know what each package contains.[17]

In the following year, it was reported, a colonist brought:

a wooden house, containing several rooms, which ... was found to be all but useless, owing to its bulky structure, and the unseasoned quality of the timber, which caused it to shrink under the influence of the climate.[18]

E.W. Andrews, an emigrant of 1839, had a different sort of complaint. His purchase was a combined dwelling and warehouse which he found much too elaborate by the standards of the colony. He decided to leave out the flooring, which few warehouses in Adelaide contained, and to have doors and windows made locally in order to save the good ones he had brought out.[19] Finally, and surely unfairly, these houses were alleged to be particularly subject to infestation:

Few of the wooden houses sent from Britain answered the expectations of the importers or fulfilled the promises of the builders; and many of those which still survive and are inhabited are also infested, being very complete and convenient repositories for many of the noxious and *innocuous* tribes. The matched linings of some of the houses secure the free tenantry from every art of ejectment short of pulling down ...[20]

Fewer portable houses were imported by the middle 1840s, less because of these complaints than because the initial demand had been met in Adelaide and the Victorian gold rushes had not yet begun. But, during this period, Singapore and other eastern sources began to play a significant role in the Victorian market. St Ninians in Brighton, built in 1839, is believed to have been of Singapore teak,[21] and a house in Williamstown, built before 1840, was framed in cedar in the round and inscribed with Chinese characters.[22] The first unequivocal contemporary reference is to Singapore Cottage, built in Little Lonsdale Street, Melbourne, before 1841.[23] It was only after the economic recession at Port Phillip in the 1840s, however, that imports became large – a notable example being a batch of two-storey houses brought out in 1848 and built at Geelong as 'Singapore Terrace'.[24] It is probable that the Singapore makers directed their attention temporarily to the Californian gold-rush in 1848–50, though there the only specific references are to houses from Hong Kong. It seems that some houses come also from India, as had Denbigh in 1818: a house of 1850 which stood until modern times at 46 Moor Street, Fitzroy, was said to be of Indian teak.[25]

The Victorian gold-rushes once more attracted these imports, on such a scale that a single firm in 1853 ordered

Chief Justice Martin's house at Judge's Bay, Auckland, by Peter Thompson, before 1843.

Germain Nicholson's house, St Kilda, near Melbourne, believed to have been imported from California, 1850.

Centre: Argyle Cottage, formerly Singapore Cottage, Melbourne. A sketch by Georgiana McCrae, 1841.

200 houses of cedar from Singapore.[26] The Geelong merchant Alexander Fife actually went to Singapore and chartered at least three ships to bring houses to Geelong,[27] and in some cases carpenters were brought out with the houses. Louis Ah Mouy was one of these and came out from Singapore in 1851 under contract, built six houses of 'Singapore oak' in South Melbourne and Williamstown, then went on to become a successful miner and speculator and a very prominent citizen.[28] Apart from the numerous Singapore houses which reached Melbourne and Geelong, some at least were brought to South Australia, where there still survives The Cedars, Myrtle Bank, a 'Singapore cedar' house imported by W. Hunter.[29] One house recently discovered at Mentone, near Melbourne, had been moved there in 1900 from a site in Collingwood where it had been first put up in the 1850s. It was built of exotic timbers, some of them inscribed with Chinese characters of a semi-literate nature, and it retained a Morewood & Rogers galvanized-iron tile roof. Otherwise it was much altered, and it has been again relocated to another site in Collingwood. Such imports virtually ceased after 1855, with the possible exception of some 'teak framed and panelled houses' which arrived with ex-servants of the East India Company, and which were said to have come from India.[30]

Housing for the gold-rush

The scale of importation to Melbourne increased dramatically with the discovery of gold. The value of imported wooden houses, which had risen from £623 in 1848 to £28,777 in 1852, now increased ninefold to £246,371 in 1853. They comprised 15,960 packages, half of which came from Britain:

	£
Great Britain	123,538
British colonies in North America	828
British colonies elsewhere	100,014
United States of America	20,981
Foreign states	1,110
Total	246,371[31]

The British houses were not merely those of the big London manufacturers Manning and Thompson, for other makers had established themselves, especially in the main seaport towns. There was also a major inland establishment at Gloucester, that of William Eassie, from which, after the Australian gold discoveries:

enormous quantities of wooden houses, doors, windows, mouldings, and other wooden materials used in house buildings, have been prepared by machinery, packed and shipped for the markets of Melbourne, Geelong and Sydney.[32]

Three cottages of oak which survived at Brighton until relatively recently, are supposed to have come from Wales,[33] and a chapel of oak was imported from Scotland in the later 1850s by the squatter, William Taylor, of Overnewton, Victoria.[34] One house of only 2.7 by 1.8 metres was imported from Glasgow,[35] but there was a combined house and shop of even smaller plan area, although two-storeys high, on Melbourne's Eastern Market Reserve (where the Southern Cross Hotel now stands). This measured only 2.25 by 1.8 metres, but

Osborne House, North Melbourne, 1854, believed to have been imported from the United States. Top: A detail of the porch. Above: Sections cut from the wall studs, showing Roman numerals used in the erection sequence.

Cottage for Dr De La Montaigne, Fishkill Landing, by Calvert Vaux and/or A.J. Downing, 1850s, from Calvert Vaux's book Villas and Cottages.

Top: A timber house believed to have been made in California and erected in South Yarra about 1855.

whether it was also from Scotland is unknown.[36]

Almost as many buildings were imported from British colonies as from Britain itself. A number would have been from Singapore and the other eastern sources mentioned above, but others would have been from within Australasia. Nathaniel Hailes of Adelaide is said to have made large profits from buying 'prefabricated wooden huts' and selling them on the Victorian diggings.[37] These were probably of overseas origin, but as early as 1838 John Crawford & Company were making portable houses for sale in Adelaide,[38] and undoubtedly others were made in the Australian colonies. By 1849 three Sydney makers, William Beaumont, J. Rossiter and Benjamin James, as well as others, were making portable wooden buildings, probably mainly for California, and George Atkinson of Hobart also sent houses there.[39] Again, in 1850 the Hobart architect James Thomson called tenders for fifty timber-framed houses to be sent to the Californian goldfields.[40] A striking case of re-export came from New Zealand, where seven complete houses of American and New Zealand pine had been made for the Southern Whale Fishery Company's station at Port Ross, in the Auckland Islands: when the Victorian market boomed, they were diverted to Melbourne and auctioned. The largest of these contained fifteen rooms measuring up to 6 by 5 metres.[41]

British colonies in North America accounted for only a small proportion of the imports, but one combined house and store is known to have been brought from Nova Scotia by John Laurens, and put up in Spencer Street, West Melbourne.[42] A significant proportion came from the United States, either re-exported from California or sent direct from points of manufacture in the east, notably Boston. A prominent example of the former was the very large house of Germain Nicholson, brought from California in 1850, even before the Victorian gold discoveries, and erected at St Kilda.[43] The merchant George Francis Train, himself from Boston, imported quantities of building materials as well as whole prefabricated structures from his home port. One of the most conspicuous of these was the large store of two and a half storeys occupied by his own firm of Caldwell, Train & Co., which is visible in early views of Sandridge (Port Melbourne).[44] Recent work has identified what is probably one of these North American buildings. Osborne House at 456 Victoria Parade, North Melbourne, is a two-storeyed house clad in 'shiplap' – horizontal boarding rebated to allow each board to fit over the one below, with a recessed channel at the joint, but with the faces flush, very like the later 'chamferboard' of Queensland. The wood of the frame has been identified as American white pine, *pinus strobus*,[45] and the form of the porch has been traced to a design in the 1857 American pattern-book, *Villas and Cottages*, by Calvert Vaux.[46]

The contributions of European and other countries were relatively slight. It appears that a number of Norwegian wooden houses from Christiana (now Oslo) reached Adelaide in 1854.[47] F. Bauer, a German-born merchant at Geelong, brought in twelve four-roomed houses from Hamburg in the same year,[48] and the much larger house at Newtown, The Heights, may also be a German import of that year. Sydney also saw some Hamburg-made houses, for the French consul, M. Bordier, had ordered four oak ones from the Paris *Exposition* of 1855, which he put up at Hunter's Hill.[49] European manufacturers only became active in response to the demands of the Crimean War, when large numbers of huts made at Cilli, Austria, were dispatched from Trieste to Balaclava in December 1854.[50] Even then Britain remained the dominant manufacturer, largely because William Eassie's works, already geared to Australian demands, were able to be diverted to war production.[51] One of the last European houses to arrive was a two-storey one of Baltic timber which reached Melbourne in 1856 on the *Goffredo Marneli* from Genoa.[52]

'*Papier-Mache Village for Australia*', by C.F. Bielefield. Illustrated London News, 6 August 1853.

Top: The Chalet, in Hunters Hill, is the last survivor of a group of four timber houses made in Hamburg and ordered at the Paris Exposition of 1855.

Paper houses and other experiments

Timber was the most widely used material for portable houses, but it was by no means the most technically interesting. At the time of the gold rushes it was reported:

Wooden houses, lined with galvanized iron, in thin sheets, have been sent out from Scotland, and they will probably find eager purchasers. Iron houses have been forwarded in large numbers from several ports, and they possess many recommendations, of which one is, that they can be cheaply and rapidly erected and removed. Houses formed of slabs of slate have also been proposed, and one company has been formed for their construction.[53]

This last material, papier mâché, is perhaps the most interesting. C.F. Bielefeld, already well-known in England as a manufacturer of papier mâché architectural ornaments, had in 1851 patented an improved papier mâché board to be used for panelled walls in the cabins of steamships,[54] and for complete portable buildings. In his system of building, as it had developed by 1853, the walls were panels set between grooved uprights, similar to Manning's timber houses, and the outer surface was sheeted in either plain or corrugated iron. The floor was a system of square frames into which were set joists, with flooring boards fixed into square sections, and the roof was also built up in rectangular panels. The provisional patent specification was not confined to the use of the papier mâché as the inner lining material,[55] and the whole idea might be thought of as fanciful, were it not for a brochure put out by Bielefeld with references to buildings which he had constructed at his works near Staines.

In July 1853 a number of periodicals (quoted in Bielefeld's brochure) reported on his model paper village, in which everything but the framework, flooring and doors was said to be of papier mâché. There were ten buildings including two-roomed cottages, a storehouse 24 metres long incorporating living quarters, and a villa of nine rooms, 3.3 metres high, with caryatid chimney-pieces of papier mâché in the principal rooms. The buildings had been commissioned by one Seymour, who was taking them with him to Australia,[56] and though there is no specific confirmation of their arrival, imports of papier mâché to Victoria reached £955 and £1,190 in 1853 and 1854, and there are a few contemporary ratebook references to paper or cardboard houses in Melbourne suburbs. Two papier mâché houses had been built in Albert Street, East Melbourne by 1855,[57] and two in Geelong, of which at least one was by Bielefeld.[58] Part of the consignment may also have been dismembered to become the 'Patent Composition Boards, suitable for roofing, lining, &c., and adapted to the colony', which were shown at the Melbourne Exhibition of 1854.[59]

A number of other more or less exotic materials were used. Of the slate houses referred to in the 1853 report little is known, except that their existence is confirmed by some of the slate from imported cottages, mainly built in Collingwood, being subsequently recycled into billiard tables.[60] Moreover two portable slate houses were put up in Geelong by the architect J.L. Shaw.[61] The system may have been based on panels set in iron frames like the method developed in 1852 by the English architect James Edmeston for making buildings of glazed clay slabs. Edmeston's first creation was a handsome clock tower sent to Geelong in 1854.[62] There was also the so-called 'portable brick house' produced by E. Smallwood of Camden Town in 1853, and though there is no specific evidence of it reaching Australia, it was certainly designed for export. This house consisted apparently of a timber frame covered in metal-tongued deal wainscoting, on the face of which were hung tiles with the appearance of bricks.[63] This is in accord with the English vernacular tradition of geometric tile hanging.

Another proposal was for hollow brick cottages, of which one of two rooms could be supplied for £25 in London or £90 in Melbourne, and one of seven rooms for £75 and £100.[64] This was the plan of a company set up in London as the 'Melbourne and Colonial House

Investment Company' which also, as we shall see, interested itself in iron buildings. The plan would seem to have been to use extruded hollow terracotta blocks of the sort made in England by Lewis Hertslet, who was one of the company directors. Most remarkable was the establishment in 1854 of a Melbourne company to manufacture 'Patent Portable Brick Houses'. They consisted of brick panels screwed to timber supports, perhaps rather like Smallwood's in principle. One was actually put up as a demonstration model at Emerald Hill (South Melbourne).[65]

Rather more prominent than these exotic systems were buildings of zinc – the most popular prefabrication material after timber and iron. Numbers of examples can be

'Portable brick' building by E. Smallwood (probably a chapel).

Top: Papier mâché villa designed by C.F. Bielefield.

identified in advertisements and rate books, but none has survived; possibly because zinc is soft and readily destroyed, perhaps also because it is a tempting material to re-use, and most of all, no doubt, because it was expensive, and could be sold back to the manufacturers for re-use at half the new price. A small amount of zinc sheeting, seamed together at the edges, was found beneath the bark roof of the Angahook bark hut at Airey's Inlet, Victoria, presumably dating from the 1850s, and perhaps part of one of these zinc buildings. This relic was destroyed in the great bushfires of 1983.

Zinc buildings seem to have been made in London by 1839, and advertised for use by emigrants to Australia.[66] There is no evidence of any arriving, but there were wooden-framed houses clad in zinc at the Californian gold-rushes,[67] and it is likely that they were made by

James Middlemass of Edinburgh, who was responsible for most of those sent to Australia. Middlemass's buildings were described in the *Edinburgh Post*:

The Roof is sustained at the centre by an iron tye-rod, screwed up to iron stretchers, acting as stents, with a plat in the centre, where the roof exceeds 12 feet in width. The walls are composed of overlapping panels, along which iron rods pass at 3 feet from the ground, and, again at the eaves, along the whole sides, through metal eyes, and are screwed up from the extreme ends, so as to tighten and compact the structure. The walls are secured to the ground by cramp irons or brackets, having holes for pegs or screws, to attach them to sleepers of wood, or by which they may be batted down to sleepers of stone.[68]

By September 1853 Cowan Collender & Caldwell of Melbourne were advertising themselves as the Australian agents for Middlemass's patent 'portable metallic houses and shops', and Westgarth, Ross & Co. had 'patent metallic houses and stores' for sale in sizes which suggest that they were also manufactured by Middlemass.[69] There were, however, other makers of zinc buildings who advertised for the Australian market.[70] Boydell & Glasier of the Anchor Iron Works at Smethwick, near Birmingham, and at Hawley Crescent, Camden Town, made them on a system using 'patent grooved wooded iron standards' as the uprights and 'patent inodorous felt' (probably Croggon's) as insulation. Zinc buildings were also made in a number of European countries from which they may have been exported to the Australian colonies,[71] and zinc houses of unknown origin were being advertised in Adelaide in 1854.[72]

Iron, the wonder material

Iron was to be the medium for the most technically interesting prefabrication, and although Australia never saw cast-iron fronted commercial buildings on the scale of those in America, there are a few cast-iron faced buildings, and many with cast components such as columns. Overwhelmingly, however, rolled wrought iron was used – both plain and galvanized, and flat as well as corrugated. Some corrugated iron store buildings reached Adelaide by 1839,[73] but the material was expensive, and such importations must have been rare. Again, the Californian gold-rush brought into full production some leading manufacturers who were next to turn their attention to Australia – probably J.H. Porter of Birmingham (though he had made buildings for export at earlier dates), and certainly John Walker of London and E.T. Bellhouse of Manchester. After these came Samuel Hemming of Bristol and probably Francis Morton of Liverpool, in response to the Australian market itself. Morewood and Rogers may or may not have made complete buildings before the Australian boom, but they were well established as leading makers of corrugated iron and as galvanizers, with their own patent process of coating the iron with tin before the final coat of zinc.

All of these manufacturers are more or less represented by surviving buildings, though not necessarily houses, and it is necessary to consider at least the more distinctive features of their products. J.H. Porter is known more for industrial buildings with arched corrugated roofs than he is for houses, though some of his warehouses may have

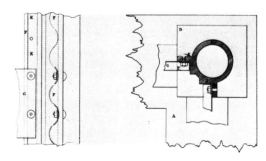

Iron work. Top: A detail from E.T. Bellhouse's British patent of 1853. Centre: A house formerly at Fitzroy, attributed to Bellhouse. Above: Part of the small enclave of iron houses in South Melbourne erected in the early 1850s. Below: Samuel Hemming's Clift House Manufactory, Bristol.

contained integral dwellings. They are based on cast-iron stanchions shaped to allow for horizontal wall girts and for wrought-iron cross-ties to be placed across the span of the arch, and they tend to have conical skylights, that can be opened, at the crown of the roof. John Walker had a more varied output, including timber houses, but the one identifiable surviving house, at Inverleigh, approached true system building.[74] The walls are framed in 51 by 51 millimetre angle iron with one flange pointing inwards, so that the other flange appears on the external face, and overlaps the panels of corrugated iron which fill the frame. All joints with the bottom member are made with gussets, and at the top is a wrought-iron tie-rod across the simple pitched roof, and the pairs of rafters have their own collar ties consisting of ungalvanized strap-iron. Only the iron shell of this house survives, measuring 9.80 by 8.51 metres, and nothing is known of the plan or of any timber components or lining materials.

E.T. Bellhouse's system with its main framing members of cast iron, differs again. His columns are hollow-backed, so that a piece of timber can be placed in them from behind, and a lining of horizontal boards fixed to it if required. Whatever the shape of the column – it may be a half-round or a half-square on the front – it has side flanges which are shaped to accord with the corrugations of the iron spandrels, which in this case run horizontally in the panels. The eaves gutter has an inside flange which similarly fits the corrugations of the adjacent roofing iron. He even made cast-iron ridge pieces shaped to fit the corrugated iron on either side, though of these there are no examples surviving. Another aspect of technical interest is his use of cast-iron window frames, paned in the traditional manner, but with sections of four panes in the middle which open as a unit on a horizontal pivot. This seems to reflect practice in the cotton-mills of Manchester, where Bellhouse had been a millwright.

Samuel Hemming became interested in the market after constructing a light portable house for a son who was emigrating to Australia. His system was less distinctive than the others, consisting simply of timber framing clad in galvanized corrugated iron. The business, however, became very big, his works conveying the impression, it

was said, of a whole town rising and falling in a week, for he made not only houses but shops, warehouses, hotels and churches.[75] Each one was actually built, the components marked, and then the whole thing dismantled and packed, using the intended floor-boards or lining boards to form crates..The joinery was all of timber, and the scale of production was so large that the stove used to season it was itself a substantial building. Of Hemming's houses there survive at least one and possibly two, the more doubtful one being Marsh House, Yapeen, Victoria, built in 1854 or 1855. It is attributed to him only because of a general resemblance to his works in its external appearance, and the use of elements like Venetian shutters. It conforms to his method of construction but, probably because it is two-storeyed, it has some cast-iron stanchions, in the form of angles at the corners and Ts elsewhere. The other house is Wingecarribee at Bowral, New South Wales, which was illustrated in one of Hemming's published broadsides and is much more distinctive and architecturally pretentious, though less representative of his work. It includes a cast-iron parapet and urns, and panelled wooden pilasters at intervals in the main wall surface.[76] This building is supposed to have been ordered in 1853 by J.M. Oxley, son of the explorer, but not erected until 1857 due to labour and transport problems.[77] Hemming's published illustration, however, indicates that it was made for the London-based Melbourne and Colonial House Investment Company, for which he seems to have made a number of structures.

Buildings on this scale of pretension are rare, but even Wingecarribee is excelled by two houses and various other buildngs made of solid plate rather than corrugated iron. Such elaborate iron fronts had begun to be made on a large scale in New York for commercial buildings, but Glasgow companies appear to have been the source of all those that came to Australia. The prominent Melbourne merchant, William Westgarth, seems to have ordered his while on a trip home in 1853–54, but it did not arrive until well into 1855, when it was put up, as Tintern, on the site where it still stands.[78] It is within the loop formed by Tintern Avenue, Toorak, a thoroughfare which was created by a later subdivision of Westgarth's

The Loren iron house, originally in North Melbourne, now at Old Gippstown, Moe.

Wingecarribee, Bowral, manufactured about 1853 and erected about 1857.

Corio Villa, Geelong, designed by Bell and Miller, manufactured probably by Robertson & Lister of Glasgow in 1854, and erected about 1856.

The conservatory of Rippon Lea, Elsternwick; the semicircular structure at left was designed by Lloyd Tayler & Fitts and cast in iron in Glasgow, 1897.

Centre: A timber house made in Belgium and erected in Hunters Hill about 1855. It is now in Burwood.

grounds, and stands in such good condition that it is difficult to find the joints where the plates butt together, or to detect a trace of rust. The impression is that of a stuccoed masonry building, for the walls are about 0.3 metres thick – the iron being about 13 to 19 millimetres thick, with a large cavity and a lath and plaster inner face – the rooms are large, up to 9 by 6 metres, and the ceilings 4.25 metres high.[79]

Tintern was made by P. & W. McLellan of Glasgow,[80] but about the authorship of the equally substantial but more elaborately decorated Corio Villa at Geelong, there is some uncertainty. The Glasgow firm of Lister & Co., then Robertson & Lister from about 1853, and later Robertson & Co., were extensive prefabricators in cast iron, beginning with street urinals in 1853.[81] In 1854 Robertson & Lister made two iron churches, of differing but related designs, for export to Sydney.[82] One of these can be identified as the Macquarie Street Free Presbyterian Church, which was finally dismantled in 1899, and had an elaborate plate-iron front, but side walls of corrugated iron running horizontally between vertical iron stanchions.[83] An illustration of a similar church, apparently the other one of the pair, appears in the brochure of another manufacturer, C.D. Young & Co.[84] It would seem that C.D. Young & Co. had taken over the prefabrication business of Robertson & Lister (there are indications that they similarly took over that of E.T. Bellhouse, or else acquired some of his designs or stock): buildings illustrated in Young's brochure may therefore be ones originally made by Robertson & Lister.

Corio Villa is an elaborate iron house which can be identified, with some variations, with an illustration in C.D. Young's brochure, which was discovered only in 1971 by Sutherland Lyall.[85] Young identified the house as having been built for 'the late Mr Gray, Colonial Land Commissioner at Geelong', and Dr E.G. Robertson was able to identify this person as the police magistrate W.N. Gray, who died at Hamilton in 1854.[86] Robertson was aware of the tradition that the house had been left unclaimed at the Geelong wharf for some time before being bought by Alfred Douglass and erected, but he did not know of the statement by one of Douglass's granddaughters that this was because the person to whom it was sent had died[87] – the link completing the chain of evidence.

Corio Villa is another structure with the main elevations of plate iron, but the back wall, like the sides of the Macquarie Street church, has corrugated iron running horizontally between stanchions. The same combination seems to characterize the other major works of Robertson & Lister and C.D. Young, including the other main surviving example, the Legislative Council Chamber in Macquarie Street, Sydney. The reason why Corio Villa merits such detailed consideration is that, with its provenance established, it can be attributed to the architects Bell & Miller, who are named as the designers of five related buildings in the C.D. Young brochure.[88] The brochure illustration was described as 'a Country Villa, in a new style of architecture, with Verandas to correspond', and this is scarcely an exaggeration, for there is nothing else quite like this house. The verandah pillars, the valance and the barge are all of heavy-looking cast-iron open-work containing vegetable motifs such as the rose, something resembling a harebell or Scottish bluebell, a clover or possibly a shamrock, and one other unidentifiable species, all presumably intended as a pantheon of themes from the British Isles, although it does not (contrary to Geoffrey Drinnan's account[89]) include the Scotch thistle. Internally, too, the soffits and linings of the arched openings in the passage are treated with vegetable ornament in papier mâché. The ceilings were also prefabricated in papier mâché, and the joinery in mahogany.

Using the prefabs

The importation of houses, not only of iron, but of timber and other materials, dwindled to the merest trickle after 1854, but the many that had been imported were now being used, though often not as was originally intended. Despite the greatest demand having been as a result of the gold-rushes, transport costs ensured that very few buildings reached the gold-fields or other inland areas, and most stayed in the coastal towns, especially Melbourne and

unnecessarily elaborate, or otherwise unsuited to the locality for which it was destined. Makers like Bellhouse made an attempt to meet this sort of situation by offering wall linings, and even flooring, as optional elements in the package. There are no known examples of surviving buildings which definitely relied upon earthen rather than wooden floors, but there are some lined in ways which were probably not intended by the original manufacturers. The house formerly at 49 Moor Street, Fitzroy, and now at the National Trust's South Melbourne site, is confidently attributed to Bellhouse, but when acquired had a lath and plaster lining and no sign of his system of horizontal boarding. Nor were there ceiling joists resting in the sockets provided by his system, for a lath and plaster ceiling had been installed somewhat higher up. Even where the buildings were lined, they were often criticized for being inordinately hot, especially the iron ones, and makers like Samuel Hemming would either supply or recommend the use of patent asphalt felt, or recommend a nogging of baked or sun-dried bricks. One occupier of a

Design No. 14 from C.D. Young & Co., Illustrations of Iron Structures for Home and Abroad: 'Iron Cottage with handsome cast iron front', made for W.N. Gray.

Geelong.[90] Here there were problems caused by the Building Acts. The Melbourne Building Act had been introduced mainly with the aim of discouraging the spread of fire, but was drafted in terms of timber and masonry construction, with no thought given to iron. Timber buildings could be put up only if they were isolated – set a prescribed distance from the boundaries of the site – but some of the first iron buildings were permitted to run to the boundaries as it was assumed that they were fireproof. This assumption had, however, been given the lie by the disastrous fires of San Francisco in 1850, which destroyed some major prefabricated iron buildings, and in Melbourne the Act was soon used to restrict iron construction. Thus even buildings which had been custom-ordered for the centre of Melbourne had to be diverted to suburbs, like St Kilda, outside the scope of the Act.

In some cases it was claimed that the cost of erection, using expensive local labour, exceeded the purchase and shipping costs; in others, the building was thought to be

Manning house in Melbourne in 1854 praised the building, but complained that it was too low:

the pitch of my rooms is only 8 feet high, and in summer we have the thermometer from 90 to 100 in the shade; it has been 97 in our sitting-room, on the shady side. The roof is a great difficulty, also: mine is now covered with 3/4-inch deal boards, thin canvass, and over all tin tiles painted. It will make a watertight roof, but it may be very hot, so that suggestions might be made as to ventilation.[91]

A number of makers were reported to supply various items of furniture and equipment, especially stoves, with their houses. But as they did not manufacture these items, this was little different from the immigrant making his selection from the regular suppliers. Our most detailed knowledge of this comes from the journal of Samuel Vaughan, whose Manning cottage has been referred to above. Vaughan noted that he was taking no lining paper or canvas, but had obtained or proposed to obtain from Norwoods of Dean Street, New North Road, London, bedroom papers at sixpence to one shilling a piece; red granite staircase papers from eightpence to one shilling and threepence; sitting-room papers from one shilling to one and ninepence; 'Common Decorations for Sitting

Mine manager's house at Whroo, Victoria, believed to be that imported from America by J.T. Lewis, above 1860.

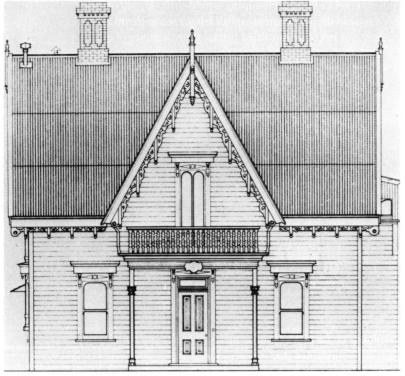

Redwood, an imported Pasadena-style bungalow from California, erected in Rosebery in 1915-16.

Centre: 'American Cottage', Coburg, about 1880. A measured drawing of the east front.

Rooms' (probably items such as paper friezes and centre flowers) and common white marble ceiling papers. He recorded the address of Gordon & Smith of Nottingham, patentees of a 'domestic gas apparatus' and of W. Patten, the London agent for J.C. Stokes's improved water closet, complete with brass sunk handle, stoneware trap, basin glazed white inside, round valve cranks, lever and wire. Another address he listed was that of Edward Healey, of the firm of John Dewrance & Co., but, as they were patentees of a range of inventions from the aneroid barometer to a means of preventing overheating in engine bearings, it is not clear what interested Vaughan. Two other things which he seems to have been concerned to bring with him were a supply of tacks and soda water.[92]

It remains to consider how these buildings survived in use. Of those in papier mâché, zinc, brick and slate, not a trace is known to survive. Two of the larger corrugated-iron houses survive in good condition and are occupied, and of the great mass of smaller ones some were occupied into relatively modern times, well after World War II, but those few that survive today are mostly vacant shells, · sheds or museum exhibits. The timber buildings have fared much better, and although many cannot be definitely identified as being of prefabricated origin, of those which can, a large number are occupied, including a handful of those made by Manning.

Importation did not cease with the Crimean War but it became very much the exception rather than the rule. One manufacturer of iron structures who rose to importance in this later period was Francis Morton, of Liverpool and London, who maintained a Sydney agency and who exported fences, gates and telegraph posts, especially to north Queensland: but no houses have yet been identified. Similarly, Andrew Handyside & Co. of Derby sent a major bridge to Queensland, and possibly others to different Australian destinations, but although they sent elaborate dwellings to India and elsewhere, there is no evidence of any reaching Australia. A number of other English makers continued to advertise houses for exportation, especially to the colonies, but cannot be traced in Australia. In the domestic market, iron conservatories and ferneries probably far exceeded actual houses in quantity. The house, Rippon Lea, in Melbourne, had a number of such structures, but one which survives is of particular interest because, although it bears the brand of George Smith's Sun Foundry of Glasgow, it seems to have been made to the design of the Melbourne architects, Lloyd Tayler & Fitts, in about 1896.

Prefabrication in timber also ceased to play any very significant role in Australia after the mid-1850s, but there are occasional references to local manufacture and others to imports from America. Twenty-five portable wooden houses for the police were made locally, tenders for which were called in 1856 by Charles Pasley, the Victorian Commissioner for Public Works.[93] There may yet have been wooden buildings imported from Britain, where William Cooper Ltd of London was still making buildings both for home consumption and export, about the turn of the century,[94] and advertised in Queensland provincial newspapers.[93]

J.T. Lewis, a mine owner at Whroo, imported an

American-made house in about 1860, which remained sufficiently portable to be moved within a few years to a new site a short distance away. It was of wood, single storeyed, with French windows, and surrounded by a verandah, and his son was to describe it, significantly enough, as having the character of a bungalow – but this was written in retrospect, long after that term had come into common use.[96] By contrast American Cottage, in the Melbourne suburb of Coburg, is a two-storey house with steep pitched roofs, weatherboard cladding, and elaborate fretwork to the eaves and barges, as well as very American-looking windows. It seems to be made principally of oregon and to date from 1880.[97] Of about the same date were two two-storeyed houses at Morphettville, South Australia, imported from the United States by Sir Thomas Elder, of Elder Smith & Co., apparently as an investment.[98] In 1881 the Melbourne biscuit manufacturer Thomas Swallow moved to Queensland to develop the sugar industry, and on his wife's initiative ordered a timber house of a chalet design which was put up near Cairns.[99] In 1883 the importers Lorimer Rome & Co. of Melbourne were selling 'Elford's Patent Portable Houses' which were made mainly of Californian redwood in numbered pieces.[100] In 1890, buildings by the Grand Rapids Portable House Co. of Michigan were shown at the New South Wales Agricultural Society Exhibition, and were available through a local agent, William Fleming, but none has been traced.[101] The most significant of this series was the Pasadena-style bungalow imported in 1915 by a Sydney real estate agent, Richard Stanton, to test local acceptance of the style and of the idea of timber buildings of this character.[102]

Meanwhile the development of north Queensland, with its special conditions of separate railway lines running inland from the main seaports, particularly suited the use of prefabricated houses from Brisbane and elsewhere. Thus there was a revival of local prefabrication in the first decade of this century by Brisbane manufacturers like James Campbell and Sons, and Brown and Broad.[103]

It would be out of place to discuss here the military hospitals and barracks which were prefabricated in the two world wars, but World War II in particular gave rise to a revival in the use of prefabricated houses in Australia as a solution to the shortage of housing and the shortage of conventional building materials. During the war the firm of Vandyke Brothers, of Punchbowl, New South Wales, brought into production their 'Sectionit' system, based on standard wall panels of 1.8 by 0.6 metres incorporating doors or windows as required. The panels were clad externally and internally in asbestos cement, and could be combined in a variety of forms, although the layout of a strip containing the bathroom, kitchen and laundry remained constant in nearly all the plans used in 1943. Initially these plumbed areas were floored in 0.6-metre square pre-cast concrete slabs, but later on larger slabs were cast *in situ*. The remaining wooden floors also seem to have evolved from the first form, in which the joists were precut, to that described in 1950, when panels of 1.8 metres wide and up to 5.4 metres long were framed in hardwood and then sheathed in tongued and grooved cypress pine boarding.[104]

An advertisement from Builder, *1854.*

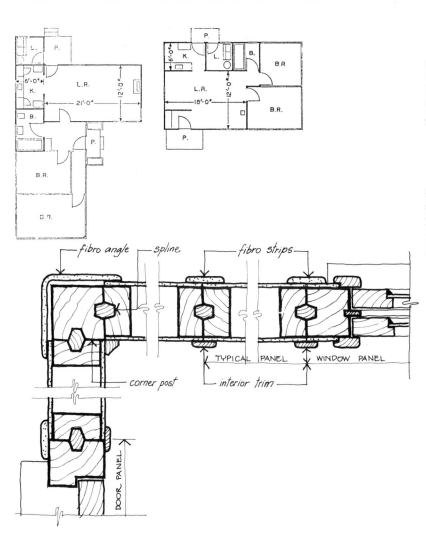

The 'Sectionit' system. Centre: Two of Vandyke Brothers' 'Sectionit' house plans, 1943, as published in America. Above: Plan of a typical wall detail of the 'Sectionit' system.

After World War II

At the conclusion of the war a number of other prefabrication factories were set up. The Commonwealth government, faced with a national housing shortage and a surplus of munitions factories, sponsored the factory building of metal houses. The Beaufort Home was designed in 1946 by the technical staff of the Beaufort Division of the Department of Aircraft Production, and was developed through the Victorian Housing Commission. It was at first intended to use aluminium, but zincanneal sheet, which was thought to be available in sufficient quantity, was chosen instead. Like the 'Sectionit' system it was based on a 0.6 metre grid, and it used a frame of 16-gauge steel sections clad in 18-gauge spot welded sheet steel, and packed with 50 millimetres of rock-wool. The steel proved to be in such short supply that the project was terminated after only about two hundred houses had been built.[105] Other timber prefabrication factories had also been established by 1950, one in New South Wales by Veneer and Plywood Pty Ltd, with developmental assistance from the Commonwealth Experimental Building Station in Sydney,[106] and another in Hobart by John Paine Pty Ltd.[107]

The importation of houses also resumed. The Stex organization of Sweden combined with Puurakenne and Puutalo of Finland in an attempt to develop a house for the Australian market. Through the East Asiatic Company, Australia, Pty Ltd they brought out six trial houses and erected one at Canberra and the rest near Sydney. Two were pre-cut, two panelized and two of mixed construction, and from this experience was evolved the 'cell-house' system, in which whole sections of rooms, incorporating walls, floors and ceilings, were assembled in a factory and then moved to prepared foundations on the site and joined together.[108] What degree of acceptance this achieved is not clear. A large volume of buildings was sent from Britain. Hawkesley Constructions of Gloucester had, by late 1951, sent about £1½ million worth, not just of houses, but of schools, offices and hospitals. These were panelized, with each panel framed in light alloy extrusion and braced with timber, faced externally with ribbed light alloy sheeting, and internally with hardboard or plasterboard.[109] As with the Beaufort Home this construction seems to have evolved from aircraft building techniques. H. Newsum, Sons and Co. of Lincoln were able to make similar sales to the Australian government of a more conventionally constructed timber house on a standard rectangular plan designed by an Australian architect, A.B. Armstrong, and developed by one of their own staff, James Riley. The frame was panelized, but in such a way that the vertical board cladding did not show the joints, and the roof was clad in aluminium. The concrete stumps and hardwood bearers were obtained locally rather than sent from Britain.[110]

Victoria again proved to be a major market. In 1948 the Minister for Transport, Colonel W.S. Kent-Hughes, was concerned to provide housing for 1,000 British workers to be brought out by the Victorian Railways. Proposals for prefabricated or pre-cut houses were invited from firms in England, Sweden and Austria, and Simms Sons and Cooke of Nottingham were chosen as principal con-

tractors for a pre-cut house yet to be designed. In January 1949, Yuncken, Freeman Brothers, Griffiths and Simpson, in association with Baxter Cox and Associates, of Melbourne, were appointed architects, and mass importation began. Other government departments took advantage of the scheme, until by late 1950 over 2,000 houses were being imported at the rate of forty per week. All the timbers were kiln-dried, most parts being of Swedish whitewood, and the 'weatherboards' – actually vertical boards – were primed before dispatch. The roofing was at first of Trafford tile pattern asbestos-cement sheeting, but

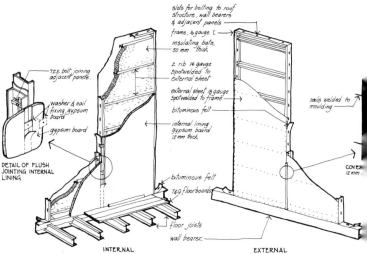

The Beaufort House project, 1946. Top: A demonstration house erected in the Treasury Gardens, Melbourne. Above: Drawings of the Beaufort prefabrication system.

a specially designed interlocking aluminium sheeting was developed to replace this. There was a substantial Australian component in each house, including not only stumps, bearers and joists, but also gas or electric stove and canopy, and electrical and plumbing installations.[111]

These post-war houses take us a long way from the nineteenth-century portable house, and it is not necessary to follow them any further except to say that importation of houses from overseas soon virtually ceased, although some British systems such as the 'Terrapin' continued to be imported or manufactured locally under licence, mainly for non-domestic buildings. Local manufacture of timber houses has continued on a reduced scale to serve distant or dispersed markets, but has not been distinguished by major design or technical innovations. Precasting of concrete dwellings, however, was becoming more sophisticated, and its fortunes were interlocked with the programme of importing houses. In 1952 there were drastic cuts in Commonwealth funding for state public works, and Victoria, now encumbered by £5 million-worth of overseas contracts which could not be dishonoured, had to drastically slash its concrete house production.[112]

The Concrete House Project was perhaps the most remarkable of all the ventures in prefabrication for the Australian market – as remarkable for its technical success as for its ultimate social failure. It originated in the experiments of T.W. Fowler, a surveyor, on his farm at Werribee South, where early in the 1920s he began building concrete dairy sheds and farm buildings, and developed a system of casting the walls, complete with the required openings, on horizontal tables next to their place of erection. The slabs were typically 76 millimetres thick, and could be tilted up and placed on previously prepared concrete piers. When the newly established Victorian Housing Commission held a competition in 1939 for the design of houses, the second and fourth placegetters, A.C. Leith and Frank Heath, both designed their entries for the Fowler system. In 1940 Fowler was given contracts to build twenty-eight houses, and then further houses were built by Fowler or by others using his plant under licence. Fowler died in 1942, and the plant was leased to a firm of builders, still operating manually, using six fixed tables and requiring about twenty-eight men to produce three houses each week. By 1944, however, the plant was lent to the Housing Commission, which began to invest in mobile cranes and tilting tables to raise the slabs to the vertical positon.

By 1945 the Commission was employing between eighty and a hundred men on concrete house production, and it took a lease of the Commonwealth factory at Holmesglen which had been making armoured vehicles and tank turrets during the war. Here the mechanization of the Fowler system into a full industrial production line was developed, requiring that components should now be transported to the site after casting. In 1944–46, 596 concrete houses, a quarter of the Commission's total production, were manufactured. By October 1948 the total had reached 1,000, by March 1950, 2,000, and by May 1951, immediately before the financial squeeze, 3,000. Buildings now began to grow upwards. The houses built had all, with one partial exception, been single-storeyed. In 1952 two-storey structures with 100-millimetre walls were first built. In 1959 a four-storey block was put up at Jordanville and tested under lateral load, resulting in a decision to introduce positive connection between wall and floor slabs. In 1957, building regulation approval was given for three-storey units, and an application was lodged for five-storey ones. In 1958–59 four-storey blocks were built consisting of two levels of two-storey maisonettes, one above the other, but these were un-

satisfactory and were phased out within two years to be replaced by four-storey blocks of three-bedroom flats.

In about 1960 the four-storey blocks began to be placed on stilts in an attempt to provide more open space at ground level, and in 1961–62 an eight-storey block was built to suit an unusual sloping site at Kensington, where access could be had to the middle level. Finally, in 1963, tenders were called for two twenty-storey blocks in either steel frame, *in situ* concrete, or pre-cast load-bearing panels supplied by the Commission. The pre-cast panels proved the cheapest, and were used. By 1963–64 the

Thirty-storey flats of precast and post-tensioned concrete, erected for the Housing Commission of Victoria in South Melbourne, 1965–69.

project was tooling up for wholesale twenty-storey production, and then in 1966–69 a thirty-storey block was built in South Melbourne.[113] It was not long after this that the whole high-rise programme was phased out. It had been remarkably successful in a technical sense – though there were many defects of which tenants in the flats complained – but it was a form of housing which proved, as elsewhere in the world, socially destructive and alienating. It is a fitting, if a sad point, at which to leave the story of prefabrication in Australia.

IN RECENT YEARS much has been written about the distinctive character of Queensland houses, of their special vernacular charm or their uniqueness. The various models which generally have been advanced as the unique Queensland house are not forms unique to that state, nor even to Australia, while the most popular and widely promoted image, 'a large sprawling structure on round timber stumps with an extensive, deep, shaded verandah filled with trellis', was never a dominant house type in Queensland.

Nevertheless most Queensland houses built before the 1930s are identifiably different from those of southern states. Their undeniable visual impact comes from the combination of a small number of characteristics used in the construction of an equally small number of house types, which through their frequent repetition are easily recognized as 'Queensland houses'.

Detached housing for all

A distinctive feature of Queensland housing that seldom receives comment is that, from the outset, individual detached dwellings were the norm.

The pattern of land-holding, determined by the nature of subdivision and of ownership, is the most basic cultural

dence was the Queensland government's immigration scheme introduced in 1860. In order to promote the influx of suitable labour, each free adult immigrant received on arrival a Land Order to the value of £18, followed two years later by a further grant of £12. It was hoped thereby to encourage small farmers to settle in the newly surveyed agricultural districts. This was only partially successful, however, and many immigrant artisans stayed in Brisbane, using their land orders to purchase a residential allotment.

The detached timber houses of early Brisbane were quite different from the southern housing pattern, exemplified in Melbourne inner suburbs such as Fitzroy, where wealthy investors purchased areas of land as large as 8 to 10 hectares at the first land sales, which they then subdivided and resold profitably to smaller entrepreneurial middlemen, who in turn further subdivided and resold, until houses with the smallest street frontage – narrow terraces – were constructed as rental accommodation for the poorest of the working class. The process was of course accelerated by the tremendous need for accommodation in Melbourne after the 1851 gold discoveries.[2]

The pattern of detached timber housing had thus been firmly established in Queensland for two decades before

THE QUEENSLAND STYLE 14

element of the urban landscape. In marked contrast to the other colonial capitals, working-class families in nineteenth-century Brisbane were housed in detached houses, and they often owned both land and house.

Climate is often put forward as the explanation of the lack of terrace housing in Queensland but this ignores the realities of economics: the low land prices, government land grants, the pattern of subdivision, and such factors as building regulations and insurance requirements. The main influences on building in early Queensland were economic – the price of land, the cost of building materials and the rate of wages. These were complemented by government policies concerning both immigration and land sales.

The population of early Brisbane was so small that residential land prices were correspondingly low. A working-class family could purchase sufficient land and build a small, cheap house. In the suburb of Petrie Terrace, opened in the 1860s, blocks of land were often 9.6 perches (243 square metres) and some few even as small as 7 perches (177 square metres).[1] The houses on these meagre sites were on the whole detached and owner occupied, however, not rental accommodation.

A major factor enabling such working-class indepen-

A house in Ipswich that epitomizes the Queensland style. Its exposed timber frame is protected by a verandah on three sides, and the whole house is raised on widely-spaced stumps with decorative timber slatting between. There are no chimneys.

the passing in 1885 of the Undue Subdivision of Land Prevention Act, which set the minimum size of Brisbane residential allotments at 16 perches (.04 hectares) and it was not considerations of the thermal environment of workers' homes which determined this size, but rather the fire risk in a timber city. A complementary consideration was the health problem arising through lack of drainage on these overcrowded sites.

The Undue Subdivision Act of 1885 did not specifically prohibit the construction of terrace housing, but it meant that individual units could not be sold. The prospect of tying up large amounts of capital in rental property was not attractive to most investors. One result seems to have been the construction of a small number of semi-detached pairs, usually of timber with a brick party-wall, intended for rental, but on sites of 32 perches (.08 hectares), which allowed sale if desired. Examples of this unusual form in Brisbane include Astrea, built in 1887 and Brighton Terrace, built in 1889.[3] More commonly, however, groups of between three and eight identical detached timber houses were the preferred style. Brisbane did not entirely miss the construction of terrace housing, and a few terraces survive, but they are large, two-storey houses, usually of brick, built with expensive detailing to serve as superior rental accommodation for professional, middle-class tenants. Among them are The Mansions built in 1889[4], Cook Terrace, 1888–89, Petrie Mansions, built about 1890, and Harris Court, 1885. In the smaller towns of Queensland, terrace housing was unknown.

Walls of timber

In 1861, the first Queensland census showed that 5,964 dwellings had outer walls of timber, representing some 88 per cent of all Queensland houses. This dominance of timber was maintained for almost a century and it is still one of the most noteworthy features of Queensland housing, except in the newest suburbs.

In the first two censuses, a distinction was made between weatherboard (sawn timber) and slab (hand split timber). The census figures show that, while the more primitive slab buildings comprised more than half of all Queensland dwellings, their distribution was not even − only 6 per cent were in Brisbane, the remainder being in rural and more isolated areas.

This concentration of better quality, more permanent housing in Brisbane is also reflected by brick being the second most popular building material, while for the colony (and later state) as a whole, canvas was the second most common material. By 1881 the percentage of timber houses in Brisbane was greater than the colony's average; early in the twentieth century over 90 per cent of Brisbane houses had timber walls.

The dominance of timber as a wall material in Queensland is explained above all by its availability. The east coast of Queensland had an abundance of trees whose timber was suitable for construction. Steam-powered sawmills were established in Brisbane in the 1850s, and at the new port towns along the coast, and sawn timber was by far the cheapest building material available to the new immigrants. Supplementing the produce of local sawmills, timber was also imported in substantial quantities into the new colony.

In the earliest days after their arrival, immigrants put up 'places of shelter of the most temporary nature' but these soon were replaced in the towns by houses of timber. The historian Traill described the first private residence built in Brisbane, Captain Coley's house, as a modest structure: 'a humble weatherboard, low-ceilinged cottage, the shingled roof partly covered with creepers'.[5]

Social pressure to erect a substantial dwelling was not so great in remoter rural areas, and even in 1871 the report accompanying the Queensland census noted that 'in the bush, whether on stations or in mining districts, in very many cases the structures that do duty as habitations are often of the rudest materials and construction'. But as reef mining assured the permanence of a gold-field, as stock and crops brought assured income to farmers, they too emulated the town dwellers in 'constructing their dwelling of sawn timber, many of them neatly built, and in some cases well painted'.

Timber houses were also easy to build. Whether a new settler was constructing his own house or had employed a carpenter, a method was evolved in Brisbane in the early years which was so economical of both materials and labour that no alternative was seriously considered for the next sixty or seventy years. This was the use of the timber stud-frame sheathed with a layer of lining boards.

Timber was the cheapest available material for Queensland house building until the 1950s. Economy, and not the Queensland climate, must be regarded as the major reason for the widespread construction of timber houses. The mild Queensland climate, however, did favour the prolonged use of huts of inferior materials, as the statistician noted in 1871: 'It must, however, be admitted that the climate of this Colony enables people to tolerate without inconvenience very inferior house accommodation', and again in 1876: 'indeed there can be little doubt that in such a climate as we possess, persons may live almost out of doors during the greater part of the year'. The low heat capacity of a thin wooden wall is indeed climatically suitable to Queensland housing. By 1891 the statistician was observing that:

in a climate like this in summer both [brick and stone] houses absorb the heat from the sun during the daytime and continue warm almost through the night, making the interior uncomfortable to the inhabitants, while the wooden house, if warmed at all, soon cools after the sun goes down.

While timber was pre-eminent in Queensland, it was important also in the housing of other states, particularly in country towns and on rural holdings. Until the 1920s wood accounted for 50 per cent of New South Wales dwellings. Economic factors outweighed climatic considerations in other states too, as in 1947 timber houses still comprised 36 per cent in New South Wales, 59 per cent in Victoria and 70 per cent in Tasmania.

The stud frame and its timber lining

Queensland houses were constructed of sawn timbers using a technique now generally known as stud framing. Light vertical members or studs, typically 100 millimetres by 50 millimetres, were spaced along the perimeter at approximately 450 millimetres to 600 millimetres apart. The studs were tenoned, and usually skew nailed as well, into top and bottom plates giving a fairly rigid frame. This was further strengthened by one or two cross braces (50 millimetres by 25 millimetres) let in flush with the inside face of the studs. The whole was then sheathed with a single layer of boards, usually chamfer-boards, fixed horizontally. Vertical tongue-and-groove boarding became common later in the century.

In any search for the origins of the Queensland house, there are thus two separate issues to consider − the timber stud frame and the single layer timber wall.

The timber frame of Queensland houses bears some resemblance to the American 'balloon frame', and the two have been linked in the architectural literature. Problems arise, however, when trying to establish a direct influence, not least because the American term has been so loosely employed. Since the 'invention' of the balloon frame in Chicago in 1832,[6] the term seems mainly to have been used to imply a timber frame held together by skew nailing − clearly a form of inferior construction, and one never used in Queensland housing, where studs were mortised into top and bottom plates and skew nailed as well. Current research suggests that balloon frame construction may not have been as extensive in America as was previously assumed.[7] In addition the suggested importation of the technique from the Californian goldfields to Victoria and then to Queensland cannot be substantiated. Timber frame houses were being built in

The characteristic low-profile Charters Towers dwelling, its verandahs more capacious than the house itself. The walls are minimal – mere vertical boarding on widely-spaced studs with a single intermediate rail.

A trellis-swathed house at Babinda. Its fine proportions and delicate decoration result from the perfect solution of the climatic problem – the wide verandahs and the encouragement of air movement.

Top and centre: Two symmetrical houses. The top one, at Roma, has a square ventilator. The other is at Emerald.

Above: The Italianate style. Bay window sashes rise high into wall cavities in the squat tower of Dovercourt, Brisbane.

Left: Kirkstow, Brisbane, designed by G.H.M. Addison and built in 1889. It has deep verandah friezes of trellised timber.

Queensland before the first gold was discovered in 1867 at Gympie, as well as in Victoria prior to 1851.

The concept of American balloon framing as an ancestor to the Queensland house entered Australian architectural history in 1968. Described as a frame of widely spaced light timbers with heavy square corner posts and rough timber sheathing, brought from America in 1851, it was then said to have been made even lighter in Australia, leading to a fragile skeleton of sticks or timbers quickly knocked together with rough butting, a minimum of skill and a handful of nails.[8] While this may be a description of jerry-built houses on the Victorian gold-fields, the technique is quite different from the light, but closely-spaced and carefully constructed stud frame of Queensland houses. It seems unlikely, therefore, that the American balloon frame played any role in Queensland building.

Instead of explaining the Queensland house as developing from imported or introduced techniques, it has been seen by some as a unique and distinctive vernacular style – but this concept comes largely from the experience of other states which were settled long before technological advances such as steam-powered sawmilling machinery. In the southern states, construction of slab-walled buildings was common and different techniques were devised using various lengths of split timber placed either horizontally or vertically.

Slab building, however, played no great role in Queensland housing since major settlement only took place from the 1860s, when sawn timber was becoming readily and cheaply available. This is not to deny that slab buildings were constructed in the state; but they were usually in remote locations where transport was difficult and expensive, on gold diggings where only a temporary residence was envisaged, or in cases of straitened finances. In southern Queensland slab dwellings may be found such as Remfry's hut at Slab Hut Farm, built in about 1873, one of the few slab buildings still in the original location; or the slab house at Magnolia Farm, built in 1893 by a newly-arrived family of Irish immigrant farmers.

The Sinnamon farm near Brisbane demonstrates the early sequence of building in Queensland. The Sinnamons were a large immigrant family who arrived in 1863; first they erected a substantial slab hut; then, in 1869, a house was begun, with hand-adzed timber frame and pit-sawn weatherboard cladding. These two houses relied on abundant local timber and a supply of labour from the many sons of the family. By 1887, however, when another house was required, they chose to build a standard stud-framed Queensland house.[9]

The above sequence also occurred sometimes on pastoral properties but even there after 1870 it was not common. In the ports and towns milled timber from Brisbane was among the first cargoes, and it was far easier to construct a

Two houses built for tropical Bundaberg. Above: A late nineteenth-century building with an eclectic ensemble of Federation motifs. The gables are ventilated to promote air movement in the roof spaces.

Below: A traditional symmetrical house with elegant timber decoration.

house of such standardized components than to start laboriously felling trees, and splitting slab. Furthermore, those slab buildings still in existence in north Queensland show evidence, not of a naive builder, a bushman with a tomahawk under his belt, but of trained carpenters using traditional methods adjusted to cope with the material at hand. The hut at Wambiana, or the former Bowen River Hotel, the homesteads at Peak Downs and Retro are examples of adaptation of carpentry techniques to slab structures. Robert Gray's house at Hughenden had the frame erected by the overseer and a carpenter, and Gray dressed and put in many of the lengths of horizontal slab for walls.

The time factor clearly shows that the Queensland stud frame was not a local development. In Brisbane there are no known relics of houses of the 1840s, and only a few, built of brick or stone, from the 1850s, prior to the introduction of steam sawmilling. But there are refer-

Original timber features on this Townsville house include stumps with ant caps, batten arches, and the fence with a gateway frame. This roof shape is sometimes termed a 'bungalow' in north Queensland.

ences to timber-framed houses erected in the late 1850s, and, by the 1860s, timber-framed houses were commonly erected, although not often with the frame exposed. The Queensland timber house, even in the early 1860s, was definitely a product of British technology, and leading figures in its distribution were the Brisbane sawmillers and builders' suppliers, Pettigrew, Petrie and Campbell, who produced the standardized studs and boards, and soon even windows, doors and hardware. This meant that throughout the colony houses could be erected quickly and cheaply using a familiar system.

In the embryonic ports to the north, even the earliest houses were similarly timber stud-framed structures – such as John Black's house in Townsville, built in 1864 but now demolished. In January 1865, six months before the settlement at Townsville was gazetted and named, the first builder had arrived, Charles Francis Hodel, bringing with him 'building materials to meet the demands for residences'. From these new ports bullock teams supplied remote inland pastoral properties and gold-fields. One biographer recalled:

the wonderful variety of goods which Robert Philp sent out by bullock and horse teams to the settlers in such distant areas as Winton before the railway was built. Sawn timber, windows and doors, galvanised iron, flooring boards and champher [sic] boards for building their houses, furniture of various kinds to make them comfortable.[10]

No real search for the antecedents of the Queensland stud frame had been undertaken until Peter Bell's recent survey of north Queensland houses, in which he argues convincingly for an origin in the British building tradition. In medieval Britain the majority of houses were built of wood. Refinements over the years included the British balloon frame, and by the seventeenth century there had developed, particularly in south-west England, the technique of 'late-framing', an example of this being Kent's 1776 drawings for 'Two Studd Work Cottages'. With some reservations this may be regarded as an ancestor of eighteenth-century timber houses of the eastern United States: and in Queensland, where the majority of immigrants were from English villages, it is entirely plausible that this technique was imported.[11]

One of the earliest descriptions of a timber-framed house in Queensland is that for the Tide Surveyor's house, built at Moreton Bay in 1858, which had:

The outside walls of the house to be framed of 4″ × 3″ pine studs and top plates and 4″ × 4″ hardwood sills, with batten braces halved into studs; the studs to be fixed 18″ apart and tenoned into beads and sills ... The whole to be covered with wrought chamfered weatherboards of pine with 2″ beaded stops at angles. [This house had] the Sitting Room and Passage lined

with 1/2″ match boarding put on vertically, on the walls. The remainder of the Rooms to be lined with the best unbleached calico secured with trimmed tacks to the studs and ceiling joists and covered entirely with wallpaper ...[12]

The frame exposed

These specifications prefigure the other aspect of Queensland housing, the exposed frame, which may be its one claim to distinction. While the origins of the practice of exposed framing may never be definitely determined, there are four possible sources.

Firstly, there is economy. It has now become commonplace to think of extreme summer temperatures in Queensland and to regard the climate as 'tropical' and hence demanding; but early immigrants to Queensland reacted differently. They steadfastly refused to acknowledge the higher temperature, and attempted to maintain styles of dress, habits, customs and diet unvaried from those of 'Home'. They also considered the climate, unlike that of Britain, to be remarkably benign – which in terms of housing allowed economies unthinkable in colder regions. Fireplaces were not essential for warmth, and walls – no longer needed to insulate but merely to provide privacy and security for possessions – could be made as thin and cheap as possible. The practice of single wall internal partitioning, with the lining to the more important room, was already well established in nineteenth-century Britain. It is a short step to doing the same to walls

This early two-room Charters Towers house shows a front verandah enclosure, walls sheeted with corrugated iron, back verandah enclosure, further extension, and new concrete stumps. The decorative metal window hoods remain.

around the perimeter, with the frame exposed to the verandah. By the 1870s, this was standard building practice in Queensland.

A second and related source for the exposed frame has been postulated, based on the resemblance to houses in the West Indies and southern States of America, notably the French-settled Louisiana. There the technique of timber framing, similar to British half-timbering, known in Louisiana as *briquette-entre-poteaux*, consisted of heavy squared posts framed into a timber sill, set on a brick base-wall, with heavy diagonal braces between each pair of posts, infilled with brick-nogging and then plastered over.[13] This is an improbable source for the timber frame, when the traditional British half-timbering must have been familiar to the majority of immigrants to Queensland, and when similar 'half-timbering' techniques are recorded around 1800 in New South Wales. The late eighteenth century French/American tradition, however, is important to Queensland housing in another way, and will be returned to in the discussion on elevation.

A third influence on the exposed timber frame is the production in Britain of prefabricated buildings for her colonies – not the better documented buildings of iron, but the earlier prefabricated timber-framed dwellings. When Governor Phillip arrived in New South Wales in 1788, he wisely brought with him a house from England. This was a timber frame with waterproofed walls of oilcloth which proved not an entirely satisfactory shelter from the elements. In 1790 the timber-framed 'moveable

Metal window hoods. Below: On a house in Charters Towers. Right: A window in an exposed-frame wall in Townsville, with a strip of boarding above the hood.

hospital' arrived in Sydney, and a few such examples must have led Governor King, in 1804, to have prefabricated buildings made in Sydney for erection at Newcastle and in Tasmania. At the embryonic penal settlement of Moreton Bay, the commandant's first cottage, erected in 1824, was similarly brought from Sydney. In the opening decades of the nineteenth century, in India, South Africa and Sierra Leone, as well as in the Australian colonies, prefabricated buildings from Britain arrived – simple precut timber frames, premade doors and windows, and boards for sheathing.[14] A great advance was made on this system in 1830 with John Manning's Portable Colonial Cottage for Emigrants, an ingenious system of interchangeable modular panels, but for the development of Queensland housing it is the work of his competitor Peter Thompson which is of more relevance.

Peter Thompson, a London carpenter and builder, is better known as the supplier of a number of temporary English churches,[15] but his initial importance is as the producer of 'Emigrants' houses' for export. These were timber framed, weatherboard clad, complex in plan, outline and roof form. They used decorative barge-boards and finials and pedimented doors, and thereby they appealed to middle-class emigrants much more than the straightforward, austere and working-class Manning cottages. Two well-documented examples of Thompson houses are Woodlands outside Melbourne, erected in 1843 for W.P. Greene and family;[16] and in New Zealand, Chief Justice Martin's house at Parnell, erected in the same year.[17] In addition to dwellings Thompson also produced framed churches, chapels and schools for export to various colonies. When overseas trade waned in the mid-1840s he turned his attention to the home market.

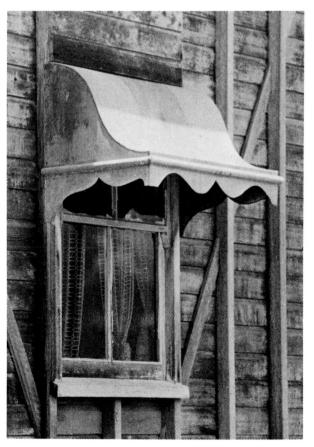

A house designed for occupation by the family of a Queensland Railways employee at Richmond, north Queensland.

There has been little research into the possible introduction of prefabricated houses to early Queensland, but there could not have been many. The construction system of these houses, however, well established in England and widely advertised in trade journals and newspapers is important. It included a studwall frame, sheathed with boarding and with boarded ceilings, often incorporating lean-to verandahs. Even before 1850 Andrew Petrie in Brisbane was making precut timber frames for portable buildings[18] and by the time of Queensland's separation the standard components for such houses need not have been imported from England, but were produced in Brisbane and shipped to new settlements to the north.

For a final inspiration for the Queensland stud frame we turn to the Romantic Revival in Britain, to religious rather than domestic architecture, and in particular to the group, formed in 1836 in Cambridge, later known as the Ecclesiologists. Their publication, *The Ecclesiologist*, begun in 1841, became one of the most important English architectural periodicals and had an enormous influence on church building.[19]

While they later promoted Gothic as the only true Christian architecture, during the early years of the 1840s emphasis was placed more on rural simplicity, seemly architecture, and plainness ('Let mean materials appear mean'). In New Zealand the Anglican Bishop Selwyn had direct Ecclesiological connections and with his architect Laidley Thatcher produced such buildings as St John's College Chapel, built in 1847 in Auckland, an exposed frame timber building with decorative cross bracing. Lewis draws attention to similar buildings, an exposed frame wooden church for Tristan de Cunha, built about 1850, and the church at Tarraville in Victoria, 1856.[20] Thompson's use of timber in his temporary churches in London had won Ecclesiological approval, because of their resemblance to medieval half-timbered buildings.

One of the earliest examples of the decoratively cross-braced exposed frame timber church in Queensland is the Methodist Church at Bundamba, said to date from 1865.[21] A variation on the style is the striking St David's Church, built in 1866 at Lutwyche, Brisbane, and designed by Richard Suter: a building with fairly widely spaced and solid exposed stud framing, sheathed internally (and at the same time braced) by diagonally fixed boarding. The Anglican Church of St David at Allora, built in 1870, had an ornate facade of many small cross-braced panels, since covered with weatherboard. The nearby St Augus-

The front verandah of the Railway house in Richmond, on the line to Mount Isa. It is now demolished.

tine's, built in 1871, at Leyburn, has a similar pattern of bracing. Probably the best known example of a cross-braced timber church in Queensland is St George's, 1876, Beenleigh. It was in the 1870s also that the exposed, diamond-patterned stud frame appeared in houses. It is best, however, not to overemphasize the role of Ecclesiological influences on such decorative cross-bracing. The result could have evolved merely through an inventive carpenter's decorative use of braces and nogging within the restrictions of stud framing for portable buildings, as is possibly the case with the ornate 'portable ballroom' at Bathurst in New South Wales.

The visual impact of cross-braced stud framing is, as noted previously, similar to traditional European half-timber construction, but this must be regarded as a very distant ancestor, rather than a direct influence on Queensland construction. It does seem, however, that the imitation of medieval half-timbering in the cross-braced stud frame was enhanced by what was probably a fortuitous feature – the properties of Queensland timbers. The dark brown hardwood studs and braces were highlighted against the pale pine of the softwood lining boards. The

architect Richard Suter took pains to maintain this contrast, as in his specifications for the School and Residence at Allora, built in 1867, which included painting 'the studs a dark brown similar to the natural colour, the boarding a light cream colour of yellowish tint as near as possible to the natural colour'.[22]

The Queensland use of the exposed timber stud frame may owe something to all of these influences – from the British tradition of light framing, as well as the older half-timbering, and its promotion by the Ecclesiologists; the ideas imported from the southern United States and/or the West Indies; and the practice of construction of portable or prefabricated buildings.

The initial propagation of the exposed stud frame may have come from the Queensland Board of Education.[23] Their first architect, Richard Suter, who had trained in the British tradition and also spent some time in the West Indies before coming to Brisbane in the 1860s, seems to have played a seminal role in the use of both the cross-braced timber wall and elevation on high stumps. Schools may well have served as models for better quality houses in country areas.

The spread of the stud-frame building system throughout the colony of Queensland was a result of technological advances in production (which brought about

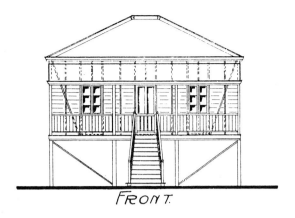

FRONT.

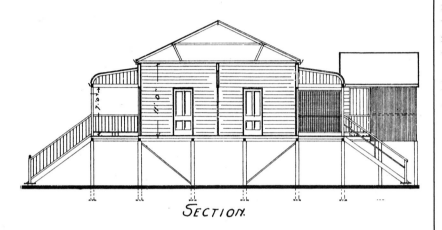

SECTION.

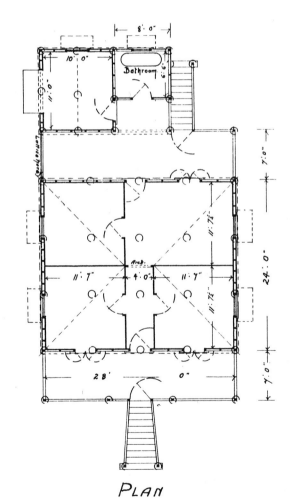

PLAN

Note. Circles on plan denote
position of square blocks.

colonial mass-production of standardized building componets – studs, boards, doors, windows, all simple and
light) coupled with the steam age of sea transport (which
enabled such componets to be shipped to northern ports)
and the importation from Britain of the other essentials,
roofing iron and nails.

Regional variation

Regional variations in the Queensland stud frame may be
noted on a broad scale. Its history seems to progress from
churches and schools to domestic building.

In north Queensland decoratively cross-braced timber
churches are unusual and few survive while simple stud-
framed churches abound (St James and St Marks, Townsville; St Teresa's, Ravenshoe). Stud-framed churches are
not exclusive to the tropics, however, and can be found in
the south (Roma presbytery; Indooroopilly Church of
England). Two northern cross-braced examples which
have not survived were the Salvation Army churches of
Bowen and Hughenden. A practice encountered in a
number of northern churches is the use of timber 'buttresses', which might be interpreted either as part of the
Neo-Gothic stylism favoured by the Ecclesiologists (St
Patrick's, Brandon, has ornate scroll-work timber buttresses), or perhaps as a precaution against tropical
cyclones. It is unwise to regard buttresses in any case as
a local feature, since they are also to be found further
afield, for example on St Paul's, Steiglitz (near Geelong).

Throughout the state, house walls protected by verandahs have single-skin exposed framing. House walls
exposed to the weather are usually boarded on the outside
in the south, whereas in north Queensland they are commonly lined only on the inside with chamfer-board, the
gable being covered with weatherboards, which extend
in tongues down to window hoods.

The north Queensland house is the essence of simplicity,
and ornament is kept to a minimum. In houses with
surrounding verandahs, it is mainly in the south that the
decoratively cross-braced house wall is found, although
several examples are known from both northern and
western Queensland – houses at Barcaldine, Charters
Towers, Richmond, and a striking, though non-domestic
use, the former Bank of New South Wales at Cooktown.

Two reasons may be advanced to explain the regional
imbalance in the use of cross-braced framing. Firstly, it
may be simply a matter of diffusion of an idea. If the idea
was Suter's as has been postulated and the schools built by
the Board of Education were the result, then one could
expect the style to be predominant in the south-east of
Queensland.[24] Secondly, there was criticism of cross-
bracing on the grounds that rainwater was retained in the
angles formed by the exposed timbers, leading to deterioration of the building fabric. In the north, where
rainfall is heavier and temperatures higher, this is clearly
an undesirable situation.

*A design by the State Advances Corporation, executed in
1915. The high, timber-framed house has four rooms and two
verandahs, with a separate kitchen and bathroom accessible
from the rear verandah. The front and rear walls have exposed
stud frames.*

Iron roofs

The settlement of Queensland coincided with the ready availability throughout the Empire of the new products of the industrial revolution and, not surprisingly, technology was a major determinant of Queensland housing. Steam-powered timber mills supplied the timber for the stud frame and walls, which were assembled with the use of inexpensive machine-made nails. The use of these instead of the old hand-made product brought about a building revolution. The iron roof, however, had probably the greatest effect on construction, as very light vertical members and light roof beams and rafters were all that

which accounted for 85 per cent of dwellings; in rural areas throughout the state bark roofs predominated.

The growth of Brisbane, as a free settlement and as the capital of the new colony, had coincided with the availability in Australia of 'an entirely new material in house building, namely metal', as the Government Statistician of New South Wales referred to the sheets of corrugated galvanized iron then being imported from Britain. There were only 183 such metal roofs in Queensland in 1864, but the relatively low cost of corrugated iron, together with its many advantages, led to its use almost universally for house roofs from 1870. By 1921 more than 90 per cent

A house at Longreach, in Queensland's western central district. The enclosing verandah is larger than the house itself.

was necessary to support the sheets of corrugated iron which were unquestionably the dominant roofing material used in Queensland.

Materials of the roof were recorded only at the censuses of 1864 and 1921, and from 1947 onwards. From such scanty data a dynamic change is nevertheless obvious. In 1864 builders in Queensland relied virtually entirely on locally produced and native materials, and almost 50 per cent of houses had bark roofs, while another 40 per cent were roofed with shingles. Brisbane houses generally used the more durable, and more weather-proof shingles,

of Queensland houses had roofs of corrugated iron.

Sheets of corrugated iron were available, as an import from Britain, from the earliest days of the colony. A metal roof, being light and quickly fixed in place, was not as labour-intensive as one of bark or shingles; in addition the other advantages of an iron roof were remarkable. It allowed a safe supply of clean drinking water, unlike that obtained from organic roofs. It was completely waterproof, as well as fireproof, and did not harbour snakes, vermin and insects as did inferior roofs.

In 1864, when there were only 183 houses in Brisbane with metal roofs, there were already ten iron roofs in the new port of Bowen, which had only been settled in May that same year. There are a few rare examples still in existence where an iron roof was erected over an earlier shingled roof but, as the pictorial record shows, metal roofs were used on virtually every Queensland house for the remainder of the century and longer.

Before leaving the use of 'tin', it is worth noting briefly its use in Queensland as a wall material. Again this is not as revolutionary as would at first seem. Iron houses were imported in considerable numbers in southern colonies. Victoria still has a number of imported prefabricated iron houses ranging from the grand iron-plate Corio Villa at Geelong to modest corrugated-iron workers' cottages in Brunswick and South Melbourne. There were some prefabricated iron industrial buildings imported from Britain to Queensland, but there is no evidence of prefabricated

such evidence readily available from historical sources.

One useful table in the censuses is that giving the number of rooms in private dwellings. Rooms enumerated were living-rooms, bedrooms and kitchen; excluded were bathroom, pantry, store and outhouses, unless these were also occupied. Unfortunately this question was not included in census schedules until 1901. The majority of Queensland houses then comprised four or five rooms which, it may be assumed, were a living-room, kitchen, and two bedrooms, with a dining-room or third bedroom as the fifth. This additional information overcame, to a large extent, the objection which had been raised in the 1876 census, that 'under the same head there is often the greatest possible difference, from the spacious mansion to the

A one-roomed house of corrugated iron. Several of these were built at Irvinebank, north Queensland, around 1912, for mine workers.

iron houses in that colony. By 1871, however, there were 155 houses recorded with metal walls, and use of the material as walls for local timber-framed houses increased markedly, so that by 1921 it ranked as the second most common material for walls of Queensland houses. The Census Report of 1901 commented that:

although iron is unsuitable for dwellings in these places (western and northern Queensland), on account of the heat, yet it is often the material for walls and roofs most easily obtainable, and the cheapest and easiest to build with of any materials available, whilst it has the advantage, also, of being waterproof.

Roof shape and house plan

While information on the external materials of the Queensland house is extremely valuable, it does not reveal anything about the house type, its shape and size, nor is

rough slab or unsightly gunyah'.

One-roomed dwellings were either tents or crude huts, both common on the mining frontier of northern Queensland, but not of further interest in the present survey. There are rare cases of later, solidly-constructed one-roomed huts such as the tiny corrugated-iron residences erected in 1914 for the mine workers at Irvinebank, or the stud-framed hut known in Herberton as Bishop Feetham's house. In cases such as these, however, the one-roomed hut served merely as a bedroom and for storage, since meals were eaten elsewhere.

The apparent multiplicity of Queensland houses can be

resolved into only two types. The smaller of these was the two-roomed cottage, a house form with origins in rural Britain. Under a gable roof was a core, about 6 metres by 3 metres, comprising two rooms – a larger living-room into which the centrally placed front door opened, and a smaller bedroom. Two windows placed symmetrically at the front gave light to each room. One of the advantages of two-roomed cottages was their portability as was found when the mines closed in Ravenswood and Charters Towers.

All these cottages in Queensland had a front verandah; a few also had verandahs at one or both sides, but these were usually a later addition. Extension of two-roomed cottages occurred invariably to the rear, where there was a front verandah.

In Brisbane, until the 1880s, houses of this type almost always had an attic with dormer windows, but by 1890 this was an uncommon feature. North Queensland four-roomed houses never had attics.

Difficulty arises about whether such a dwelling should be designated a cottage or a house. Nineteenth-century usage seems to have accepted both these terms, whereas current use favours the term cottage for the attic style, and, in most cases, for the simple four-roomed house. Yet the same building with side verandahs would be called a house. There seems to have been a different use by class as well, middle-class people lived in 'houses' and working-class families in 'cottages'. This is of considerable sociolog-

A four-roomed house in Charters Towers, showing a typical 'conversion'. Asbestos-cement sheeting has been applied over the formerly-exposed framework and encloses the front verandah. The original wide window hoods have been taken off and replaced.

combination of skillion, gable and tank roofs, and walls of corrugated iron. A most unusual example of the two-roomed or cottage plan used for a two-storey house, with two rooms on each level, was built by Rooney in Townsville in the 1880s.[25]

The other dwelling is the four-roomed house. Generally a square core of about 6 metres or larger, it was divided into four rooms, commonly with a central hallway at least between the first two rooms. A steeply hipped or a pyramidal roof covered the core, and again there was always a

ical interest, but for the purposes of this survey we have simply adopted Bell's suggestion of restricting 'cottage' to the two-roomed style.

The roof over the core of a four-roomed house was a pyramid or almost a pyramid ending at a short ridge. By the turn of the century a hipped gable roof became common and a basic style difference emerged in southern Queensland. Here one front room was extended forward into what had been verandah space, and roofed with its own gable, giving an asymmetrical facade. In southern Queensland this was the prevalent house type; in the north the symmetrical style with front verandah remained the major house type.

The remarkable feature of the basic four-roomed house is that even the largest houses conformed to this plan – they had a few very large rooms in the core, and a detached wing at the rear containing kitchen and servants' rooms. Wealthier people had larger rooms, but not necessarily more rooms. Their money went sometimes into brick walls but always conspicuously into brick foundations, wider verandahs, an ornate gable in the verandah roof over the entrance, cast-iron balustrading, and extra timber detailing. Houses of this style in the north range in age from Rosebank, built in 1886 to Warringah, 1912, and in the south include such well-known examples as Miegunyah, 1884–85, Roseville, 1885, Dovercourt, built in about 1870 and Hughesville, 1890.

The style seems to have reached its acme in Brisbane in the middle to late 1880s. A design feature of particular note – which is also found in similar houses in southern states – is the use in the front rooms of bay windows, whose lower sash reached to floor level, and slid telescopically into a recess in the ceiling, allowing direct access to the front verandah. To accommodate the extra height required, a small tower-like section of roof was constructed above the bay window, giving a more complex roof-line than the straight pyramid-plus-verandah.

The suggestion has been frequently advanced that the Anglo-Indian bungalow was a model for this kind of house. But a very distinctive feature of the Indian bungalow, 'a European version of the Bengal double-roofed house',[26] is that the wall section between the two separate elements (core and verandah) incorporates clerestory windows to admit light to core rooms, or at least small vents to cool by exhausting hot air from the roof space. This pattern seems virtually unknown in Queensland and only two such possible examples have emerged from extensive research. These are the former house at Dalmore near Longreach of which nothing more is known, and Dr Chapman's house Duncragan at Townsville, now altered beyond recognition.[27]

The elevated house

There is a general and mistaken belief that all Queensland houses are elevated 2 metres or more on stout tree trunks, known locally as 'stumps' or 'blocks'. The use of piles, pillars, or piers, to support a floor, was well established building practice long before Queensland was settled. Here, as elsewhere under pioneer conditions, the earliest huts had merely bare earth floors. As soon as conditions permitted construction of a better class of dwelling, however, solid raised floors were required for which the natural choice of material was timber. In order to provide a foundation for the timber floors, a grid pattern of very low stumps was laid out with a spacing of as much as 2.5 metres. These supported the bearers, which in turn held joists to which the floor was fixed. Again it must be stressed that this was not a Queensland innovation. Better quality houses elsewhere had long been built on brick or stone footings, and the average cottages tended to use low piles for foundations.

Many reasons have been advanced to account for elevation in Queensland, but they are mainly rationalizations, or advantages discovered well after the practice was firmly established. On the steep hills of Brisbane it was often necessary to secure a level floor by having one side of the house at ground level, the other 4 metres or even

more above. An excellent and very early example of this is to be found in Brisbane in William Stephens' house, The Grange, built in 1864 probably to the design of Richard Gailey, an architect newly arrived from Ireland. The timber house core is elevated above the ground some 3 metres on a base of hand-made brick comprising two sub-floor 'cellar' rooms. Around the perimeter the floors of the encircling verandah are supported on tall and solid squared timber blocks ranging in height on the sloping site from 4 metres at the front of the verandah to 1 metre at the rear corner.[28]

Once the practice of elevation was well established, many other reasons gave it added advantages which in the opinion of residents far outweighed any considerations of appearance. An enquiry made in 1944 by the Queensland Bureau of Industry found nearly fifty reasons for high stumps.[29] These included benefits of extra space for laundry, children's play, storage, work, summer living, coolness, avoidance of damp, freedom from insects, and finally control of 'white ants'.

The disadvantage of a steep site included little usable garden area, but one advantage soon became apparent – the underfloor space provided extra area for many activities such as laundry, storage, bathing, children's play and later car parking. Over the years it was realized that elevation was a very cheap means of gaining such extra space, and the practice became more and more common, so that by the 1880s houses even on level sites were erected elevated on 2 metre to 3 metre stumps.

This was more often a feature of working-class housing, and middle-class houses remained mainly low-set. The claim that elevation makes a house cooler because it catches more breeze is difficult to justify. There may be some slight increase in wind strength at 2 metres above ground, but it is unlikely to be discernible by occupants.

The sub-floor space is however a valuable area for summer living, particularly during the day, as the whole house structure functions as a double roof, insulating the area from strong sunlight and high temperatures. In addition, the absence of solid walls means that cooling breezes are not impeded, so that this is the coolest part of the house. In working-class houses this takes the place of the wide shaded verandahs of the large houses.

The avoidance of damp in sub-floor space is a clear benefit of better ventilation, although an increase to 2 metres would not bring a noticeable improvement over a 1-metre elevation. Freedom from insects is a more dubious reason, based on a popular myth that mosquitos fly less than a metre above the ground – scientifically, and by experience, shown to be untrue.

Elevation emerged as a means of controlling termites ('white ants') as early as 1838, when four prefabricated

Above: This Charters Towers house has been fully sheeted and enclosed. Decorative tinwork at the roof corners and the batten arches give a suggestion of its former appearance.

Below: This four-roomed house in Charters Towers has a verandah along one side, as well as the usual front verandah. The additional shade is typical of Charters Towers and further inland.

buildings at Port Essington, erected on (2.4 metre) piles, proved far superior to those locally-built at or close to ground level. It is unlikely however that early Brisbane builders considered the termite a menace, as they would have been unfamiliar with their depredations.

A further reason for elevation was more apparent in northern Queensland: the very heavy rains of the wet season led to boggy and even minor flood conditions. Here houses were raised at a safe height above the water level – examples such as Chillagoe, Burdekin plantation houses, and a number in the Herbert River area.

Settlers in the early sugar-growing areas of north Queensland seem to have been influenced by the popular Victorian idea of miasma inducing sickness, and sought to escape fevers by elevation another reason for building on high stumps. This belief had similarly caused the wealthiest men in Brisbane to build their houses high on the tops of various hills.

Allied to this is the suggestion of the influence on Queensland housing of architectural style in early French Louisiana where the miasma theory was a factor in the erection of distinctive elevated plantation houses. A few remaining homes such as the Home Place built in 1801, or the J.B. Valle house, 1800, show a style with main living area raised high above the ground, while these rooms have French windows opening onto a *galerie* or verandah. While the similarity with Queensland is noteworthy, further research is necessary to determine links between these two building traditions.

Elevation became more popular with time in Queensland, but was never universally adopted. Analysis of 330 north Queensland houses built before 1920 showed 28 per cent to be high set, and Bell's recent survey of almost 4,000 early houses in various north Queensland towns revealed only 37 per cent high set. Since many of these had been relocated or restumped since erection, this was probably a slightly higher proportion than original.

The fashionable verandah

It is also widely believed that all Queensland houses have wide encircling verandahs and that these are evidence of a particular adaptation to a hot climate. As with so many other aspects of Queensland housing, the verandah is neither a regional feature, nor even a national one.

As a result of British experience in India, the verandah was imported back to Britain in the late eighteenth century where it became popular despite a climate in which it was totally unsuitable. As Southey wrote in 1807:

Here is a fashion lately introduced from better climates, of making verandahs, verandahs in a country where physicians recommend double doors, and double windows as precautions against intolerable cold.[30]

Above: A two-roomed timber house built in Townsville in 1884–85, with a rear extension built about 1887. Note the protective boarding in the gable and over windows.

Below: Camona, in Brisbane, was built in 1896 by James Campbell, a prosperous builders' supplies merchant whose house testifies to his extensive timber milling investments.

A low-set four-roomed timber house with verandahs on three sides. Decorative ironwork adorns each corner of the roof as well as the ventilator. Timber decoration ranges from a simple dowel balustrade to capitals on the verandah posts and unusually ornate brackets.

A house erected in Brisbane by the Workers' Dwellings Scheme in 1913. The sloping site gives prominence to the stumps and the sub-floor space between them.

In this, as in so many other matters of taste and fashion, practical considerations were often overlooked or ignored.

The verandah filled a social need even in England, and was popularized by architects of the Picturesque mode. Though criticized by some as 'a mere excrescence in design ... and so far tolerable only for small villas and cottage residences where no style is attempted', the verandah had by the 1870s in England become an indispensable social adjunct. As George Elliot parodied: 'He has all the qualities that would make a husband tolerable – battlements, verandah, stables'.[31]

So it was from India, mediated by more than half a century of use in Britain, that the verandah came to Queensland, as it had somewhat earlier to the other colonies. The fact that it was a fashion, rather than a necessity, is shown by its extensive use on houses of all sizes and in all of the Australian colonies. The meanest of single-fronted, single-storey terraces in Sydney or Melbourne had its verandah, even when this faced south and made the house consequently colder and darker. In the boom years of Victoria's 1880s, even formerly chaste Georgian terraces were frequently embellished with cast-iron-edged verandahs or balconies.

The Queensland verandah should be viewed therefore as an obligatory contemporary design feature with its origins in immigrants' conventional taste. It was necessary symbolically, as it was 'proper', for a house to have a front verandah; and psychologically, since it signified the 'front' of the house, as well as a kind of 'barrier' between public and private; and finally since it was a cheap means of shelter against rain and sun for a dry place to sit alfresco, attached to sitting-rooms on the ground floor.

Clear evidence that the verandah, even in northern Queensland, is not climatically indispensable comes from its widespread enclosure. In Bell's survey, only 7 per cent of houses still had an open front verandah, the others being enclosed above with louvres of glass or wood or with casements, and below with asbestos sheet or boards. This is typical also of the houses of southern Queensland. Surveys of existing housing stock similarly show that the encircling verandahs, regarded as a 'trademark' of the Queensland house, occur on fewer than 20 per cent of houses.[32] Over half of all early Queensland houses have a verandah at the front only. It is worth noting here too that the four-verandahed house style with steep pyramid roof is certainly not confined to Queensland but seems to be a British colonial style – as existing and former houses show in South Africa, Sierra Leone, India, the West Indies and elsewhere in Australia.

Other decorative finishes

There are some early houses in Queensland whose verandahs are open, flanked only by the pillars supporting the roof (Lucerne, built in 1862; Wilston House built in the 1870s; Ormiston House, 1864; Lota House, 1862) but this loggia style is unusual. In most cases the verandah is enclosed with some form of balustrading about one metre in height. For this purpose cast-iron panels found some use in the south (Woollahra, 1868; Ralahyne, 1888), at

This Townsville house has had its verandah enclosed with timber louvres and lattice, and an extra shading device has been added. Roof ventilators now rarely survive in Queensland houses.

first imported and later of local manufacture. Cast iron was also made at some northern foundries, but was not commonly used for domestic buildings.

Much of the visual appeal of the verandahed house comes from the balustrades, for which the most common material was timber and, at first, light timber in quite intricate patterns (Newstead House, 1845; Stromness, 1870s). By the 1880s however, most balustrading was made from simple dowel held by upper and lower rails. Unfortunately the majority of Queensland houses have lost the decorative detail of balustrades, posts and brackets when verandahs were later enclosed.

Cast iron was sometimes also used for verandah brackets and valances, and for ridge crestings and finials, but this domestic use was confined, as with iron balustrading, to southern Queensland. The few cases of such use in the north are found in Charters Towers and may almost be enumerated individually.[33] Verandah posts in the grander houses were often heavy Doric columns, sometimes in pairs, but in ordinary timber houses, evenly-spaced 100 millimetre by 100 millimetre posts were employed. The posts themselves were stop-chamfered from above the balustrade to about 300 millimetres below the verandah eaves, where a moulded timber capital and fretwork bracket were placed, for decorative rather than structural effect. The timber brackets featured scroll and leafwork in various patterns, often delicate and intricate. By the 1890s rising costs led to a simpler bracket which could be saw-

An old four-roomed house with surrounding verandahs now enclosed. The decorative window hoods remain, and the deep 'verandah-shade' so common in Charters Towers appears here.

cut without prior drilling for fretwork. The Art Nouveau movement brought some sinuous designs and the use of elegant curved timberwork framing verandah bays, but there are very few domestic examples of such work outside the Brisbane area.

Other timber decoration found on large houses included brackets under the soffit of the main house roof (Roseville, Hughesville) as well as ornate gable infill detailing incorporating flowers, animals or geometric designs (numerous examples include Carvarmore, Waldheim and Miegunyah), fretwork infill for window-hood brackets, and elegant finials. Lattice verandah screens were not as common as is popularly believed, but were used more frequently in the north than in Brisbane.

The naked stumps beneath the house were perhaps regarded as visually unattractive. More importantly however, the space when open could not be used for secure storage. The practice therefore was introduced of enclosing this sub-floor space with battens — sometimes placed diagonally, often set back one row of stumps from the perimeter with crescents of battens used decoratively between the outer stumps.

Interior timber decoration included fretwork panels in the transom above internal doors, and fretwork ceiling rosettes. Chamferboards used for single-layer walls had a row of beading at the bottom of each board on the reverse side. A few houses exist where extra wide boards also have a median row of beading, to give the illusion of two boards (for example, Bellevue homestead).

One of the most engaging and distinctive features of Queensland houses is the elaborate tinwork of the metal window-hoods and roof ventilators. The latter, which

were seen more often in the past, were used to exhaust hot air from the roof space of the steeply pitched main roof over the house. Re-roofing, whether after storm damage or simply to replace corroded iron, often led to the removal of ventilators, but sufficient remain to give an indication of the variety of shape, size and decoration.

Sheet metal window-hoods were used on the western side of houses with no side verandah. Generally speaking, hoods of north Queensland are much deeper than those of the south, shading the whole upper half of the sash window. Their efficacy in reducing internal temperature is highly questionable. A rare example has been noted from Charters Towers of sheet metal cut into shaped

A house in Charters Towers with verandahs enclosed with sheets of ripple-iron that can be propped open.

brackets attached to verandah posts.[34] Pressed metal sheeting was used internally as ceiling material in some houses built in the 1920s and later.

Tents and other dwellings

Regional variation in materials is very small in Queensland where timber and corrugated iron predominate. Of major significance is a group of stone homesteads constructed in the 1880s and extending through central inland Queensland from Richmond to Winton to Longreach. These are all in the colonial Georgian idiom; long low buildings, often only one room deep, surrounded by verandahs. Built mainly of freestone, they include Manfred Downs, Rockwood built in 1882, Elderslie, 1881, Oondooroo, 1883, and the interesting combination of stone and pit sawn planks at Mount Cornish built in the 1870s and 1890s.[35]

The origins of these homesteads are generally ascribed to a shortage of timber. Virtually all houses in the nearby towns, however, are of timber, brought from the coast or from Brisbane. A probable influence was the presence of a group of skilled stonemasons, possibly from South Australia, who moved from one property to another, using locally available building stone. Folklore attributes this construction to Italians, Germans and Chinese but there is no factual foundation for this belief. These stone homesteads are an obvious group for further research, and stand apart from the Queensland timber tradition which has here been our concern.

Another interesting group of homesteads, many of which are now abandoned, were built in the area south and west of Winton, extending into the Channel Country and across the border into South Australia. These were constructed of *pisé* (or rammed earth) again in the basic 'Colonial Georgian' style.[36] In this case, the extreme distance from transport coupled with lack of local timber or stone does seem to have been a causal factor in the choice of material. Again this is a regional group where further study would lead to new insights into pioneer building techniques and styles.

The use of corrugated iron as a wall material has already been commented on. There are more iron-walled houses in northern and western Queensland than in the south, which reflects the makeshift attitude and the lesser social pressure away from the capital city.

Although tents figure largely in the history of Queensland housing, this aspect has not been examined here. It is worth noting however that the British army tent is sometimes claimed to be the ancestor of the Queensland house.[37] This reasoning may be derived from J.L. Kipling's assertion in 1911 that early British residents in India, who lived most of their time in tents, later built their houses there on the model of the Indian service tent. Research has shown, however, an indigenous prototype for the Anglo-Indian bungalow[38] – the tent cannot be readily placed in a postulated sequence of development in India, much less so in Australia. It should also be recalled that tents continued to be used extensively in Australia long after the house style of core and surrounding verandahs was well established.

North Queensland does claim one house-style evolved from the formerly ubiquitous miner's tent, the 'tent-houses' erected in Mt Isa in the 1930s. These comprised a light timber frame to which were attached canvas walls and roof, with a second separate timber frame around the perimeter supporting a corrugated-iron roof.[39]

Around the house

Large, shady, exotic trees, often mangoes, are found on the western side of the Queensland house. Trees were rarely planted at the front, the garden there being reserved for a more formal arrangement of flowering annuals, and small shrubs, such as hibiscus and croton. Some larger urban houses have a group of royal palms spaced evenly along the front boundary, and on large southern properties the Bunya pine was a popular choice to line driveways or boundary fences at a considerable distance from the house. Other plants, including native species and the popular bougainvillaea vine, are more recent introductions to Queensland gardens.

Urban allotments were enclosed with picket fences at the front and split palings at the side and rear, although these are now a rarity. The corrugated-iron cylindrical water tank on a stand was a general accompaniment to Queensland houses, but is now seldom found except in rural and inland situations.

The later 'Queensland style'

By the 1920s verandahs had fallen from fashion for new houses and roofs had become more complex. A distinctive style of house then emerged with two or three front gables, the apex infilled with asbestos sheet embellished with vertical stripes, open porches, weatherboard walls and casement windows glazed with Arctic glass, often green, purple or yellow. These solidly-built, well-designed houses still had spacious rooms, high ceilings, good ventilation, together with the contemporary modern advantages of an internal kitchen and bathroom. They perhaps come closest to representing a genuine Queensland style. Increasingly in demand, they are already, in the parlance of local real estate agents, termed 'Queenslanders'.

Hughesville, a fine timber house built about 1890 on the outskirts of Brisbane. It has escaped alteration because it is still the home of the daughter of the original owner. The design is a Queensland version of the Italianate style. The tower-like projection of the bay above the verandah roof accommodates a floor-length upward-sliding sash window.

GLOSSARY

aedicule: a small house or room. Also, the enframing of a window or door by columns and a pediment.

anthemion: ornament based on honeysuckle buds.

antis: a term usually applied to a portico or space where the supporting columns are arranged between walls or pilasters. Such columns are described as 'in antis'.

apse: a semicircular or polygonal termination or recess usually used as a sanctuary in a church.

arcade: a series of arches supported on piers or columns.

architrave: a beam forming part of a Classical entablature. Also, the moulded trim around a doorway or a window.

arcuated: the use of arches or the arch principle in a building.

ashlar: masonry of squared and tooled stones laid with fine mortar joints between the blocks.

astylar: the term applied to a facade without columns or pilasters.

bagging: a process of applying a thin mortar to the face of a brick or stone wall with coarse material such as a hessian bag.

balconette: a small balcony.

baluster: a pillar or column supporting a hand-rail or coping. A series of balusters is called a balustrade.

barge-board: a sloping board fixed to the verge of a gable to cover the ends of the horizontal roof timbers. It may be plain or decorated.

barrel vault: a simple continuous vault, usually in the shape of a half-cylinder. Also called a tunnel vault or a waggon vault.

bay window: a curved or faceted window projecting from a building. A curved bay is called a bow window. If the bay commences above ground level it is called an oriel window.

bellcast: a Scottish term used for a roof the lower part of which has a slightly flatter pitch than the rest.

belvedere: a building or part of a building designed to afford a view.

board-and-batten: wall sheeting of boards or planks butted together lengthwise, with battens or strips of timber covering the joints.

bracketed eaves: the overhanging edge of a roof which is supported or appears to be supported by decorative brackets or corbels at intervals along the wall below.

cam or **came:** a metal strip, usually of lead, used to join the separate pieces of glass in a decorative window.

campanile: the Italian word for a bell-tower.

cantilever: a horizontal beam projection unsupported at outer end.

casement: a window sash hinged on one side.

castellated: built with battlements, as in a wall with a parapet employing gaps or indentations (embrasures) flanked by raised portions (crenellations).

chinoiserie: the name given to the use of Chinese motifs in European architecture, especially in the Georgian period.

clerestory or **clear-storey:** an upper stage in a building having windows above an adjacent roof; windows placed between roofs of two different levels.

cluster housing: contiguous houses, particularly on sloping land, which permits the exploitation of different floor levels.

collar tie: a horizontal timber member joining two opposite rafters, about half-way between the wall plate and the ridge of the roof.

colonnade: a sequence of columns and their superstructure.

condominium: the American term for a home unit.

console: a scrolled corbel or bracket.

coping: a capping course at the top of a masonry wall or balustrade, usually finished with a slope to cast off rain.

corbel: a block projecting from a wall to support a beam or other feature.

cornice: in Classical architecture, the top, projecting section of an entablature. Also, a projecting decorative feature along the junction of an internal wall and ceiling, or along the top of an external wall, or around the outer curve of an arch.

Cosy corner: see **ingle-nook**.

Cottage orné: a picturesque and artfully rustic house, usually asymmetrical in appearance.

Courses: parallel and usually horizontal layers of bricks, stones, slates, tiles, shingles, etc.

coved ceiling: a ceiling curved at its junction with the walls.

crenellation: see **castellated**.

crown glass: window glass cut into panes from a large disc, called a 'crown table', which is formed while the glass is hot and soft.

cupola: a dome or spherical shape, especially when used on a circular or polygonal base crowning a roof or a turret.

curtilage: the area of landscape enclosing a house and its outbuildings.

cylinder glass: glass made by forming an elongated bubble which, while still hot and soft, has its ends cut off and is slitted along its length so that it lies flat. After cooling, the sheet is cut into panes.

dado: the lower part of a wall, when finished or decorated differently from the wall above.

dentils: small rectangular blocks used in rows, like teeth, as part of the decoration of a cornice. Such a cornice is said to be dentillated.

diaper: an all-over pattern of painted or carved elements, usually of small square or lozenge shapes.

doorcase: the whole surround of a door, including the thickness of the wall which the door penetrates (the reveal) and the architraves.

dormer: a vertical window projecting from a sloping roof, so named because traditionally it provided light for a sleeping compartment such as a dormitory.

double pile: a building that is two rooms in depth.

dressings: accurate or decorative surrounds, usually of stone or brick, to a window, doorway or building corner.

earth-covered buildings: buildings which have their floors and a large proportion of their walls and roofs protected by earth, so that, typically, soil covering the walls and roofs is of sufficient depth to support vegetation and modify internal air temperatures.

earth-integrated buildings: the term used where significant portions of buildings are in thermal contact with the surrounding earth, e.g. earth-covered and earth-sheltered structures.

earth-sheltered buildings: buildings whose walls, but not roofs, are protected or hidden by mounds of earth.

egg-and-dart: an enrichment, usually on Classical mouldings, consisting of alternate egg-like and dart-like shapes. Also called egg-and-tongue.

elevation: an external face of a building. A geometrical drawing of the same.

encaustic tiles: earthenware tiles decorated with coloured clays before firing. Much used in the Middle Ages, and revived in the Victorian period.

entablature: in Classical architecture, the upper part of an Order, i.e. all of the horizontal members supported by a column, comprising architrave, frieze, and cornice.

entasis: the slight swelling of a Classical column to emphasize its load-bearing function and to counteract the optical illusion that a straight column is concave.

fanlight: the glazed part of a doorway above the door. In Georgian times it often had radiating glazing bars suggesting a fan, but the term is used for an above-door panel of any shape whether fixed or openable.

fascia: a flat, on-edge member which trims the eaves of a roof. Usually it is fixed to the ends of the rafters and also supports the eaves gutter.

finial: an embellishment, usually spiky in form, at the apex of a gable, pinnacle or spire.

French window or **French door:** a window reaching to floor level, or nearly so, and opening in casement fashion.

fret: an ornamental band consisting of right-angled straight lines. Such a pattern, cut in thin timber by means of a fret-saw, is called fret-work, and the same term is applied generally to interlaced or open-work decoration, no matter what the material.

frieze: the middle division of a Classical entablature. Also, the decorated band along the upper part of a wall below the cornice.

frontispiece: the main facade of a building or its principal entrance bay.

gable: the triangular portion of a wall between the enclosing lines of a sloping roof. A gablet is a small gable.

gambrel roof: a roof having a gablet near the ridge, and the lower part hipped; also called a half-hipped roof. See **Jerkin-head roof** and **mansard roof**.

glulam: timber structural members made of laminated components glued together.

half-timbering: walls built of timber framework, the spaces between the frame members being filled in with other materials such as wattle-and-daub or nogging.

ingle-nook: a room recess, usually containing a fireplace and, often, built-in seats. Also called a chimney-corner and a cosy corner.

in-situ: in place, at the site.

intaglio: pressed or incised decoration.

jalousie: a door or window shutter with louvres or slats sloping upwards from the outside to exclude rain and sun, while admitting air.

jerkin-head roof: a roof which is hipped from the ridge halfway to the eaves, and gabled from there down. See **gambrel roof.**

keystone: the central wedge-shaped voussoir of an arch.

label mould: a projecting moulding across the top of a window or doorway, for the purpose of diverting rainwater running down the wall face away from the opening. Also called a hood-stone, weather moulding and drip-stone.

lichgate or **lychgate:** a roofed gate to a churchyard, originally intended to provide pallbearers with some protection from the weather pending the arrival of the priest.

loggia: an open gallery or arcade; an outdoor room.

machicolation: a parapet gallery projecting on brackets from the outside of a castle wall or tower, with openings in the floor through which (in its original Medieval form) missiles and liquids could be discharged upon an enemy below.

mansard roof: a roof with two pitches – a gentle slope at the top and a steep lower slope. It was devised by the French architect J.-H. Mansard to provide roomier attic space, and dormers are often provided. Known in the United States as a gambrel roof.

midden: the term used for an Aboriginal refuse heap, chiefly of shells.

mullion: a vertical framing member dividing a window.

nogging: the filled panels between the members of a timber frame. Nogging was traditionally made of brickwork or stonework. In light framework, a nogging is a horizontal piece fixed between vertical members.

oeil-de-boeuf: a round ('bull's-eye') window.

off-form concrete: concrete with no applied finish except the imprint left by the formwork after it has been stripped.

off-saw: the term applied to timber as cut by the saw.

ogee: a double curve, like the letter S; an arch or moulding made up of a convex curve and a concave curve.

order of architecture: in Classical architecture, a column and its entablature, including all the parts and the proportions between them. The Greek Orders were Doric, Ionic and Corinthian, while the Roman ones were Tuscan, Doric, Ionic, Corinthian and Composite. The classification originated with Vitruvius Pollio, an architect of ancient Rome.

oriel: see **bay window.**

palmette: an ornamental motif resembling a palm leaf.

pantile: a roofing tile S-shaped in cross-section.

parapet: a wall built up higher than the eaves line of a roof, either to hide the roof surface or to provide safety for the users of a flat roof.

pargetting or **parging:** the plastering of a wall with mortar as the erection of the wall proceeds. Particularly used for the inside surfaces of a chimney flue. See also **bagging.**

pavilion: a light, ornamental building. Also, a projecting subdivision of a larger building which terminates or completes its composition.

pediment: a decorative feature finishing the gable of a Classical building. Also, a similar feature above a door or window. A pediment may have a straight or curved top.

piano nobile: main floor of a house, containing reception rooms.

pilaster: a rectangular column attached to a wall as though it were partly buried in the wall, and conforming with one of the Orders.

pit closet: a small detached building for human defecation, built over a pit and moved when the pit has nearly filled.

plinth: the slightly projecting base of a column or a building.

podium: a continuous projecting base or pedestal.

portico: a porch supported by columns and open on at least one side. A portico often has a pediment.

purlin: in traditional roof construction, a horizontal member offering intermediate support to sloping rafters.

quoin: the external angle of a building. Where stones form the angle they are called quoin-stones or quoins.

rebate: a longitudinal step-shaped recess, as in a door jamb to receive the door. Sometimes spelt 'rabbet', and also known as a check.

retrofitting: adapting an existing building for better energy efficiency.

rinceau: an ornamental motif consisting of scrolls of foliage.

roughcast: an external coating of rough material, traditionally applied in two layers of lime mortar, the second of which, containing gravel, crushed stone or pebbles, is thrown on. Also called pebbledash.

roundel or **rondel:** a round or oval-shaped medallion-like ornament.

rustication: stone walling comprising ashlars with exposed faces rough or textured, or where the ashlars are smooth-tooled with deep or greatly-emphasized joints.

sash: a frame holding the glass of a window. The term sash-window is generally applied to a window which slides up and down. See **casement.**

segmental arch: an arch in the shape of an arc but less than a semicircle.

shingle: a thin rectangular piece of wood, terracotta, asbestos-cement or other material used for covering roofs or walls. Clay shingles were made in Australia from 1788, but the heyday of terracotta shingles was brought on by the Arts and Crafts movement. In New South Wales and Victoria, timber shingles were commonly split from billets of casuarina, ironbark or cypress pine; in Tasmania long shingles of peppermint gum were common.

sidelight: the narrow vertical window beside a front entrance door.

single pile: the term applied to a building that is one room in depth.

soffit: the under-surface of a beam or similar architectural member, a staircase, or the eaves of a roof.

soldier course: a course of brickwork with each brick laid on its end so that its greatest dimension is vertical.

squinch: an arch or infilling across the interior angle of two contiguous walls, to provide support for a ceiling, roof or tower above.

stabilized earth: prepared earth to which a stabilizing agent such as Portland cement or bitumen emulsion is added.

strapwork: decoration simulating interlaced bands such as cut leather.

string course: a moulding or projecting band running horizontally across a facade.

stucco: a thin decorative finish, traditionally composed of lime and sand, applied in two coats to external walls. The term was originally used for all plasterwork, though stucco did not usually include gypsum in its ingredients. Portland cement began to be used as an ingredient in the second half of the nineteenth century. Stucco was employed as an economic medium for the modelling of architectural features in lieu of stone, which it was often made to imitate.

swag: an ornamental festoon in the form of a piece of cloth, usually with flowers, fruit or foliage, draped over two supports.

tabula rasa: literally, an erased tablet. Figuratively, the human mind at birth viewed as having no innate ideas. Architecturally, an inspired concept awaiting realization.

terracotta: a baked form of fine brick earth, used for floor tiles, wall decorations and, especially in the Federation period, for roofing tiles.

terrazzo: fragments of coloured marble, mixed with cement mortar and laid over a solid base. When the mixture has set, it is abraded to a smooth finish, and may also be polished.

tile-hanging: fixing tiles on to a wall to keep out the weather.

tongue-and-groove: a joint between the edges of boards (e.g. floor boards) to form a smooth surface. The tongue on one board fits into the groove of its neighbour.

trabeated: constructed by the post-and-beam method.

transom: a horizontal framing member dividing a window.

treillage: trellis-work, usually of timber or iron.

turret: a small tower, usually round or polygonal.

tympanum: the triangular area enclosed by the mouldings of a pediment.

valance: pendulous drapery around a bed or across a window head. In building, a decorative panel or strip under a roof verge, usually between verandah posts.

vermiculation: a worm-eaten appearance given to stone-work by tooling and carving.

voussoir: a wedge-shaped stone or brick, making up the curve of an arch.

REFERENCE NOTES

CHAPTER 1

1. L.L. Robson, *The Convict Settlers of Australia*, Melbourne University Press, 1973, p. 18.
2. Philip Cox and Clive Lucas, *Australian Colonial Architecture*, Lansdowne, 1978, p. 8.
3. John Shute, *First and Chief Groundes of Architecture*, London, 1563.
4. David Watkin, *English Architecture, a Concise History*, Thames & Hudson, 1979, p. 97; Isaac Ware translated Palladio's treatise into English in 1738 as *The Four Books of Adrea Palladio's Architecture*, and a facsimile of this, by Dover Books, is still in print.
5. John Summerson, *Georgian London*, 3rd edition, Barrie & Jenkins, 1978, p. 29.
6. Mark Girouard, *Life in the English Country House*, Yale University Press, 1978, p. 8.
7. Quoted in Nathaniel Lloyd, *History of the English House*, Architectural Press, 1976, p. 88.
8. *ibid.*, p. 133.
9. *ibid.*, p. 109.
10. Miles Hadfield (ed.), *A Book of Country Houses*, Hamlyn, 1969, pp. 26, 27.
11. Mark Girouard, *op.cit.*, p. 122.
12. Nathaniel Lloyd, *op.cit.*, p. 130.
13. Philip Cox and Clive Lucas, *op.cit.*, p. 175.
14. Dan Cruickshank and Peter Wyld, *London: the Art of Georgian Building*, Architectural Press, 1977, p. 1.
15. Joan Kerr and James Broadbent, *Gothick Taste in the Colony of New South Wales*, David Ell, 1980, p. 41.
16. J. Mordaunt Crook, *The Greek Revival*, R.I.B.A., 1968, p. 5.
17. Nikolaus Pevsner, *The Buildings of England: London*, Penguin, 1952, p. 209.
18. David Watkin, *op.cit.*, p. 150.
19. Mary Mix Foley, *The American House*, Harper Colophon, 1980, p. 134.
20. Marc-Antoine Laugier's *Essai sur l'Architecture* (1753) was an early exposition of Neoclassic theory which condemned pilasters (and all Renaissance elements) and advocated free-standing columns.
21. David Watkin, *op.cit.*, p. 134.
22. Peter Kidson *et al.*, *A History of English Architecture*, Pelican, 1965, p. 253.
23. *ibid.*, p. 259.
24. David Watkin, *op.cit.*, p. 146.
25. Tony Evans and Candida Lycett Green, *English Cottages*, Weidenfeld & Nicolson, 1983, p. 94.
26. Philip Cox and Clive Lucas, *op.cit.*, p. 132.
27. Joan Kerr and James Broadbent, *op.cit.*, p. 20.

CHAPTER 2

1. Amos Rapoport, 'Australian Aborigines and the Definition of Place', in Paul Oliver, ed., *Shelter, Sign and Symbol*, Barrie & Jenkins, 1975, p. 39.
2. William Dampier, *A New Voyage Round the World*, quoted by Rex & Thea Rienits, *A Pictorial History of Australia*, Paul Hamlyn, 1969, p. 16.
3. Rex & Thea Rienits, *op. cit.*, pp. 16, 20.
4. Watkin Tench, *Sydney's First Four Years*, first published 1789, reprinted by Angus & Robertson, 1962, p. 47.
5. George B. Worgan, *Journal of a First Fleet Surgeon*, Library Council of NSW, 1978, p. 16.
6. Isabel McBryde, *Aboriginal Prehistory in New England*, Sydney University Press, Sydney, 1974, p. 9.
7. The Rous, Perry and Mitchell observations are quoted in McBryde, *op.cit.*, p. 8.
8. A.P. Elkin, *The Australian Aborigines*, Angus & Robertson, Sydney, 1979, p. 50.
9. Fay Gale, 'A Social Geography of Aboriginal Australia', in D.N.

Jeans (ed.), *Australia: A Geography*, Sydney University Press, 1977, p. 357.
10. Amos Rapoport, *op.cit.*, pp. 40–1.
11. H.M. Cooper, *Australian Aboriginal Words*, South Australian Museum, 1974, *passim*; Sidney J. Baker, *The Australian Language*, Sun Books, 1977, p. 80.
12. M.J. Meggitt, quoted in Rapoport, *op.cit.*, p. 41.
13. W.C. Wentworth, *A Statistical, Historical and Political Description of the Colony of New South Wales*, London, 1819, pp. 56, 57.
14. Andrew Crombie, c. 1860, quoted in Peter Freeman, *The Homestead: A Riverina Anthology*, Oxford University Press, Melbourne, 1982, p. 17.
15. Watkin Tench, *op.cit.*, p. 140.
16. Captain John Hunter, *An Historical Journal of Events at Sydney and at Sea*, Angus & Robertson, 1968, p. 269.
17. Watkin Tench, *op.cit.*, p. 189.
18. *ibid.*, p. 200.
19. *ibid.*, p. 201; *Historical Records of New South Wales*, 2, p. 797.
20. Isadore Brodsky, 'Bennelong Profile', pp. 54, 55.
21. David Collins, *An Account of the English Colony in New South Wales*, London, 1798, p. 275.
22. *ibid.*, p. 433.
23. Public Records Office 2: Colonial Office 201/5, p. 274; *Extracts of Letters from Arthur Phillip, Esq., to Lord Sydney*, 1791, p. 22.
24. For Wyatt, see Morton Herman, *The Early Australian Architects and their Work*, Angus & Robertson, 1954, p. 8; and Philip Cox and Clive Lucas, *Australian Colonial Architecture*, Lansdowne, 1978, p. 5. For Nathan Smith, see John White, *Journal of a Voyage to New South Wales*, Angus & Robertson, 1962, p. 113; and Miles Lewis, 'Architecture from Colonial Origins', in *The Heritage of Australia*, Macmillan, 1981, p. 74.
25. George B. Worgan, *op.cit.*, p. 34; William Bradley, *A Voyage to New South Wales*, facsimile, Sydney, 1971, p. 84; Philip G. King, *Journal*, 29 January 1788.
26. *ibid.*, p. 53.
27. Drawing no. 28, attributed to the Port Jackson Painter, c. 1792, Watling Collection, British Museum (Natural History).
28. Thomas Watling, *Letters from an Exile*, London, c. 1792.
29. John Cobley, *Sydney in 1788*, Hodder & Stoughton, 1963, p. 104; *Historical Records of New South Wales*, 2, p. 745; *Journal Royal Australian Historical Society*, vol. 5, 1918–19, p. 458; Sergeant James Scott, *Journal*, 10 November 1788.
30. Peter L. Reynolds, *The Evolution of the Government Architect's Branch*, unpublished Ph.D. thesis, University of New South Wales, 1972, pp. 4–15.
31. *Naval Chronicle*, London, 1809, p. 388.
32. Robert Irving, *The First Australian Architecture*, unpublished M. Arch. thesis, University of New South Wales, 1975, pp. 384–6.
33. *ibid.*, pp. 328–56
34. National Trust of Australia (NSW), *Old Government House, Parramatta, N.S.W.*, Dunhill, 1977, not paginated.
35. Helen Proudfoot, *Old Government House*, State Planning Authority of NSW, 1971, pp. 19–24.
36. Carolyn R. Stone and Pamela Tyson, *Old Hobart Town and Environs, 1802–1855*, Pioneer Design Studio, 1978, pp. 39–53.
37. *South West View of Sydney*, c. 1800 (Dixson Gallery), and *Sydney from the West Side*, c. 1799 (private collection); both attributed to Thomas Watling.
38. *Sydney Gazette*, 2 April 1803. Refer also to *Grimes's Plan of Sydney*, 1800.
39. *Australian Dictionary of Biography*, vol. 1, pp. 126–7.
40. Drawing in Colonial Office Papers, CO/201/17; Royal Australian Historical Society *Newsletter*, September 1977, pp. 5–6; Joseph Fowles, *Sydney in 1848*, Ure Smith, 1962, plate 12A(2).
41. Letter from William Neate Chapman, Norfolk Island, to his brother, 20 November 1795, Mitchell Library.
42. *Australian Dictionary of Biography*, vol. 1, pp. 202–6; John Eyre, *View of Sydney from the East Side*, no. 2, aquatint, 1810.
43. *Australian Dictionary of Biography*, vol. 2, pp. 546, 547; John Eyre (attrib.), Sydney Cove, West Side, watercolour, c. 1810; A. West, *View of Part of the River of Sydney*, 1813.
44. *Australian Dictionary of Biography*, vol. 2, pp. 128–31; D.R. Hainsworth, *The Sydney Traders*, Cassell, 1971, pp. 72, 73.

45. John Eyre (attrib.), *Sydney Cove, West Side*, watercolour, c. 1810; Jas. Meehan, *Plan of the Town of Sydney*, 1807, Lot 91.

46. *Australian Dictionary of Biography*, vol. 2, pp. 373, 374; Westpac Bank Archives.

47. James Broadbent, 'Early Sydney Houses, Examples of Pattern Book Architecture', in *Art Association of Australia: Architectural Papers 1976*, AAA, 1978; Joan Kerr and James Broadbent, *Gothick Taste in the Colony of New South Wales*, David Ell, 1980, p. 35.

48. Robert Irving, *op.cit.*, pp. 162–72; Miles Lewis, 'Architecture from Colonial Origins', p. 74.

49. James Broadbent, *op.cit.*, 'Early Sydney House . . .', pp. 62, 63; Philip Cox and Clive Lucas, *op.cit.*, p. 126.

50. Examples and descriptions have been supplemented by reference to James Broadbent, *op.cit.*, Joan Kerr and James Broadbent, *op.cit.*; Marton Herman, *op.cit.*; Philip Cox and Clive Lucas, *op.cit.*; Australian Heritage Commission, *The Heritage of Australia*, Macmillan, 1981; and M. Barnard Eldershaw, *The Life and Times of Captain John Piper*, Ure Smith, 1973.

CHAPTER 3

1. F. Lancelott, *Australia as it is: its Settlements, Farms and Goldfields*, 2 vols, London, 1852, vol. II, p. 76.

2. J.C. Loudon, *Encyclopaedia of Cottage Farm and Villa Architecture and Furniture, &c.*, London, 1833, p. 34.

3. E. & R. Jensen, *Colonial Architecture in South Australia*, Adelaide, 1982, p. 19.

4. L.A. Meredith, *Notes and Sketches of New South Wales*, London, 1844, p. 35.

5. In a series of articles in the *Australasian Builder and Contractor's News*, May–June, 1887.

6. Loudon, *op.cit.*, p. 61.

7. Terry & Oakden, *What to Build and How to Build It*, Melbourne, 1885, p. 7.

8. J. Thomson, *Retreats*, quoted in Christopher Hussey, *The Picturesque*, plate XXVI, 1.

9. Calvert Vaux, *Villas and Cottages*, first published 1857, 2nd ed., New York, 1864, p. 232.

10. E. and R. Jensen, *op.cit.*, pp. 174, 278, and 280, include the conflicting dates and attributions.

11. The illustration is a photograph of 1864, held by the St Kilda Council. The story of Charnwood is confusing, but for the tender notice see the *Argus*, 25 October 1855, and for discussion see H.W.L. Schuchard, 'Old Mansions of St Kilda: Charnwood and other Fine Houses', *Argus*, 20 June 1937, and H.W. Raggatt, 'A Study of the Development of St Kilda from the beginning till 1873', B. Arch. Research Report, Melbourne University, 1978, p. 39, dates and attributions.

12. Charles Parker, *Villa Rustica* (2nd ed., London 1848) illustrates scrolls flanking elements like bell-cotes and statuary niches (pl. LXVI) and a chimney-back with a sort of fiddle shape, as if it had swallowed a pair of scrolls (pl. LXVIII).

13. *ibid.*, pl. LXV.

14. Jensen, *op.cit.*, pp. 120, 211, 216–17.

15. La Trobe Library, State Library of Victoria, LT612. An almost identical painting by Tibbits is also in a private collection.

16. An illustration, brought to my attention by Mr Terence Lane of the National Gallery of Victoria, appears in 'A Saunter through a fashionable suburb: by Ixion', *Australasian*, 30 July 1892, p. 232. More recently still, a good photograph has been found in an album in a private collection.

17. From recent research in England by Mrs Jessie Serle.

18. The characteristic scroll occurs in a terrace house at the corner of George and King Streets, East Fremantle, of about 1904, illustrated in M.P. Morison and J. White (eds), *Western Towns and Buildings* (Perth 1979), p. 121. This building has not so far been positively attributed to Hitchcock, but he lived in Fremantle at the time and there can be no serious doubt. Hitchcock's responsibility is documented for a house in Canning Road, East Fremantle, built for Dr White in 1904–5, which had panels of vermiculation and other lush Hitchcockian details. I am indebted to Miss M.P. Morison for copies of Hitchcock's certificate of completion and a photograph of some of the decorative cement work.

19. Allan Willingham, 'Barwon Park, Winchelsea, Victoria, Historic Structures Report', mimeographed typescript, Melbourne 1980, pp.

45–53, ref. *Geelong Advertiser*, 4 June, 1869.

20. For example Wylie & Biers call tenders for a *cottage orné* at Gardiner (Malvern) for Adolphus Haller, in the Melbourne *Argus*, 25 September 1859, p. 7.

21. George Tibbits 'The So-Called Melbourne Domestic Queen Anne', *Historic Environment*, vol. 2, no. 2, 1982, p. 11 (note that an incorrect illustration is reproduced).

CHAPTER 4

1. J.A. La Nauze, *Alfred Deakin: A Biography*, Angus & Robertson, 1979, p. 183 (quoting the Melbourne *Age* of July 27, 1899).

2. B.K. de Garis, '1890–1900', *A New History of Australia*, ed. Frank Crowley, William Heinemann, Melbourne, 1980, third reprint of 1974 edition, pp. 235–41.

3. Geoffrey Blainey, *The Tyranny of Distance*, Sun Books, Melbourne, 1971, fourth reprint of 1966 edition, p. 294.

4. Andrew Saint, *Richard Norman Shaw*, Yale University Press, New Haven and London, 1977, second printing of 1976 edition, pp. 201–10.

5. C.B. Purdom, *The Letchworth Achievement: From the establishment of the first Garden City to the recent dramatic defeat of a take-over*, J.B. Dent & Sons Ltd, London, 1963, pp. 1–30.

6. Vincent Crow, *Haberfield: The Development of its Character*, no. 4 in *Scrapbook* series of booklets published by the Ashfield District Historical Society, 1978, pp. 4–5.

7. Anthony Price, *Dacey Garden Suburb*, B. Arch. thesis, University of New South Wales, 1969, pp. 22–3.

8. Colin Bond, and Hamish, Ramsay, *Preserving Historic Adelaide*, Rigby Ltd, Adelaide, 1978, pp. 67–71.

9. Margaret Betteridge, *Australian Flora in Art, from the Museum of Applied Arts and Sciences, Sydney*, Sun Books Ltd, Melbourne, 1979, pp. 5–15.

10. William Richard Lethaby, *Philip Webb and his work*, Raven Oak Press, London, 1979, reprint of 1935 edition with revisions and new material, pp. 86–118.

11. Saint, *op.cit.*, chapter 3 deals with Norman Shaw's 'Old English' country houses; chapters 4, 5 and 6 deal, among other things, with his 'Queen Anne' work.

12. Vincent J. Scully, Jr, *The Single Style: Architectural Theory and Design from Richardson to the Origins of Wright*, Yale University Press 1965, fourth printing of 1955 edition, p. 10.

13. Arnold Lewis, and Keith Morgan, *American Victorian Architecture*, Dover Publications Inc., New York, 1975, plates II.25, II.28–29, III.1, III.3–4, III.6–10, III.13–14, III.16, III.18–28, III.30–31, III.33.

14. Scully, *op.cit.*, pp. 130–54.

15. Lionel Lambourne, *Utopian Craftsmen; The Arts and Crafts Movement from the Cotswolds to Chicago*, Astragal Book, The Architectural Press Ltd, London, 1980, pp. 36–52.

16. Phillippe Garner, *Glass 1900*, Thames and Hudson Ltd, London, 1979, plate 4.

17. For example: *Palliser's New Cottage Homes and Details*, Da Capo Press, New York, 1975. This reprint of the 1887 edition illustrates a large number of designs for which plans, details and specifications could be obtained by mail order.

18. For example: *Late Victorian Architectural Details*, American Life Foundation Study Institute, Watkins Glen, New York, (undated). A facsimile edition of an 1898 catalogue, developed from the first edition of 1871, originally entitled *Combined Book of Sash, Doors, Blinds, Mouldings, Stair Work, Mantels and All Kinds of Interior and Exterior Finish*.

19. *Seventy Years of Wunderlich Industry*, Halstead Press Pty Ltd, Sydney, 1957, p. 47.

20. Hermann Muthesius, *The English House*, Granada Publishing Ltd, London, 1979, an abridged English translation of *Das Englische Haus*, first published in three volumes in 1904–5, pp. 192–3.

21. Robin Boyd, *Australia's Home: Its Origins, Builders and Occupiers*, Melbourne University Press, 1952, pp. 56–69.

22. *The Australasian Builder and Contractors' News*, 10 September 1887, pp. 286, 308 (as noted in B.Arch. research paper on Harry Chambers Kent, by Bela Hatossy, University of New South Wales, 1974).

23. George Tibbits, 'The So-Called Melbourne Domestic Queen Anne', *Historic Environment*, vol. 2, no. 2, 1982, pp. 12–16.

24. Of the architects mentioned in this chapter, the following were

born in England: Robert Haddon, J.J. Talbot Hobbs, E. Jeaffreson Jackson, Howard Joseland, Henry Kemp, James Peddle, G. Temple Poole, J. Spencer-Stansfield, John Sulman, B.J. Waterhouse. J. Horbury Hunt was born in Canada. Robin Dods, born in Brisbane, lived and worked in Britain for some years. Beverley Ussher, born in Melbourne, visited Britain and the Continent for about two years after completing his articles. William Richards, the builder and designer of the houses in The Appian Way, Burwood, Sydney, was born in England.

25. Ian Molyneaux, (for the Western Australian Chapter of the Royal Australian Institute of Architects), *Looking around Perth: A guide to the architecture of Perth and surrounding towns*, Wescolour Press, East Fremantle, 1981, p. xviii.

26. John and Ray Oldham, *George Temple-Poole: Architect of the Golden Years, 1885–1897*, University of Western Australia Press, 1980, pp. 26–8, 45–7, 58–9.

27. Tibbits, *op.cit.*, pp. 5–34.

28. Crow, *op.cit.*, p. 11.

29. Robin Boyd, *Victorian Modern*, The Architectural Students' Society of the Royal Victorian Institute of Architects, July 1947, pp. 15, 23.

30. J.M. Freeland, *The Making of a Profession: A History of the Growth and Work of the Architectural Institutes in Australia*, Angus & Robertson in association with the Royal Australian Institute of Architects, Sydney, 1971, pp. 54–75.

31. J.M. Freeland, *Architect Extraordinary: The Life and Work of John Horbury Hunt, 1838–1904*, Cassell Australia, 1970, pp. 98–9.

32. *ibid.*, pp. 99–100.

33. *ibid.*, pp. 100–1.

34. George Sydney Jones, 'Another Castle in Spain' and 'Castles in Spain: being the ideas of certain architects with regard to the homes they would build for themselves', *Art and Architecture*, May 1906, pp. 69–73, and June 1906, pp. 107–9.

CHAPTER 7

1. M. Ross-Macdonald, *Life in the Future*, Doubleday, 1977.

2. *ibid.*

3. *Energy Conservation in Building Design*, American Institute of Architects Research Corporation, Washington DC 1974.

4. B. James, 'Energy strategy alternatives to nuclear power', *Habitat* 4, 5, April 1977.

5. S. Bolland, 'Energy economy in housing design', *RIBA Journal*, June 1977.

6. A. Bernatzky, 'Climatic influences of greens and city planning', *Anthos*, 1, 1966, p. 29–34.

7. G. Robinette, *Plants/People/and Environmental Quality*, US Dept of Interior, National Park Service, Washington DC, 1972.

8. P. Soleri, *Arcology*, MIT Press, Cambridge, Massachusetts, 1973.

9. *ibid.*

10. P. Soleri, *Matter Becoming Spirit: The Arcology of Paolo Soleri*, Anchor/Doubleday, 1973.

11. C. Jencks, *The Language of Post-Modern Architecture*, rev. ed., Academy Editions, London, 1978.

12. Paul-Alan Johnson, Dr Bruce Judd and Geoffrey Le Sueur, *The Integrated House, Prototype Experimental Dwelling for the Future*, Residential Research Unit, Faculty of Architecture, University of New South Wales, 1984.

13. E. Schumacher, *Small is Beautiful*, Sphere Books, London, 1973.

14. J. Ballinger, M. Smart and T. Shotbolt, *Bonnyrigg Solar Village*, Solarch, Graduate School of the Built Environment, University of New South Wales, 1982.

15. M. Parnell and G. Cole, *Australian Solar Houses*, Second Back Row, Sydney, 1983, p. 126.

16. M. Wells, 'Nowhere to go but down', *Progressive Architecture*, 46, 1965, p. 174–9.

17. B. Mollison and D. Holmgren, *Permaculture One*, Ealing, Corgi, 1978.

18. Western Australian Museum, private communication.

19. D. Mulvaney, *The Prehistory of Australia*, rev. ed., Penguin, 1975.

20. J. Allen, J. Golson, and R. Jones, *Sunda and Sahul*, Academy Press, London, 1977.

21. P. Finch, and I. Auhl, *Burra in Colour*, Rigby, 1973.

22. *ibid.*

23. F. Leechman, *The Opal Book*, Ure Smith, 1961.

24. *Climatic Averages Australia*, Bureau Meteorology, Dept Sc. Consumer Affairs, Canberra, Australian Government Publishing Service, 1975.

25. P. Vin Wake, *Opalmen*, Reed, Sydney, 1969.

26. *Census of Population and Housing*, Australian Bureau of Statistics. Canberra, Australian Government Publishing Service 1976.

27. S.A. Baggs, 'Underground housing for the Australian region: user attitudes, remote prediction of periodic ground temperature and the role of certain landscape factors in soil temperature modification', unpublished doctoral thesis in the School of Landscape Architecture, University of New South Wales, 1981.

28. S.A. and D. Baggs, *Australian Earth Covered Building*, University of New South Wales Press, 1984.

29. *ibid.*

30. S. Baggs, 'Terratecture', *Architecture Australia*, 72, 4 July 1983, pp. 60–7.

31. G. Birkerts, *Subterranean Urban Systems*, Ann Arbor, Industrial Dev. Div. Ins. of Science and Technology, 1974.

32. S. Baggs, 'Lithotecture around the World', *Geotecture*, 14 July 1984, pp. 31–47.

33. J.J. Greenland, 'Alternative technology in the architecture and geotecture of China,' in S.A. Baggs, *Proceedings, Australasian Papers. First International Conference on Energy Efficient Buildings with Earth Shelter Protection, 1–6 August*, University of New South Wales, Unisearch, App. C1–C5, 1983.

34. C. Moore and G. Allen, *Dimensions: space, shape and scale in architecture*, Architectural Record Books, New York, 1976.

35. P. Ehrlich and A. Ehrlich, *Population Resources Environment*. Freeman, San Francisco, 1972.

CHAPTER 8

1. Alec Clifton-Taylor, *The Pattern of English Building*, Faber & Faber, 1972, p. 32.

2. D.W. Berry and S. H. Gilbert, *Pioneer Building Techniques in South Australia*, Gilbert-Partners, Adelaide, 1981, p. 68.

3. Granville Wilson and Peter Sands, *Building a City*, Oxford University Press, Melbourne, 1981, p. 11.

4. Much of the information about brickmaking came from Dr George Gibbons, in lectures given in the Graduate School of the Built Environment, University of New South Wales.

5. John Woodforde, *Bricks to Build a House*, Routledge & Kegan Paul, 1976, p. 1.

6. A house by John Gawler, architect, described by Neil Clerehan in the *Age*, Melbourne, 27 February 1961.

7. *Sun*, Sydney, 30 December 1983, p. 14.

8. Philip Cox and Clive Lucas, *Australian Colonial Architecture*, Lansdowne Editions, Sydney, 1978, p. 28.

9. Clifton-Taylor, *op.cit.*, p. 287.

10. Miles Lewis, *Victorian Primitive*, Greenhouse Publications, Melbourne, 1977, p. 43; Judy Birmingham, Ian Jack and Dennis Jeans, *Industrial Archaeology in Australia: Rural Industry*, Heinemann, 1983, p. 101.

11. Birmingham *et al.*, *ibid.*, p. 102.

12. Lewis, *op.cit.*, p. 52.

13. Peter Freeman, *The Homestead: A Riverina Anthology*, Oxford University Press, Melbourne, 1982, p. 82.

14. *ibid.*

15. *ibid.*, p. 83.

16. Birmingham *et al.*, *op.cit.*, p. 102.

17. *ibid.*

18. Australian Heritage Commission, *The Heritage of Australia*, Macmillan, Melbourne, 1981, p. 4/52.

19. Lewis, *op.cit.*, p. 34.

20. Alistair Knox, *Alternative Housing*, Albatross, 1980, pp. 31, 150.

21. Brian Woodward, 'Earth Construction', in *Traditional Building Technology*, Graduate School of the Built Environment, University of New South Wales, 1979, p. 8/3.

22. Lewis, *op.cit.*, pp. 40–2.

23. *ibid.*, p. 9.

24. Philip Cox and J.M. Freeland, *Rude Timber Buildings in Australia*, Thames and Hudson, 1969, p. 9.

25. Judy Birmingham, Ian Jack and Dennis Jeans, *Australian Pioneer*

Technology: Sites and Relics, Heinemann, 1979, p. 180.

26. *ibid.*

27. R.A. Salaman, *Dictionary of Tools*, Allen & Unwin, 1976, pp. 54–6.

28. *Sydney Gazette*, 9 December 1804.

29. Birmingham *et al.*, *Sites and Relics*, p. 181.

30. Barron Field's *Geographical Memoirs*, 1825, quoted in L.A. Gilbert, 'Botanical Investigation of New South Wales, 1811–1880', Ph.D. thesis, University of New England, Armidale, 1971, pp. 176–7.

31. For Mathew's arrival, see the *Census* of 1828, where he is described as a settler. For the Clanville mill see *Ku-Ring-Gai*, Kuringai Historical Society, 1973, p. 5. For Cowan Saw Mill see *Sydney Gazette*, 25 February 1828.

32. W.A. Bayley, *Blue Haven: Centenary History of Kiama Municipality, New South Wales*, Kiama Municipal Council, 1960, p. 22.

33. Historical Records of Australia, vol. 7, p. 693.

34. *Sydney Herald*, 5 June 1840, p. 1; J. Raymond, *New South Wales Calendar and General Post Office Directory for 1837*, W. Moffit, 1837, p. 49.

35. J.M. Freeland, *Architecture in Australia*, Penguin Books, 1974, p. 117; see also Chapter 14 in this book, The Queensland Style.

36. *Parramatta & Hills News*, Parramatta, 9 July 1982.

37. Captain Arthur Phillip, *The Voyage . . . to Botany Bay*, John Stockdale, 1789, p. 105.

38. Lewis, *op.cit.*, p. 20.

39. *ibid.*, pp. 59–66.

40. *ibid.*

41. *ibid.*

CHAPTER 9

1. Eliza Shaw, quoted in Mary Durack, *To be Heirs Forever* Constable, London, 1976, p. 40.

2. Georgiana McCrae, *Georgiana's Journal*, ed. Hugh McCrae, Angus & Robertson, Melbourne, 1937, p. 37.

3. R.D. Murray, *A Summer at Port Phillip*, Edinburgh, 1843, p. 193.

4. Morton Herman, *The Early Australian Architects and Their Work*, Angus & Robertson, Sydney, 1954, p. 7.

5. A.B. Facey, *A Fortunate Life*, Penguin, 1981, p. 194.

6. Rachel Henning, *The Letters of Rachel Henning*, ed. David Adams, Penguin, 1963, p. 94.

7. Facey, *op.cit.*, p. 19.

8. Henning, *op.cit.*, p. 32.

9. *ibid.*, p. 142.

10. *ibid.*, p. 218.

11. *ibid.*, p. 224.

12. William C. Wentworth, *Australasia*, London, 1823.

13. Philip Cox and Clive Lucas, *Australian Colonial Architecture*, Lansdowne, Sydney, 1978, p. 149.

14. Joseph Lycett, *Views in Australia . . .*, London, 1824, p. 43.

15. Eugene Delessert, *Souvenirs d'un Voyage a Sydney*, Paris, 1847, p. 140.

16. Lycett, *op.cit.*, p. 44.

17. Richard Twopeny, *Town Life in Australia*, first published 1883, Penguin Colonial Facsimile, 1973, p. 40.

18. W.D. Rocke, *Remarks on House Furnishing and House Decoration*, Melbourne, 1874, p. 40.

19. Twopeny, *op.cit.*, p. 41.

20. *ibid.*, p. 42.

21. *ibid.*, p. 43.

22. 'Beryl', 'Art in the Home', in *Illustrated Sydney News*, 6 March 1890, p. 8.

23. Clive Lucas, 'Colour—the Fourth Dimension in the Restoration of the Nineteenth Century Interior', in *Historic Interiors*, Sydney College of the Arts, 1983, p. 37.

24. L.J. McQ., 'The Tribune', *Australasian Decorator and Painter*, 1 November 1906, p. 35.

CHAPTER 10

1. Katharine Kirkland, *Life in the Bush*, (Appendix I of *Flowers in the Field* by Hugh Anderson, Hill of Content Publishing, Melbourne, 1969, p. 180.

2. F. Marian McNeill, *The Scots Kitchen*, Granada, Great Britain, reprint 1979, p. 19.

3. Anne Gollan, *The Tradition of Australian Cooking*, Australian National University Press, Canberra, 1978, p. 21.

4. Katharine Kirkland, *op.cit.*, p. 180.

5. Anne Gollan, *op.cit.*, p. 33.

6. Margaret Weidenhofer (ed.), *Garryowen's Melbourne*, Thomas Nelson, Australia, Adelaide, 1967, p. 13.

7. J. Seymour Lindsay, *Iron and Brass Implements of the English Home*, Alec Tiranti, UK, enlarged and revised edition 1964, p. 7.

8. F. Marian McNeill, *op.cit.*, p. 68.

9. Isaac Batey, 'The Pioneers of Sunbury District', unpublished manuscript, La Trobe Library, 1907, p. 24.

10. William Howitt, *Land, Labour and Gold or Two Years in Victoria*, Lowden, Kilmore, 1972, p. 208.

11. Pamela Statham (ed.), *The Tanner Letters*, University of Western Australia Press, Western Australia, 1981, p. 10.

12. Isaac Batey, *op.cit.*, p. 27.

13. Mrs Charles Clacy (ed. Patricia Thompson) *A Lady's Visit to the Gold Diggings of Australia in 1852–53*, Lansdowne, Melbourne, 1963, p. 94.

14. Mrs McKinnon of Yandoit, conversation with author, 1978.

15. Arthur C. Slater of Hawthorn, conversation with author, 1970.

16. Henry Lawson, 'Getting Back on Dave Regan' in *The Prose Works of Henry Lawson*, Angus & Robertson, reprint 1980, p. 513.

17. Katharine Kirkland, *op.cit.*, p. 180.

18. William Evans, ed., *Diary of a Welsh Swagman, 1869–1894*, Sun Books, Melbourne, reprint 1977, p. 125.

19. George Francis Dow, *Every Day Life in Massachusetts Bay Colony*, Benjamin Blom, New York, 2nd ed. 1967, p. 92.

20. W. Fearn-Wannan, *Australian Folklore*, Lansdowne Press, Adelaide, reprint 1976, p. 168.

21. J. Seymour Lindsay, *op.cit.*, p. 33.

22. George Francis Dow, *op.cit.*, p. 93.

23. G.E. Evans, *Ask the Fellows Who Cut the Hay*, Faber, London, this edition 1969, pp. 56, 57.

24. Mrs E. Cowell, conversation with author, 1973.

25. Jane Vince Pendergast, *Pioneers of the Omeo District*, Riall Bros, Melbourne, 1968, p. 42.

26. Observed in the manager's house at Ercildoun, Victoria, April, 1982.

27. Doreen Yarwood, *The English Home*, B.T. Batsford Ltd, London, 3rd Impression 1964, p. 230.

28. F. Lancelott, *Australia As It Is*, Vol II, Colburn and Co., London, 1852, p. 138.

29. Letter from the Director of Historic Houses Trust, NSW, 15 June 1982.

30. Jenni Calder, *The Victorian Home*, B.T. Batsford Ltd, London, 1977, p. 88.

31. Doreen Yarwood, *op.cit.*, p. 308.

32. G.F. James, ed., *A Homestead History*, Oxford University Press, Melbourne, 3rd edition, revised, 1969, p. 170.

33. Jane Vince Pendergast, *op.cit.*, p. 42.

34. Richard Twopeny, *Town Life in Australia*, Penguin Books, *Australia* facsimile edition, reprint 1976, p. 44.

35. Ellison Westgarth, unpublished letter, 9 March 1855, La Trobe Library.

36. E. Chivers, 'In the Days of Queen Victoria' in *Weekly Times*, July 17 1974, p. 42.

37. *Official Catalogue of Intercolonial Exhibition*, 1866–67, class IV, section II, p. 354.

38. F. Lassetter & Co. Ltd, *Catalogue of Ranges, Stoves, Grates, Mantelpieces, Fenders, Gasfittings, etc.*, Sydney, c. 1896, p. 11.

39. *Australia in the Good Old Days*, Facsimile pages from Lassetter's Commercial Review, no. 26, 1911, Ure Smith, Sydney, 1976, p. 173.

40. John Danks & Son Pty Ltd, *Catalogue of Stoves*, c. 1930, p. 16.

41. *James McEwan & Sons Illustrated Catalogue*, Heritage Publications facsimile edition, n.d. Melbourne, p. 61.

42. John Keep & Sons Ltd, *Catalogue of Ironmongery*, 1904, p. 183.

43. *Metters' Fuel Stove Sectional Catalogue*, May 1926, p. 10.

44. A.B. Facey, *A Fortunate Life*, Penguin Books, reprint 1981, p. 123.

45. John Danks & Son Pty Ltd, *op.cit.*, pp. 3–14.

46. Theodora Fitzgibbon, *A Taste of Ireland*, Pan Books Ltd, London, reprint 1970, p. 27.

47. *ibid.*, pp. 27, 59.

48. Judith Brown, 'Early Days in South Australia' in *Australasian Antique Collector*, IPC Business Press, nineteenth edition 1979, p. 60.

49. Lucille M. Quinlan, *Here My Home, Life and Times of John Stuart Hepburn, 1803–1860*, OUP, Melbourne, 1967, p. 59.

50. G.F. James, ed., *op.cit.*, p. 49.

51. Jane Vince Pendergast, *op.cit.*, p. 42.

52. Mariel Lee, 'Seventy Years Ago', in *Meteor*, School Paper no. 808, March 1970, p. 29.

53. Peter Taylor, *A Taste of Australia*, Pan Books Pty Ltd, Sydney, 1980, p. 8.

54. John Moffat's *Bill of Loading* for shipment to Hopkins Hill, 1859, unpublished manuscript at La Trobe Library.

55. Mrs E. Cowell of Melbourne, conversation with author, February, 1973.

56. Ralph Edwards and L.G. Ramsey, eds, *The Connoisseurs Complete Period Guide*, The Connoisseur, London, 1968, p. 910.

57. John Moffat's *Inventory* for Hopkins Hill, 1872, unpublished manuscript at La Trobe Library.

58. J. Seymour Lindsay, *op.cit.*, pp. 33, 34.

59. Flora Thompson, *Lark Rise to Candleford*, Penguin Books, London, reprint 1979, p. 430.

60. Theodora Fitzgibbon, *A Taste of Scotland*, Pan Books, London, reprint 1971, p. 102.

61. J. Seymour Lindsay, *op.cit.*, p. 33.

62. William Westgarth, *Personal Recollections of Early Melbourne and Victoria*, George Robertson & Company, Melbourne and Sydney, 1888, p. 45.

63. J.H. Walsh, *A Manual of Domestic Economy*, G. Routledge & Co., London, 1857, p. 152.

64. Henry Lawson, 'Joe Wilson's Courtship' in *Prose Works*, pp. 325, 326.

65. Henry Lawson, 'The Hero of Redclay' *op.cit.*, p. 263.

66. Henry Lawson, 'The Drover's Wife', *op.cit.*, p. 89.

67. Australian Council of National Trusts, *Historic Houses of Australia*, Cassell, Melbourne, 1974, p. 93.

68. Georgiana McCrae, ink sketch, La Trobe Library.

69. W. Griffiths of Barwite, Victoria, conversation with author, August 1973.

70. G.F. James, ed., *op.cit.*, p. 170.

71. M.S.A. and M.R.A.S., *The Grammar of House Planning*, A. Fullarton & Co., Edinburgh and London, 1864, p. 40.

72. Richard Twopeny, *op.cit.*, p. 34.

73. Maie Casey, *An Australian Story 1837–1907*, Sun Books Pty Ltd, Melbourne, 1965, p. 40.

74. John Cornforth, 'Victorian Lanhydrock – I' in *Country Life*, IPC Magazines, London, February 16 1978, p. 382.

75. Australian Council of National Trusts, *Historic Homesteads of Australia*, Cassell, Melbourne, 1969, p. 279.

76. Richard Twopeny, *op.cit.*, pp. 35, 36.

77. M.S.A. and M.R.A.S., *op.cit.*, p. 53.

78. F. Lancelott, *op.cit.*, p. 79.

79. W. Fearn-Wannan, *op.cit.*, p. 150.

80. Philip E. Muskett, *The Art of Living in Australia*, Eyre and Spottiswoode, London, 1893, p. 256.

81. Wallace Malcolm Mortimer, *The History of Wonnangatta Station*, Spectrum Publications, Melbourne, 1981, p. 32.

82. H.A. McCorkell, (ed.), *The Diaries of Sarah Midgley and Richard Skilbeck*, Cassell, Melbourne, 1967, pp. 59, 60.

83. Philip E. Muskett, *op.cit.*, p. 251.

84. Isabella Beeton, *Book of Household Management*, Ward, Lock, London, 1890, p. 39.

85. F. Marian McNeill, *op.cit.*, p. 69.

86. Eileen E. Ewing, 'Mother's Iron Wash Tubs' in *Weekly Times*, 11 September 1974, p. 47.

87. Henry Lawson, 'Wanted by the Police' in *Prose Works*, p. 576.

88. Henry Lawson, 'The Selector's Daughter' *op.cit.*, p. 303.

89. M.L. Holbrook, M.D., *American Cookery with an Australian Appendix*, E.W. Cole, Book Arcade, Melbourne, 1888, p. 45.

90. Hal Porter, *The Watcher on the Cast-Iron Balcony*, Faber & Faber, London, 1963, p. 55.

91. Henry Lawson, 'New Year's Night' in *Prose Works*, p. 258.

92. F. Lancelott, *op.cit.*, p. 79.

93. G.F. James (ed.), *op.cit.*, p. 170.

94. Robin Boyd, *Australia's Home*, Penguin Books, Melbourne, reprint 1968, p. 245.

95. Mrs Freda Cook, in an unpublished letter to Mrs Fay Bolton referring to Campaspe Villa, Kyneton, 25 April 1966.

96. Allen Mansfield, 'Plumber's Day Book (1876–1881)', unpublished manuscript, Victoria.

97. Hal Porter, *op.cit.*, p. 55.

98. Eileen Ewing, *Weekly Times*, 17 December 1975, p. 25.

99. John D. Keating, *The Lambent Flame*, Melbourne University Press, Melbourne, 1974, p. 110.

100. Allen Mansfield, *loc.cit.*

101. John D. Keating, *op.cit.*, p. 110.

102. Wimpole's *Visitors Guide to Melbourne*, A.H. Massina & Co., Melbourne, 1881, p. lxxxix.

103. M.L. Holbrook, *op.cit.*, p. 2.

104. *ibid.*, p. 12.

105. John D. Keating, *op.cit.*, p. 110.

106. F. Lassetter & Co., *op.cit.*, p. 28.

107. John Danks & Son, *op.cit.*, p. 28.

108. State Savings Bank of Victoria, *Design Book Timber Dwellings*, January 1936.

109. Peter Cuffley, *A Complete Catalogue and History of Oil and Kerosene Lamps in Australia*, Pioneer Design Studio Pty Ltd.

110. Dymphna Cusack (ed.), *Mary Gilmore: a Tribute*, Australasian Book Society, 1965, p. 60.

111. Mrs E. Cowell, conversation with the author.

112. Wallace Malcolm Mortimer, *op.cit.*, p. 32.

113. Isabella Beeton, *op.cit.*, p. 38.

114. Wallace Malcolm Mortimer, *op.cit.*, p. 32.

115. Philip E. Muskett, *op.cit.*, p. 251.

116. Isabella Beeton, *op.cit.*, p. 38.

117. Dymphna Cusack, (ed.) *op.cit.*

CHAPTER 11

1. Watkin Tench, *Sydney's First Four Years*, Angus & Robertson, reprint 1961, p. 262; John White, *Journal of a Voyage to New South Wales*, Angus & Robertson, reprint 1962 p. 158; George B. Worgan, *Journal of a First Fleet Surgeon*, Library of Australian History, 1978, p. 12.

2. Howard Tanner, 'The Art of Gardening in Colonial Australia', in *Proceedings of the First Garden History Conference*, National Trust of Australia, Victoria, 1980, p. 16.

3. Derek Clifford, *A History of Garden Design*, Faber, London, 1962, p. 15.

4. John Harris, *The Garden—A Celebration of One Thousand Years of British Gardening*, Victoria and Albert Museum, London, 1979, p. 40.

5. Beatrice Bligh, *Cherish the Earth*, Ure Smith, Sydney, 1973, p. 6.

6. Oline Richards, *Proceedings of the First Garden History Conference*, National Trust of Australia, Vic., 1980, p. 64.

7. Bligh, *op.cit.*, p. 16.

8. 'Mr. Macleay's Garden', catalogue of an exhibition at Elizabeth Bay House, Sydney, August 1981, p. 3.

9. Joan Kerr and James Broadbent, *Gothick Taste in the Colony of New South Wales*, David Ell Press, Sydney, 1980, p. 38.

10. Thomas Shepherd, *Lectures on Landscape Gardening in Australia*, William McGarvie, Sydney, 1836, p. 2.

11. Shepherd, *op.cit.*, p. 2.

12. J.C. Loudon, *The Suburban Gardener and Villa Companion*, London, 1939.

13. Ann Drysdale, 'Diary, 1839–54,' MS9249, La Trobe Collection, State Library of Victoria.

14. Paul Fox, in a lecture delivered at the Art Gallery of New South Wales, 1983.

15. Clifford, *op.cit.*, p. 184.

16. Howard Tanner and the Australian Gallery Directors Council, *The Art of Gardening in Colonial Australia*, AGDC, 1979, p. 52.

17. *Australian*, 24 June 1876. Quoted in Tanner and the AGDC, *op.cit.*, p. 52.

18. Robin Boyd, *Australia's Home*, Melbourne University Press, Melbourne, 1952, p. 60.

19. R.E.N. Twopeny, *Town Life in Australia*, Elliot Stock, London, 1883.

CHAPTER 13

1. My summary of the evidence on this house is reproduced by Anne Bickford in *Kalori Quarterly Newsletter*, no. 3/76, September–November 1976, pp. 15–17.

2. Rachel Roxborough, *Early Colonial Houses of New South Wales*, Sydney 1974, pp. 99–100.

3. Miles Lewis, 'Lonsdale's Cottage' (mimeograph report, National Trust of Australia, Victoria, 1981 76pp. *passim*.

4. Captain John McArthur (to Sir Charles Fitzroy), 12 April 1848 *Historical Records of Australia*, series I, vol. 26, October 1847–December 1848, Sydney, 1925, pp. 373–4.

5. J.C. Loudon (ed.), *Encylopaedia of Cottage, Farm and Villa Architecture*, London, 1833, secs. 509, 513.

6. Alexander Tolmer, *Reminiscences of an Adventurous and Chequered Career at Home and in the Antipodes*, 2 vols, London, 1882, vol. I, p. 131.

7. Henry Capper, *Capper's South Australia, &c.* 3rd ed. of his *South Australia*, London, 1839, advertisements p. 12.

8. John Stacpoole, *William Mason, the first New Zealand Architect*, Auckland, 1971, p. 32; Stacpoole, *Colonial Architecture in New Zealand*, Wellington &c, 1976, pp. 23–4.

9. Miles Lewis, 'Jolimont', in *Historic Houses of Australia*, Melbourne, 1974, pp. 85–95.

10. Journal of Samuel Bradford Vaughan, 1852, in the possession of Mrs W.J. Kendall, Malvern. The house was put up in Mona Place, South Yarra, and subsequently moved to Queenscliff, where it stands at 78 Mercer Street, altered beyond recognition externally, but with part of the panelling visible inside.

11. Ida Darlington, 'Thompson Fecit', *Architectural Review*, vol. CXXIV, no. 740 September 1958, pp. 187–8, for a general account of his career. For Thompson's terracotta block church at Redhill, near Reigate, see *Builder*, vol. XI, no. 548, London, 6 August 1853, p. 507.

12. Henry Capper, *South Australia. Extracts from the Official Dispatches, &c*, London, 1837, p. 66. These can probably be identified with the '72 huts provided by the Commissioners' which were incuded in the cargo of the *Tam O'Shanter*, according to L.J. Ewens, *The Establishment of Trinity Chapel, Adelaide*, paper read to the Pioneers' Association of South Australia, 1953, p. 6.

13. *Builder*, vol. I, no. 6, London, 18 March 1843, p. 70.

14. Henry Capper, *Capper's South Australia, &c*, London, 1839, advertisements p. 16; see also the similar text in John Stephens, *The Land of Promise, &c.*, London, 1839, advertising sheets, n.p.

15. Stacpoole, *Colonial Architecture*, pp. 25–7.

16. Peter Lovell, 'Woodlands Homestead Complex: an Historic Structure Report: the Building Fabric', mimeograph report, Melbourne, 1981, pp. 18, 13, and for the flooring in the western rooms and long corridor, pp. 51, 55, 59, 62, 69.

17. George C. Morphett, *The Life and Letters of Sir John Morphett*, Adelaide, 1936, p. 64.

18. R.G. Jameson, *New Zealand, South Australia, and New South Wales, &c* London, 1842, p. 12.

19. Journal of E.W. Andrews, 3 September 1839. In the possession of Mrs Bryce Andrews, Stonyfell.

20. *Builder*, vol. IV, no. 161, London, 7 March 1846, p. 110, in notes taken from the *South Australian Register* and *Adelaide Observer*.

21. Esme Johnson, 'Ghosts of St. Ninians', *Australian Home Beautiful*, vol. II no. 2, 1 February 1933, p. 29. For a slightly more extensive acount of these exotic buildings see my 'The Singapore Cottage', *Unibeam*, Singapore, vol. X, 1980–1, pp. 90–1.

22. W.P. Evans, *Port of Many Prows*, Melbourne, 1969, p. 129 illustrates the house; more detail is given in Evans's typescript notes on the history of Williamstown, p. 22.

23. Hugh McCrae (ed.) *Georgiana's Journal*, Angus & Robertson, Sydney, 1934, pp. 23, 120, 235.

24. 'Garryowen' (Edmund Finn), *Chronicles of Early Melbourne*, Melbourne 1888, vol. I, p. 33.

25. Mary Lloyd & Clare Lewis, 'Portable Buildings', B. Arch. History thesis, University of Melbourne 1959, p. 26 and pl. 23.

26. H.G. Turner, *A History of the Colony of Victoria*, 2 vols, London 1904, vol. I, p. 369.

27. Peter Alsop, address to the Institution of Engineers, Melbourne, 17 July 1979.

28. Yong Ching Fatt, 'Louis Ah Mouy (1826–1891)', in *Australian Dictionary of Biography*, vol. 3, Melbourne 1969, pp. 19–20.

29. E. & R. Jensen, *Colonial Architecture in South Australia*, Adelaide 1980, pp. 105–6.

30. W.P. Evans, typescript notes, *loc.cit.*, pp. 24–5.

31. *Illustrated London News*, vol. XXVI, no. 722, 6 January 1855, p. 14.

32. *Statistical Register for the Colony of Victoria*, quoted by J.B. Cooper, *Victorian Commerce 1834–1934*, Melbourne, 1934, p. 12.

33. Patricia Weetman, 'Brighton – as it was in the early "fifties"', *Woman's World*, vol. XIV, no. 160, 1 April 1934, pp. 22ff.

34. Wendy Milsom, 'Fortunes waxed—house grew', *Age*, 20 August 1971.

35. *Melbourne Auction Mart*, 23 December 1853.

36. *Argus*, 23 March 1853.

37. Douglas Pike, *Paradise of Dissent*, Melbourne, 1967 [1957], p. 451, ref. *South Australian Register*, 27 April and 19 July 1852.

38. Jensen, *loc.cit.*, p. 15, ref *South Australian Register*, 13 October 1838, 10 August 1839.

39. George Bateson, *Gold Fleet for California*, Sydney, 1963, pp. 82–3, 102.

40. Harley Preston, 'James Alexander Thomson (1805–1860)', in *Australian Dictionary of Biography*, vol. 2, Melbourne 1967, pp. 527–8.

41. *Melbourne Auction Mart*, 21 February 1853.

42. Alexander Sutherland (ed.), *Victoria and its Metropolis* (2 vols, Melbourne, 1888), vol. II, p. 482.

43. J.B. Cooper, *The History of St Kilda*, 2 vols, Melbourne, 1930, vol. I, p. 278.

44. G.F. Train, *My Life in Many States and Foreign Lands* (New York, 1902), p. 132; D. & A. Potts, *A Yankee Merchant in Goldrush Australia*, London and Melbourne, 1970, p. xiv.

45. By Mr Hugo Ilic, wood anatomist, of the CSIRO.

46. Calvert Vaux, *Villas and Cottages*, New York, 1864 [1857], p. 140. The identification is made by Anne Neale, 'The American timber Cottage in Australasia', B.Arch research report, Melbourne University, 1982. While Vaux's porch is comparable with that of Osborne House, Neale points out that the distinctive motif, that of three semi-circular arches with the central one larger than the side ones, had already been used in a different context in Richard Upjohn's villa for Edward King, Newport, Rhode Island, of 1845. It was published in A.J. Downing, *The Architecture of Country Houses*, New York, 1850, facing p. 34.

47. Jensen, *op.cit.*, p. 107, ref. *South Australian Register* 15 April 1854.

48. W.R. Brownhill, *The History of Geelong and Corio Bay*, Melbourne, 1955, pp. 331–2.

49. J.B. Cleland, 'Section Built Manning Cottages', *Proceedings of the Royal Geographical Society of Australia (South Australian Branch)*, vol. LIX, 1958–9, pp. 51–2, quoting James Jervis; also Philip Cox and John Freeland, *Rude Timber Buildings in Australia*, London, 1969, pp. 57, 203.

50. *Illustrated London News*, vol. XXVI, no. 723, 13 January 1855, p. 32.

51. *Illustrated London News*, vol. XXV, no. 716, 9 December 1854, p. 575; *Builder*, vol. XII no. 617, London, 2 December 1854, p. 622.

52. *Argus*, 28 June 1856, p. 7.

53. *Argus*, 14 December 1853.

54. *Builder*, vol. IX, no. 4, London.

55. *ibid.*, vol. XI, no. 535, 7 May 1853, p. 299.

56. *Portable Buildings Designed and Built by Charles F. Bielefeld, Patentee, &c*, London, 1853. While the buildings illustrated would appear to be mainly those of Seymour's village, there is also a rather charming church shown in a view and a plan. Bielefeld quotes reports in the *Morning Post, Morning Chronicle, Daily News, Illustrated London News, Era, Windsor and Eton Express Public Ledger* and *The Times*. The most significant is that of the *Illustrated London News*, vol. XXIII, no. 630, 6 August 1853, p. 80, which gives a picturesque view of the village, not reproduced by Bielefeld.

57. Winston Burchett, *East Melbourne 1837–1977*, Melbourne, 1978, p. 161.

58. Alsop, *loc.cit.*

59. *Official Catalogue of the Melbourne Exhibition 1854*, p. 11.

60. *Australian Encyclopaedia*, 10 vols, Sydney 1962, vol. I, p. 501, *s.v.* Billiards.

61. Alsop, *loc.cit.*

62. *Illustrated London News*, vol. XXV, no. 721, 30 December 1854; Brownhill, *op.cit.*, pp. 126–32.

63. *Builder*, vol. XI, no. 550, 20 August 1853, p. 544.

64. *ibid.*, no. 536, 19 May 1853, p. 318.

65. *Mount Alexander Mail*, 15 September 1854.

66. Stephens, *loc.cit.*, advertising sheet, n.p. The Messrs Hewetson were offering 'Zink roofing, sheds, flats, terraces, and other buildings'.

67. J.D. Borthwick, *Three Years in California*, Edinburgh, 1852, p. 44.

68. Quoted *Builder*, vol. XI, no. 531, London, 9 April 1853, p. 238.

69. *Argus*, 3 September 1853.

70. *Murray's Australian Circular*, no. 3, July 1853, p. 31; J.S. Prout, *An Illustrated Handbook of the Voyage to Australia*, London, n.d., advertisements, n.p.

71. Deydier, of Vaurigard, near Paris, showed ornamental zinc structures such as summerhouses at the Great Exhibition of 1851: *Art Journal Illustrated Catalogue of the Industry of All Nations 1851*, London, 1851, p. 147.

72. Jensen, *op.cit.*, p. 107 ref. *South Australian Register*, 15 April 1859.

73. Letterbook of E.W. Andrews, in the possession of Mrs Bryce Andrews, Stonyfell, 23 September 1839 and 11 October 1839; Capper, *Capper's South Australia*, p. 38; *South Australian*, 2 March 1841 (for the destruction of one by fire); G.C. Morphett, *Life and Letters of Sir John Morphett*, Adelaide, 1936, p. 106.

74. The building is the discovery of Mr Peter Alsop, of Geelong.

75. *Illustrated London News*, vol. XXIV, no. 669, 18 February 1854, p. 141.

76. I rely again on Mr Peter Alsop, who has visited the house and taken detailed notes on its construction.

77. M.J. Freeland, *op.cit.*, pp. 113–14.

78. Mrs Westgarth wrote to her mother on 9 March 1855 that the house had not yet arrived: 'Three Westgarth Letters', *La Trobe Library Journal*, vol. II, no. 8 (October 1971), p. 108.

79. *Builder* vol. XII, no. 619, London, 16 December 1854, p. 642.

80. The *Glasgow Commonwealth* report named the makers as 'W. & P. M'Lellan', but Mr S.W. Johnston of the University of Glasgow Library has advised me that it was as P. & W. McLellan that they became a public company in 1872.

81. *Builder*, vol. XI, no. 546, London, 23 July 1853: the company is here named as Lister & Co., however Mr C.W. Black, City Librarian at the Mitchell Library, Glasgow, has advised that Robertson & Lister appear in the directories from 1848 as smiths, &c.; in 1853 at an additional address as iron house builders; and by 1855, as Robertson & Co., they conduct both activities at the second address, in Parliamentary Road.

82. *ibid.*, vol. XII, no. 592, 10 June 1854, p. 326.

83. There are a number of contemporary photographs of this church, one of the best being in a published album of 1872: *Photographs of Public and Other Buildings*, p. 92.

84. Charles D. Young & Co., *Illustrations of Iron Structures for Home and Abroad*, held in The RIBA Library, London.

85. Lyall communicated his discovery to both Dr E.G. Robertson and Professor Gilbert Herbert, each of whom published it.

86. E.G. Robertson, 'Cast Iron Ornamentation', *Victorian Historical Magazine*, vol. XVII, no. 4, November 1971, p. 692.

87. Note by Mrs E.M. Sampson, in the possession of Mrs W.G. Jones of Ocean Grove.

88. Gilbert Herbert, 'Some Problematic Iron Buildings of the Eighteen Fifties', mimeographed typescript, Haifa 1972, pp. 7–9.

89. Geoffrey Drinnan, 'Corio Villa', B.Arch history thesis, Melbourne University, 1949.

90. Even in 1843, John Cotton, who had brought a house with him from England, found it would be far too expensive to cart it to his property on the Goulburn, and as bricks were now cheap in Melbourne he would have to sell it at a loss. R.V. Billis & A.S. Kenyon, *Pastures New*, Melbourne, 1930, p. 225.

91. *Builder*, vol. XII, no. 605, London, 9 September 1854, p. 59; a very similar complaint about a Manning house was quoted from the same journal, by the *Australian Builder*, no. 27, 4 September 1856, p. 216.

92. Journal of Samuel Bradford Vaughan.

93. *Australian Builder*, no. 10, 7 May 1856, p. 77.

94. Nigel Kendall, 'The House of 500 Houses in the Old Kent Road', *House and Garden*, vol. XXVI, no. 263, October 1971, pp. 106–7.

95. Personal communication from Peter Bell, Adelaide, 14 June 1984.

96. J.B. Lewis, untitled MS 'This goes back to about 1865 . . .', in the possession of R.B. Lewis, Frankston.

97. The building is in Station Street; there are conflicting accounts, like that in the *Age*, 11 November 1957, which attributes it to a local builder.

98. Personal communication from Sir Edward Morgan.

99. J.W. Collinson, *More About Cairns: the Second Decade*, Brisbane, 1942, pp. 152–5.

100. *Argus*, 15 September 1883, p. 2.

101. *Australasian Ironmonger*, vol. V, no. 5, 1 May 1890, p. 131.

102. J.M. Freeland, *Architecture in Australia, a History*, Cheshire, 1968, pp. 228–9.

103. Peter Bell, *Miasma, Termites and a Nice View of the Dam: the Development of the Highest House in North Queensland*, History Department, James Cook University of North Queensland, 1984, p. 47.

104. 'Prefabrication Down Under', *Architectural Forum*, vol. 79, November 1943, pp. 75–7; 'Australian Prefab', *ibid.*, vol. 86, March 1947, pp. 122, 124; 'House out of Factory', *Architecture*, Melbourne, vol. 38, no. 4, October–December 1950, pp. 122–3.

105. 'The Beaufort Home – Prefabricated in Steel', *Architecture*, *ibid.*, pp. 132–3.

106. 'Mass-produced All-timber House', *ibid.*, p. 135.

107. 'Tasmanian Prefabrication Project', *ibid.*, pp. 130–1.

108. 'The Cell-house System', *ibid.*, p. 129.

109. 'Prefabricated Buildings for Australia', *Architects' Journal*, vol. 115, no. 2980, 10 April 1952, p. 448.

110. 'The Riley Newsum Factory-Made House', *Builder*, vol. 181, no. 5663, 31 August 1951, p. 124.

111. '"Operation Snail" The Victorian Pre-Cut Housing Project', *Architecture*, vol. 38, no. 4, October–December 1950, pp. 124–8.

112. H. Bechervaise, 'History of the Concrete House Project', B. Arch. history thesis, Melbourne University 1970, p. 18.

113. This account is based principally on Bechrvaise, *op.cit.*, *passim*, but also on other sources such as 'Housing in Victoria', *Architecture*, vol. 34, no. 2, April–June 1945, pp. 180–5.

CHAPTER 14

1. See P. Skinner, 'The Development of Petrie Terrace 1861–1901, unpubd B.Arch. thesis, 1979, University of Queensland.

2. B. Barrett, *The Inner Suburbs*, Melbourne University Press, Melbourne, 1971, chs 1 and 2.

3. R. Sumner, *More Historic Homes of Brisbane*, National Trust of Queensland, 1982, pp. 80–1.

4. J. Hogan, *Historic Homes of Brisbane*, National Trust of Queensland, 1979, pp. 38–9.

5. W.H. Traill, 'Historical Sketch of Queensland' in *Picturesque Atlas of Australasia*, A. Garran, ed., facsimile edition Paul Hamlyn, 1980, p. 40.

6. P.E. Sprague, 'The Origin of the Balloon Frame', *Journal of the Society of Architectural Historians*, XI, 4, December 1981, pp. 311–19.

7. An extensive treatment of these arguments is to be found in P. Bell, *Houses and Mining Settlement in North Queensland 1861–1920*, unpubd Ph.D thesis, 1982, James Cook University, ch. 3.

8. J.M. Freeland, *Architecture in Australia*, Penguin Books, Ringwood, 1972, p. 117.

9. *See* Sumner, *More Historic Homes*, pp. 10–20.

10. H.C. Perry, *Memoirs of the Hon. Sir Robert Philp*, Watson Ferguson, Brisbane, 1923, p. 115.

11. P. Bell, *op.cit.*

12. For details of this house and much other valuable information see D. Watson, *The Queensland House* (National Trust of Queensland, 1981), 5.4. The construction of the Tide Surveyors house is closely analogous to earlier Melbourne construction: e.g. F.M. White's Model School Specification of 1852, see L. Burchell, *Victorian Schools*, Melbourne University Press, Melbourne, 1980, pp. 45–8.

13. Watson, *op.cit.*, 7.5.

14. G. Herbert, *Pioneers of Prefabrication*, John Hopkins University Press, Baltimore, 1978, ch. 2.

15. I. Darlington, 'Thompson Fecit', *Architectural Review*, September 1958, pp. 157–8.

16. R. Sumner, *Woodlands*, unpubd report to National Parks Service, Melbourne, 1981.

17. J. Stacpoole, *Colonial Architecture in New Zealand*, A.H. Reed, Wellington, 1975, p. 25–7.
18. D. Watson, *op.cit.*, 9.3.
19. This suggestion was first advanced by Dr Miles Lewis. See his 'Architecture from Colonial Origins', *The Heritage of Australia*, Macmillan, Melbourne, 1981, p. 82.
20. *ibid.*
21. P. Hyndman and M. Baker, *An Approach to Queensland Vernacular Architecture*, National Trust of Queensland, 1975. While this compendium of photographs cannot be regarded as reliable, it gives a few interesting selected examples, quoted here.
22. D. Watson, *op.cit.*, 5.7.
23. *ibid.*, 5.6–5.8.
24. *ibid.*
25. Bell, *op.cit.*
26. S. Nilsson, *European Architecture in India 1750–1850*, Faber, London, 1969, p. 187.
27. A.J. Wallwork, 'Four early timber houses in Townsville', *Architecture in Australia*, vol. 57 no. 1, pp. 96–100.

28. R. Sumner, *op.cit.*, pp. 106–9.
29. R. Boyd, *Australia's Home*, Penguin Books, Ringwood, 1968, p. 212n.
30. Quoted in A. King, 'The Bungalow, Part 1', *Architectural Association Quarterly*, vol. 5, 1973, pp. 6–26.
31. *ibid.*
32. R. Sumner, 'Settlers and Habitat' in *Tropical Queensland, Monograph no. 6*, Geography Department, James Cook University, p. 18; and P. Bell, *op.cit.* ch. 5.
33. R. Sumner, 'Influences on Domestic Architecture in Charters Towers', *Queensland Heritage*, 3(4), 1976, pp. 38–48.
34. P. Bell, personal communication.
35. R. Sumner, 'Local Materials in early North Queensland Housing', *LINQ*, 4(3 & 4), 1975, pp. 1–12.
36. *ibid.*
37. P. Newell, 'Evolution of the small house in Queensland', *Courier Mail*, 11 May 1959, p. 15 of supplement.
38. King, *op.cit.*, p. 14.
39. Hogan, *op.cit.*, p. 119.

SOURCES OF ILLUSTRATION

The authors wish to thank those who have supplied or kindly given permission for the use of the photographs, drawings, paintings and maps which illustrate this book. All of the pictures not specifically acknowledged were supplied by the contributors or the compiler. The sources of the other illustrations are abbreviated in the list that follows:

AOT Archives Office Tasmania; BM British Museum (Natural History) London; DM David Moore, Sydney; FB Frank Bolt, Brisbane; HS Harry Stephens, Sydney; IG Irvine Green, Melbourne; JMF J.M. Freeland, Sydney; MD Max Dupain, Sydney; ML Mitchell Library, Sydney; MU Melbourne University; NLA National Library of Australia, Canberra; NT National Trust of Australia; PB Peter Bell, Brisbane; RAHS Royal Australian Historical Society; SLV State Library of Victoria; UNSW University of New South Wales.

Front cover Max Dupain; back cover Historic Houses Trust NSW; 1 JMF; 2 JMF; 6 MD; 15b Watling Collection, BM; 16 UNSW; 17t UNSW; 17b UNSW; 22tl JMF; 22b Nan Kivell Collection, NLA; 25t RAHS; 28 UNSW; 29 UNSW; 32t JMF; 32b JMF; 34t RAHS; 34b Nan Kivell Collection, NLA; 35 ML; 36 Watling Collection, BM; 37t ML; 37b Watling Collection, BM; 39 Watling Collection, BM; 41t ML; 41c Nan Kivell Collection, NLA; 41b ML; 42t ML; 43t Allport Collection, State Library of Tasmania; 43b NT, New South Wales; 44 ML; 44–45 Miles Barne; 45 ML; 46b John Hawkins; 47 RAHS; 48 RAHS; 51t RAHS; 52b JMF; 54b JMF; 55 JMF; 56t JMF; 56b JMF; 58t JMF; 58b RAHS; 60t JMF; 60b JMF; 63 JMF; 64 NLA; 66 MU Archives; 67 *Australian Builder*, 2 October 1856; 68t J C Loudon, *Encyclopaedia*, p 61; 68b SLV; 69 AOT; 70l AOT; 70r Leake Papers, AOT; 71b SLV; 72 St Kilda City Council, Victoria; 73; 76b Margaret Pitt-Morison and John White; 77t NT, Victoria; 77b H. Licht, *Architektur Deutchlands*, 1882; 78 AOT; 80t St Kilda City Council, Victoria; 81t J L Tarbuck, *Builder's Practical Director*; 82b *Building and Mining Journal*, 31 December 1892; 83 HS; 90 HS; 91 HS; 93t Architectural Press, London; 93c W Hawkings Ferry, *The Buildings of Detroit*; 93b The University Press, New Haven, Connecticut; 94 Lionel Lambourne, *Utopian Craftsman*; 98b JMF; 103t Peter Hartog; 103b JMF; 109 JMF; 111 Harry Stephens; 112t JMF; 116b MD; 121 Ian Stapleton; 122 JMF; 123b Ian Stapleton; 124 Government Printing Office of New South Wales; 132 *Decoration and Glass*, May 1938; 135 Ian Stapleton; 136b HS; 138t Ian Stapleton; 139 Ian Stapleton; 141t *Decoration and Glass*, May 1938; 143t Ian Stapleton; 144 DM; 148t MD; 150c *Age*, Melbourne; 150b DM; 152t DM; 152b Ken Woolley; 153 DM; 154 DM; 156 Morrice Shaw; 157t JMF; 157b Morrice Shaw; 158 MD; 160 MD; 161 MD; 162 DM; 163t Don Gazzard; 163c Don Gazzard; 165t Robin Blume; 166t Gregory Burgess; 166b Gregory Burgess; 167 Gregory Burgess; 168t David Liddle and *Crafts Magazine*; 168b David Liddle and *Crafts Magazine*; 171 Michael Campbell; 174 Leon Byass; 175t Robert Mair; 175b Robert Mair; 176 Koppers Australia Pty Ltd; 177 ECA Space Design Pty Ltd; 181t ECA Space Design Pty Ltd; 181b ECA Space Design Pty Ltd; 185t Mike Shepherd; 185b Mike Shepherd; 194t Diderot, *Encyclopaedia*; 194b Edward Dobson, *Bricks and Tiles*; 195t Pyne's *Microcosm*; 195b Appleton, *Cyclopaedia of Applied Mechanics*; 199b HS; 200 JMF; 202 Salaman, *Dictionary of Tools*; 203 Weston Collection, Wollongong Library; 204t SLV; 204c Mrs Lance Rawson, *Australian Enquiry Book*; 204b Frank Tozer; 206t JMF; 206bl JMF; 208l JMF; 208r JMF; 210 B HS; 212t IG; 212b IG; 215t Historic Houses Trust of New South Wales; 216 IG; 217t IG; 217b IG; 220 ML; 221t ML; 221bl UNSW; 223 IG; 224 IG; 225 IG; 227t IG; 227bl IG; 227br IG; 228t IG; 228bl IG; 228br IG; 232 Historic Houses Trust of New South Wales; 236b HS; 237b HS; 240 Kyneton Historical Society; 241 JMF; 243t JMF; 246t HS; 246b HS; 248 Laurie Le Gay; 250t UNSW; 250b Latrobe Collection, SLV; 251t JMF; 253t JMF; 254t Andrew Pfeiffer; 254bl JMF; 255b; 257 JMF; 258 *Building*, June 11, 1910; 259r Ted Rotherham; 260t JMF; 260b JMF; 262 JMF; 263 JMF; 266b JMF; 267t HS; 267b Department of Housing and Construction; 268t RAHS; 270 RAHS; 272–273 JMF; 272b HS; 273b HS; 274t Latrobe Collection, SLV; 274b Art Gallery of South Australia; 276t Western Australian Museum; 276c ML; 276b Loudon, *Encyclopaedia*; 277b Royal Historical Society of Victoria; 279b Calvert Vaux, *Villas and Cottages*; 280b Illustrated London News, 6 August 1853; 281t Bielefield, *Portable Buildings*; 281b *Builder*, 20 August 1853; 282t British Patent Specification No 609, 1853; 282cl by courtesy of Mrs Mein; 282b Latrobe Collection, SLV; 283b Hilary Lewis; 285 *Young's Catalogue*, Design No 14; 286t by courtesy of Mrs K Allan and Miss G Haines; 286c Greg Missingham; 278t *Builder*, 1854 issues; 287c *Architectural Forum*, November 1943; 287b Harry Stephens; 290 FB; 293t FB; 293b JMF; 294 FB; 295t JMF; 295c JMF; 295b FB; 296t JMF; 296b JMF; 297 PB; 298 PB; 299l PB; 299r PB; 302 State Advances Corporation of Queensland; 303 JMF; 304 Cairns Historical Society; 305 PB; 306t PB; 306b PB; 308t PB; 309t John Oxley Library, Brisbane; 309b Workers' Dwellings Scheme Annual Report, 1925; 310 PB; 311 PB; 312t JMF; 313 FB.

BIBLIOGRAPHY

Adams J.R.P., *Distinctive Australian Homes*, Sydney, 1925.

Apperly, Richard and Lind, Peter, *444 Sydney Buildings*, Angus & Robertson, Sydney, 1971.

Australian Council of National Trusts, *Historic Homesteads of Australia*, Cassell, Melbourne, volume 1, 1969, volume 2, 1976.

Australian Council of National Trusts, *Historic Houses of Australia*, Cassell, Sydney, 1974.

Australian Heritage Commission, *The Heritage of Australia*, Macmillan, 1981.

Beeton, Isabella, *Book of Household Management*, Ward, Lock, London, 1861, and 1890.

Beiers, George, *Houses of Australia*, Ure Smith, Sydney, 1948.

Berry, D.W. and Gilbert, S.H., *Pioneer Building Techniques in South Australia*, Gilbert Partners, Adelaide, 1981.

Bligh, Beatrice, *Cherish the Earth*, Ure Smith, Sydney, 1973.

John J.-G. Blumenson, *Identifying American Architecture*, American Association for State and Local History, Nashville, 1977.

Boyd, Robin, *Australia's Home*, Melbourne University Press, Melbourne, 1952.

Boyd, Robin, *The Australian Ugliness*, Penguin, Mitcham, 1963.

Broadbent, James, *The Golden Decade of Australian Architecture*, David Ell, Sydney, 1978.

Cannon, Michael, *Our Beautiful Homes: New South Wales*, c. 1906, reproduced by Today's Heritage, Melbourne, n.d.

Casey Maie, *et al.*, *Early Melbourne Architecture, 1840 to 1888*, Oxford University Press, Melbourne, 1953.

Caudill, W., Lawyer, F. and Bullock, T., *A Bucket of Oil*, Cahners, Boston, 1974.

Cox, Philip and Lucas, Clive, *Australian Colonial Architecture*, Lansdowne, Sydney, 1978.

Cox, Philip and Stacey, Wesley, *The Australian Homestead*, Lansdowne, Melbourne, 1972.

Cuffley, Peter, *Cottage Gardens in Australia*, The Five Mile Press, Canterbury, 1983.

Elkin, A.P., *The Australian Aborigines*, Angus & Robertson, Sydney, revised edition, 1979.

Evans, Ian, *The Australian Home*, Flannel Flower Press, Glebe, 1983.

Evans, Ian, *Restoring Old Houses*, Macmillan, Melbourne, 1979.

Evans, Ian, Lucas, Clive and Stapleton, Ian, *Colour Schemes for Old Australian Houses*, Flannel Flower Press, Glebe, 1984.

Facey, A.B., *A Fortunate Life*, Penguin, Ringwood, 1982.

Fitch, James Marston, *American Building: the Historical Forces that Shaped it*, Schocken Books, New York, 2nd edition, 1973.

Fleming, John, Honour, Hugh and Pevsner, Nikolaus, *The Penguin Dictionary of Architecture*, Penguin Books, Harmondsworth, 1966.

Forge, Suzanne, *Victorian Splendour: Australian Interior Decoration 1837–1901*, Oxford University Press, Melbourne, 1981.

Fowles, Joseph, *Sydney in 1848*, facsimile by Ure Smith, Sydney, 1966.

Freeland, J.M., *Architect Extraordinary – the Life and Work of John Horbury Hunt: 1838–1904*, Cassell, Melbourne, 1970.

Freeland, J.M., *Architecture in Australia: A History*, Penguin, Ringwood, 1974.

Freeman, Peter, *The Homestead: A Riverina Anthology*, Oxford University Press, Melbourne, 1982.

Girouard, Mark, *Life in the English Country House*, Yale, 1978.

Gollan, Anne, *The Tradition of Australian Cooking*, Australian National University Press, Canberra, 1978.

Griffiths, G. Nesta, *Some Houses and People of New South Wales*, Shepherd Press, Sydney, 1956.

Hadfield, M., ed., *A Book of Country Houses*, Hamlyn, London, 1969.

Herman, Morton, *The Architecture of Victorian Sydney*, Angus & Robertson, Sydney, 1956.

Herman, Morton, *The Blackets*, Angus & Robertson, Sydney, 1963.

Herman, Morton, *The Early Australian Architects and Their Work*, Angus & Robertson, Sydney, revised edition, 1970.

Hogan, Janet, *Building Queensland's Heritage*, National Trust of Queensland and Richmond Hill Press, Richmond, 1978.

Holister, G. and Porteous, A., *The Environment*, London, 1976.

Irving, Robert, Kinstler, John and Dupain, Max, *Fine Houses of Sydney*, Methuen, Sydney, 1982.

Jensen, E. and R., *Colonial Architecture in South Australia*, Adelaide, 1982.

Johnson, Donald Leslie, *Australian Architecture 1901–1951.*, Sydney University Press, Sydney, 1980.

Johnson, Donald Leslie, *The Architecture of Walter Burley Griffin*, Macmillan, Melbourne, 1977.

Kerr, Joan, *Edmund T. Blacket, Architect, Sydney*, National Trust, 1983.

Kerr, Joan and Broadbent, James, *Gothick Taste in the Colony of New South Wales*, David Ell, Sydney, 1980.

Kidson, Peter, Murray, Peter and Thompson, Paul, *A History of English Architecture*, Penguin, Ringwood, 1965.

Knox, Alistair, *Alternative Housing*, Albatross, Sutherland, 1980.

Lambourne, Lionel, *Utopian Craftsmen: The Arts and Crafts Movement from the Cotswolds to Chicago*, Architectural Press, London, 1980.

Lewis, Miles, *Victorian Primitive*, Greenhouse, Carlton, 1977.

Lloyd, Nathaniel, *A History of the English House*, Architectural Press, London, 1975.

Loudon, J.C., *An Encyclopaedia of Cottage, Farm and Villa Architecture*, London, from 1833.

Molyneux, Ian, *Looking Around Perth: A Guide to the Architecture.*, Wescolour Press, East Fremantle, 1981.

Moore, C. and Allen, G., *Dimensions: Space, Shape and Scale in Architecture*, Architectural Record Books, New York, 1976.

Morgan, E.J.R. and Gilbert, S.H. *Early Adelaide Architecture*, Oxford University Press, Melbourne, 1969.

National Trust of Australia (NSW), *William Hardy Wilson, a 20th Century Colonial*, National Trust of Australia, 1980.

Pitt-Morison, Margaret and White, John, eds, *Western Towns and Buildings*, Perth, 1979.

Rawson, Mrs Lance, *Australian Enquiry Book*, 1894, facsimile by Kangaroo Press, Kenthurst, 1984.

Robertson, E. G., *Sydney Lace*, Georgian House, Melbourne, 1960.

Robertson, E. G., *Victorian Heritage*, Georgian House, Melbourne, 1960.

Roxburgh, Rachel, *Early Colonial Houses of New South Wales*, Ure Smith, Sydney, 1974.

Saini, Balwant and Joyce, Ray, *The Australian House: Homes of the Tropical North*, Lansdowne, Sydney, 1982.

Saunders, David, ed., *Historic Buildings of Victoria*, Jacaranda, Melbourne, 1966.

Schumacher, E., *Small is Beautiful*, Sphere Books, London, 1973.

Scully, Vincent J., Jr, *The Single Style*, Yale, New Haven, 1965.

Sharland, Michael, *Stones of a Century*, Oldham, Beddome and Meredith, Hobart, 1952.

Smith, Bernard and Smith, Kate, *The Architectural Character of Glebe, Sydney*, University Co-operative Bookshop, Sydney, 1973.

Stannage, C.T., ed., *A New History of Western Australia*, University of Western Australia Press, Perth, 1981.

Stapleton, Ian, *How to Restore the Old Aussie House*, John Fairfax Marketing, Sydney, 1983.

Stapleton, Maisy, ed., *Historic Interiors*, Sydney College of the Arts Press, Sydney, 1983.

Stones, Ellis, *Australian Garden Design*, Macmillan, Melbourne, 1971.

Summerson, John, *Georgian London*, Barrie & Kenkins, London, 1978.

Tanner, H., ed., *Architects of Australia*, Macmillan, Melbourne, 1981.

Tanner, H., ed., *Converting the Wilderness: The Art of Gardening in Colonial Australia*, Australian Gallery Directors Council, 1979.

Tanner, H., *Towards an Australian Garden*, Valadon, Woollahra, 1983.

Tanner, Howard, Cox, Philip, Bridges, Peter, and Broadbent, James, *Restoring Old Australian Houses and Buildings: An Architectural Guide*, Macmillan, South Melbourne, 1975.

Twopeny, Richard, *Town Life in Australia*, 1883, Penguin, Ringwood, 1973.

Ure Smith, Sydney, and Stevens, Bertram, eds, *Domestic Architecture in Australia*, Sydney, 1919.

Watkin, David, *English Architecture: A Concise History*, Thames & Hudson, London, 1979.

Watson, D., *The Queensland House*, National Trust, 1981.

Wilson, Granville and Sands, Peter, *Building a City: 100 Years of Melbourne Architecture*, Oxford University Press, Melbourne, 1981.

Hardy Wilson, W., *Old Colonial Architecture in New South Wales and Tasmania*, 1924, facsimile by Ure Smith, Sydney, 1975.

INDEX

(numbers in italics indicate illustrations)